AMERICAN MUSICALS IN HISTORICAL CONTEXT

AF620904

AMERICAN MUSICALS IN HISTORICAL CONTEXT

FROM THE AMERICAN REVOLUTION TO THE 21ST CENTURY

Thomas A. Greenfield

methuen | drama
LONDON • NEW YORK • OXFORD • NEW DELHI • SYDNEY

METHUEN DRAMA
Bloomsbury Publishing Plc, 50 Bedford Square, London, WC1B 3DP, UK
Bloomsbury Publishing Inc, 1359 Broadway, New York, NY 10018, USA
Bloomsbury Publishing Ireland, 29 Earlsfort Terrace, Dublin 2, D02 AY28, Ireland

BLOOMSBURY, METHUEN DRAMA and the Methuen Drama logo are trademarks of Bloomsbury Publishing Plc

First published as *American Musicals in Context* by Greenwood 2021

This edition published in Great Britain by Methuen Drama 2026

Copyright © Thomas A. Greenfield, 2021, 2026

Thomas A. Greenfield has asserted his right under the Copyright, Designs and Patents Act, 1988, to be identified as author of this work.

For legal purposes the Acknowledgements on p. viii constitute an extension of this copyright page.

Cover design and illustration © Aisling Repp

All rights reserved. No part of this publication may be: i) reproduced or transmitted in any form, electronic or mechanical, including photocopying, recording or by means of any information storage or retrieval system without prior permission in writing from the publishers; or ii) used or reproduced in any way for the training, development or operation of artificial intelligence (AI) technologies, including generative AI technologies. The rights holders expressly reserve this publication from the text and data mining exception as per Article 4(3) of the Digital Single Market Directive (EU) 2019/790.

Bloomsbury Publishing Plc does not have any control over, or responsibility for, any third-party websites referred to or in this book. All internet addresses given in this book were correct at the time of going to press. The author and publisher regret any inconvenience caused if addresses have changed or sites have ceased to exist, but can accept no responsibility for any such changes.

No rights in incidental music or songs contained in the work are hereby granted and performance rights for any performance/presentation whatsoever must be obtained from the respective copyright owners.

A catalogue record for this book is available from the British Library.

A catalog record for this book is available from the Library of Congress.

ISBN: HB: 978-1-3505-7586-8
PB: 978-1-3505-7585-1
ePDF: 978-1-3505-7587-5
eBook: 978-1-3505-7588-2

Typeset by RefineCatch Limited, Bungay, Suffolk

Printed and bound in Great Britain

For product safety related questions contact productsafety@bloomsbury.com.

To find out more about our authors and books visit www.bloomsbury.com and sign up for our newsletters.

In loving memory of

Alice Hermoine Rogstad

(1947–2025)

When she could barely walk and

then, when she could not walk at all,

she marched

until she finally finished the fight.

CONTENTS

ACKNOWLEDGMENTS

I am very grateful to Dom O'Hanlon, senior publisher at Methuen Drama, for suggesting the idea of an updated paperback edition of *American Musicals in Context*. It has been a pleasure to work with him and his associates at Methuen. The moment I mentioned the project to Dr. Melanie Blood, theater professor and academic Dean at SUNY Geneseo, she said, "You have to add *Suffs*." She was absolutely right, of course, but it hadn't hit me yet. Many thanks to Dean Blood, whose chapter on *Hair* from the original text appears in this revised edition. I was delighted that SUNY Geneseo history professor Dr. Justin Behrend, who did such exceptional work as the consulting historian on the original book, agreed to re-enlist for this project. In addition, he is co-author with me for the new chapter on *Suffs*. I cannot imagine having completed this edition without him. Professor Charlie Freeman, Distinguished Teaching Professor of Physics at SUNY Geneseo, serves as advisor on all things nuclear and is second author with me on the updated chapter on *Atomic*.

This edition is the progeny of the original. I am delighted to acknowledge again the superb work of editors Marian Perales and Cat Lafuente, formerly with ABC-CLIO & Greenwood, who shepherded me through the rigors of developing the first edition. Kurt Fletcher and Stephen Padalino, both Distinguished Teaching Professors of Physics at SUNY Geneseo, provided important guidance on the first edition. The enthusiastic support of Dr. Robert Doggett, former Chair of the Department of English, and now-retired department secretary Michele Feeley manifests itself in this edition as it did in the earlier book. The same can be said for my former student research assistants, Erin M. Carlo and Lila Klatz.

I concluded the acknowledgements in the original edition, written in April 2020, as follows:

> For 47 years, I have had the good fortune to be sheltering in place, one way or the other, with Alice Hermoine ("Moine") Rogstad. During the final months of work on the book as the COVID-19 virus swept over the nation we, like so many others, transitioned from "No Place Like Home" to "No Place *But* Home." I scarcely noticed the difference. I love you, Sweeps.

Moine passed away this year. I still love you, Sweeps, and I miss you. This time the difference is profound.

Thomas A. Greenfield
Avon, New York
October 13, 2025

INTRODUCTION

> I cordially detest history in the theatre. History is ghoulish and prosaic and odiously encyclopedic.
>
> Anonymous critic, *American Magazine* review of Rodgers and Hart's *Dearest Enemy*, 1925

> The United States could not help having a master narrative, in view of the dramatic quality of its remote origin and its enhancement by large, diverse immigrations.
>
> Denis Donoghue, "The American Narrative," 2012

American musicals weave themselves throughout the American Narrative, the nation's ongoing chronicle of its own history. Like all open-ended stories, the American Narrative assembles countless seemingly disconnected experiences and seeks out themes and forms best suited for the telling. America's Narrative encompasses many recurring themes. Among the most common is conflict between competing national values; that is, actions for the common good should guide political behavior, yet individual freedom should dominate political life (Chafe 2012). Other themes explore self-evident yet enigmatic truths rooted in the European Enlightenment that we adapted for our national creed: freedom, equality, and justice (Parini 2012). The American Narrative also embodies themes of self-correction as "one story after another fails to cope with the ongoing mystery it faces" (Wood 2012). Such narratives expose earlier omissions and distortions as well as question whether the American Narrative is the sense-making, truth-telling story we claim it to be.

American theater: an ambitious immigrant

American theater, an insatiable American storytelling form, shapes and is shaped by the American Narrative. Deeply rooted in the nation's history as a British colony, American professional theater owes its very existence to England. America's first professional actors were British. They arrived as early as 1703 and staged plays, often with musical accompaniment, in spaces they found in theatre-less cities such as New York and Charleston. Some new arrivals worked as troubadours and traveling wits, recruiting local townsfolk to join them in performances staged in courthouses, taverns, and barns. Owing to strong Puritan influences in New England, America's nascent theatrical activity gravitated to the mid-Atlantic and southern colonies. Williamsburg, Virginia, boasts a credible claim as home to the first American theater constructed for that purpose in 1716 (Wyatt 1941). Others followed in Philadelphia (1724), New York City (mid-1730s), and Charleston (1736).

Actor/producers Thomas Kean and Walter Murray, whose nationalities apparently defy authoritative sourcing, had a short-lived but noteworthy producing career. One prominent theater historian claims their 1749 Philadelphia production of Joseph Addison's English tragedy *Cato* "marks the point of origin for North American theatre" (Shaffer 2007). Another credits their 1750 New York production of Jon Gay's *The Beggar's Opera* as the first professional musical produced in America (Kenrick 1996).

The Hallam Brothers' London Company of Comedians was the single most influential colonial-era theater company. Arriving in 1752, the Hallams toured the colonies for years, eventually renaming themselves the American Company owing to the colonies' growing antipathy toward England. On April 24, 1767, the Hallams staged the first-ever professional production of an American-authored play: *The Prince of Parthia* by

Philadelphian Thomas Godfrey. Set entirely in ancient Persia, the play marked an undistinguished debut for American playwrighting. On April 16, 1787, in New Yok City, the Hallams mounted a more promising roll out of American playwrighting: Royall Tyler's *The Contrast*, the first professionally produced hit comedy by an American author (Shaffer 2007).

The Contrast owes much to eighteenth-century English Comedy of Manners traditions (aka Restoration comedy). Restoration comedy bequeathed to American theater a warehouse of now-familiar comic tropes: an appealing young leading couple's troubled romance plays out over a secondary flirtation between an older or plain comic-relief couple; stodgy puritanical patriarchs and wealthy stuffed-shirts get their comeuppance; witty young women outsmart every male authority figure in their path; over-educated preening fops meet their match in plain-spoken clever lads. Like Restoration British comedy, *The Contrast* is set in locations familiar to the audience. Not the stuff of midsummer night dreams or distant kingdoms, the Comedy of Manners roams the towns, streets, and riverbanks its audience knows well. Years later, American playwrights, composers, and lyricists would take notice.

The Contrast first introduced American theater to its national narrative. After the Revolutionary War, Americans actively debated the new nation's economic philosophies, educational aspirations, and moral standards: "Into these troubled waters dove Royall Tyler to engage the cultural debate . . . *The Contrast* is all comic satire. The original situation comedy . . . each character's story illustrates something of an American crisis, and its heroine, Maria, articulates the American dilemma herself: her pursuit of happiness against (her father's) old world conventions" (Roe 2009).

The popularity of *The Contrast* made a good case for American theater as a worthy contributor to the American Narrative. Now, just add music.

Cue the orchestra, cue the chorus

The professional American musical owes its musicality to diverse sources, with European opera, especially nineteenth-century operetta, principal among them: "The very idea of a theater in which music is an essential dramatic element, the *dramma per musica or* 'music drama,' is the foundational idea of all European operatic traditions and Broadway as well" (Blood 2010). The early forms of classical European opera first appeared in Florence, Italy, around the sixteenth century. England began creating its own operas in the late seventeenth and early eighteenth centuries. In the 1850s, new forms of operatic theater arose throughout Europe. "[They] were lighter than opera in music, or plot, [or both], and often included spoken dialogue in alternation with the sung material" (Garber 2010). Arthur Sullivan was the English composer most closely associated with the new "light opera" or "operetta" forms. During the 1860s and 1870s, successful New York City productions of operettas by French-German composer Jacques Offenbach and Austrian composer Johann Strauss II created opportunities for English-language artists to tap into a new American operetta market. Enter Arthur Sullivan and collaborator playwright/lyricist W. S. Gilbert.

Gilbert and Sullivan began collaborating in London in the early 1870s. In 1878, their London production of *H.M.S. Pinafore* created a sensation. They promptly opened a Broadway production in January 1879. The New York *Pinafore* was so popular that Gilbert and Sullivan opened two more Broadway productions that year: *The Sorcerer* and *The Pirates of Penzance*. Much of *Pinafore*'s acceptance in America is attributable to Gilbert's hands-on (arguably tyrannical) direction of the London production. He drilled his actors in naturalistic acting and precise comic timing, virtually unknown approaches in operetta production: "[Gilbert's] advanced concept of musical staging exerted an enormous influence on later musical theater in America" (Greenfield and Hanrahan 2010).

By the 1890s, some American operetta composers had risen to prominence, Irish-born Victor Herbert (1859–1924) most notably among them. Collaborating with various lyricists, Herbert's most influential operetta scores—including *Babes in Toyland* (1903), *Naughty Marietta* (1910), and *Sweethearts* (1913)—tended toward "serious, exotic, and romantic plots with music to suit" (Blood 2010).

While operatic traditions gave form to the American musical, it was vaudeville's broad palette of music hall entertainments that Americanized it. "Vaudeville was the first truly massive entertainment in the United States. It had varieties that appealed to all classes and both genders. It created ethnic stereotypes even as it gave new immigrants a place to bond with their countrymen and gain exposure to American ideals" (Kattwinkel 2010). Vaudeville's range of performance forms, some of American origin, became increasingly popular during the mid- and late nineteenth century. Blackface minstrel shows, an energetic music-comedy-dance amalgamation performed by whites "made up" as caricatured Black people, established a distinctly American entertainment form while leaving a correspondingly damaging racist legacy. Other vaudeville entertainment styles arose from taverns, saloons, and burlesques that catered to working-class men. These shows often featured ribald comics, singers, and attractive "exotic" female dancers. With expanding markets for family-friendly entertainment, vaudeville producers signed minstrel and music hall entertainers, beer garden musicians, classical operetta soloists, and novelty acts—acrobats, magicians, and jugglers from circuses and fairs. Perhaps predictably, attractive showgirls also became staples of family-friendly shows, "suggestive rather than bawdy" to accommodate audience demographics.

By 1900, various forms of vaudeville-style performances had created sensations in cities and small towns across the country. The business itself, however, was so widespread that "it needed a monopoly to come in and manage its bookings and presentations" (Maslon and Kantor 2008). Two major vaudeville producer/theater owners, B. F. Keith and E. F. Albee, merged in 1906. In so doing, they nationalized the vaudeville industry, consolidating bookings, artists contracts, theater ownership, and management of shows produced under their aegis. The Keith–Albee merger nationalized "big time" professional vaudeville much as producers in New York's Theatrical Syndicate had nationalized professional operetta and prestige drama ("legitimate theater") ten years earlier.

By 1910, nationalized management of musical (and non-musical) stage production, combined with Manhattan's Tin Pan Alley's dominance of commercial song production, established the foundation of modern American musical theater: a tightly organized industry supporting a fluid evolving art form. Vaudeville entertainments, literary plays, and operetta productions began to influence each other both in New York City and on the road: "Elements from these traditions coalesced into a complex hybrid of narrative plot, song, and dance that was variously known as 'musical plays,' 'book musicals,' or simply 'musicals.' Operettas with humorous plots and light musical numbers had already introduced the term 'musical comedies' into the American theater lexicon" (Blood 2010).

American musical theater grew as New York City continued its ascendency as the nation's leading industrial, economic, and cultural metropolis. In 1904, the *New York Times* opened its mid-town office, giving the theater district its iconic name, Times Square. That same year, ex-vaudevillian George M. Cohan established himself as the first American musical theater "superstar," writing, directing, composing, and starring in *Little Johnny Jones*. The show featured Cohan's immortal hit showtunes, "Yankee Doodle Boy" and "Give My Regards to Broadway."

In 1907, producer Florenz (Flo) Ziegfeld premiered his legendary variety revues, the *Ziegfeld Follies*. Running annually for twenty years (with several one-offs thereafter), Ziegfeld's *Follies* transformed the American musical and the entertainment industry. With opulent staging that surpassed many lavish Broadway operettas, *Ziegfeld Follies* decimated the uncultured, on-the-cheap stigma attached to vaudeville-style entertainment. The *Follies*' signature attraction was the Ziegfeld Girls lineup: "glorious specimens of American womanhood . . . in chiffon and silk, feathers and lace" (Martin 1996). *Ziegfeld Follies* attracted wealthy audiences and patrons, news reporters, gossip columnists, photographers, an aura of Jazz Age chic, and practically everyone pursuing a musical stage career. *Ziegfeld Follies*' alumni comprise a Who's Who of American musical stage entertainment from the 1900s through the 1950s: composer/lyricists Victor Herbert, Irving Berlin, Jerome Kern, Oscar Hammerstein II, and E. Y. (Yip) Harburg; comics Fanny Brice, Eddie Cantor, Ed Wynn, Will Rogers, Bob Hope, W. C. Fields, and Bert Lahr; dancers Bert Williams, Marilyn Miller, and Gypsy Rose Lee; and actor/singers Paul Robeson, Claire Luce, Al Jolsen, Sophie Tucker, and Josephine Baker.

The book musical

A "Golden Age of American musicals" arose with the creation of the book musical, widely considered the definitive, uniquely American modern theatrical form. The book musical emphasizes realistically crafted dialog spoken by characters who act on discernible motivations. A central coherent linear plot drives the action. Music, lyrics, dance, lighting, and set design unify the presentation and represent logical extensions of the characters, situations, and plot (Mroczka 2013). The origin of the book musical is credited to Jerome Kern (1885–1945) and Oscar Hammerstein II's (1895–1960) *Show Boat*, which premiered in 1927. Temporally, the "Golden Age" usually refers to the approximately twenty-year period in which the book musical dominated American musical theater, beginning with Richard Rodgers (1902–79) and Hammerstein's *Oklahoma!* (1943) and ending in the mid-to-late 1960s (sometimes identified with the opening of *Fiddler on the Roof* in 1964). A partial list includes Rodgers and Hammerstein's *Oklahoma!*, *Carousel* (1945), *South Pacific* (1949), *The King and I* (1953), *The Sound of Music* (1959); Alan Jay Lerner and Frederick Loewe's *Brigadoon* (1947), *My Fair Lady* (1956), and *Camelot* (1960); Meredith Wilson's *The Music Man* (1957); and Leonard Bernstein, Stephen Sondheim, and Arthur Laurents' *West Side Story* (1957).

Golden Age book musicals nationalized the American musical in several respects. In the heyday of teenage-oriented 1950s and early 1960s rock and roll, these shows generated hundreds of mature popular hit songs, many of which became American standards. The shows inspired important Hollywood studio film adaptations, including *West Side Story* (1961), *My Fair Lady* (1964), and *The Sound of Music* (1965). The most successful book musicals entranced America's regional, community, and school drama groups, who raced to produce them locally. Despite the occasional faraway setting, such as Austria, England, or Siam (Thailand), American theater embraced the book musical as its national shining star . . . for a time.

Beyond the book

In the late 1960s, the book musical ceded credibility and relevance to rapidly changing socio-political forces and emerging new art forms. The Civil Rights Movement, Vietnam War protests, a resurgence of American feminism, and a fledgling gay rights movement demanded changes in standard narratives and images presented in popular culture. Increasingly, the big-time book musical seemed frozen in amber. Twenty-five years after *Oklahoma!* the book musical had stuck largely to escapist romantic comedy formulas. It was practically oblivious to racial diversity, impervious to concepts of sexuality outside heteronormative relationships, and conspicuously reluctant to engage current political issues. The book musical dated itself artistically as well. Plotlines seemed stale. Commercial rock music, no longer a production line for white teenagers' dance tunes, had evolved into an artistically sophisticated diverse cultural force. By the late 1960s, rock music began to "[usher] out the supple rhythms and modulations of the Romantic style of Tin Pan Alley that had served the musical theater well for six decades" (Blood 2010).

Contemporary fiction, visual art, music, and dance were veering away from "realistic" representation and familiar linear forms. Musical theater artists sought new directions as well. Galt MacDermot, Gerome Ragni, and James Rado's *Hair* (1968) brought the rock musical into being. Stephen Sondheim's *Company* (1970) pioneered the now popular "concept musical," which discards traditional plotline and unifies a show around fluid exploration of central themes. In the 1980s, American musical theater faced a challenge to pre-eminence in its own country when Scottish producer Cameron Mackintosh unleashed the "European Megamusical." Mackintosh's major productions—Andrew Lloyd Webber's *Cats* (Broadway, 1982), *The Phantom of the Opera* (Broadway, 1988); and ClaudeMichel Schönberg's *Les Misérables* (Broadway, 1987)—exported a new European operatic spectacle to American theater. Lush scenery, lavish costumes, and exotic orchestration overwhelmed melodramatic plots and characters. American audiences loved these extravaganzas. *Phantom*, *Cats*, and *Les Mis* have perched comfortably atop the list of Broadway's longest running shows for decades.

America's answer to grand-scale megamusical production emerged in the 1990s from an unlikely source: Disney Theatrical Productions. With access to the vast Disney Company catalog of revered stories and characters, Disney staged and marketed original shows that invited comparison with Mackintosh's megamusical success. Disney's *The Lion King* (1997) and *Beauty and the Beast* (1994) achieved "megamusical-level" success, and Mackintosh himself co-produced Disney's long-running musical *Mary Poppins* (2006).

It is tempting to embrace the idea that "nearly every [musical] falls into one of two categories: either a book musical or a concept show" (Green 2012). While oversimplified, the point speaks knowingly to the fact that artistic clashes between innovation and tradition frequently reach a mutual, if uneasy, accommodation. Nearly eighty years after the premiere of *Oklahoma!* the old-style American book musical still "does business." Between 2015 and 2020, *Oklahoma!*, *Carousel*, and *The King and I* had well-received Broadway revivals. *Fiddler on the Roof*, *Hello Dolly!*, and *My Fair Lady* were booked for 2020 national tours (suspended due to Covid-19 related restrictions). More recent innovative hit productions, such as *Hamilton* (2015) and *Newsies* (2012), follow book musical text-based coherent storylines while offering representations of race, gender, and socioeconomics that speak to contemporary American sensibilities. The American musical has countless American stories yet to tell. Compulsive storyteller that it is, it will find or invent anew forms suited for the telling.

Broadway and Covid, 2020–2025

In the second week of March 2020, the World Health Organization labeled Covid-19 a pandemic, the Trump administration declared a national emergency due to Covid, and states began implementing shutdowns to prevent spread of the disease. All Broadway theaters in New York went dark on Thursday, March 12. Notable musicals that shut down immediately included *Aladdin*, *The Book of Mormon*, *Chicago*, *Come From Away*, *Dear Evan Hansen*, *Hadestown*, *Hamilton*, *The Lion King*, *The Phantom of the Opera*, *Waitress*, and *Wicked*. The theater community resolved to be up and running again with a full season in 2020–1, but the shutdown had a solid run of its own. No Broadway musicals reopened again until September 2, 2021, with *Waitress* and *Hadestown* breaking the nearly eighteen-month quarantine. (Bruce Springsteen had opened a limited return engagement of *Springsteen on Broadway* in June.) Many more shows returned later in September, but re-engagement of artists and audiences after an eighteen-month separation came slowly, and full recovery was not guaranteed.

The 2018–19 Broadway season, the last twelve-month season before shutdown, boasted an all-time high of nearly $1.83 billion in ticket sales, $130 million over the previous season. The $1.83 billion reverberated throughout the City injecting $14.7 billion into New York City's economy and supported approximately 9,600 jobs in theater and related enterprises (Ben-Anchor and Conlon 2021).

The shutdown dealt the city a devastating blow. Broadway & Touring Broadway losses were estimated at $5.5 billion through Labor Day 2021. Approximately 175,000 jobs tied directly or indirectly to Broadway productions were lost or put at risk as tourist traffic to New York City shrank from over 66 million visitors in 2019 to 23 million in 2020 (Arst 2021). The psychological toll of unprecedented unemployment in a field where job insecurity is the norm took center-stage in midtown coffee talk, theater news, and even an occasional college thesis. When restrictions were lifted in September 2021, the first glimmers of hope were tinged with reasonable pandemic-weary skepticism. While the 2021–2 season was inspiring for reopening shows, gross ticket sales for the forty-two-week shortened season were $845 million, a drop of over 50 percent from the last full season.

The closing of big name shows in 2022 and 2023 exacerbated pandemic public relations woes. *Dear Evan Hansen*, *Come from Away*, and *Tina* all closed in 2022 after strong pre-Covid runs. *The Phantom of the Opera*'s closing in 2023 made international news as the longest running Broadway show in history. Covid had set Broadway ticket sales back as much as a decade (Cudd 2024).

Even though the closing of *Phantom* and the lingering effects of Covid were arguably the two biggest Broadway news stories in 2022–3, signs of a rebound generated some justified optimism. Seasons 2022–3 and 2023–4 had flat attendance sales at just over $1.5 billion each. Nonetheless, each season nearly doubled the gross receipts of the dismal attendance and revenue numbers for 2021–2. Doomsday predictions of a ten-year recovery or worse were muted although not dispelled altogether.

Building on the solid re-openings of established audience favorites including *Hamilton*, *Chicago*, and *The Lion King*, new successes pointed toward better days ahead. *MJ*, the Michael Jackson jukebox musical, is the lynchpin of the Covid-era premieres. It opened on Broadway in February 2022 and as of this writing has had over 1,600 performances and counting. Close on *MJ*'s heels is *& Juliet*, in which a feminist critique of Shakespeare hero worship receives a full-on musical comedy staging. In October 2025, *& Juliet* celebrated its third year on Broadway and was still drawing full and nearly full houses. *Kimberly Akimbo*, which also opened in 2022, did not recoup its investment during its 612 performances but won four major Tony Awards including Best Musical. Through exceptionally good press and word of mouth, *Kimberly Akimbo* helped draw young audiences back to the theater and garnered goodwill for Broadway through its timely positive message of finding fulfillment and joy in the face of great adversity.

For 2024–5, momentum from the previous two partial comeback seasons combined with screen star power and election year politics to give Broadway some of its best gross revenue and attendance numbers in history: $1.89 billion in gross ticket sales, a new record; 14.6 million in attendance, the second highest ever ("Broadway Season Statistics" 2025). Two limited-run plays drove the season's "buzz." A 2025 revival of *Glengarry Glen Ross*, David Mamet's Pulitzer Prize-winning drama about cutthroat competition in a Chicago real estate office, landed a casting coup of three major male stars best known for their work outside of theater. Kieran Culkin led the field fresh off an Oscar win (*A Real Pain*) and a Prime Time Emmy (*Succession*). Bob Odenkirk, having become a television star in his fifties with *Breaking Bad* and *Better Call Saul*, had the central role of Shelley "The Machine" Levene. Bill Burr, a comedian/provocateur best known for his television comedy specials, talk show appearances, and podcasts, drew press for his well-received Broadway debut.

For political relevance, nothing in 2024–5 matched film star and Democratic Party activist George Clooney's play *Good Night and Good Luck*. Clooney adapted the late CBS journalist Edward R Murrow's 1953 conflict with his own network as he attempted to hold the late Republican Senator Joe McCarthy publicly accountable for his infamously slanderous "witch hunt" investigations against alleged "communists" and "fellow travelers." Clooney clearly intended the audience to apply the crisis unfolding on stage to President Donald Trump's concurrent hostilities directed at leading newspapers and news broadcast companies. A hit show in pre-sale tickets alone, *Good Night and Good Luck* became the first Broadway play ever to gross over $4 million in its first week.

Suffs, another new musical in 2024–5 that failed to recoup its financial investment on Broadway, made political news nonetheless. Shaina Taub's song-filled retelling of American suffragists' historic fight to win the 19th Amendment and universal suffrage for American women weighed in on the perennial political debates over women's rights and gender equality. However, when former Secretary of State, Senator, First Lady, and President Donald Trump's 2016 Democratic opponent Hillary Rodham Clinton signed on as a lead producer and promoter, she gave *Suffs* a robust political cache that enhanced the historical and educational mission Taub clearly intended for the musical. (See *Suffs* chapter in this book.)

Once the season's gross ticket sales and attendance figures were finalized, Broadway League President Jason Laks was jubilant:

> There is so much to celebrate about the 2024–2025 season. Looking back, it was never a given that audiences would return to their seats or that every theatre's lights would come back up. [It took] hard work and imagination . . . to bring the magic of Broadway back.
>
> *"Broadway Season Statistics" 2025*

Laks also cautioned that rising production costs posed challenges to further recovery but stopped far short of sounding an alarm. Rising production costs had been a familiar complaint at least as far back as the 1980s and 1990s, when expensive spectacle-driven European Megamusicals (*Cats*, *The Phantom of the Opera*) and Disney Theatrical Productions' lavish stage adaptations of Disney animated films (*Beauty and the Beast*, *The Lion King*) found their first successes on Broadway.

Nevertheless, writing in September 2025 (early in the fall cycle of 2025–6), Michael Paulson of the *New York Times* insisted that the season's dismal profit picture demanded immediate crisis management:

> The Broadway musical is in trouble ... None of the 18 commercial musicals that opened on Broadway last season have made a profit yet . . . *Tammy Faye*, *Boop!*, and *Smash* each cost at least $20 million to bring to the stage, and each was gone [within] four months. (Paulson 2025)

Paulson notes that beloved classics fared no better in new revivals. A $26 million *Cabaret*, a $19.5 million *Gypsy* (co-starring the eminently bankable Audra McDonald), and eventual Tony winner for Best Revival of a Musical, *Sunset Boulevard*, at $15 million all closed early. Noting that production costs now routinely prohibit even otherwise successful shows from meeting expenses, Paulson warned that Broadway's current business model, if not fixed immediately, will soon result in significant reductions in the number and variety of shows opening on Broadway, leading to serious repercussions for theater workers, audiences, investors, and the city itself.

By the end of November 2025, some industry observers found cause for a brighter assessment of the current season while not discounting Paulson's unforgiving analysis of the profit picture. After a somewhat sluggish October, Broadway went into overdrive in November. A full three weeks before the Thanksgiving week rush, all thirty-four shows on Broadway saw gains from the previous week—a "rarity" as *Playbill* noted. Importantly, not only did the predictable musical behemoths, #1 *Hamilton* and #2 *Wicked*, thrive, but, as if in defiance of Paulson's argument, a revival of the campy Benny Andersson, Björn Ulvaeus, and Tim Rice 1988 musical *Chess* opened that week and grossed a spectacular $2 million, ranking #3 for the week, overleaping such juggernauts *The Lion King* and *MJ*. November also saw the jarring announcement that Steven Schwartz's musical *The Queen of Versailles*, starring Kristin Chenowith, would close unexpectedly in December owing to mounting losses despite garnering solid attendance and "decent" box office receipts. The news offered a grim reminder of Paulson's warning that even new shows with seemingly everything going for them (i.e., the composer/lyricist and original "Glinda" of *Wicked*) and respectable box office sales are financially vulnerable in the current economic climate.

Nonetheless, a successful Thanksgiving week capped a sufficiently strong November to warrant some positive year-end assessments. Writing in *Playbill*, Logan Culwell-Block proclaimed that "[Broadway is] on track for this season to outpace even last season's historic highs . . . so far beating the same period from last season by more than 10%" (Culwell-Block 2025). Jessica Morrison writing in Red94 concurred adding that "consistency of the numbers signals that Broadway's recovery has stabilized, well into the 2025–2026 season . . . [as theaters] continued drawing audiences night after night . . . to a diverse lineup of both legacy musicals and fresh productions" (Morrison 2025).

Further reading

Arst, Gregg. 2021. "Case Study Covid-19: Economic Impact on Broadway." *Medium*, March 11, https://greggarst.medium.com/covid-19-case-study-the-economic-impact-on-broadway-cb2726b666c0.

Ben-Anchor, Sabro and Rose Conlon. 2021. "For Broadway Performers a Year of Unemployment and Reflection." *Marketplace*, April 2, https://www.marketplace.org/story/2021/04/02/broadway-reopening-pandemic-shutdown-unemployment.

Blood, Melanie. 2010. "Musicals." In *Broadway: An Encyclopedia of Theater and American Culture*, edited by Thomas A. Greenfield. Santa Barbara: ABC-CLIO.

"Broadway Season Statistics." 2025. *The Broadway League*, https://www.broadwayleague.com/research/statistics-broadway-nyc/.

Chafe, William H. 2012. "Is There an American Narrative & What Is It?" *Daedalus*', Winter 2012. https://www.amacad.org/daedalus/american-narrative.

Cudd, Shannon. 2024. "Broadway Theater Attendance Hasn't Bounced Back Two Full Seasons After COVID." *Fast Company*, May 28, https://www.fastcompany.com/91131299/broadway-theater-attendance-flat-2023-2024-season-post-covid.

Culwell-Block, Logan. 2025. "Grosses: *Harry Potter* Is Broadway's Top Post-Thanksgiving Earner, and More From Last Week's Broadway Grosses." *Playbill*, December 9, 2025, https://playbill.com/article/harry-potter-is-broadways-top-post-thanksgiving-earner-and-more-from-last-weeks-broadway-grosses.

Garber, Michael G. 2010. "Operetta." In *Broadway: An Encyclopedia of Theater and American Culture*, edited by Thomas A. Greenfield. Santa Barbara: ABC-CLIO.

Green, Sarah. 2012. "The Wicked Stage: Book Musicals vs. Concept Musicals—Are They Both under Threat?" *A Younger Theatre*, January 8, 2012, https://www.ayoungertheatre.com/the-wicked-stage-book-musicals-vs-concept-musicals-are-they-both-under-threat/.

Greenfield, Thomas A. and Mary Hanrahan. 2010. "Gilbert and Sullivan." In *Broadway: An Encyclopedia of Theater and American Culture*, edited by Thomas A. Greenfield. Santa Barbara: ABC-CLIO.

Hanning, Barbara Russano and Herbert Weinstock. 2020. "Opera." *Encyclopaedia Britannica*, https://www.britannica.com/art/opera-music.

Kattwinkel, Susan. 2010. "Vaudeville." In *Broadway: An Encyclopedia of Theater and American Culture*, edited by Thomas A. Greenfield. Santa Barbara: ABC-CLIO.

Kenrick, Jon. 1996. "1700–1865: Musical Pioneers." *Musicals101.com*, http://www.musicals101.com/1700bway.htm.

Martin, Douglas. 1996. "Former Ziegfeld Follies Girl Recalls the Glory Days." *New York Times*, October 18, 1996.

Maslon, Laurence and Michael Kantor. 2008. "Vaudeville and Broadway." *PBS/WNET*, December 2, 2008, www.pbs.org/wnet/makeemlaugh/comedys-evolution/history-vaudeville-and-broadway/31/.

Morrison, Jessica. 2025. "Broadway Shows NYC Ticket Sales Soar to $40.6 million Week, Here's Why *Hamilton* Keeps Beating *Wicked*." *Red94*, November 27, 2025, https://www.red94.net/news/12398-broadway-shows-nyc-ticket-sales-soar-to-40-6m-week-here-s-why-hamilton-keeps-bea/.

Mroczka, Paul. 2013. "The Golden Age of the American Book Musical, Part 1 Defining the Genre." *The Broadway Scene*, May 28, 2013. http://broadwayscene.com/the-golden-ageof-the-american-book-musical-part-1defining-the-genre/.

Parini, Jay. 2012. "The American Mythos." *Deadelus*, Winter 2012, https://www.amacad.org/daedalus/american-narrative.

Paulson, Michael. 2025. "The Broadway Musical is in Trouble." *New York Times*, September 25, 2025.
Roe, Alex. 2009. "The Contrast." *Metropolitan Playhouse: The American Legacy*, www.metropolitanplayhouse.org/contrastessay.
Shaffer, Jason. 2007. *Performing Patriotism: National Identity in the Colonial and Revolutionary American Theater.* Philadelphia: University of Pennsylvania.
Wood, Michael. 2012. "The Other Case." *Deadelus*, Winter 2012, https://www.amacad.org/daedalus/american-narrative.
Wyatt, Edward A., IV. 1941. "Three Petersburg Theatres." *The William and Marty Quarterly* 21, no. 2 (April): 83–110.

CHRONOLOGY

Early America to 1900

Date	Event	Musical
1776, June 11	The Second Continental Congress in Philadelphia assigns a committee of delegates to draft a *Declaration of Independence*. Thomas Jefferson drafts the document on behalf of the Committee.	*1776*
1776, July 2	While debating Jefferson's draft of the *Declaration*, the Continental Congress formally declares independence from Great Britain on behalf of the American colonies.	*1776*
1776, July 2	General William Howe, Commander-in-Chief of British forces, arrives in Staten Island and begins planning a summer invasion of New York City.	*Dearest Enemy*
1776, July 4	The Second Continental Congress ratifies the final text of the *Declaration of Independence*. Signing by delegates is completed on August 2, 1776.	*1776*
1776, August 27–October 28	British General William Howe's land and sea forces attack New York City. Fighting occurs intermittently in Brooklyn, throughout Manhattan, and north of the city limits. The Battle of New York is a major victory for the British, who occupy the city for seven years.	*Dearest Enemy*
1776, December	Benjamin Franklin arrives in Paris to secure diplomatic and military support from France in America's war for independence against Britain.	*Ben Franklin in Paris*
1777, September 19–October 17	Patriot troops win a major victory over British forces at Saratoga, New York. The American victory helps Benjamin Franklin persuade France's King Louis XVI to support America's war for independence against Britain.	*Ben Franklin in Paris*
1787–8	Alexander Hamilton, James Madison, and John Jay write eighty-five essays, the *Federalist Papers*, to persuade citizens to support ratification of the U.S. Constitution. Hamilton writes fifty-one of them. To this day, the *Federalist Papers* remain foundational documents for interpreting the Constitution.	*Hamilton*
1790–1	Alexander Hamilton, first Secretary of the Treasury, proposes the basic principles for the U.S. economy. His "Financial Plan," four reports to Congress, advances policies to retire the country's Revolutionary War debt, establishes the United States as a credit-worthy international trading partner, and charters a national bank run by the federal government.	*Hamilton*
1804, July 11	Vice President Aaron Burr mortally wounds Secretary of the Treasury Alexander Hamilton in a pistol duel. Burr serves out his term as vice president but thereafter leaves public life in disgrace.	*Hamilton*
1814, March 26–27	General Andrew Jackson of the Tennessee militia defeats the Red Stick Creek Indians at the Battle of Horseshoe Bend. Jackson's victory compels the Red Stick Creeks to turn over to the federal government over 20 million acres of tribal land that now comprises much of Alabama and Georgia.	*Bloody Bloody Andrew Jackson*

Date	Event	Musical
1815, January 8	Andrew Jackson's outnumbered troops crush larger, better equipped British forces attempting to seize the port of New Orleans. Jackson's victories at Horseshoe Bend and the Battle of New Orleans propel him to national prominence and pave the way for his eventual election as president.	*Bloody Bloody Andrew Jackson*
1828, November	Andrew Jackson is elected seventh president of the United States. He is the first president raised in poverty and the first member of the Democratic Party to win the presidency.	*Bloody Bloody Andrew Jackson*
1836, April	The town of Lowell is officially chartered as a city by the state of Massachusetts. Named for local textile industrial magnate Francis Cabot Lowell, the city provides an early model for future American one-industry and one-company towns.	*The Cradle Will Rock*
1860, November 8	Abraham Lincoln is elected 16th president of the United States and the first-ever elected from the Republican Party. He campaigns in opposition to the spread of slavery, but abolitionists, such as Frederick Douglass, fear he would never support outlawing slavery altogether.	*The Civil War*
1863, January 1	President Abraham Lincoln issues the *Emancipation Proclamation*, declaring that slaves in rebellious states "henceforward shall be free." The *Proclamation*, while not ending slavery, repurposes the Union effort in the Civil War toward expanding freedom in America.	*Shenandoah, The Civil War*
1863, March	The Confederate government formally legalizes the practice of impressment—the seizure of slaves, food, horses, or other "commodities" from individuals—to support the Confederate Army's fight against the North. Impressments alienate many landowners, contributing to the hoarding of scarce resources and diminishing enthusiasm for the fight in the last two years of the Civil War.	*Shenandoah*
1863, August 10	Frederick Douglass makes the first of three personal visits to President Lincoln at the White House. The two men develop a mutual admiration. Historians believe the president's admiration for Douglass strengthened Lincoln's resolve to see slavery abolished.	*The Civil War*
1880s–1920s	Over 20 million people emigrate to America, most of them from Europe. Beginning in 1892, the European immigrants arrive at the processing center at New York's Ellis Island.	*Ragtime, War Paint, Atomic*
1890, February 18	The National American Woman Suffrage Association (NAWSA) is established. The leaders of two rival suffrage groups—the American Woman Suffrage Association and the National Woman Suffrage Association—merged to form NAWSA. Elizabeth Cady Stanton was the first President of NAWSA. She was succeeded by Susan B. Anthony in 1892. While the merger did not end all disputes within the suffrage movement, the unification facilitated development of state-based suffrage chapters affiliated with a single, national organization.	*Suffs*
1895, September 18	Booker T. Washington delivers what came to be known as "The Atlanta Compromise" speech, asserting that vocational training presents Blacks with a better opportunity for economic security than education for the professions. His position draws criticism from W. E. B. Du Bois, who faults Washington for defending Blacks' economic subordination to whites.	*Ragtime*

Chronology

Turn of the century: the Gilded Age through the Depression

Date	Event	Musical
1899, July 20–August 2	New York City's "newsies," boys who sell newspapers on the streets, strike against newspaper publishers Joseph Pulitzer and William Randolph Hearst over unfair compensation. With strong public support, the newsies win concessions from the publishers and bring nationwide attention to the exploitation of child laborers.	*Newsies*
1900–20	Led by Henry Ford, automobile manufacturers revolutionize American society, transforming the automobile from a novelty for the rich into a necessity for the middle class. From 1900 to 1920 U.S. individual automobile ownership jumps from approximately 8,000 to 800,000.	
1903, July 7	Labor activist Mary Harris ("Mother") Jones leads the 19 "Children's Crusade," a three-week march of striking adults and children textile mill workers from Philadelphia to New York City. The march brings national attention to outrageous treatment of child mill and factory workers. Jones' activism generated widespread awareness of the issue and leads to the passage of state and national child labor laws.	*Newsies*
1913, March 3	NAWSA organized the first national suffrage protest march in Washington, D.C., the day before President Woodrow Wilson's Inauguration.	*Suffs*
1915, June 5	The Congressional Union, an offshoot of NAWSA created by Alice Paul and Lucy Burns, formed the National Woman's Party (NWP) to better mobilize women voters in the states that had already adopted women's suffrage. Their singular focus was on ratifying a constitutional amendment, and, to that end, they pressured Democratic leaders, especially President Wilson. The NWP picketed the White House in 1917 and 1918 and sent organizers to several states during the during 1919–20 ratification campaign.	*Suffs*
1915, August 16	Several prominent men, including a former governor, kidnap Leo Frank from jail and lynch him in Marietta, Georgia. A Jewish factory superintendent convicted two years earlier of murdering a teenage girl in his employ, Frank is kidnapped while awaiting the results of an appeal of his conviction. Overt antisemitism attendant to his original arrest, conviction, and lynching draws national outrage over Frank's case, which remains a defining point in the history of American antisemitism.	*Parade*
1920, August 18 and 26	On August 18 the Tennessee legislature approved the proposed 19th Amendment to the Constitution prohibiting denial of voting rights based on sex and, thus, guaranteeing American women their voting rights. As the 36th state to have done so, Tennessee's endorsement meant that national ratification had been achieved. Eight days later, on August 26, Secretary of State Bainbridge Colby formally accepted the women's suffrage amendment as passed and certified it as the 19th Amendment of the Constitution	*Suffs*
1928	Helena Rubinstein sells her American cosmetics company to Lehman Brothers bank for $7.3 million ($110 million in 2020). At the time, it is the largest sale to date of an American company that is entirely self-made and solely owned by a woman.	*War Paint*
1931, March 25	Nine African American males aged thirteen–twenty, are arrested near Scottsboro, Alabama, and falsely charged with raping two white women. Blatant racist injustice attendant to their trial sparks international outrage. The "Scottsboro Boys" spend years in jail, even as appeals lead to significant Supreme Court rulings on behalf of the trial defendants' rights in court. The Scottsboro case is an important precursor to the Civil Rights Movement of the 1950s and 1960s.	*The Scottsboro Boys*
1932, November 7	The U.S. Supreme Court invalidates the convictions of the Scottsboro Boys due to the Alabama court's failure to ensure "effective counsel" for the defense. In *Powell v. Alabama*, the Supreme Court finds that egregious incompetence on the part of court-appointed defense attorneys violated the defendants' constitutional right to legal representation at trial. The ruling sets "effective" legal representation as a standard for meeting a criminal defendant's 6th Amendment right to a fair trial. This precedent impacts criminal courtroom practices nationwide for decades.	*The Scottsboro Boys*

Date	Event	Musical
1935, August 14	President Franklin D. Roosevelt signs the controversial Social Security Act into law. The Act provides ongoing payments to retirees over the age of sixty-five based on their earnings during their lifetime.	*I'd Rather Be Right*
1937, February 5	President Franklin D. Roosevelt introduces the Judicial Procedures Reform Bill. Hoping to "stack the Supreme Court" in his favor, Roosevelt's bill would permit him to expand the number of Supreme Court justices with new appointees sympathetic to his policies. Bipartisan opposition to the bill ensures its failure. Roosevelt's attempt to "stack the court" marks his lowest point of popularity during his presidency.	*I'd Rather Be Right*
1937, May 26–August 16	Unionized steel workers vote to strike at three independent Ohio-based steel companies, collectively known as "Little Steel." The protracted strike leads to several violent incidents for which labor and management blame each other. Sixteen people die in strike-related violence, making the Little Steel strike one of the deadliest labor–management conflicts in American history.	*The Cradle Will Rock*
1938, June 25	President Franklin Roosevelt signs the Food, Drug, and Cosmetic Act into law. The Act constitutes the first review of federal food and product safety in thirty-two years. It brings the previously unregulated commercial cosmetics industry, long suspected of using potentially hazardous ingredients, under federal regulations for labeling ingredients and meeting safety standards. The Act also requires pre-market safety testing for new drugs.	*War Paint*

World War II–twenty-first century

Date	Event	Musical
1941, December 7	Japan's air and naval forces launch a surprise attack on Pearl Harbor, Hawaii, headquarters of the U.S. Pacific Fleet. Over 2,400 Americans are killed. Seven of the fleet's eight lead battleships are sunk or disabled. On the following day, President Roosevelt delivers his famous "Day of Infamy" speech to Congress, seeking a declaration of war against Japan, which was duly passed by Congress that afternoon.	*Allegiance*
1942, February 19	President Roosevelt signs Executive Order 9066, authorizing military construction of detention camps in the United States. The order paves the way for the arbitrary incarceration of 110,000 American residents of Japanese ancestry.	*Allegiance*
1944, June 22	President Franklin D. Roosevelt signs the Servicemen's Readjustment Act ("the GI Bill"), providing financial support to returning war veterans seeking higher education and new housing. African Americans suffer widespread discrimination in GI Bill-supported home purchases, a contributing factor to *de facto* housingsegregation in cities and suburbs throughout the country.	*Raisin*
1945, August 6–August 9	The United States drops two atomic bombs on the Japanese cities of Hiroshima and Nagasaki, killing over 100,000 people immediately. Japan surrenders on August 15, ending the Second World War. The bombing of Japan marks the beginning of the "Nuclear Age."	*Atomic*
1947–91	The Cold War begins after the Second World War and ends with the 1991 dissolution of the Soviet Union. A perpetual state of rivalry and hostility short of direct armed conflict, the Cold War between the United States and Russia shapes international politics for over forty years.	*Atomic*
1957 August	The first African American family moves into the all-white suburb of Levittown, Pennsylvania. Daisy Myers, Bill Myers, and their three children face nine days of violent protests by white residents, much of it occurring on and around their property. International coverage of the "out of control" residents' conduct draws public attention to widespread racial discrimination in the postwar suburban real estate business.	*Raisin*

Date	Event	Musical
1964, August 7	Congress passes the "Gulf of Tonkin Resolution" authorizing President Lyndon Johnson to "take all necessary measures" against armed forces aligned with the pro-communist government of North Vietnam in its war with South Vietnam. The resolution escalates America's role in the war from military advisor to active combatant.	*Hair*
1967, January 14	Dr. Timothy Leary addresses the San Francisco Human Be-In. His mantra "Tune in, turn on, drop out" becomes the motto of the Hippie movement. The speech cements Leary's legacy as a cultural icon of Hippie drug culture.	*Hair*
1969, June 28	New York City police raid the Stonewall Inn, a popular gay bar in Greenwich Village. Incensed over ongoing police actions against local gay establishments, patrons and supporters riot in protest for six nights. The protests catalyze a national movement for LGBQT rights.	*Falsettos*
1973, December	The American Psychological Association (APA) removes the diagnosis of "homosexuality" from its official diagnostic publication, the *Diagnostic and Statistical Manual of Mental Disorders*. The APA decision recognizes a spectrum of human sexual attraction, regardless of gender, as normal rather than disordered.	*Falsettos*
1976, February 19	President Gerald Ford officially repeals President Franklin D. Roosevelt's Executive Order 9066, which authorized the incarceration of over 110,000 Americans of Japanese descent during World War II.	*Allegiance*
1986, March 12	The State of Georgia awards a posthumous pardon to Leo M. Frank, a Jewish businessman notoriously lynched in 1915 while awaiting appeal of his controversial murder conviction. The Georgia Board of Pardons and Paroles makes no judgment on Frank's guilt or innocence but acknowledges that he was denied justice.	*Parade*
1991, November 7	Professional basketball star Earvin "Magic" Johnson announces he has tested positive for the HIV virus and retires from basketball. Publicity surrounding his announcement generates an increase in reporting and public discourse on AIDS. Johnson's announcement results in documented improvements in Americans' social awareness, attitudes, and behaviors with respect to AIDS-related issues.	*Falsettos*
2001, September 11	On "9/11," nineteen men hijack four commercial airplanes and direct them toward American targets. Two planes destroy the Twin Towers of New York City's World Trade Center. A third hits the Pentagon in Washington, D.C. The fourth crashes in a Pennsylvania field. Approximately 3,000 people die in the attacks, most in the Twin Tower explosions. The attack is orchestrated by Osama bin Laden and carried out by Al Qaeda, the militant Islamist organization he leads. "9/11" is the defining event of George W. Bush's presidency and a foundational experience for America's "Millennial" generation.	*American Idiot*
2003, March	The United States leads a military invasion of Iraq, quickly defeating Iraqi forces and toppling the government of President Saddam Hussein. Subsequently, U.S.-led occupation forces in Iraq confront years of persistent attacks from armed insurgents. Over time, initial support for the Iraq War erodes, tarnishing the presidency of George W. Bush (2001–9).	*American Idiot*

CHAPTER 1
ALLEGIANCE (2012)

Book by Marc Acito (1966–), Jay Kuo, and Lorenzo Thione (1978–)
Music and Lyrics by Jay Kuo
World Premiere: Old Globe Theater, San Diego, September 7–October 21, 2012
Broadway: November 8, 2015–February 14, 2016

Songs*

"Prologue"
"Wishes on the Wind"
"Do Not Fight the Storm"
"Gaman"
"What Makes a Man"
"I Oughta Go"
"Get in the Game"
"Should I?"
"Allegiance"
"Ishi Kara Ishi"
"With You"
"Paradise"
"Higher"
"Our Time Now"
"Resist"
"This Is Not Over"
"Resist" (Reprise)
"Stronger Than Before"
"With You" (Reprise)/442nd Battle
"Nothing in Our Way"
"Itetsuita"
"Victory Swing"
"How Can You Go?"
"What Makes a Man?" (Reprise)
"Still a Chance"

*Order of songs and listed reprises may vary slightly among published scores, cast recording, and production programs.

Overview

Allegiance is a fictionalized story inspired by childhood recollections of Japanese American actor George Takei. Born and raised in California, Takei and his family spent over four years incarcerated in a World War II federal detention center (commonly known as a "camp"). After Japan attacked America's military installation at Pearl Harbor, Hawaii, on December 7, 1941, Takei became one of over 110,000 Japanese and Japanese American men, women, and children ordered to evacuate their homes in West Coast states and remain confined to inland camps for the duration of the war.

Allegiance is structured as a classic "memory play." Most of the action is composed of a detailed personal recollection, or "flashback," to a distant past (1941–5 in a Wyoming detention center) framed between a prologue and an epilogue set in more recent times (December 2001, in California). *Allegiance* tackles head-on the challenges of getting the story of Japanese American internment out to the American public during and after the war. The musical establishes as one of its central themes the deep-seated reluctance on the part of many internees to revisit painful memories and confront unresolved resentments associated with the internment years. No less challenging has been the struggle to integrate the history of the internment years into the broader American historical narrative following the war. *Allegiance* assigns to one fictional family, the Kimuras, the task of giving voice to the generally unknown stories of camp detainees. At the same time, the creators of *Allegiance* assign themselves the task of filling critical gaps in America's war-era history.

From the opening scene, *Allegiance* confronts the paradox of performing a story that resists its own telling. In the prologue, the first actual mention of the history of the internment, voiced by the posthumous spirit of camp survivor Kei Kimura, alludes only to "a time that no one speaks of anymore." Kei's younger brother, Sam Kimura, a camp survivor and an army veteran, has for fifty years refused to speak of his sister or any of his long-buried memories of World War II. In a nod to ancient Greek tragedy, a messenger presents Sam with news of his sister's passing, which suddenly forces his suppressed recollections to surface against his will.

As the prologue fades out, the history "no one speaks of" unfolds. *Allegiance* tries to deliver an uncomfortable history lesson through reassuringly familiar musical theater conventions. The libretto provides the Kimura family with recognizable storylines and relatable character conflicts that call to mind previous Broadway hits. Prior to the attack on Pearl Harbor, youthful Sam (Sammy in the flashback) and Kei long to free themselves from parental authority and strike out on their own (*Funny Girl*, *Fiddler on the Roof*, *In the Heights*). Once interred in the camp, they both take up politically hazardous flirtations that blossom into perilous love affairs (*South Pacific*, *West Side Story*, *Memphis*, *Miss Saigon*). Loving elders offer words of wisdom to the young (*South Pacific*, *The Sound of Music*, *Raisin*). Even in the wasteland of a detention camp, a community dance party advances the plot, clarifies rivalries, and gives the ensemble a chance to show off its dancing chops (*Grease*, *Hairspray*, *Phantom of the Opera*).

By design, the easy familiarity of *Allegiance*'s character types and song styles contrasts with the unsettling background of displacement and incarceration of more than 110,000 Americans based on their race. The creators of *Allegiance* assume their audience knows more about wartime Nazi activities in Europe (the background for such musicals as *Cabaret* and *The Sound of Music*) than it does about Washington's wartime activities with respect to Japanese Americans. To compensate, the writers embed within the show short vignettes and narrators' expositions to provide historical background for situations that members of the Kimura family encounter. In contrast to *Bloody Bloody Andrew Jackson* or even parts of *Hamilton*, the creators of *Allegiance* generally avoid comedic turns when presenting historical information. *Allegiance* relegates most of its comedy to its characters' repartee, romantic flirtations, and ironic commentary about camp life. Part of the show's explicit educational mission is to make the case for integrating critical but little-known points on the "internment timeline" into the audience's general knowledge of American history. For *Allegiance* these points include the Roosevelt administration's evacuation and internment orders to "Persons of Japanese Ancestry" (1942); a resistance movement in the camps that was triggered when thousands of detainees refused to sign a mandatory government "Loyalty Questionnaire" (1943); and the heroic accomplishments of the 442nd Regimental Combat Team, a segregated Japanese American army unit that was among the most decorated regiments in the entire war (1943–6). In addition, the writers also knew that their story could inform political debate over immigration, which figured prominently in the 2016 presidential election campaign already underway when *Allegiance* opened on Broadway.

For the most part, composer and lyricist Jay Kuo minimizes purposing his lyrics toward the show's political messages and historical background. The music's main function is to enhance the Kimura family members' storylines and emotions. There are, however, some noteworthy exceptions. The title song "Allegiance" speaks of sharp differences of opinion among detainees on whether to comply with the government's demand that interned adults sign a coercive loyalty oath while still incarcerated. "Paradise," performed by detainees for each other at a camp dance, mocks a Japanese American civil rights leader's slavish support of government internment policies. "Victory Swing" undercuts America's self-congratulatory celebrations at the end of the war with a satiric yet sobering reminder that America fought tyranny overseas while imposing tyranny at home. "Resist" articulates a major argument behind many camp resistance movements: Japanese Americans should not be subject to the draft until their civil rights have been restored, including the release of all camp detainees. At the same time, the song offers a rebuttal: military service is the best way to secure freedom for all Japanese Americans.

While not specifically historical in nature, other songs in *Allegiance* provide some cultural context to the internment. *Allegiance* implies that people who directly resisted hostile government action were working at odds with certain traditional Japanese teachings. Various moments and songs in the show discourage direct confrontation with adversity but counsel instead patience, endurance, and a transcendent long view. The song "Gaman," which Kuo has identified as a signature song in the score, speaks directly to this principle. The word "Gaman" itself is Japanese for "to endure with dignity." The lyrics speak of burying rather than expressing one's pain. The spoken word "Gaman" functions in the show as a salve against seemingly unbearable hardship but does so as a whispered reassurance and not a cry of protest. The song "Ishi Kara Ishi" ("stone by stone") offers an understated coping mantra for having infinite patience: "[A] mountain can be moved stone by stone" (Kuo 2016).

A subtext of *Allegiance*'s narrative, then, is a clash of competing virtues: Japanese traditions of long-term patience in the face of adversity against the exigency of direct action in defense of civil rights. Nowhere in the show is this conflict more clearly portrayed than in two songs featuring Tatsuo, Sam and Kei Kimura's father. At the first sign of hostilities directed against Japanese Americans, Tatsuo counsels patience and endurance as he sings the song "Do Not Fight the Storm": "Keep your head down . . . we must wait and see" (Kuo 2016). Yet, when he receives his Loyalty Questionnaire while incarcerated, that final insult breaks his patience. Tatsuo sings "Allegiance," in which he defies the government mandate, refuses to sign the questionnaire, and is taken to a maximum security segregation center in California.

Kuo's score respectfully honors those traditions of quiet dignified forbearance, but *Allegiance* suggests that direct action makes for better American politics as well as more engaging American musical theater.

Plot synopsis

The play opens with a prologue set in California on December 7, 2001. World War II veteran Sam Kimura (played by George Takei in both New York and Los Angeles), in full uniform, is about to participate in a Pearl Harbor Day celebration. A woman enters to tell Sam that his older sister Kei has just died. She introduces herself to Sam as the executor of Kei's estate and presents Sam with an envelope bequeathed to him by his late sister. Sam berates the woman for bringing up his painful family history that includes an unexplained fifty-year estrangement from Kei. Kei's spirit appears and urges Sam to open the envelope, confront the past, and heal old family wounds.

Sam rebuffs Kei's pleas as the prologue dissolves to the main action of the play—memories dating back to Sam's youth in California, in December 1941. A joyful Japanese American farm community prepares for a festival in celebration of their annual harvest and success in America. Teenage Sam (Sammy) and big sister Kei are vibrant young adults affectionately teasing and bantering with each other as they help with festival preparations.

During the festival, the Kimura family sings of their hopes for the future ("Wishes on the Wind"). Tatsuo, a widowed Japanese immigrant and proprietor of the family farm, offers traditional parental wishes for his children: a husband for Kei and "respect" via good grades and career success for Sammy. Yet Sammy and Kei each wish for "new dreams with new mysteries" of their own. Ojii-chan, the Kimura siblings' grandfather and family patriarch (also played by Takei) observes the proceedings with quiet dignity. The celebration ends abruptly as President Roosevelt's announcement of Japan's attack on the U.S. military installation at Pearl Harbor (the iconic "Date That Will Live in Infamy" speech) blares over a loudspeaker.

Tatsuo sings of imminent danger ("Do Not Fight the Storm") as staged vignettes interspersed with choruses depict the first wave of government sanctions against Japanese Americans. The military starts rejecting Japanese American men seeking to enlist, classifying them as "enemy aliens." FBI agents enter Japanese American homes investigating possible contact with "nationals" in Japan. The federal government orders "all people of Japanese ancestry" to evacuate the West Coast and be transported to relocation centers. Evacuees lose abandoned property to speculators and thieves. Japanese American civil rights leaders urge cooperation when ordered to surrender civil liberties "to keep America safe" (Kuo 2016). When the song ends, several months have passed, and the Kimuras are resettled in Heart Mountain Relocation Center in Wyoming.

In Heart Mountain, Sammy and Kei begin to grow apart. American loyalist Sammy, to Tatsuo's chagrin, is an enthusiastic follower of the controversial Japanese American Citizens League (JACL) spokesperson Mike Masaoka. A real historical figure, Masaoka is an unapologetic advocate for accommodating the government and cooperating with internment policies. By contrast, Kei falls in love with Frankie Suzuki, the camp's leader of the resistance movement. Defying Sammy's wishes that she, too, fully cooperate with the government, Kei joins Frankie in the resistance.

Sammy organizes group social events for the camp population ("Get in the Game"). He stages a camp dance that dissolves into open confrontation between resisters (led by Frankie) and accommodationists (led by Sammy), with each faction angrily accusing the other of harming the cause of Japanese American advancement. Further complicating the Kimuras' life, Sammy falls in love with Hannah Campbell, a white nurse on the staff at Heart Mountain. The two sing of their perilous interracial relationship ("I Oughta Go"). But love conquers all and their romance flourishes.

Protests in Heart Mountain and other camps as well as Mike Masaoka's lobbying efforts in Washington move federal officials to allow "loyal" Japanese Americans to enlist in the military. However, the government first requires all interned adults to sign an invasive Loyalty Questionnaire that many find degrading. Sammy signs eagerly, but Tatsuo can tolerate no further offenses to his dignity ("Allegiance"). Tatsuo refuses to sign and is transferred to the government's "segregation center" for Japanese Americans at Tule Lake, California. Sammy stays true to his principles but fears his father is ashamed of him for his unabashed loyalty to America.

The army designates its 442nd Regimental Combat Team as a segregated unit for Japanese American soldiers. As Sammy departs Heart Mountain for the army, he and Hannah pledge to stay true to each other during his absence. Sammy serves heroically in the 442nd Regiment. Wounded in action and awarded the Purple Heart, he becomes famous for his military exploits and is featured on the cover of *Life* magazine. Now a soldier-celebrity, Sammy stirs national controversy by publicly condemning camp resistance movements at the urging of Mike Masaoka and the JACL.

While Sammy fights overseas, resisters Kei and Frankie pursue their romance in Heart Mountain. Hannah reaches out to befriend Kei, who is suspicious of Hannah's intentions and wary of her romance with Sammy. Hannah wins Kei's trust, convincing Kei that she loves her brother and their family. Kei confides to Hannah that she is pregnant with Frankie's baby. The women vow to look out for each other while remaining true to themselves ("Stronger Than Before"). Frankie, now a familiar troublemaker in the eyes of camp officials, fights with a camp military policeman in Hannah's nursing station; the officer's gun goes off accidentally killing Hannah. Shortly thereafter Ojii-chan dies of a heart attack, at peace in his camp garden.

Radio announcements report America's bombing of Hiroshima, the end of the war, and the release of camp detainees. As couples swing dance in celebration, Mike Masaoka praises the government on behalf of Japanese Americans for releasing the detainees, giving each of them $25 plus a bus ticket home, and predicting for Japanese Americans "bright hopes for the future" (Kuo 2016).

Home from the war but still in uniform, Sammy reunites with his family, unaware of all the family news that awaits him. Kei informs Sammy that Hannah died in camp. She and Frankie are now married with a daughter named after Hannah (Hanako). Enraged, Sammy denounces Kei for marrying a traitor and holds both Kei and Frankie responsible for Hannah's death. As Sammy turns to leave the reunion, Kei physically tries to stop him. She accidentally tears his Purple Heart from his uniform as he storms out the door.

The epilogue returns the play to 2001. Still in uniform, Sam has reluctantly attended Kei's funeral accompanied by the executor, who persuades him to open the envelope she still carries. It contains the *Life* magazine featuring his cover story and the Purple Heart Kei had torn from his uniform. The executor reveals herself to be Hanako, Kei and Frankie's daughter and, of course, Sam's niece. Honoring her mother's dying wish, Hanako implores Sam one last time to forgive all remaining resentments and make the Kimura family whole again ("Still a Chance"). Sam finally relents. He embraces his niece, expresses regret for his years of silent bitterness, and tearfully heals the family wounds.

Critical reception

An early version of *Allegiance* premiered with little national attention in San Diego in 2012. The highly revised finished version of the musical had two major initial theatrical runs, each receiving a decidedly different critical reception. *Allegiance* ran on Broadway at the Longacre Theatre from November 8, 2015, to February 14, 2016. In 2018, it premiered in Los Angeles in a limited run from March 1 to April 1. The Los Angeles production, staged at the Japanese American Cultural & Community Center (JACCC) with a new director and different lead actors, fared far better with critics than did the Broadway production.

Between the New York and Los Angeles runs, a film of the Broadway production—marketed as *George Takei's Allegiance: The Broadway Musical on the Big Screen*—was released for two one-night showings in movie theaters across the country on December 13, 2016, and again on February 19, 2017. Ticket sales for the two showings exceeded expectations, giving the producers some welcome relief from the disappointing Broadway run. As noted above, Takei played Sam and Ojii-chan in both the New York and Los Angeles productions. His star power left a strong impression on reviewers of both productions.

Practically every reviewer who saw the Broadway production praised Takei's stage presence, sometimes mounting his name into their review headline. Despite the casting of Tony Award winner and Disney film powerhouse Lea Salonga as Kei (*Miss Saigon*, *Mulan*), Takei was *Allegiance*'s undisputed star on Broadway. Yet the adoration of Takei sometimes worked against the show. The New York reviews tended to use Takei's endearing and warm presence as a foil to launch critical barbs against the production as a whole.

The *New York Times* set a tone that echoed through many Broadway reviews—George Takei notwithstanding, an important but cluttered history lesson is ill served by a mediocre, derivative book and score: "Allegiance struggles to balance both [entertainment and instruction] . . . and doesn't always find an equilibrium." The *Times* also reprimanded composer-lyricist Jay Kuo for packing the score with too many echoes of better earlier shows, "as if Kuo has long kept 'Les Misérables' and 'Miss Saigon' on permanent rotation on his iPod" (Isherwood 2015). The *New York Daily News*' review, "George Takei Lends Luster to New Broadway Musical," bestows virtually all of its positive notices on Takei while dismissing the overall production as "a jumble" (Dziemianowicz 2015). Several other reviewers reprised these themes. *Time Out New York* complained that the show "crumples things badly [weakened by] . . . generic, clunkily worded ballads and anthems" (Cote 2015). *The Chicago Tribune* followed suit: "Music and lyrics by Kuo [seem] alas, wholly out of sync with its subject matter, especially when directed at such breakneck speed" (Jones 2015).

The *Guardian* offered a more forgiving if mitigated review, conceding that the "unexceptional" book, score, and lyrics "tend toward the generic." However, the review found the emotional impact of Sam and Hanako's reconciliation in the epilogue sufficiently moving to salvage the show: "The trials and indignities of the past are finally allowed some small redemption" (Soloski 2015). Linda Winer, writing for the highly influential Long Island-based *Newsday*, provided a rare enthusiastic review among the city's major press outlets. While the highest praise she could muster for the score was that it is "serviceable," Winer was having none of the carping over *Allegiance*'s obvious debts to other musicals. For Winer the buffet of familiar "anthems, simple melodic lines, and some obvious rhymes with a few lighthearted '40s boogie-woogie numbers . . . signify Americana." As for one of the show's signature songs, "Gaman," titled and based on the Japanese word meaning "to endure with dignity," Winer was all in: "This may not make it as a kill-for-a-ticket boffo-Broadway slogan, but, for me, that simple concept sells the show" (Winer 2015).

The pans and faint praise from New York critics took their toll, and *Allegiance* closed early on Broadway, having lost money and failed to impress audiences or critics. Opening in the same Broadway season as *Hamilton*, which won eleven Tony Awards including Best New Musical that year, *Allegiance* stood little chance in the annual competition for Tony honors and New York media adulation. The show received no Tony nominations at all.

The producers had hoped to benefit commercially from the nation's focus on immigration issues during the 2016 presidential primary campaigns, which ran concurrently with their show. Upon reading an interview in which then Republican primary frontrunner Donald Trump equivocated when asked if he would have supported Japanese American internment in World War II, George Takei and the show's producers invited Mr. Trump to see *Allegiance* as their guest. Mr. Trump never responded. However, the producers held a reserved orchestra seat for him each night of the Broadway run as a reminder of the relevance of their historic tale (Acito, Kuo, and Thione 2018).

The relatively few favorable reviewers of the New York run might have felt much more at home when *Allegiance* was staged in Los Angeles. Only Takei and Greg Wantanabe (Mike Masaoka) reprised their roles from the original Broadway cast. The Los Angeles production was held in the Aratani Theatre in the JACCC. Many factors likely accounted for the sea change in critical response to the New York show. Local casting, a less formal venue, California's central role in Japanese American internment history, Takei's California childhood roots, post-presidential-election sensitivities to issues of inclusion, and Los Angeles' longstanding support for the JACCC likely all contributed to Takei and company's relatively happy California homecoming.

The *Los Angeles Times* signaled that the L.A. critics, while generally mindful of the show's shortcomings, were willing to give *Allegiance* a chance to breathe: "[*Allegiance* is] an acknowledgment of collective pain. That's a heavy burden for any show to bear . . . but it is brave for making the attempt." The *Times* further praised *Allegiance's* innovative handling of historical information and found its familiar, conventional Broadway style to be "traditionally entertaining" (Miller 2018).

The *LA Weekly* went further in defense of the show, declaring in its headline that a post-2016 election *Allegiance* is "newly relevant," insisting that the Los Angeles production of the show had found its proper time and place: "The sometimes . . . unwieldy tale of how the United States summarily [incarcerated] 120,000 Japanese Americans—including 37,000 Angelinos—today seems harrowingly near" (Raden 2018). The Los Angeles-based blog critic for *Onstage.com* also hailed the timely importance of the musical. Furthermore, the review saw no reason to take issue with the score or the book, which had taken a pounding in the New York reviews: "[*Allegiance*] is . . . a winningly-presented production that valiantly attempts to put a well-deserved spotlight on one of American history's most shameful occurrences" (Quintos 2018).

Between the Broadway and Los Angeles runs, *Allegiance* found an intermediary public life in the form of two one-night showings in neighborhood movie theaters across the country. Promoting the film under the banner of "*George Takei's Allegiance*," Fathom Events, a company specializing in marketing single-night filmed features to movie theaters, distributed the show nationwide on December 13, 2016. The single night's showing yielded the most commercially successful event Fathom had ever produced in its fourteen-year history, grossing over $1 million (Vankin 2016). A second one-night theatrical release, on February 19, 2017, grossed a very respectable $784,000 ("George Takei's *Allegiance*" 2017). It is very likely that more people saw *Allegiance* in those two one-night theater showings than those who saw the live Broadway and Los Angeles productions combined.

Historical accuracy and context

Evacuation orders and the aftermath of the attack on Pearl Harbor

Considering the compression of stage time (evacuations occurred throughout the spring of 1942 and many people were sent to holding centers prior to internment), *Allegiance* offers a generally creditable depiction of the evacuation, with exceptions.

What is often referred to as the "evacuation order," Presidential Executive Order (E.O.) 9066, was issued on February 19, 1942. Technically, E.O. 9066 was not an evacuation order—a distinction *Allegiance* does not clarify. However, it granted authority for the War Relocation Authority (WRA), the federal agency overseeing the evacuation and internment, to create domestic "military exclusion zones" from which "any or all persons may be excluded" (Roosevelt 1942). While E.O. 9066 did not specify any racial group or geographical region, it created an obvious pretext for politicians and military commanders in Western states to operationalize long-standing racist attitudes against Japanese Americans living in the region. Multiple federal and local investigations conducted prior to Pearl Harbor provided no substantive evidence of subversive activity among Japanese Americans. To the contrary, Japanese Americans were clearly and overwhelmingly loyal Americans. Nevertheless, at the urging of Western-based military commanders, in March 1942 the WRA created under a separate order two exclusion zones covering nearly all of California and parts of Washington, Oregon, and Arizona. Over 110,000 people of Japanese ancestry were evacuated and assigned to detainee camps located further inland.

Accounts of the internment often conflate E.O. 9066 and the subsequent evacuation and internment orders into a single directive. *Allegiance* does so as well. However, as *Allegiance* points out, Japanese Americans feared retaliation for Pearl Harbor prior to E.O. 9066. Tatsuo warns of danger immediately upon learning of the Pearl Harbor attack: "This will not be good for us" (Acito, Kuo, and Thione 2016). Oral accounts verify that fear and dread of racist reprisals swept through Japanese American communities in Western states before the E.O. 9066 was issued, a fact that might readily account for the conflation of the order creating the exclusion zones and the evacuation orders themselves into a single event (Tateishi 1984, 6–7).

In 1982, the Commission on Wartime Relocation and Internment of Civilians, a bipartisan federal commission that reviewed the history and impact of E.O. 9066, determined there was no justification or military necessity for the U.S. government's systematic removal and detention of Americans of Japanese descent. Their report concluded that the government had not only acted against people of Japanese ancestry without evidence of disloyalty but also had been motivated by government officials' race prejudice, war hysteria, and complicity in the massive injustice (Yamato 2012).

Yes-Yes, No-No: The Loyalty Questionnaire

In light of the complexity of the Loyalty Questionnaire's impact on camp life, *Allegiance*'s representation of events surrounding the Questionnaire is commendable and generally accurate. The Questionnaire (officially "Statement of United States Citizen of Japanese Ancestry") was distributed by the WRA in 1943. Its presumptive function was to assess whether detainees, including newly draft-eligible males, would swear allegiance to the United States and renounce allegiance to Japan. All adults in the camps were required to sign the Questionnaire or risk criminal penalties, including possible separation from families, criminal conviction, or even deportation. *Allegiance* makes clear that the Loyalty Questionnaire deeply intensified already conflicted feelings among Japanese Americans about whether to cooperate with the internment or openly resist. But the musical does not go into detail as to why this document was so potently controversial.

The new level of tension generated by the Questionnaire is admirably highlighted in Tatsuo and Sammy's heated father–son duet, the title song "Allegiance." Sammy wants to please his father but is also eager to answer yes, join the military, and defend America against the Japanese. But Tatsuo, having previously counseled passive tolerance ("Do Not Fight the Storm"), is now outraged to the breaking point: "Today! I answer 'no' and 'no'" (Kuo 2016).

Tatsuo's refusal, "no and no," is in itself a historically important signifier. The phrase refers to camp shorthand of "Yes-Yes" or "No-No" to distinguish between those who complied with the Questionnaire and those who refused. The paired responses invoke two particularly infamous items: questions 27 and 28. Question 27 demanded to know whether detainees, if called upon to do so (i.e., drafted), would be willing to serve in military combat units. Many feared that by answering yes they would be de facto enlisting in the military. Question 28 required all adult detainees to swear allegiance to the United States while renouncing "*any form of allegiance*" to Japan (emphasis added). The wording struck many as entrapment. Answering no was automatically a crime but answering yes might criminalize routine future activity such as visiting Japan or even writing letters to friends and family. Thousands of detainees throughout the camps refused to sign even in the face of likely criminal prosecution. Numerous camp resistance efforts arose in direct response to the Questionnaire. Many people referred to resisters as "No-No Boys," alluding to questions 27 and 28. The term endured for decades with double-edged implications, stigmatizing "No-Noes" [*sic*] as "uncooperative" and disloyal to America.

Life inside the camps: Whose Heart Mountain is this?

Allegiance assigns itself the daunting task of staging a two-hour depiction of life in an internment camp that on some level represents more than 100,000 life experiences from ten different camp locations. Complicating the challenge is the fact that, although the Kimura family is fictionalized, the *Allegiance* camp is not. Heart Mountain in Wyoming was an actual camp and, like the other nine sites, had its own unique identity and lore within the collective memories of the men and women incarcerated there. Claiming artistic license, the creators of *Allegiance* freely acknowledged incorporating into their story scenes inspired by events in other camps.

Professional theater reviewers raised no objections against the writers for taking such liberties. However, some camp survivors and historians objected strenuously to what they considered to be *Allegiance*'s inappropriate distortions of life at Heart Mountain. The harshest detractors focused primarily on two areas of inaccuracy: (a) a hyper-militarized depiction of Heart Mountain's operations, including overinvolvement of military police in camp life, and (b) representation of Heart Mountain camp resistance efforts as anarchistic and violently confrontational.

Heart Mountain did have a military presence, as did all internment camps in the Western states. However, the real Heart Mountain was managed by civilian administrators and staff. Military personnel were assigned to secure the perimeter and were not authorized to "police" camp life, for example, register new detainees, oversee detainees' daily life, or draw a gun on residents to impose discipline—all of which occur in *Allegiance*. The implication that Heart Mountain was operated by military authorities is probably based on events from Tule Lake camp in California. Tule Lake opened as a regular internment camp but was redesignated as a "segregation center" for the WRA camp system in 1943. It was converted to a high security penal facility, where detainees from other camps, such as Tatsuo in *Allegiance*, were transferred and held for giving "incorrect" responses on the Loyalty Questionnaire or other offenses. Once converted, Tule Lake had ten times the number of military personnel as Heart Mountain.

However, notwithstanding that Heart Mountain's administration provided detainees with paid work, camp stores, social activities, education, and health care on the premises, a number of Heart Mountain detainees recalled "concentration camplike" treatment at this camp. Complaints of mistreatment included staff theft of detainees' food or goods, some violent confrontations between staff and detainees, and inadequate shelter against the brutal Wyoming winters.

Critics' objections to *Allegiance*'s depiction of camp resistance activity focus on the historic work of the Heart Mountain Fair Play Committee (FPC), a unique and distinctive movement within the panoply of camp resistance efforts. The writers of *Allegiance* had stated publicly that they never intended to offer a site-specific history of Heart Mountain, so criticisms of "inaccuracy" with regard to the staging of Heart Mountain resistance efforts may be beside the point. However, the critics' substantive objections themselves are worth noting.

Allegiance does depict accurately the fact that many accommodationist detainees, such as Sammy Kimura, openly condemned camp resistance movements as misguided and unpatriotic, especially resisters like the FPC who mobilized opposition to wartime military policies. Further, *Allegiance* does presume to honor the FPC, identifying the committee by its historic name and underscoring its members' principled convictions and sacrifices for justice. Moreover, *Allegiance* can rightly claim that FPC did not have a monopoly of Heart Mountain resistance activity: "Acts of resistance, large and small . . . violent and non-violent . . . were ubiquitous at the Heart Mountain concentration camp" (Matsumoto 2016). Nevertheless, *Allegiance*'s critics point out that the show's staging of the FPC's activities—including lots of secrecy paired with violent clashes among the FPC and its adversaries—sacrifices historical accuracy for theatricality. One can imagine the creators of *Allegiance* determining that FPC's legalistic, civil-disobedience approach to resistance made for remarkable history but uncompelling theater.

Life in the camps: Who was Mike Masaoka?

Although he never spent a day in a camp, Mike Masaoka held more influence over camp life than any other single Japanese American. The only expressly non-fictional character in *Allegiance*, Masaoka was the controversial spokesperson, leader, and Washington lobbyist for the JACL during the war. Few historical facts about Masaoka's policies and political influence are in dispute. However, interpretation and assessment of Masaoka's legacy remains controversial even today. *Allegiance* weighs in on that controversy and is pointedly critical of Masaoka for demonizing resisters and legitimizing Japanese Americans' forfeiture of civil rights as a patriotic contribution to the war effort. Yet, while largely condemning Masaoka for much of the suffering borne by the Japanese American community during the internment, *Allegiance* implicitly affirms the validity of some of Masaoka's ultimate goals.

Even prior to Pearl Harbor, Masaoka's political vision for equality and acceptance for Japanese Americans centered on his unshakable belief in "cheerful" cooperation with all government demands. His advice to his countrymen and women to "prove [ourselves] worthy of equal treatment" through humility and eagerness to cooperate earned him both admiring followers and appalled detractors within the Japanese American community (Niiya 2018). His public philosophy never wavered even after Pearl Harbor, evacuation, internment, the drafting of detainees, and the camp resistance movements.

Although granted a few sympathetic stage moments where he sincerely, if ineffectually, advocates for better treatment of Japanese Americans, *Allegiance*'s Masaoka is an unappealing politician: condescending, dismissive of dissent, and unnuanced in his thinking. His tailored business attire contrasts jarringly with the plain clothing worn by detainees and visually aligns him with the Washington bureaucrats and politicians overseeing internment policy. Throughout the play, Masaoka's statements in support of government policies reek of hypocrisy. He speaks nobly of "sacrifices" that every Japanese American but himself appears to be making: "In a time of war, it is necessary to forego some civil liberties . . . trust in the fairness of the American way" (Acito, Kuo, and Thione 2016).

Yet, while *Allegiance* echoes real criticisms of Masaoka that have circulated throughout the Japanese American community for decades, the show implicitly reinforces much of what Masaoka tried to accomplish. The story's hero, Sammy Kimura, a fierce critic of the Heart Mountain resistance, is Masaoka's chief acolyte on stage. However, as a man Sammy is everything that the "stage Mike Masaoka" is not—likeable, sincere, self-sacrificing, and principled. In contrast to Masaoka, who, like Sammy, volunteered for wartime army service, once we see Sammy in his military uniform we never see him out of it. In an effort to bring some balance to Masaoka's portrayal, the writers have Masaoka address the audience at the end of the play. In an abbreviated version of postwar statements the real Mike Masaoka made on various occasions, "stage Masaoka" responds to critics and, implicitly, to the musical itself: "[Many believed] I betrayed my people, but I and I alone held the fate of 120,000 lives in my hands. I confronted government officials who wanted to deport us, to have us sterilized . . . everything I did—everything—I did for the good of my people" (Acito, Kuo, and Thione 2016).

Allegiance creditably honors feelings of lasting resentment that built up around Masaoka during and after the war, while acknowledging that his legacy remains a subject of controversy. Yet the epilogue, in which a uniformed Sam Kimura is finally reconciled with his family and his wartime past, embraces much of Masaoka's vision. The real Mike Masaoka predicted all along that the benefits of wartime cooperation and military service would come to Japanese Americans after the war was over, as would equality, respect, and healing. One can envision the real Mike Masaoka in the audience applauding enthusiastically when his devoted follower, war hero Sam Kimura in full military uniform, forsakes his past bitterness and finds acceptance and reconciliation.

Sammy's *Life* magazine cover story

Sammy's *Life* magazine cover story touting his heroics in battle is entirely fictional. This made-up plot point, although seemingly innocuous, actually misrepresents important aspects of American race relations and media culture in the 1940s.

At the time of the Pearl Harbor attack, approximately 5,000 Japanese Americans were serving actively in the U.S. military. Immediately following the attack, the U.S. Selective Service System ceased drafting or accepting volunteer enlistments of Japanese Americans. They had all been reclassified for Selective Service as 4C: "enemy aliens" not qualified for military service because of race or ancestry. This prohibition against Japanese Americans serving in the armed forces represented a setback for Mike Masaoka and the JACL, who viewed the war with Japan as a golden opportunity for Japanese Americans to demonstrate their patriotic loyalty to a suspicious, predominantly white American public. The JACL successfully lobbied Washington officials to allow Japanese Americans, including camp detainees, to serve in the military—supporting the creation of a segregated military unit similar to the "Negro units." (The government agreed on the condition that camp detainees would be required to sign what became the Loyalty Questionnaire.)

Sammy's fictitious *Life* magazine cover story appears in the musical after Sammy signs "yes" on his Loyalty Questionnaire and sets off from Heart Mountain to join the army. Serving heroically in combat and earning a Purple Heart, Sammy is the subject of national press coverage—including the *Life* magazine cover photo portrait fully visible to the audience. Although Sammy's *Life* magazine cover is a critical prop in the Kimura family storyline, no Japanese American soldier received anything comparable to the press attention bestowed upon Sammy in *Allegiance*.

Sammy's cover story misrepresents the reality of America's wartime media culture. During the war no Asian American member of the military appeared on a cover of any of the "major weeklies": *Life* magazine, *Time* magazine, and *Look* magazine (bi-weekly in the case of *Look* magazine). Since televisions were not yet commonly available, visually appealing national magazine cover photographs provided the equivalent of today's viral images. They heavily influenced national news coverage, dinner conversations, and workplace small talk. A Japanese American combat soldier appearing on the cover of *Life* magazine would have been elevated to a level of fame comparable to that of leading politicians, movie stars, sports legends, and a handful of white military heroes who did appear on those covers. It never happened.

Sammy's cover story is likely an outsized variation of an article that *Time* magazine published in 1944 profiling a Japanese American gunnery sergeant named Ben Kuroki (1917–2015). Appearing on page 78, the article earned Kuroki notoriety among Japanese Americans in particular. The JACL encouraged Kuroki to visit camps, recruit detainees, and criticize resisters—events reenacted by Sammy in *Allegiance*. But no Asian American soldier emerged from the war as a national "name" celebrity ("Ben Kuroki" 1944).

The conspicuous attention *Allegiance* affords Sammy's cover story belies a history of servicemen and women of color being grossly under-represented as recipients of major military service awards. By 1946, Congress had approved only one Medal of Honor for an Asian American soldier and no Medals of Honor to African Americans for service in World War II. Petitions submitted to Congress over the course of forty-five years led to reviews which concluded that racism was a determining factor in the virtually all-white roster of World War II era awardees. In 2000, seven African Americans and twenty-two Asian Americans and Pacific Islanders were finally awarded Congressional Medals of Honor for their service in a ceremony at the White House (Niiya 2014; Clinton 2000).

Thomas A. Greenfield

Further reading

Abe, Frank, dir. 2000. *Conscience and the Constitution*. San Francisco: Independent Television Service. DVD.

Acito, Marc, Jay Kuo, and Lorenzo Thione. 2016. *Allegiance*. Video recording, February 6, 2016 at Longacre Theatre, 132 minutes. Theatre on Film and Tape Archive, New York Public Library for the Performing Arts.

Acito, Marc, Jay Kuo, and Lorenzo Thione. 2018. "Marc Acito, Lorenzo Thione, and Jay Kuo Talk Importance of *Allegiance* Musical." *YouTube*, 9:41, March 9, 2018.

"Ben Kuroki—American." 1944. *Time Magazine*, February 7, 1944.

Clinton, William J. 2000. "Remarks on Presenting the Congressional Medal of Honor to Asian-American Heroes of World War II." *American Presidency Project*, University of California Santa Barbara, June 21, 2000.

Cote, David. 2015. "*Allegiance:* Theater Review." *Time Out New York*, August 14, 2015.

Dziemianowicz, Joe. 2015. "'*Allegiance*' Review: George Takei Lends Luster to New Broadway Musical." *New York Daily News*, November 8, 2015.

"George Takei's *Allegiance*." 2017. *Box Office Mojo*.

Isherwood, Christopher. 2015. "Review: '*Allegiance*,' a Musical History Lesson about Interned Japanese-Americans." *New York Times*, November 8, 2015.

Jones, Chris. 2015. "'*Allegiance*' on Broadway Is Inspired by Life of George Takei." *Chicago Tribune*, November 8, 2015.

Jones, Jennifer Locke, curator. 1990–2001. "A More Perfect Union: Japanese Americans & the U.S. Constitution." *Smithsonian National Museum of American History*.

Kuo, Jay. 2016. "*Allegiance*: Original Cast Recording." Broadway Records, *YouTube*, 1:08:21, February 15–17.

Masaoka, Mike and Bill Hosokawa. 1987. *They Call Me Moses: An American Saga*. New York: William Morrow and Company.

Matsumoto, Mieko. 2016. "Heart Mountain." *Densho Encyclopedia*, April 1, 2016, https:// encyclopedia.densho.org/ Heart%20Mountain/.

Miller, Daryl H. 2018. "George Takei & Co. Pledge an '*Allegiance*' to Teaching WWII History." *Los Angeles Times*, March 1, 2018.

Niiya, Brian. 2014. "Japanese Americans in Military [sic] During World War II." *Densho Encyclopedia*, last revised March 5, 2014.

Niiya, Brian. 2018. "Japanese American Creed." *Densho Encyclopedia*, last revised January 11, 2018.

Quintos, Michael L. 2018. "Review: George Takei Returns to '*Allegiance*' for Its Superb Los Angeles Premiere." *OnStage Blog*, March 3, 2018.

Raden, Bill. 2018. "Newly Relevant Musical *Allegiance* Depicts an American Wartime Crime against Its Citizens." *LA Weekly*, March 6, 2018.

Roosevelt, Franklin D. 1942. "Executive Order 9066: Authorizing the Secretary of War to Prescribe Military Areas." *National Park Service*.

Soloski, Alexis. 2015. "*Allegiance* Review: George Takei Can't Save Broadway's Mediocre Pledge." *Guardian* (U.S. edition), November 8, 2015.

Tateishi, John. 1984. *And Justice for All: An Oral History of the Japanese American Detention Camps*. New York: Random House.

Taylor, Allen. 2011. "World War II: Internment of Japanese Americans." *Atlantic Monthly*, August 21, 2011.

Vankin, Deborah. 2016. "George Takei's Broadway Musical '*Allegiance*' Breaks a Theater-Screening Record." *Los Angeles Times*, January 6, 2016.

Winer, Linda. 2015. "'*Allegiance*' Review: George Takei on WWII Japanese-American Camps." *Newsday*, December 8, 2015.

Yamato, Sharon. 2012. "Commission on Wartime Relocation and Internment of Civilians." *Densho Encyclopedia*, June 25, 2012, https://encyclopedia.densho.org/Commission%20on%20Wartime%20Relocation%20and%20Internment%20of%20Civilians.

CHAPTER 2
AMERICAN IDIOT (2009)

Music by Green Day (as credited on the Broadway *Playbill*)
Lyrics by Billie Joe Armstrong (1972–) *(Unless otherwise noted)*
Book by Billie Joe Armstrong and Michael Mayer (1960–)
World Premiere: Berkeley Repertory Theatre, Berkeley, California, September 15, 2009
Broadway Run: St. James Theatre, April 20, 2010–April 24, 2011

Songs

"American Idiot"
"Jesus of Suburbia"
"City of the Damned"
"I Don't Care"
"Dearly Beloved"
"Tales of Another Broken Home"
"Holiday"
"Boulevard of Broken Dreams"
"Favorite Son"
"Are We the Waiting"
"St. Jimmy"
"Give Me Novacaine"
"Last of the American Girls/She's a Rebel"
"Last Night on Earth"
"Too Much Too Soon"
"Before the Lobotomy"
"Extraordinary Girl"
"Before the Lobotomy" (Reprise)
"When It's Time"
"Know Your Enemy"
"21 Guns"
"Letterbomb"
"Wake Me Up When September Ends"
"The Death of St. Jimmy"
"East 12th Street"
"Nobody Likes You" (lyrics by Mike Dirnt)
"Rock and Roll Girlfriend" (lyrics by Tré Cool)
"We're Coming Home Again"
"Whatsername"

Overview

American Idiot is a 2009 sung-through musical adaptation of the landmark punk-influenced concept album of the same name. Released in 2004, the album—written, performed, and produced by veteran punk rock band Green Day—achieved critical acclaim for not only its artistic merit but also its searing social commentary—qualities the musical's creators sought to enlarge upon in the theatrical adaptation.

The album and the musical presented a jarring portrait of embittered, angst-ridden suburban Millennials, born around 1981–96, and the debilitating socioeconomic decay confronting them as they enter adulthood. Moreover, the *American Idiot* album had been among the first popular culture platforms that expressed disapproval of the American government's post-9/11 wars in the Middle East, which had commenced in March 2003 with the American-led military invasion of Iraq. Between the 2004 release of the album and the

2009 world premiere of the musical, the album's stature as social criticism, historical artifact, and anti-war protest had grown steadily, as its social commentary and themes of youthful alienation and disillusionment seemed increasingly reflective of the times.

The *American Idiot* album's smoldering undertones of resentment against the American government's invasion of Iraq resonated with increasing effect as public support for the Iraq War effort, resting comfortably over 60 percent in 2003, plummeted to below 40 percent going into the 2008 presidential election (Rosentiel 2008). Over time, young audiences, music critics, and Green Day band members themselves increasingly framed the album as a direct repudiation of the Bush administration's conduct in the Iraq War, even though only one of the original album's thirteen songs, "Holiday," is expressly an anti-war song.

The album's treatment of its predominant theme—young adults' alienation from vapid, conformist suburban life—reflected a level of artistic maturity compared to the band's earlier punk-steeped mosh pit style rants and jests. However, over time the album moved surprisingly close to mainstream cultural discourse, as journalists and educators discovered disturbing socioeconomic developments facing middle- and working-class Millennials: findings that corresponded in tone and content with much of what emanated from Green Day's album. *American Idiot* hit singles such as the title track "American Idiot," "Jesus of Suburbia," and "Are We the Waiting" provided broadly accessible reference points for emerging social crises among young adults: crippling student debt, upswings in substance abuse, widespread unemployment and underemployment, depression, premature burnout, as well as disillusionment with the seemingly endless wars in the Middle East. (A Harvard University opinion study on Millennials, pointedly entitled "Growing Up with Green Day," asserted that the *American Idiot* album and musical functioned as a "rude awakening" for Millennials and "political allegory" for "coming of age in the post-9/11 era . . . as the nation was engaged in armed conflict overseas and battling [the 2007–8] recession" [Wang 2014].)

The musical's loosely structured plot follows a year in the lives of three suburban Millennial childhood friends on the threshold of adulthood. Johnny (the lead character), Will, and Tunny, all from Jingletown, U.S.A., renounce the idiotic banality and false promises of their suburban upbringing. They agree to escape to an unnamed city, vowing to carve out meaningful lives for themselves. Will, upon learning that his girlfriend Heather is pregnant, remains in Jingletown and mounts an ill-fated attempt to make a go of suburban family life. In the city, Johnny falls victim to a pernicious heroin addiction (personified by his depraved alter ego St. Jimmy). He survives his addiction, but his tortured behavior drives away the woman he loves (Whatshername). Chronically depressed, Tunny binge-watches television and becomes entranced by army recruitment TV ads for America's all-volunteer forces fighting in the Middle East. He volunteers for combat overseas, where he loses a leg but falls in love with his military nurse. The plot ends with a homecoming reunion of the three young men and old friends back in the suburbs. The final scene, while hardly optimistic, evokes a degree of reassuring affirmation, but affirmation mitigated by hard-wrought loss and an arduous coming of age.

The music, attitudes, and themes of the *American Idiot* musical and album are rooted in 1970s British and American punk culture which, like other youth movements, "practiced a wide array of social dissent through shared behavioral, musical, and costume orientations" (Clark 2003). Originally an homage to urbanism, 1970s American punk culture's foundational bands, such as New York City's Ramones or Los Angeles' Black Flag, modeled and mirrored punk's self-marginalized youth rebellion. Half-shouted stripped-down, guitar-and-drum rhythm-driven songs invoked 1950s rock and roll's unwelcome intrusion into American culture (too loud, too fast, musically incompetent). Punk fashion featured torn jeans, shirts, and tops. Those going for a more iconoclastic look added other "disreputable" fashion choices, including fluid and ambiguous gender display, unconventional hair stylings, body art, and piercings—anything that might invoke a parent's validating primal scream: "You're not going out dressed like *that* are you?" Early punk expressions of political dissent tended toward the visceral: profanity-laced rages, sarcastic dismissiveness, sweeping nihilistic condemnations, largely void of nuance or reflection. To the extent that punk culture sought reaction beyond its own adherents, it did so "through an ability to shock and dismay, to disobey prescribed confines of class, gender, and ethnicity" (Clark 2003). By the time *American Idiot* premiered on Broadway in 2010, however, punk's disruptive impact on American culture had long ceased to shock. "The punk prairie fire" that began in the 1970s and blazed a trail of disorderly oppositionalism in rock music, gender identity display, pop fashion, and political dissent had settled, if not always comfortably, into mainstream American culture. During the 1980s, metal bands, music videos, and a youth-market-savvy fashion industry had neutralized, if not normalized, punk's visual weapons. Foundational punk musicians such as the Ramones, Blondie, and England's The Clash had been inducted into the rock and roll Hall of Fame, enshrined as pillars of the industry they once reviled.

Punk's nihilistic social commentary, for all its 1970s anti-social fervor, was culturally marginalized during Ronald Reagan's presidency (1981–9). By the mid-1980s, African American hip-hop artists such as Public Enemy and NWA dominated American youth-protest music. Moreover, LGBTQ+ rights activists responding to the AIDS crisis in the 1980s set an issue-focused legislative agenda for urban political dissent. Following a similar pattern, when *American Idiot* opened on Broadway in 2010, opposition to President George W. Bush's 2003 decision to invade Iraq—a highly controversial minority position when Green Day released the *American Idiot* album—had in fact become a mainstream majority political opinion.

Green Day and *American Idiot* did not find their way to Broadway as much as Broadway found its way to them. Tom Hulce and Michael Mayer, producer and director respectively of the raucous, coming-of-age Broadway musical *Spring Awakening* (2006), greatly admired *American Idiot* and understood the music's kinship with their show. In 2007, having swept the Tony Awards with eight wins, including Best Original Musical for *Spring Awakening*, Hulce and Mayer wanted their next show to be a musical adaptation of the *American Idiot* album. Mayer eventually pitched the idea to Green Day songwriter and front man Billie Joe Armstrong.

Green Day's members, "un-punkishly" ambitious and openly success-driven since their teens, were no less so as multi-millionaires at the top of their game in their mid-thirties. They had pondered adapting *American Idiot* to film but eventually abandoned that idea. Having themselves described the album as "a punk rock opera," the band was intrigued with the idea for a musical stage adaptation, although they had never seriously considered it on their own. After seeing Mayer's work in *Spring Awakening* on Broadway and attending a professional workshopping of the expanding score for an *American Idiot* musical, Armstrong became increasingly enamored of the project—to the point of stepping into the role of St. Jimmy several times on Broadway.

With a one-year run and over 400 performances, the cultural impact of *American Idiot* did not come close to matching the cultural influence of the album. However, the musical represents a theatrical breakthrough as the first *truly* American style punk Broadway musical. More importantly, as music critics eventually wrote ten-year and fifteen-year anniversary retrospectives on the album, the 2009 musical added to a growing consensus among popular culture critics: as a harbinger of post-9/11 youth disillusionment and an ear-splitting alert to weakening socioeconomic fault lines, *American Idiot* in all its forms had "kick-started 21st Century protest music" (Clark 2019).

Plot synopsis

At the start, a flashing collage of blaring television soundbites emanates from an otherwise darkened stage that is infested with TV screens. News snippets of 9/11 response speeches by President George W. Bush (2001), the Indian Ocean tsunami that killed 225,000 people (2004), and North Korea's first nuclear weapon's test (2006) quickly establish the musical's time period and dystopian overtones. Approximately twenty Millennials from the fictitious suburb of Jingletown, U.S.A., staring at the screens, turn them off one-by-one and sing a frenzied, self-aware anthem of frustration and social alienation ("American Idiot").

Stepping forward, three friends—Johnny, Will, and Tunny—proceed to Will's apartment, where they hang out, drink beer, smoke weed, and, by turns, lament, lash out at, and mock their tedious existence ("Jesus of Suburbia"). Out of beer, the trio heads to a 7-Eleven, where they ascend the store's roof. The three men watch their peers hanging out in the parking lot below and conclude that their friends' lives are no better than their own ("City of the Dead"). Fed up with dismal suburban life and the apathy it engenders in himself and his friends, Johnny challenges all of them to care about life and the broken world "from Anaheim to the Middle East" ("I Don't Care").

While Johnny, Tunny, and Will hatch a plan to escape the suburbs and move to the city, Will's girlfriend, Heather, discovers she is pregnant ("Dearly Beloved"). As the three men say goodbye to their friends and board a city-bound bus, Heather confronts Will with news of her pregnancy. Will remains in Jingletown with Heather as Johnny and Tunny depart, leaving suburbia for city life ("Tales of Another Broken Home," "Holiday").

Once in the city, Johnny and Tunny settle into a shabby hotel room. Johnny spends his nights walking the streets of the city alone. One night he notices a woman, whom he calls Whatsername, opening an apartment window several floors above him. He is immediately captivated by her ("Boulevard of Broken Dreams"). In the hotel room, Tunny, binge-watching television, has grown disenchanted with the city's own brand of boredom. He becomes intrigued by wartime military recruitment television ads and the hyper-masculine "sex machine" image they portray of soldiers in combat. Imagining himself in such a role ("Favorite Son"), Tunny enlists in the army ("Are We the Waiting"). Johnny, disatisfied with his lonely city life as well, conjures up an insidious imaginary alter-ego called St. Jimmy, who encourages him to take pills and shoot heroin for the first time ("St. Jimmy").

Back in the suburbs, Will sits depressed, withdrawn, drunk, and stoned. Progressing in her pregnancy, Heather struggles to connect with Will, but to no avail. Tunny is deployed to war in the Middle East and is soon hospitalized with a badly wounded leg ("Give Me Novacaine").

Since first spotting her a few months earlier, Johnny has struck up a passionate affair with Whatsername. He writes a postcard to Will about his strong feelings for her ("Last of the American Girls/She's a Rebel"). St. Jimmy appears and, threatened by Johnny's love for Whatsername, urges Johnny to shoot heroin. He does so and persuades Whatsername to shoot up with him.

In Jingletown, Heather has given birth to a baby girl. Will is still depressed and remains detached from both Heather and the baby ("Last Night on Earth"). Fed up with Will's emotional abandonment, Heather, holding their baby, walks out on him ("Too Much, Too Soon").

Tunny, wounded in battle in the Middle East, has been taken to a military hospital, where he shares a room with three other wounded soldiers ("Before the Lobotomy"). Hallucinating on morphine, Tunny falls in love with his nurse and engages in a dream-like aerial ballet with her ("Extraordinary Girl"). Tunny's hallucination soon fades, and we see him on his hospital gurney writhing in pain ("Before the Lobotomy [Reprise]").

In the city, Johnny proclaims his love for the sleeping Whatsername ("When It's Time"). When Johnny refuses an additional hit of heroin, St. Jimmy, furious at the refusal, tries to split up Johnny and Whatsername. St. Jimmy's aggression frightens Johnny, rendering him delusional and paranoid. Succumbing to his terror, Johnny takes another hit ("Know Your Enemy"). Whatsername pleads with Johnny to abandon his path of self-destruction and embrace their relationship.

At the military hospital, Tunny's nurse, Extraordinary Girl, dresses Tunny's post-operation wounds following the operation to amputate his wounded leg. Heather appears across stage with her baby, having permanently left Will, who remains despondent on his couch ("21 Guns"). Johnny writes a note to Whatsername telling her that he has chosen drugs over their relationship. Infuriated, Whatsername confronts Johnny, telling him that St. Jimmy is an invention of his self-destructive mind. Disgusted by Johnny's downward spiral, Whatsername, unleashing a word storm of invective, tells Johnny she is leaving him ("Letterbomb").

Seven months after accepting their challenge to start caring about life, Johnny, Will, and Tunny each sits alone in their respective rooms, wearily playing guitar and acknowledging that they have hit rock bottom ("Wake Me Up When September Ends"). St. Jimmy revisits Johnny, who struggles to resist him. Johnny's resistance pushes St. Jimmy towards a metaphorical suicide ("The Death of St. Jimmy"). Apparently drug-free and freed from St. Jimmy's hold on him, Johnny seeks out and takes a traditional office job. Finding no satisfaction with that change, Johnny realizes that moving to the city was a mistake ("East 12th Street"). Will remains on his couch, wallowing in solitude ("Nobody Likes You"). Heather enters and introduces Will to her new rock-star boyfriend ("Rock and Roll Girlfriend"). Upset at the encounter, Will leaves and seeks solace at a 7-Eleven.

To his surprise, Will finds Johnny and Tunny at the 7-Eleven. Johnny has sold his guitar to buy a bus ticket home. Tunny has returned from the warfront with his nurse, the Extraordinary Girl. The three friends share an intense reunion that transitions to a gathering of their friends from Jingletown. Heather, her baby, and her boyfriend appear; Heather uneasily allows Will to introduce his child to his friends ("We're Coming Home Again").

One year later, Johnny reflects upon the lessons learned during his time in the city and since his return. He accepts his shortcomings, exhibits some maturity, reconciles himself to having lost his true love, and expresses a conspicuously non-punkish forward-looking, if measured, sense of self-affirmation ("Whatsername").

Critical reception

American Idiot premiered at the Berkeley Repertory Theatre in Berkeley, California, on September 15, 2009. Originally scheduled for a five-week run, the production broke box office records for the house and garnered rave reviews, a showing that earned it a five-week extension at Berkeley. Charles McNulty of the *Los Angeles Times* praised the "visually mesmerizing" production for melding "latter-day mainstream punk with cutting-edge musical theater craft" (McNulty 2009). *SF Gate*, the sister-site of the *San Francisco Chronicle*, complimented the cast and creative team for mounting a "pulsating wall of sound [of] sheer energy," driven by "Broadway-quality pipes, stage-rattling, thrashing choreography, flying bodies and walls crammed with pulsating video and projected images" (Hurwitt 2009). Karen D'Souza of San Jose's *Mercury News* immediately saw the show's Broadway potential: "[I]f there's any justice in the world it will head east shortly" (D'Souza 2009).

However, *American Idiot*'s book did not sit well with the California reviewers, even those who thought highly of the show. Disparaging its faulty narrative and weak dialog, critics belittled the creators' self-imposed burden of including every song from the *American Idiot* album plus additional songs from Green Day's 2009 album, *21st Century Breakdown*. The *Los Angeles Times* condemned "loosely tied wisps of narrative" as not even constituting a book (McNulty 2009). Similarly, *Mercury News* called the narration "clunky" for failing to "stand up against the lyrics" (D'Souza 2009). *SF Gate* agreed: "It isn't much of a story, more like concepts imposed upon songs proclaiming nihilistic disillusion" (Hurwitt 2009).

American Idiot transferred from Berkeley to Broadway on April 20, 2010. Opening with many members of the Berkeley cast and crew, the Broadway production received a positive critical reception, if not quite the power surge it received in California. The *New York Times* called *American Idiot* "a thrillingly raucous and gorgeously wrought Broadway musical" (Isherwood 2010). The *Chicago Tribune* concurred, stating that *American Idiot* "delivers a thick, gorgeous head rush of a musical soundscape without current Broadway parallel" (Jones 2010). Most critics were also quick to make comparisons between *American Idiot* and other musicals (i.e., *Spring Awakening*, *Hair*, *Rent*, and *The Who's Tommy*) with similar rock opera style and themes of youthful alienation.

The cast earned kudos for their energy and talents. The *Hollywood Reporter* praised John Gallagher Jr. (winner of the Tony Award for Featured Actor in *Spring Awakening*) as "impressively dynamic as Johnny" and lauded the entire cast as equally compelling (Scheck 2010). The *New York Times* commented on the cast's "galvanizing intensity" and their ability to "transmit with aching clarity" the show's more reflective songs (Isherwood 2010). Critics further praised the stage design and technology that gave the show a "fierce aesthetic charge" (Isherwood 2010). *Newsday* hailed director Michael Mayer's visual conception as "a nonstop, sky-high concert/collage of embedded video screens and metal staircases . . . and [an occasional] person hanging in the air" (Winer 2010). *Newsday* also singled out excellent work by scenic designer Christine Jones and lighting designer Kevin Adams. The *Chicago Tribune* praised choreographer Steven Hoggett, "who found a swooping, stuttering organic vocabulary that makes headbanging quite a beautiful act" (Jones 2010). Critics also praised musical arranger Tom Kitt for creating "lush, harmony-laden arrangements" of the Green Day songs that "work in a theatrical context without sacrificing their guitar-fueled crunch" (Gardner 2010).

As it had in Berkeley, Broadway's *American Idiot*'s book failed to impress. The *New York Times* found it distractingly simplistic, "drawn in brash, primarycolored strokes" (Isherwood 2010). The *Washington Post* also derided the flat story: "It's surprising how a show with enough imaginative candlepower to light a stadium can appear to have invested so little energy in illuminating its characters" (Marks 2010). The *Chicago Tribune* was similarly dismissive of the playwrighting: "[*American Idiot*] has mercifully few lines of dialogue or strained connective tissue" to flesh out the characters. The *Hollywood Reporter* went so far as to suggest that weaknesses in the narrative threatened the success of the entire musical: "it's a thin premise on which to base a musical, and the book . . . never manages to make us care about the fate of its thinly drawn characters" (Scheck 2010). The *New York Theater Guide* gave the show one of its few full-on pans, asserting that the intervening years between the album and the musical had "dated" the music and ultimately rendered the show mainstream: "the music has become what it resisted" (McCall 2010).

American Idiot on Broadway fared reasonably well among its peers, receiving three Tony nominations—Best Musical, Best Scenic Design, and Best Lighting Design—and winning in the two latter categories for Christine Jones and Kevin Adams, respectively. Michael Mayer won a Drama Desk award for Outstanding Direction. The production had a Broadway run of a year and 424 productions—not a hit but a modest success, considering composer/lyricists Green Day's distinctively non-Broadway background. A national tour ran from December 2011 to July 2012. The *Toronto Star* extolled the touring show as the "first great musical of the 21st century" and "one of the most exciting musicals you've ever seen" (Ouzounian 2011).

American Idiot, punk culture's mainstream American musical theater debut, doubtless appalled punk purists if for no other reason than the show earned sufficient acclaim and box office sales to justify itself and encourage future ventures in the same vein. Nonetheless, the prevailing positive critical reception was nicely encapsulated by the *Los Angeles Times*: "Even if *American Idiot* did not spin a fully satisfying yarn, its roar is still irresistible" (McNulty 2009).

Historical accuracy and context

"Idiot Nation" Millennials: punk and disorderly

Large numbers of angst-stricken, alienated suburban Millennials at the turn of the twenty-first century gravitated toward the recent resurgence of punk music and culture, which by 2000 had acquired far greater cultural influence than had its 1970s punk antecedent. No longer niche or cult music, recordings and concerts by rock star punk bands such as Green Day, The Offspring, and Blink-182 provided a vehicle for large-scale excoriation of suburban parental hypocrisy. Millennials lashed out at the familiar agents of suburban banality: education, mass media, middle-class dress and social codes, sexual repression, boredom, and careerism. They did so collectively through music and, often, individually through anti-social and even self-destructive behavior at school, work, and home.

If twenty-first-century Millennials openly despised the established adult world and the adults that ran it, the feeling appeared to be mutual. Millennials' disruptive and apathetic behavior—or perception of such behavior—roiled adults across the generational spectrum, especially where workplace performance was concerned. By 2005, social commentators ranging from thirty-year-old Generation Xers to sixty-five-year-old Baby Boomers began weighing in.

Self-help author Simon Sinek vilified Millennials as victims of "failed parenting strategies: too many were told that they were special [all the time] . . . Some kids got participation medals . . . for coming in last" (Sinek 2017). A thirty-two-year-old entrepreneur published a controversial business editorial entitled "What's Wrong with My Millennial Employees?" and proceeded to answer her own question: they don't follow through, they take things for granted, they are cocky, and they think they are exempt from rules (Jimenez 2012). The title of a professor's book left little to the imagination: *The Dumbest Generation: How the Digital Age Stupefies Young Americans and Jeopardizes Our Future* (Bauerlein 2008).

Defenders responded along two contradictory lines. Many dismissed the sweeping insult as ludicrous on its face: "My generation started the trend of communicating through blogs and social networks. Every Fortune 500 company has jumped on our bandwagon . . . [We] process information in a much more streamlined fashion than any previous generation" (Hershatter and Epstein 2010). However, a second group conceded that perceptions of Millennial social disfunction reflected reality. Nevertheless, they slammed critics' moralistic attacks on Millennials' character as counterproductive and misinformed about important socioeconomic trends. This second group had a point and evidence to back them up.

As early as the 1990s, sociological research revealed troubling signs of socioeconomic disintegration in predominantly white American suburbs to a degree previously unknown in these post-World War II "planned communities." Long considered safe havens from the presumptive scourges of urban housing shortages, social instability, and poverty, fifty-year-old suburbs "with their shoddy construction and hastily installed infrastructure" were visibly crumbling (Florida 2017). Physical deterioration was only a surface problem. Additional findings over the same period revealed steadily collapsing social structures and cultural guardrails, resulting in upswings in suburban crime, unemployment, illegal and dangerous drug use, anxiety, and anti-social behavior among young adults. These findings mirrored conclusions from concurrent studies of youth self-identifying as punk from which researchers concluded that "the implications of suburban life appeared to provide a stage on which punk rock thrives . . . providing a [means of] resisting boredom by dissenting with a purpose" (Chuang and Hart 2008).

Journalists eventually hit upon this troubling synthesis of punk culture, Millennial alienation, and socioeconomic suburban decay. Millennial author Ryan Holiday wrote in response to castigations of his peers:

> The economic situation for millennials is not a good one. Thirty-six percent of our generation still lives with their parents. Unemployment for millennials is twice the national average . . . [many] aren't even bothering to learn how to drive . . . student loan debt, rising above $1 trillion, [is] surpassing credit card debt.
>
> *Holiday 2015*

A similar process of synthesis went into the writing of the songs for *American Idiot*. Composer Armstrong has said that the struggle to find coherence among disparate destabilizing forces in the wake of 9/11 was central to the band's conception of the album: "[We were] trying to make sense out of a big mess. You're trying to find something to believe in, but it's difficult when you're getting bombarded with useless information. So it's just [about] trying to find your identity and your individualism in the midst of all that" (Montgomery 2010).

In research and discussion of the socioeconomic forces confronting their entry into adulthood, Millennials, in addition to being the subject of such scrutiny, increasingly asserted themselves as participants, critics, and arbiters of the debates at hand. By the time *American Idiot* the musical opened in Berkeley, many Millennials had come to identify Green Day as providing an essential voice in the national conversation. For citizens of "Idiot Nation" (the bands' official fan club), the album became nearly akin to sacred text.

There were precious few Millennial punks working as full-time Broadway critics in 2010. Thus, the lasting legacy of *American Idiot* diverges from the concerns of most Broadway opening critics as the following *American Idiot* "peer reviews" demonstrate.

- "*American Idiot* traces the evolution of the millennial generation and canonizes the generation's journey to understand how to engage in our nation's political system" (Wang 2014).
- "*American Idiot* (and especially 'Jesus of Suburbia') is an artifact and reflection of suburban culture" (Chuang and Hart 2008).
- "[Green Day] saw the world around them cowering in paranoia and fear, struggling to come to grips with the post-9/11 world . . . they were the perfect band in the perfect place to call the world out" (Bray 2014).
- "We don't just love the songs but [the band's] entire existence . . . Green Day sinks its claws in and leaves its mark, forever earning the affection of fans who age alongside the band" (Johnson 2016).
- "In 1994 Green Day pointed the way forward for alternative rock" (James 2017).

"The Army that you have": Iraq, Tunny, and recruiting the all-volunteer army

Over time, the *American Idiot* album earned a larger reputation than the musical for protesting against President George W. Bush and the Iraq War, notwithstanding that the musical focuses far more intensively on post-9/11 American politics than does the album. Retrospective essays on its 2004 release seemed to retrofit the album as an explicit anti-Bush screed: "crosshairs . . . on the smirking face of President George W. Bush" (Winwood 2018); "unleashing . . . Bush-bashing fury" (Schonfeld 2016); potentially "swaying the presidential election" against Bush (Long 2009). However, unlike the album which, but for the pointedly anti-war song "Holiday," broadly implies an anti-Bush position, *American Idiot* the musical confronts President Bush and the post-9/11 wars in the Middle East head-on, connecting them directly to a major character's narrative.

The musical opens with blaring yet instantly recognizable snippets from Bush's two most famous post-9/11 speeches: the "bull horn" call to cheering throngs from the wreckage of the fallen Twin Towers ("I can hear you! The rest of the world hears you") and his "War on Terrorism" speech to Congress ("either you are with us or you are with the terrorists"), delivered three and nine days respectively after the attacks of September 11, 2001. Tunny's volunteer military service and subsequent wounding in combat put a human face to Bush's 9/11 speeches and the roiling controversies that followed.

Although Tunny's combat injury and subsequent amputation present a graphic tale of young people at war, *American Idiot*'s most instructive historical commentary emanates from Tunny's response to televised military recruiting ads. Literally losing himself in gloriously heroic masculinity exuding from action-packed film clips of American troops on the ground, Tunny's response to military recruiting TV ads encapsulates an act repeated tens of thousands of times, during the peak troop buildup years, 2003–8.

During the first five years after the invasion, the U.S. Army struggled at times to meet recruitment demands of a surprisingly protracted armed conflict—one that Bush administration officials had predicted would last "weeks rather than months" ("FTN 3/16/03" 2003). Just prior to the March 2003 American-led invasion, Secretary of Defense Donald Rumsfeld announced that the Pentagon would not reinstate a draft to support the impending Middle East military action. The war would be won with an all-volunteer military.

The draft (formally the U.S. Selective Service System), established during World War I, had continuously conscripted male citizens into the army until 1973, when it was suspended in conjunction with America's drawdown of troops in Vietnam. Beyond the Bush administration's confidence that an all-volunteer military could quickly accomplish its Iraq mission, vivid memories of the American public's repudiation of the draft during the Vietnam era mitigated against reinstating it for the invasion of Iraq. The draft's negative impact on the political fortunes of presidents Lyndon Johnson (1964–9) and Richard Nixon (1969–74) was widely viewed as a warning sign for future presidents.

Initially, the administration's Iraq strategy succeeded. Public approval and military recruitments remained strong for several months, boosted by the May 2003 fall of Iraqi president Saddam Hussein's notorious regime—a direct result of the invasion. However, America's ongoing military presence in post-Saddam Iraq tested public support for the war, as officials wrestled with the challenge of making persuasive arguments for staying the course and producing evidence of military success. Administration predictions that American troops would be hailed as liberators by the Iraqi people proved wrong in the face of Iraq's diverse religious, ethnic, and regional factions whose deep-seated internecine disputes rendered peaceful unification impossible. The State Department's pre-invasion promises to unearth Saddam's hidden troves of weapons of mass destruction faltered badly. In 2004, leaked photographs of American troops illegally torturing prisoners of war in an army prison in Abu Ghraib fueled international criticism of the entire mission. Such setbacks impacted military recruiting efforts. In 2005, the army missed its recruiting quotas by almost 7,000 troops (Dao 2011). Soldiers on a mission, the U.S. Army Recruiting Command sprang into action.

From 2001 through 2005, the army's principal recruiting campaign theme ("Army of One") invoked themes of duty, self-sacrifice, and service from World War II recruitment drives. Ads featured the motto "Every generation has its heroes. This one is no different." The army replaced the campaign following the 2005 recruitment shortfall.

The army launched "Army Strong" in late 2006, the campaign that a real-life Tunny would likely have seen. "Army Strong" targeted seventeen- to twenty-four-year-olds via television exposure and a strong internet presence. (A "Straight From Iraq" website featured young servicemen and women giving upbeat personal accounts of their Middle East deployments.) A sub-theme, "Strength like no other," replaced appeals to duty with the lure of self-empowerment: "how serving can bring personal and career success later in life" by enhancing physical, emotional, and mental well-being (Elliot 2008). In *American Idiot*, the "Army Strong" ideology frames Tunny's fantasy and song "Favorite Son." Before enlisting, Tunny is mesmerized by television ads touting the physical prowess of today's "All-American" army soldier ("He's a sex machine"). Although *American Idiot* does not broadcast or sample actual army ads, Tunny's "Fortunate Son" sequence, albeit satirically exaggerated, strongly reflected the values and pitch of the updated army campaign. (The musical does not address army signing bonus incentive payments to recruits, nor controversies surrounding allegations of inconsistent payments, non-payments, and unexpected demands for repayment of bonuses that grew out of those programs.)

Less than two years after Secretary Rumsfeld professed full confidence in the all-volunteer army's ability to conduct its mission, he indicated that he might have altered his position. Answering a young officer's complaint that U.S. forces lacked key equipment to complete their Iraq mission, Rumsfeld replied, "you go to war with the army that you have . . . not the army you might want" (Page 2004). The United States declared an official end to the Iraq War on December 15, 2011, although as recently as February 2020, America maintains an active military combat presence in-country.

The Pentagon kept the "Army Strong" recruiting campaign for twelve years, replacing it in 2018 with "Warriors Wanted." In March 2023, the army returned to its best-known recruiting slogan, "Be all you can be," which had not been seen in action since January 2001.

As of this writing, all branches of the U.S. Armed Services are volunteer forces.

Green Day, punk, and rock history

As an identifiable rock music sub-genre, punk emerged in the 1970s (all three Green Day band members were born in 1972). Rooted in urban centers in the United States and London, England, 1970s punk generated the second of two rock and roll cultural exchanges between the two countries—the first being the 1960s "British Invasion." In the early 1960s, emerging British bands, most notably the Beatles and the Rolling Stones, literally studied imported American blues and early rock and roll records. Aided by foresighted promoters on both sides of the Atlantic, English rock bands "invaded" America with a "re-styled and refreshed" version of rock for an American generation "largely ignorant of its historical and racial origins" (Robbins 1999).

England's 1970s punk scene grew out of working-class protests over the nation's deteriorating economy, and particularly widespread unemployment among young adults. In America, the impetus was middle-class youth alienation from mainstream culture and middle-class society in general. Both streams of youth alienation became fixtures in punk music and remained so through punk's various iterations.

The origin of punk's anarchistic posture is generally credited to the London punk scene, exemplified by the Sex Pistols' song "God Save the Queen" (1977). The resonant shock of an open attack on beloved Queen Elizabeth II ("a fascist regime") was alarming to Americans as well as the British. The song's nihilistic recurring mantra—"No future"—became embedded in punk's DNA and, to this day, is widely considered the embodiment of punk's essential spirit. American airplay of Sex Pistols songs and a brief American tour in late 1977 gave rise to new punk scenes in other cities, including Seattle, Detroit, and San Francisco.

Through the 1970s, American punk bands generally remained true to the idiom's articles of faith: hyper-fast rhythms, half-shouted lyrics, high-volume weaponized power guitar chords, conspicuous absence of musical proficiency, anti-social nihilistic lyrics with clothing and body art to match, all performed with "bad kid" intimations (and sometimes more than intimations) of violence, substance abuse, and sexual aggression.

As a noticeable part of the rock scene, punk's 1970s first wave had only a few golden years in America. By 1980, it had lost much of its following, having splintered into sub-genres (new wave, hardcore, post-punk, etc.) and surrendered what little ground it held to disco, soft-rock, hip-hop, and even its own "descendants"—metal and grunge. By 1990, punk as a music commodity seemed to have found a permanent state of marginalization befitting its "no future" manifesto.

In the 1990s, punk experienced a resurgence (aka "punk's second coming"). Its breakout year was 1994, and Green Day its breakout band. Heretofore a northern California punk-style band with a regional following, Green Day's first major-label album *Dookie* (1994) sold one million copies within a few months, eventually becoming the best-selling punk album in history (Wilson-Taylor 2017). Appearing at the August 1994 Woodstock 25th anniversary festival, Green Day laid waste to the festival's "Summer of Love" pastoral nostalgia: "What is all this free hippie love sh—?" and more. They subsequently turned the gigantic mud field and its 500,000 drenched attendees into an outsized punk club with a crowd-thrilling, profanity-laced set. By

December 1994, Green Day was a rock music oxymoron: street-credible 1970s style punks and, simultaneously, international commercial music headliners—a first in punk history.

From *Dookie* and beyond, Green Day wrote songs with well-crafted qualities of commercial pop: insightful relatable lyrics, fueled by readily singalong hooks set to melodic "stuck-in-your-head" earworms. Yet they arranged, recorded, and performed with the volume, distortion, snarky sarcasm, and "not to be messed with" abandon of a first-rate stripped down American punk club band.

Green Day's success brought predictable dismissals from purists for whom the band's wealth and commercial music chops stood as *prima facie* evidence of betrayed principles. The derogatory press label "pop punk," which Armstrong openly despises, has followed the band for years but with no apparent artistic or commercial consequences. The Generation Xers who embraced *Dookie* in 1994 were having none it, any more than would the upcoming legion of Millennials who, ten years later, discovered revelatory versions of themselves in the music of *American Idiot*.

Thomas A. Greenfield and Christina M. Baurle

Further reading

Armstrong, Billie Joe, Green Day, and Michael Mayer. 2011. *Green Day's American Idiot*. New York: Music Theatre International.

Armstrong, Billie Joe, Green Day, and Michael Mayer. 2019. "American Idiot Broadway Part 1." *YouTube*, April 12, 2019, https://www.youtube.com/watch?v=BeskvTnhhm4.

Bauerlein, Mark. 2008. *How the Digital Age Stupefies Young Americans and Jeopardizes Our Future*. New York: TarcherPerigree.

Bray, Ryan. 2014. "Dusting 'Em Off: Green Day's American Idiot Turns 10." *COS (Consequence of Sound)*, September 12, 2014.

Chuang, Lisa M. and John P. Hart. 2008. "Suburban American Punks and the Musical Rhetoric of Green Day's 'Jesus of Suburbia.'" *Communication Studies* 59, no. 3: 183–201.

Clark, Dylan. 2003. "The Death and Life of Punk, the Last Subculture." In *The PostSubcultures Reader*, edited by David Muggleton and Rupert Weinzierl, 223–36. Oxford: Berg.

Clark, Tyler. 2019. "American Idiot at 15: How Green Day Kick-started 21st Century Protest Music." *Consequence of Sound*, September 21, 2019.

Dao, James. 2011. "They Signed Up to Fight." *New York Times*, September 6, 2011.

De La Rocha, Zach. 2007. "Zack De La Rocha Inducts Patti Smith Rock and Roll Hall of Fame." *YouTube*, Rock and Roll Hall of Fame (n.d.), https://www.youtube.com/watch?v=-dj5Rr7tYzI&t=83s.

D'Souza, Karen. 2009. "Review: Green Day's *American Idiot* Punk Extravaganza Makes a White-Hot Debut." *Mercury News*, September 16, 2009.

Elliot, Stuart. 2008. "Army to Use Webcasts from Iraq for Recruiting." *New York Times*, November 10, 2008.

Ensminger, David A. 2016. *The Politics of Punk: Protest and Revolt from the Streets*. Lanham, MD: Roman and Littlefield.

Florida, Richard. 2017. "The New Suburban Crisis." *CityLab*, May 2, 2017, https://www.citylab.com/equity/2017/05/the-new-suburban-crisis/521709/.

Fricke, David. 2009. "The Birth of Green Day's 'American Idiot.'" *Rolling Stone*, June 16, 2009.

"FTN 3/16/03." 2003. *Face the Nation*, CBS-Television, March 3, 2003.

Gardner, Elyssa. 2010. "*American Idiot* Elevates Hope Above Nihilism." *USA Today*, April 21, 2010.

Henry, Tricia. 1989. *Break All Rules! Punk Rock and the Making of a Style*. Ann Arbor, MI: UMI Research Press, 1989.

Hershatter, Andrea and Molly Epstein. 2010. "Millennials and the World of Work: An Organization and Management Perspective." *Journal of Business* 25, doi:10.1007/s10869-010-9160-y.

Holiday, Ryan. 2015. "Here's the Real Solution to Millennial Angst." *Ryan Holiday*, December 14, 2015, https://ryanholiday.net/heres-the-real-solution-to-millennial-angst/.

Hurwitt, Robert. 2009. "Theater Review: *American Idiot.*" *SFGATE*, September 18, 2009, https://www.sfgate.com/performance/article/Theater-review-American-Idiot-3217535.php.

Isherwood, Charles. 2010. "Stomping onto Broadway with a Punk Temper Tantrum." *New York Times*, April 20, 2010.
James, Darren. 2017. "How Green Day's *Dookie* Dragged Punk Rock into the Mainstream." *Louder*, November 1, 2017, https://www.loudersound.com/features/how-green-days-dookiedragged-punk-rock-into-the-mainstream.
Jimenez, Mayra. 2012. "A Gen-Xer's Rant: What's Wrong with My Millennial Employees?" *Inc.*, July 3, 2012.
Johnson, Alysson. 2016. "What Green Day Means to Our Generation." *The Young Folks*, October 13, 2016, ww.theyoungfolks.com/review/88864/what-green-day-means-to-our-generation/.
Jones, Chris. 2010. "Green Day's 'Idiot' Has Right Sound for Broadway." *Chicago Tribune*, April 21, 2010.
Long, Lacey B. 2009. "American Idiot to the American Eulogy: Green Day's Rock Operas as Apocalyptic Protest during the George W. Bush Administration." Masters dissertation, University of Georgia.
Marks, Peter. 2010. "Peter Marks Reviews 'American Idiot' on Broadway." *Washington Post*, April 21, 2010.
McCall, Tulis. 2010. "American Idiot." *New York Theatre Guide*, April 21, 2010, https://www.newyorktheatreguide.com/reviews/american-idiot.
McNulty, Charles. 2009. "Theater Review." *Los Angeles Times*, October 10, 2009.
Meissner, Daniel J. n.d. "No Future: The Conception and Evolution of Punk Music and Culture in the United States and Great Britain from 1965 to the Present." Marquette University, https://academic.mu.edu/meissnerd/punk.html.
Montgomery, James. 2010. "Green Day's *American Idiot* Musical Is Political and Personal." *MTV News*, April 21, 2010, http://www.mtv.com/news/1637563/green-days-american-idiot-musical-is-political-and-personal/.
Ouzounian, Richard. 2011. "Review: Beautiful Sound, Bitter Fury in *American Idiot*." *Toronto Star*, December 29, 2011.
Page, Clarence. 2004. "Just Answer the Question, Mr. Rumsfeld." *Chicago Tribune*, December 12, 2004
Robbins, Ira A. 1999. "The British Invasion." *Encyclopedia Britannica*, November 8, 1999.
Rosentiel, Tom. 2008. "Public Attitudes Toward the War in Iraq: 2003–2008." *Pew Research Center*, March 19, 2008.
Savage, Jon. 2019. "Punk." *Encyclopaedia Britannica*, June 14, 2019, www.britannica.com/art/punk.
Scheck, Frank. 2010. "American Idiot—Theater Review." *Hollywood Reporter*, October 14, 2010.
Schonfeld, Zach. 2016. "Does Bush-Era Protest Music Still Hold Up?" *Newsweek*, December 8, 2016.
Sinek, Simon. 2017. "Transcript of Simon Sinek Millennials in the Workplace Interview." *Ochen*, January 4, 2017, https://ochen.com/transcript-of-simon-sineks-millennials-in-the-workplace-interview/.
"Views of U.S. Military Force in Iraq: 2003–2018." March 16, 2018. Pew Research Center, www.pewresearch.org/fact-tank.
Wang, Emily. 2014. "Growing Up with Green Day: Millennials and 10 Years of American Idiot." *Harvard Political Review*, February 28, 2014.
Wheeler, Emily. 2012. "Hyper Masculinity in the Punk Scene and the Bravery of Laura Jane Grace." *The Big Takeover*, May 14, 2012, https://bigtakeover.com/essays/hyper-masculinity-in-the-punk-scene-and-the-bravery-of-laura-jane-grace.
Wilson-Taylor, James. 2017. "These Are the Ten Best Punk Rock Albums EveReleased." *Pop Buzz*, updated May 8, 2017, https://www.popbuzz.com/music/features/top-ten-best-pop-punk-albums-ever/.
Winer, Linda. 2010. "Rollers Are Rocking on Broadway." *Newsday*, April 20, 2010.
Winwood, Ian. 2018. *Smash: Green Day, the Offspring, Bad Religion, NOFX, + the '90s Punk Explosion*. New York: DaCapo.

CHAPTER THREE
ATOMIC (2013)

Book and Lyrics by Danny Ginges (1959–) Music and Lyrics by Philip Foxman (1958–)
Premiere: Staged Reading National Institute of Dramatic Arts (NIDA), Sydney, Australia, February 28 and March 1, 2013

Songs

"The Atom Bomb Is Here (1960)"	"Holes in the Donuts"
"Little Fire"	"Greater Battle"
"The Force That Lights the Stars"	"World of Grey"*
"A Risk You Take"	"Greater Battle" (Reprise)*
"There Are Lines"*	"The Atom Bomb Is Here (1945)"
"Headlights"	"The Force That Lights the Stars"
"Atom Smasher"	"Into the Bar"* (Reprise)
"Stars and Stripes"	"Only Numbers"
"Where Is Home?"	"What I Tell Myself"
"One Day"	

* Not included on the Cast Album.

Overview

Atomic is a two-act musical based on the Manhattan Project, America's successful attempt during World War II to build the first atomic bomb. Every named character in *Atomic* is an historical figure, including well-known nuclear scientists Enrico Fermi, J. Robert Oppenheimer, Edward Teller, Leona Woods, and Arthur Compton. *Atomic* also brings to the stage the unheralded Leo Szilard, also an historic figure, a nuclear scientist, and the show's principal character.

If there is a truly singular American historical event, it is the development of the atomic bomb. In July 1945, a team of American scientists, led by Compton, Oppenheimer, and Fermi among others, successfully developed and tested the first-ever nuclear weapon. Three weeks after the test, on orders from President Harry S. Truman, the U.S. Army Air Force dropped one atomic bomb on each of two Japanese cities: Hiroshima and Nagasaki, on August 6 and August 9, respectively. The devastating impact of the two bombs hastened Japan's surrender and ushered in the Atomic Age, which changed the way the world thinks about war, international relations, the environment, and even human survival.

A core topic in modern American history and the subject of countless popular culture references, the birth of the Atomic Age is not an altogether surprising subject for a full-length professional musical in the twenty-first century. However, that the first such effort was undertaken by an Australian creative team—and musical theater novices at that—was decidedly unexpected. *Atomic*, which premiered in Sydney, Australia, in 2013, recounts the tumultuous and controversial career of Leo Szilard, a relatively obscure but pivotal figure in the Manhattan Project and the development of the bomb.

The Manhattan Project was America's famous (and, for many, infamous) yet enigmatic race against Germany during World War II to develop the world's first nuclear weapon. An omnipresence throughout *Atomic*, the Manhattan Project resulted from an extraordinary collaboration between the U.S. Army and what began as a small group of top American nuclear scientists, some of whom (including Fermi, Teller, and Szilard) were recent immigrants who had fled emerging fascist governments in Europe.

The Manhattan Project officially began in 1941. Two years earlier, Szilard, a visiting nuclear physicist conducting research with Fermi at New York's Columbia University, drafted a letter to President Franklin Roosevelt warning that Hitler's scientists could soon develop an atomic bomb. The letter further requested immediate financial support for American physicists to launch a counter effort and beat Hitler to the punch. In America barely a year, Szilard had little political influence. However, Szilard's friend and former tutor from Germany was now a Princeton professor, a friend of the Roosevelts, and the most famous scientist in the world. Szilard took a trip to Princeton and persuaded Albert Einstein to sign and send the letter under his own name. After additional correspondence and red-tape delays, in 1941, Roosevelt concurred and funded what would become America's top-secret quest to build an atomic bomb.

Roosevelt's support meant the as yet unnamed project would fall under the command of the Army Corps of Engineers. The commander assigned to the project was Colonel (later General) Leslie R. Groves, head of the Manhattan District of the Corps (now called the New York District). Groves earned the assignment on the strength of his unit's most recent success: Groves' team had just completed building the Pentagon. With Groves' appointment, the project took the official name of the Army Engineers' home district, Manhattan.

From the day of Groves' appointment as head of the Manhattan Project until the dropping of the bombs on Japan in 1945, all personnel associated with the project—especially the scientists—were subject to military wartime protocols on such matters as secrecy, clearance for access to information, job assignments, and, of course, military chain of command. These protocols caused tension and resentment among some of the project scientists, a point *Atomic* takes pains to underscore in its portrait of the science team's brilliant, anti-authoritarian, political activist, and provocateur Leo Szilard.

Then, as now, science was a highly collaborative discipline; international collaborations and global sharing of information were standard practice. That all stopped with the U.S. Army in charge. *Atomic* is replete with incidents of Szilard's acts of disruption, including defying supervisors' directives and initiating petitions against military restrictions on the scientists' work. The musical's scenes of Szilard's willful violations of military protocols may seem overly dramatic, but they are indeed grounded in historical fact. Szilard was a lightning rod as well as a genuine problem for keepers of secrets and sticklers for procedure.

As work on the bomb progressed, the tasks attendant to the project expanded exponentially. Developing the best fuel for chain reactions, controlling and measuring their output, designing the actual weapon, and so on required bringing on additional staff as well as assigning tasks to various locations so that multiple phases of the project could be conducted simultaneously. Major stages of the Manhattan Project were conducted in Hanford, Washington; Los Alamos, New Mexico; Oak Ridge, Tennessee; Dayton, Ohio; and Chicago, Illinois. Focusing on Szilard, *Atomic* follows his geographical trajectory with Fermi at Columbia University in the late 1930s and then focuses on Szilard, Fermi, and others working at the University of Chicago, where Colonel Groves relocated the Manhattan Project's chain reaction research in 1942.

Atomic's most compelling historical and ethical moments involve a complicated moral debate that arose in the final months of the war: if Germany surrenders prior to developing its own atomic bomb, should the

United States drop the bomb on Japan, thereby causing hundreds of thousands of civilian casualties in a country with no nuclear capability? This is precisely what occurred in 1945. Germany surrendered on May 7, and the Manhattan Project successfully tested its atomic bomb in New Mexico on July 16. On stage as in history, Szilard championed the argument to refrain from bombing Japan—at least until Japanese leaders could see a test of the bomb's devastating power. Circulating a petition that now bears his name, Szilard received signatures of support from seventy scientists, most of whom had been involved with the Manhattan Project. However, Szilard failed to get support from his closest and most influential project associates: Fermi, Teller, Compton, Woods, and Oppenheimer. Predictably, Groves (now a general) rejected the Szilard Petition and, convinced that Szilard was disloyal to America, made it impossible for Szilard to ever work again for the only employer of American nuclear physicists at the time: the U.S. government. *Atomic* ends with forty-seven-year-old Szilard resigned to his ouster as a practicing nuclear physicist and retooling himself to become a successful researcher in biophysics, which is precisely what the real Leo Szilard did following the war.

Atomic's writer, Danny Ginges, an advertising executive and copywriter from Sydney, Australia, first read about the atomic bomb as a child growing up during the Cold War. Like many of his generation born just after World War II, Ginges found the story of America's bombing of Japan and its aftermath both fascinating and frightening. Ginges' preoccupation with the subject remained with him through adulthood. Yet, notwithstanding his lifelong interest in the atomic bomb, he never even heard of the Manhattan Project until he was in his thirties. Talking with friends, he realized that many of them knew little or nothing about it as well. Ginges' curiosity about the Manhattan Project led him to read Richard Rhodes' *The Making of the Atomic Bomb* (1986), widely viewed as the most authoritative study of the people and events of the Manhattan Project: "[I came] across this story about an unsung scientist [Szilard] and it moved me. It demanded to be told. And after years of research, writing and rewriting, the story told me it needed music." While developing his story, Ginges became increasingly committed to the feelings, conflicts, triumphs, and vulnerabilities of the people who carried the burden of the project. Ultimately, it was the emotional stories of the atomic bomb's creators that spurred Ginges to complete his work as a musical: "I never cry over dialogue, but there are songs in our show that kill me" ("Genesis" 2013). While trying to write songs for his musical, Ginges met Philip Foxman, a Sydney-based musician with an extensive background in successful rock bands in the 1970s and 1980s. Foxman shared Ginges' enthusiasm for the story, and both men felt a personal connection to Szilard. Like Szilard, both Ginges and Foxman are Jews whose families were disrupted by the war in Europe. Ginges' maternal grandparents fled Hungary with their daughter when she was a baby. Foxman's parents lived in Nazi-occupied Poland when the Russian Army liberated their town. His mother was decorated for her later work as a nurse. Both men have acknowledged that their personal connection to the historical events made them all the more eager to see Szilard's story find a larger audience.

Atomic has had productions in Australia (2013 and 2019), New York City OffBroadway (2014), St. Louis (2016), Rochester, Michigan (2016), and Denver (2018). More recently, *Atomic* has been staged in Germany (2022 and 2023). An independently produced collection of songs from the show is accessible on *YouTube* (as of November 11, 2025). Performers on the song collection include cast members from the early Australian production, although the collection does not specify that it is an original cast recording. The script and score were significantly revised after the Sydney and New York productions. Ginges and Foxman have said that the version that played in Michigan in 2016 had "the right combination of story and song" (Venhaus 2016). The playwrights and their licensing company in Sydney continue to pursue opportunities to get *Atomic* and the story of the underappreciated Dr. Szilard in front of new audiences and out of historical obscurity.

Plot synopsis

New York City, 1960

Commuters rush to work worried about the Cold War with Russia and the nuclear arms race ("The Atom Bomb Is Here [1960]").

New York City, 1954

A "Formal Gathering" at the funeral of nuclear physicist Enrico Fermi (1901–54). Surviving lead scientists on the Manhattan Project discuss the experiences they shared during the war. J. Robert Oppenheimer, Edward Teller, Leona Woods, and Arthur Compton reveal varying degrees of pride, ambivalence, and guilt about their wartime assignment. Missing is physicist Leo Szilard, another surviving member whom they describe as a relentless visionary and crusader. Teller knew Leo in Germany in the 1930s and reflects on those times.

Berlin, 1933

Leo and his wife Gertrud Weiss (Trude), a physician, fear rising antisemitism in Nazi Germany and flee to London. A nuclear physicist, Leo is hopeful for the future of atomic energy: batteries that last a century; gas tanks forever full ("The Force That Lights the Stars").

London, 1938

Leo has done notable scientific work in London and has assisted refugee scientists in finding jobs. Seeing that Britain and Germany are preparing for war, he and Trude emigrate to America. In New York, Leo introduces himself to Fermi at Columbia University when Leo recognizes the Nobel Laureate. Familiar with Leo's political activism, Fermi chastises Leo for mixing politics and science. Leo responds that scientists should publicly work for justice ("There Are Lines"). Teller, also at Columbia, informs them that German scientists have split a uranium atom and are likely to develop an atomic bomb soon. Fermi, intrigued by Leo's theories on creating an explosive nuclear chain reaction, invites Leo to join his research team at Columbia.

Columbia University, 1939

When Fermi fails to obtain federal funding to develop an atomic bomb, Leo composes a letter to President Roosevelt explaining the urgency of keeping pace with Germany. Leo persuades his old friend from Germany, Albert Einstein, now teaching at Princeton, to sign the letter. In 1941, Roosevelt approves funding for the Columbia physicists' research. A radio announces Japan's attack on Pearl Harbor.

Chicago, 1942

Army Colonel Leslie Groves, director of the newly named Manhattan Project, appoints Compton, a Nobel Laureate in Physics at the University of Chicago, to manage the scientists developing the atomic bomb. Over protests by the Columbia scientists, the Manhattan Project relocates to Chicago. Leo and Trude lament further instability in their life ("Headlights"). In Chicago, the Columbia scientists meet the only woman on the lead team, Leona Woods. She reveals her apprehensions about the potentially disastrous consequences of the project ("Atom Smasher").

In December 1942, the Chicago team successfully executes the first lab-based controlled release of nuclear energy, or chain reaction. As project research continues, the scientists complain to Compton about the military's veto power over their choice of collaborators. Compton defers to military demands for secrecy. Leo lodges protests with Washington officials and writes a letter to Mrs. Roosevelt complaining of the military's authority over scientists. Groves learns of Leo's unauthorized communications and orders Compton to fire him. Considering Leo difficult but indispensable, Compton persuades Groves to keeps Leo on the staff.

Chicago, 1943

Leo joyously informs the team that Mrs. Roosevelt promises to notify President Roosevelt of his concerns about military authority. Compton reprimands Leo for the letter, but Leo is defiant. Exasperated, Compton transfers Leo back to Columbia University. Oppenheimer is introduced as Leo's replacement. In a bar, a despondent Leo meets Paul, a young airman eager to battle the Japanese emperor. Paul inspires Leo to fight his own tyrants, supervising scientist Compton and Project Director Groves ("Stars and Stripes").

New York, 1944

Leo is jobless and depressed back in New York. Trude is empathetic but frustrated at his inertia. They learn that the U.S. government has discovered Nazi concentration camps in Europe and realize they can never go home ("Where Is Home?"). Leo learns from former colleagues that Germany is close to developing an atomic bomb. Out of moral commitment he returns to Chicago to force his way back onto the team ("The Road Back").

Chicago, 1945

A radio broadcast announces the death of President Roosevelt. Leo approaches Compton, who allows Leo to return to the project if he pledges to be cooperative. Leo agrees. Radio stations broadcast news of Germany's surrender to Allied forces. Leo tells the project team that America no longer needs the bomb since Germany has surrendered and Japan is not a nuclear threat. Oppenheimer informs Leo that, his protests notwithstanding, the project is still ongoing. Most of the Chicago team travels to Los Alamos to witness the test of the bomb. In New Mexico, Oppenheimer celebrates the "colossal astronomical power" of the successful Los Alamos test. Leo warns that deployment of the bomb will generate an arms race with Russia that could "end civilization."

The Formal Gathering, New York, 1954

The team, still recalling their shared history, salutes Leo in absentia for having accurately predicted a postwar international arms race. Several U.S. factories are currently manufacturing bombs with workers who do not know what they are making (Factory Girls sing "Holes in the Donuts").

Chicago, 1945

Leo and Trude learn that the U.S. military wants to use the bomb on Japan and that Roosevelt never told Vice-President Truman that the bomb was developed to use against Germany, not Japan. Leo protests the immoral "madness" of deploying the bomb after Germany's surrender ("World of Grey"). In Washington, Leo, believing he has support from the project leaders, petitions President Truman via the army to stage a test detonation for Japanese leaders to scare them into surrendering. Leo believes Fermi and Compton may support him but he is stunned when they publicly oppose his petition. His idea rejected, Leo realizes his career as an atomic physicist is over ("The Atom Bomb Is Here [1945]").

Washington, D.C., 1945

Diagnosed with cancer, Leo expects to die soon. He and Trude speculate that radiation experiments he conducted during the Manhattan Project could be adapted for cancer treatments. They vow to develop radiation treatment for his cancer. In a bar, Leo bumps into the airman Paul again. Paul is now a colonel and an experienced warplane pilot. As Paul exits, we see "Enola Gay" on his jacket—he is Paul Tibbetts, pilot of the *Enola Gay*, who dropped the first bomb on Hiroshima. Leo, Trude, Paul (flying over Hiroshima), and the ensemble sing of their respective feelings about the historic mission in progress ("Only Numbers"). There is a loud boom and a flash of light as Paul exits. On radio, President Truman hails the successful bombing of Hiroshima.

The Formal Gathering, 1954

We learn that Leo, now present, has spent a year hospitalized but is recovering. Toasting Fermi, each team member reaffirms their perspective on the project ("What I Tell Myself").

New York, 1960

Leo and Trude discuss their recent work with radiation, which has become part of Leo's own cancer treatment. Now a successful biologist, Leo is invited to join the prestigious Jonas Salk Institute in California. Happily preparing for another journey, Leo wonders aloud if a designated phoneline between the White House and the Kremlin might head off future nuclear wars.

Critical reception

Of the six productions staged in Australia and the United States, reviews from the 2014 New York production are the most numerous and offer the widest diversity of opinions on the show. The *New York Times*' David Rooney, granting summer OffBroadway theater its traditional license to experiment with audience sensibilities, dismisses practically everything in the New York production beyond the "capable" cast's singing: "The overstuffed show unfolds like a hurried biodrama shoehorned inside a lost, guitar-and-synthesizer-heavy 1970s rock opera." Rooney fairly identifies *Atomic*'s thesis as an attempt to "rescue from semiobscurity" Leo Szilard, the unheralded bad boy member of the star-studded lead team of nuclear physicists of the Manhattan Project. However, Rooney finds that *Atomic* undercuts its own argument with its "ambitious but dramatically diffuse" and "tonally incoherent" book. Particularly troubling to Rooney is the ending's loud, bloated, staging of the *Enola Gay*'s mission over Hiroshima, which smothers the subdued but effective final scene, wherein surviving scientists reflect on the moral complexities of their legacy (Rooney 2014). Frank Scheck of the *New York Post* dismisses out of hand the entire disconnected theater experience: "By the time a female scientist [Leona Woods] plaintively asks, 'How do you say I'm sorry to the whole world?' the triviality of the enterprise has become overwhelming" (Scheck 2014). Writing in his blog *Everything I Know I Learned from Musicals*, Chris Caggiano openly admits to picking a low-hanging fruit headline: "*Atomic* is a bomb … certainly a dud: *Atomic* wants to be both searing drama and goofy satire, and is ultimately unsuccessful at both" (Caggiano 2014).

Not all New York reviews were so unforgiving. Jonathan Mandel, writing for *NewYorkTheater.com*, is among the production's strongest admirers, eager to forgive (for the most part) *Atomic*'s shortcomings in deference to its laudable ambitions. Mandel accepts outright the creators' assumption that Szilard's is an unjustifiably untold story, and his scientific contributions to the Manhattan Project, for good or ill, demand the retelling that *Atomic* affords them. For Mandel, an otherwise admirable show fails only to the extent that the details of Szilard's story overwhelm the limited ability of a musical to convey textual and technical information: "*Atomic* is well-acted and exceptionally well-designed … a largely intelligent effort with worthwhile and thought-provoking moments. But … [the] bombardment of details [is] difficult to absorb." *Encore Theatre*'s unattributed, self-described "mixed review" is among the outright champions of Foxman's score: "Foxman delivers a variety of genres, an unusual feat for a lot of composers, many of which rock the house. His lyrics are specific to the character for whom they were written … and Foxman surely hits the mark with his original compositions" (Mandel 2014). *Time Out New York*'s Diep Tran, while somewhat more reserved than Mandel, finds that the quieter, reflective moments in *Atomic* provide a salve for the show's melodramatic simplicity, its rather forgettable songs, and some distracting "hamming it up" by Jonathan Hammond as Enrico Fermi. Sharing Rooney's lowered expectations for summer theater in New York, Tran salutes the show's redeeming qualities: "it is enjoyable and more introspective than your typical summer offering" (Tran 2014). David Finkle, drama critic for the *Huffington Post*, also finds that *Atomic*'s worthiness lies in its pursuit of ambitious ends: bringing forth the role of the unsung Szilard among the Manhattan Project luminaries. But Finkle recoils at what he perceives as *Atomic*'s misrepresentation of J. Robert Oppenheimer as a villainous counterpoint to Szilard's heroic crusade against dropping the bomb on Japan: "How [Oppenheimer] became Manhattan Project head is completely ignored, practically reducing him to the heavy in the piece, a bombastic bombing advocate" (Finkle 2014).

Ginges and Foxman report revising the script after the New York run, "getting the right combination" for the Michigan production in 2016. Nevertheless, the *Detroit Free Press*'s John Monaghan panned a show he was hoping to like: "There are probably viable ways to stage Szilard's fascinating story, but *Atomic* is not one of them. Ginges puts the events of [Szilard's] life across with all the imagination of a PowerPoint presentation … and the dialogue sounds as if it has been lifted straight from a history book" (Monaghan 2016). By contrast, *Atomic* received a uniformly strong critical reception when New Line Theatre in St. Louis staged the production in 2016. Judith Newmark in the *St Louis Post-Dispatch* felt the show handled the density of historical information effectively: "It might be the most cerebral rock musical ever written. And that's a compliment" (Newmark 2016). Reviewing for KDHX radio, Tina Farmer praised the production, accepting the show on its own terms: "History comes to life with a strong cast and an intriguing script … The show takes a personal approach, helping audiences better understand the conflict the bomb caused for those individuals responsible for its creation" (Farmer 2016). Writing for *OnStage Missouri*, Erin Karll likewise honored the higher purposes for which Ginges and Foxman strived: "History is full of amazing stories waiting to be told. *Atomic* is one of them … Danny Ginges and Philip Foxman taught the story behind the atomic bomb in a thought-provoking way" (Karll 2016).

The first Australian staging in 2013 drew a negative review from the influential *Sydney Morning Herald*. Additionally, the *Herald* foreshadowed criticism *Atomic* would face in New York for its "sprawling" overload of content:

> Filled with historical incident, *Atomic* is made dense with ethical conundrums … *Atomic*'s reliance on chest-thumping argument is no substitute for real drama. Furthermore, the show's historical lens is too wide. Fascinated by their subject [the creators] seem unable to leave anything out.
>
> *Blake 2013*)

However, Frank Hatherley, writing for Australia's *Stage Whispers* online theater magazine, celebrated *Atomic* as an "adult" musical bursting with energy: "Its visceral charge alone makes seeking out this engrossing new adult musical worthwhile" (Hatherley 2013). Sydney theater blogger Kevin Jackson admits to being "unsettled" for the first 20 minutes because of "too short" songs and a cliched flashback to pre-war Germany to stage Szilard's fear of Nazism. However, shortly thereafter Jackson "was suspended into belief and curiosity. I was completely won over … It is an entirely satisfying experience" (Jackson 2013).

Historical accuracy and context

Politics: The Cold War, the Atomic Age, the Nuclear Arms Race

In foregrounding the role of the comparatively unknown Manhattan Project physicist Leo Szilard, the creators of *Atomic* self-consciously embrace Szilard's grim prophetic warnings in the early 1940s. Szilard prophesized that deployment of the first atomic bomb would permanently alter world politics for the worse. While wartime air bombing dates back to the Italian–Turkish war (1911–12) and was common in both World Wars I and II, the atomic bombs dropped on Hiroshima and Nagasaki in August 1945 changed at least two fundamental geo-political realities. Firstly, the overwhelming power of this single weapon, in its horrifying immediate impact and devastating aftermath of radiation poisoning, empowered its owner to annihilate with a single strike heretofore unimaginable numbers of people. Secondly, once the first country proved that atomic bombs worked as designed, other nations would surely be interested in acquiring the knowledge to build nuclear weapons of their own in the interests of national security. Szilard left the details to history, but as he predicted, the bombing of Hiroshima and Nagasaki ushered in the Atomic Age and fueled the nuclear arms race that defined the Cold War.

The origin of the term "Cold War" is generally attributed to a 1947 speech by American diplomat Bernard Baruch. Although specifically referring to the sustained mistrust and rivalry between the United States and the Soviet Union after World War II, Baruch's term eventually acquired a generic meaning for any political conflict over ideology that does not lead to overt military conflict and sustains at least a modicum of diplomatic communication among adversaries. However, the term has always retained its primary application as a descriptor of diplomatic hostility between the United States and Soviet Union from end of World War II until the breakup of the USSR in 1991.

Looming over the Cold War period was a nuclear arms race between the world's nuclear superpowers, the United States and the Soviet Union—much as Szilard predicted both on stage and in real life. There would likely have been postwar political tension between Russia and the United States even without the atomic bomb, especially over expansion of their respective rival political philosophies: communism and democracy. However, the Cold War was marked by an ever-present, worldwide anxiety about possible nuclear annihilation resulting from a seemingly imminent violent confrontation between the two superpowers. Insofar as the United States and the Soviet Union each believed the other to be determined to gain strategic superiority through perpetual expansion of their respective nuclear arsenals, such fears were not unfounded.

These very fears comprise the message of *Atomic*'s opening ensemble song, set in 1960. Fearful commuters start their daily lives weighed down by the nation's anxieties about American and Soviet alleged spying operations, repeated failures of nuclear arms control negotiations, and the specter of nuclear devastation that could bring Hiroshima-like catastrophes or worse to America and the entire world. These fears manifested themselves in many aspects of American life during the Cold War years, including political campaigning, social small talk, government-distributed civil defense instructions for building personal home bomb shelters, and mandatory "duck and cover" drills for school students in the event of nuclear attack during the school day. In popular culture, commercial novels, movies, television shows, and protest songs found a responsive audience for their dystopian visions of the Atomic Age. Novels such as Patrick Frank's *Alas Babylon* (1959) and Neville Chute's *On the Beach* (1957) sold well in America and Europe. Films like *Dr. Strangelove* (1964) and *Fail-Safe* (1964) were also commercially successful. In popular music, Pete Seeger's "Where Have All the Flowers Gone?" and Bob Dylan's "Talkin' World War III Blues" kept the memory of Hiroshima alive in the music of the 1960s Vietnam War protests.

Notwithstanding the end of the Cold War in 1991, Szilard's prophecy of an ongoing global race for nuclear supremacy has been largely borne out. In 2019, the two original superpowers, the United States and Russia, possessed approximately 90 percent of the world's nuclear weapons arsenal (Kristensen and Korda 2019). However, at least six other countries each had developed substantial nuclear weapon capability or the potential to achieve it: the United Kingdom, China, France, India, North Korea, and Pakistan. It would be an overstatement to suggest, as *Atomic* does, that for years Szilard stood alone among leading scientists as *the* solitary prophet of the Atomic Age. Two months prior to circulating his petition to forestall the bombing of Japan, he had been one of five scientists in the Chicago unit to submit "The Franck Report," a formal political impact statement that foregrounded Szilard's historic petition against moving forward with the atomic attack on Japan. Furthermore, after the bombing of Hiroshima, scientists, politicians, journalists, and informed people everywhere could see contours of the new Atomic Age taking shape. However, in his field and for his time, Szilard was in many ways the self-martyring voice and visionary that *Atomic* celebrates.

Science: fission, chain reactions, and uranium

In *Atomic*, nuclear scientists often speak to each other about nuclear science. Principal among conversation topics is nuclear fission: the splitting of the nucleus of an atom into two or more smaller nuclei. This process is often accompanied by the spontaneous release of energy and other particles such as neutrons. Under the right conditions, neutrons produced in a fission event can induce fission of other nuclei, which in turn produce additional neutrons that bombard more nuclei. This leads to a self-sustaining process known scientifically and familiarly as a "nuclear chain reaction." Nuclear chain reactions are much more powerful than chemical reactions and can generate tremendous amounts of energy from a relatively small mass of fuel.

Where nuclear chain reactions are concerned, not all nuclei are created equal. *Atomic* is commendably specific, and, for the most part, clear on this point. Not all nuclei can be split (i.e., are fissionable). And not all fissionable nuclei can sustain a chain reaction which releases sufficient energy to be used in weapons or other large-scale enterprises such as nuclear power plants. A number of variables in the process of creating powerful nuclear chain reactions led the musical—as it had the original scientists—to focus their attention on the chemical element uranium.

Uranium emerged as a promising fuel because it is a fissionable element found naturally in the earth's crust. In its natural state, uranium is found in several different forms, known as isotopes. The isotope uranium-238 is the most common, comprising more than 99 percent of naturally occurring uranium. Less than 1 percent of naturally occurring uranium is uranium-235, which is a fissile isotope of uranium that can sustain a nuclear chain reaction. A significant portion of the Manhattan Project research focused on uranium enrichment, in which a sample of naturally occurring uranium is processed so that its uranium-235 content is greatly increased, making it an effective fuel for atomic weapons. Indeed, it was highly enriched uranium, consisting of large amounts of uranium-235, that fueled the powerful chain reactions used in the atomic bomb that was dropped on Hiroshima on August 6, 1945.

Atomic as historical biography

Leo Szilard

Atomic posits two theses on Szilard's behalf: 1) Szilard's historic voice as a singular clairvoyant ethicist of the Atomic era is grossly underappreciated and 2) his scientific contributions to the Manhattan Project are comparable to and unjustly overshadowed by achievements of other scientists, particularly those of Enrico Fermi. The musical makes a compelling case for Szilard as an underappreciated, pioneering moralistic philosopher/scientist for an atomically weaponized world. However, the musical's implicit effort to position Szilard as Fermi's match in the laboratory engages the difficult, perhaps unresolvable, process of assigning individual shares of credit for collaborative projects undertaken years ago in secret. Adding to the difficulty are conflicting interpretations regarding who-led-whom and fair questions about the value of such relitigation in the first place.

Atomic's overall presentation of Szilard's life is faithful to his biographical milestones. The play honors Szilard's controversial campaign in the 1930s to persuade nuclear scientists to withhold research and new patents if publication might aid Hitler's scientists in developing the first atomic bomb. Also faithfully recounted, but not staged, is Szilard's pivotal role in obtaining President Roosevelt's financial support for the Manhattan Project via the Einstein Letter (now properly the Einstein–Szilard letter) after others had failed in similar attempts. Once the Manhattan Project began, secrecy became the order of the day, but now secrecy was enforced by the army. Anti-authoritarian by nature, Szilard, on stage and in history, challenged the military's veto power over the project scientists' autonomy in selecting collaborators. Szilard's brazen disregard of protocols, such as endrunning military supervisors and protesting directly to the Pentagon, were rogue actions that created tension among his fellow scientists and elevated the military's suspicion of the project scientists, especially recent immigrants from Europe. Moreover, Szilard's supervisors' wariness over his repeated challenges to authority virtually assured failure of his 1945 petition to President Truman requesting postponement of plans to bomb Japan until the United States could demonstrate to Japanese leaders the bomb's power. Seventy nuclear scientists (but none of Szilard's most prominent colleagues) signed his petition; however military and scientific project leaders refused to forward the petition to Truman. (Truman would have certainly dismissed Szilard's petition had it reached him. Once sworn in and briefed on the Manhattan Project, President Truman showed no reluctance in using the atomic bomb against Japan.)

Atomic attributes two remarkable postwar accomplishments to Szilard: developing a new form of radiation therapy and conceiving the idea of a nuclear deterrence hotline connection between Washington, D.C. and Moscow. While the former is true, the latter is highly dubious. Barred from working as a nuclear physicist and suffering from bladder cancer, Szilard researched applications of his wartime radiation experiments for cancer treatments. He assisted in the development of radiation treatments for cancer which he undertook for his own illness (Wyner 2018). As for the hotline, there is no undisputed single originator of the Washington-to-Moscow emergency phone connection, which was a diplomatic byproduct of the 1962 Cuban Missile Crisis.

In addition to repositioning Szilard's biography in the history of the Manhattan Project, *Atomic*'s creators highlight certain characteristics of other major project scientists, using Szilard's character as the lens through which the audience views his more well-known colleagues. *Atomic*'s biographical information about Szilard's famous colleagues is, while brief, generally accurate, at times illuminating, and occasionally open to reasonable alternative interpretations.

Enrico Fermi

Szilard's most complex professional relationship in *Atomic* involves his work with Fermi. The two men are historically linked throughout the development of the atomic bomb. As the musical makes clear, they clashed frequently over Szilard's insistence that scientists factor political and ethical implications into their research.

Atomic's implication that as a laboratory scientist Szilard is Fermi's unacknowledged equal, while not entirely groundless, contradicts the prevailing view among science historians. The musical strongly implies that Fermi and Szilard were full partners at Columbia, noting that their fusion discoveries at that university came to be known as the Fermi–Szilard System (Byers 2003). However, Fermi was a senior Columbia University professor while Szilard was on temporary appointment with lab privileges at Fermi's behest. When the Columbia University team was relocated to Chicago Metallurgical Laboratory ("Met Lab") in 1942, Szilard held the position of chief physicist. However, according to the Argonne National Laboratory in Illinois, Fermi "led the team" that built the Chicago Pile 1 Reactor, "which achieved the world's first man-made controlled nuclear chain reaction" ("Chicago Pile 1 Pioneers" n.d.).

Both men were indispensable to each other's work, and their work was indispensable to the Manhattan Project. Notwithstanding *Atomic*'s heartfelt counter-narrative, Fermi remains a singular figure in the history of nuclear physics. However, there is genuine value in the attention *Atomic* brings to Szilard's unique role in the Manhattan Project.

Edward Teller et al.

Atomic devotes little attention to Teller's scientific contributions to the Manhattan Project. Closely associated with development of the hydrogen bomb in 1952, Teller's function in *Atomic* is to present polar opposite ethical positions to Szilard's—an accurate reflection of their real-life contrasting ethical stances on the Manhattan Project. More prominently than other leading nuclear scientists, on stage or in history, Teller claimed he never had regrets, second thoughts, or ambivalent feelings about developing or deploying the bomb.

Atomic accurately presents Arthur Compton as crediting his religious faith for "getting (him) through" the Manhattan Project and alludes to Compton's published statements asserting that sole ownership of nuclear power after World War II was a gift "God has seen fit to give" the United States (Byers 2002).

J. Robert Oppenheimer was so conflicted after the bombing of Japan that he confessed his feelings of guilt to President Truman, who disgustedly rebuked Oppenheimer. In *Atomic*, Oppenheimer recounts his humiliating meeting with Truman, which did in fact occur.

An earlier version of *Atomic* misrepresented Leona Woods as opposing Truman's decision to bomb Japan and signing on to Szilard's letter of protest. Woods did not sign Szilard's letter and publicly defended the bombing of Japan long after the war was over. In 2023, Mr. Ginges rewrote Woods' key scene to reflect her refusal to join Szilard in protesting Truman's actions.

Thomas A. Greenfield and Charlie Freeman

Further reading

Blake, Jason. 2013. "Atomic: The Musical—Review." *Sydney Morning Herald*, November 20, 2013.

Byers, Nina. 2002. "Physicists and the 1945 Decision to Drop the Bomb." *History and Philosophy of Physics*. Ithaca, NY: Cornell University, October 13, 2002. https:// arxiv.org/abs/physics/0210058v1.

Byers, Nina. 2003. "Fermi and Szilard." *History and Philosophy of Physics*. Ithaca, NY: Cornell University, June 3, 2003. https://arxiv.org/abs/physics/0207094v3.

Caggiano, Chris. 2014. "Review—*Atomic* the Musical Off Broadway." *Everything I Know I Learned from Musicals*, July 23, 2014, https://www.chriscaggiano.com/2014/07/review-atomic-the-musical-off-broadway-.html.

"Chicago Pile 1 Pioneers." n.d. Argonne National Laboratory, www.ne.anl.gov/About/cp1-pioneers/.

"Enrico Fermi." n.d. *Atomic Heritage Foundation Profiles: Enrico Fermi*, https://www.atomicheritage.org/profile/enrico-fermi.

"Enrico Fermi." 2004. *C250 Celebrates Columbians Ahead of Their Time*. New York: Columbia University Press, http://c250.columbia.edu/c250_celebrates/remarkable_columbians/enrico_fermi.html.

Farmer, Tina. 2016. "'Atomic' Peers into the Past with an Inside Look at the Manhattan Project Scientists." KDHK Radio, St. Louis, June 12, 2016.

Finkle, David. 2014. "First Nighter: Musicals *Atomic*, *The Mapmaker's Opera*, *ValueVille*." *Huffington Post*, July 13, 2014.

"Genesis of a Musical: *Atomic*." 2013. *Daily Review*, November 22, 2013, https:// dailyreview.com.au/genesis-of-a-musical-atomic/1096/.

Ginges, Danny, and Philip Foxman. 2018. *Atomic* (Book and Lyrics). Provided by ORiGiN™ Theatrical Pty Limited, www.origintheatrical.com.au.

Hatherley, Frank. 2013. "Review: *Atomic*." *Stage Whispers*, November 30, 2013, https:// www.stagewhispers.com.au/reviews/atomic.

Jackson, Kevin. 2013. "ATOMIC—A New Musical in the Parade Playhouse." *Kevin Jackson's Theatre Diary*, November 19, 2013.

Karll, Erin. 2016. "Review: *Atomic* Drops Powerful Truths at New Line Theatre." *onstageblog.com/reviews*, June 15, 2016.

Kristensen, Hans M. and Matt Korda. 2019. "Status of World's Nuclear Forces." *Federation of American Scientists: Issues*, Updated, May 2019, https://fas.org/issues/nuclear-weapons/status-world-nuclear-forces/.

Lanouette, William. 2011. "Einstein and Szilard in Princeton." *Center for Arms Control and Nuclear Proliferation*, February 13, 2011, https://armscontrolcenter.org/einstein-and-szilard-in-princeton/.

Lanouette, William. 2013. *Genius in the Shadows: A Biography of Leo Szilard, the Man Behind the Bomb*. New York: Skyhorse Publishing Company.

Luciebella, Michael et al. 2014. "This Month in Physics History November 10, 1986: Death of Leona Woods Marshall Libby." *APS News* 23, no. 10 (November), https:// www.aps.org/publications/apsnews/201411/physicshistory.cfm.

Mandel, Jonathan. 2014. "Atomic Review: A Musical about the Bomb." *NewYorkTheater.com*, July 13, 2014.

Monaghan, John. 2016. "Review: Atomic Produces Lots of Noise, Little Heat." *Detroit Free Press*, February 17, 2016.

"Musical Review *Atomic*." 2014. *encoretheatercompany.com*, April 4, 2014, encoretheatercompany.com/musical-review-atomic/.

Newmark, Judith. 2016. "A Serious Musical Raises Big Issues at New Line." *St. Louis Post-Dispatch*, June 7, 2016.

Rhodes, Richard. 1986. *The Making of the Atomic Bomb*. New York: Simon & Schuster.

Rooney, David. 2014. "Sing the Song Before You Drop That Bomb." *New York Times*, July 13, 2014.

Scheck, Frank. 2014. "Off-Broadway Manhattan Project an 'Atomic' Bomb." *New York Post*, July 13, 2014.

Tran, Diep. 2014. "Atomic." *Time Out New York*, July 14, 2014.

Venhaus, Lynne. 2016. "How *Atomic*'s Creators Built a Musical about Nuclear Physicists." *Belleville News-Democrat*, June 20, 2016.

Wyner, L. M. 2018. "Leo Szilard's Bladder Cancer: Survival in the Nuclear Era." *Urology* 116: 17–19, doi:10.1016/j.urology.2018.02.020.

CHAPTER FOUR
BEN FRANKLIN IN PARIS (1964)

Book and Lyrics by Sidney Michaels (1927–2011) Music by Mark Sandrich, Jr. (1928–1995)
World Premiere: Schubert Theatre (now Merriam Theatre), Philadelphia, August 1964 Broadway: October 27, 1964–May 1, 1965
215 performances (plus 13 previews)

Songs

"We Sail the Seas"	"Hic Haec Hoc"
"I Invented Myself"	"God Bless the Human Elbow"
"Too Charming"	"When I Dance with the Person I Love"
"Whatever Became of Old Temple"	"Diane Is"
"Half the Battle"	"Look for Small Pleasures"
"A Balloon Is Ascending"	"I Love the Ladies"
"To Be Alone with You"	"To Be Alone with You"
"How Laughable It Is"	"You're in Paris" (Reprise)

Overview

Ben Franklin in Paris was originally produced as a star vehicle for Broadway and film actor Robert Preston. Coming off the great success of *The Music Man* Broadway musical (1957) and film (1962), as well as two inconsequential follow-up shows, Preston sought a demanding role that would test his acting and put some distance between himself and *The Music Man*.

Coincidentally, playwright Sidney Michaels was in New York "shopping" for his new musical comedy based on seventy-year-old Ben Franklin's journey to Paris in 1776 to secure military and diplomatic support from France for the nascent American Revolution. By focusing on this important but, for many Americans, largely unfamiliar event in American history, Michaels accomplished two objectives for his portrait of Franklin: he challenged what he perceived to be a superficial popular image of Franklin as a whimsical platitude-dispensing eccentric inventor, and he separated Franklin from the other famous signatories of the *Declaration of Independence* to facilitate a nuanced representation of his title character.

Franklin's mission to France nicely accommodated Michaels' interest in spotlighting Franklin apart from the other Founding Fathers. In 1776, the American Continental Congress was almost evenly divided on whether or not they should turn their struggle against Britain's ill-treatment of the colonies into a full-scale war for American independence. However, the Congress was nearly unanimous in their belief that America could not win a sustained armed conflict against the British without a formal alliance with France or another major European power. France had been quietly sending munitions in support of the Americans since 1775, but did so reservedly so as not to alarm the British and disrupt the two European rivals' delicate diplomatic relationship.

Congress signed the *Declaration*, in part because America would be more appealing to France as a political ally if it presented itself as a sovereign independent nation rather than an aggrieved British colony. Thus, after the signing of the *Declaration*, Congress immediately launched a diplomatic mission to France—in the form of Benjamin Franklin—to secure France's recognition of America's sovereignty and win France's explicit support for the war against Great Britain. Franklin would ultimately succeed at both parts of his mission within fifteen months of his arrival in France, the time frame in which Michaels sets *Ben Franklin in Paris*.

As the person assigned to take on this mission, Franklin was uniquely qualified among the members of the Continental Congress and, arguably, all other Americans as well. In 1776, few Americans had traveled to Europe, including the prosperous aristocrats of the Continental Congress and their social peers. Franklin was an exception, having made prior trips across the Atlantic, including extended residencies in England. At the time of his arrival in Paris in December 1776, Franklin was the most famous American in the world. He was particularly admired in France for his scientific experiments as well as his popular writings.

Preston was intrigued by Michaels' uncommon approach to the role of Franklin. The musical's Ben Franklin is a buoyant, gregarious, charismatic man of many talents—not all of them admirable—on a serious mission. Carrying the fate of the newly declared independent and vulnerable American nation on his shoulders, Michaels' Franklin secretly knows, but will admit to no one, that his mission to Paris is more likely to fail than succeed. On stage, Franklin is clearly under pressure and, at times, unsure of himself—even despondent. Yet, he understands his success will depend upon his diplomatic skills, sociability, charm, convivial deceptions, and his ability to ingratiate himself with France's leaders as well the French public. Michaels' concept for his lead character generally corresponds to historical accounts of Franklin's personal and public life during his first year in France. Furthermore, Michaels infuses Franklin's dialogue with direct quotes and close adaptations from Franklin's actual writings, including witty epigrams and jests as well as thoughtful reflections on philosophy and history. Preston was delighted with Michaels' substantive, creditable, layered portrait of Franklin, and agreed to star in the show, ensuring its eventual production.

For all the attention he devoted to rendering Franklin's character, Michaels fictionalized Franklin's diplomatic mission to France beyond recognition. Glossing over Franklin's skillful alliance-building and numerous encounters with diplomats, military leaders, spies, and arms dealers, *Ben Franklin in Paris* posits a conventional romance between Franklin and a fictitious French woman as the determining factor in the success of his mission. Specifically, at the French court, Franklin encounters a fictitious elegant palace seductress (Diane) who, when unleashed upon a male world leader, can alter his politics to her whim on behalf of the French king. Franklin and Diane's on-again/off-again romance not only drives the show's plot, score, and comedic moments, but also, absurdly, secures the French king's decision to support the war for American independence. The musical's creators were clearly counting on Preston's performance as the newly-imagined Benjamin Franklin, and not the intricacies of eighteenth-century European diplomacy, to carry the production.

Michaels' and Preston's high expectations for *Ben Franklin in Paris*' Broadway opening met with their own historical complications owing to the competition they faced from rival shows. On *Ben Franklin*'s opening night, October 27, 1964, the smash hit musicals *Fiddler on the Roof*, *Hello Dolly!*, *Funny Girl*, and *What Makes Sammy Run?* were all in the first year of their Broadway runs. The results were devastating to *Ben Franklin*'s press and audience appeal. Even with an established star in a good role, the producers had picked the wrong year to open a show with a first-time Broadway composer (Mark Sandrich) and a relatively unknown actress in her first American theatrical starring role (Swedish operetta singer Ulla Sallert). When *Ben Franklin* closed on May 1, 1965, after a disappointing run of 215 performances, the hit shows that had greeted its arrival were still running. To make matters worse, they had been joined by new strong shows, including Richard Rodgers and Stephen Sondheim's *Do I Hear a Waltz?* and a revival of *Guys and Dolls*. The competition in 1964 left no room for Preston or his show to breathe, much less catch fire. The year that *Playbill* once proffered as the "Best Year Ever for Broadway Musicals" had been claimed by Zero Mostel as Tevya, Carol Channing as Dolly, and Barbra Streisand as Fanny Brice before Robert Preston's Ben Franklin even hit the boards. To add insult to injury, in 1969 the Broadway musical *1776* featured Howard Da Silva as Ben Franklin in an ensemble-cast show about the writing and ratification of the *Declaration of Independence*. The show ran for 1,000 more performances than did *Ben Franklin in Paris*, and Da Silva's Ben Franklin was very well received by audiences and critics. Preston went on to enjoy other Broadway and film successes but, when he died in 1987, he was still best remembered as "the Music Man" and not, as he had hoped, the former and first American Ambassador to France, Benjamin Franklin.

Plot synopsis

In December 1776, an American military vessel transporting Ben Franklin arrives in France greeted by well-wishers eager to meet the famous writer/inventor. Franklin disembarks with grandsons Temple (sixteen) and Benny (seven) along with a cache of his inventions. Initially coy, Franklin soon reveals his reason for coming to France: to secure France's support for the colonies in their revolution against Britain. In addition, he plans to wield his considerable charm with the Parisian public by trading on his fame derived from his writings and inventions; curry the favor of men and especially women with ties to France's centers of power; and win for himself recognition as Ambassador to France and America's first international diplomat ("I Invented Myself"). Ben and grandsons depart for their residence escorted by adoring Parisians carrying the Franklins' belongings.

Once settled, Ben and grandson Temple are granted an audience with King Louis XVI and find themselves at the Throne Room in the Palace at Versailles. King Louis seems adrift without his consort, La Comtesse Diane de Vobrillac ("Diane"), whose absence from the Throne Room unsettles him. Diane soon enters; she is elegant, beautiful, a force to be reckoned with. She informs King Louis she has been up all night pacifying a hostile Turkish diplomat: "It's settled there will be no war." Ben, recognizing where the power lies, turns his attention to Diane.

Ben and Diane immediately recognize each other, having shared a romance in London years ago. They exchange flirtatious pleasantries, interlacing diplomacy with praises for each other's charms. Smitten yet loyal to France, Diane refuses to urge the king to support the colonies because the Americans had not had a military victory over the British since Concord. This diplomatic impasse breaks the romantic mood. Diane vetoes further discussion of French support until the colonies achieve a military victory. Ben exits, handing her a pair of his bifocals to mock her political short-sightedness.

At the Franklins' Paris residence, Benny and Temple speak of their grandfather's plan to enlist them in "the cause" of currying favor with important French families. Franklin has instructed Benny to befriend children of dignitaries at his school. Ben enters, lecturing Temple on the virtue of marrying an older woman. A messenger enters informing everyone that British troops have seized Philadelphia and Congress has fled to Baltimore. They all bemoan this setback. However, Ben turns the mood around with a center-stage fighting song, "Half the Battle," inspiring all assembled to press onward.

In a Paris park, Diane attends the celebratory first-ever public flight of a "manned" hot air balloon. Tricked by Franklin's allies to christen the grounded balloon by climbing into the gondola just prior to launch, Diane and the balloon are suddenly set aloft; sending her screaming into the Parisian sky and out of the audience's sightline. The scene shifts to Diane and her balloon floating among the clouds. Ben, hiding under blankets in the gondola, reveals himself to a not-quite-shocked Diane ("Franklin … I might have known"). Literally trying to rise above their differences, the two recall fondly their former romance even as they take up their debate over French aid to the colonies. On the ground, Temple meets Janine Nicolet, a woman in her mid-twenties, who is part of a French revolutionary movement. They hit it off and mingle with the crowd for the evening.

Back at his residence, Ben hatches a plot to trick the Spanish ambassador to France into providing guns for the American Revolution. Diane enters expecting to follow up on their recent airborne romantic rapprochement. However, Ben suspects he is being lured into marriage. They quarrel again. Ben storms out again. Diane sings about the perils of love ("How Laughable It Is").

In a transition scene, the Merry Monks of Morellet Abbey cross the stage singing a novelty drinking song of elementary Latin recitations: "Hic Haec Hoc/In Vino Veritas." Ben and his entourage are discovered at the Abbey winery along with the Spanish ambassador. After several drinks, the ambassador—drunk and eager to form an alliance with the colonies—agrees to give Ben money for arms. All assembled celebrate the glories of drinking ("God Bless the Human Elbow").

Act II opens four months later at the Spanish Embassy in Paris. Janine sees Temple dancing with the Spanish ambassador's daughter. Ben accidentally bumps into her. Recognizing the famous American, Janine offers her political support, including future delivery of a small cache of guns. Ben thanks her and, unaware of her feelings for Temple, offers to find her a dance partner. Ben receives news of the colonies' victory over the British at Saratoga, which is apparently achieved with weapons procured by Franklin and shipped to America. Ben heads to Versailles to demand recognition from France. Temple sees Janine, but she runs into the night, leaving Temple with the ambassador's daughter.

At Versailles, Ben and Temple are approached by the British ambassador, Lord David Stormont. He states that their victory at Saratoga notwithstanding, the colonies will lose their war for independence, and France will never grant Ben recognition as an ambassador from a sovereign United States. Lord Stormont further asserts that Americans are becoming British Loyalists, including Ben's son, William, governor of New Jersey. The ambassador invites a somber Ben to London to make peace but without independence. Still hopeful for success in France and suspicious that he might be executed as a traitor in London, Ben declines. The ambassador exits, leaving open his London invitation.

Temple, William Franklin's son, questions Ben about his father's betrayal. Ben deflects the issue but is clearly disturbed by the news. Ben orders Temple to reject his earlier request to marry for "the American cause" and find a woman he truly loves. Temple exits in search of Janine. In turn, Ben seeks out Diane, despite not having spoken to her in four months.

Ben practically barges his way past Diane's house servants as she is reluctant to see him. He presents her with a spinning wheel (part of his original cargo) which fails to impress her. They spar verbally until he pledges his love in a lengthy two-song proposal ("Diane Is" and "Look for Small Pleasures"). She asks for a couple of days to think it over. They agree to meet at Versailles, where she will give him her answer.

At the Franklins' residence, Ben credits his victories in life to his luck with women ("I Love the Ladies"). Temple formally introduces Ben to Janine, and the gathering celebrates the couple's love. An assistant brings in the spinning wheel Ben had given Diane with a message that the she has returned the gift as "an answer of a kind." Despondent at Diane's apparent rejection and the lost hope of obtaining France's support for the Revolution, Ben decides to travel to London to seek peace with Britain even at risk of his life.

Ben goes to Versailles to see Diane and bid a courtesy farewell to the king. Diane and Ben meet in a corridor just outside the king's Throne Room. She harbors no bitterness, saying she returned the gift because Ben genuinely loves America, not her. Prepared to die for his country, Ben is resigned to his diplomatic failure and possible execution in London. Diane exits. Before entering the Throne Room, a solitary Ben professes faith that while America may fail to gain full independence in his lifetime, he is hopeful that they will do so in the future and will understand the sacrifices necessary to keep it.

A footman escorts Ben to the Throne Room doorway which opens into the giant hall. The room is magnificently decorated and packed with gloriously attired celebrants. The king sits on the throne, Diane smiling at his side. The king announces: "Benjamin Franklin … Ambassador to the United States of America." A stunned Ben turns to Diane who nods silently. Joyous music fills the room. The recognition celebration for the new and first American ambassador commences.

Critical reception

Even if *Ben Franklin in Paris* had arrived on Broadway in a mediocre season, opening night gave little indication that the show could ever take flight, second act hot air balloon notwithstanding. The *New York Times*' Howard Taubman, fully aware that Preston took the role to escape the ghost of *The Music Man*'s Harold Hill, sounded a death knell in his opening sentence: "Neither 18th-century wig nor waistcoat … [obscures the fact that this Ben Franklin] is really our old friend selling band instruments in Iowa." Taubman quickly picks the felled Preston off the mat (he is "beguiling," "charming," "winning") only to puncture what, to Preston, sat at the very heart of the project: playwright Sidney Michaels' portrait of Franklin. What Preston saw as an innovative and daring representation of this unique Founding Father, Taubman dismissed as "predictable" and possessed of a too-modern, ironically self-conscious humor for winning over the court of Louis XVI at Versailles. Damning with no praise, Taubman mentions without comment the name of Ulla Sallert, the Swedish actress playing opposite Preston in her Broadway debut as Comtesse Diane (Taubman 1964). One infers that Taubman saw in Preston and Sallert none of the on-stage chemistry to which the production devoted the bulk of its story, several songs, the signature balloon ride, and the fate of the American Revolution.

In an anonymous summative review of three new Broadway openings, *Newsweek Magazine* made Taubman's screed appear charitable by comparison. Opening the article with the unambiguous pronouncement that "a dry rot is overtaking Broadway," the magazine launched its prosecution of the 1964–5 season with *Ben Franklin in Paris* as Exhibit A. *Newsweek* condemned the entire production as "amateurish" to the point of resembling a Harvard Hasty Pudding Club skit. Specifically, Franklin's wit and wiles failed to shine through the banality of his tedious romance with Comtesse Diane ("Sad Week" 1964).

John Chapman, writing in the *New York Daily News,* was among the most enthusiastic reviewers at opening night, praising Preston's Franklin in the manner the star himself had hoped for: possessed of "humor," "dignity," and "charm" enough to carry the entire show. However, the *Daily News* also ran a review by Jack Gaver of the news service United Press International (UPI), which, while lavishing praise on Preston, had little good to say about the show as a whole. Ulla Sallert, who may have fared better receiving no mention at all from Gaver, was dismissed as a competent singer "lovely to look at" but stuck in a part that is "stuffy" and "inflexible" (Gaver 1964). If the opening night reviews stung, the Tony Awards drew blood. The show's only nomination went to Michaels for his book. Many observers were surprised that Preston, who received generally favorable notices as Franklin, did not receive a nomination for Best Actor in a Musical. Preston would rebound two years later, winning Best Actor in a Musical for *I Do! I Do!,* but by that time his Ben Franklin was all but forgotten and Harold Hill remained his signature role for the remainder of his career.

Owing in part to American popular culture's nostalgic turn for all things 1960s, critics have periodically revisited *Ben Franklin in Paris,* largely through a second listen to the original cast album. *Ben Franklin* received somewhat better treatment as time wore on, nonetheless the new jurors generally upheld the original verdict that the show, despite some under-appreciated virtues for its time, was in over its head from opening night against the likes of *Fiddler on the Roof* and *Hello Dolly!*

In 1995, Richard Traubner, writing in the *American Record Guide*, recalled the show as a "colorful turn" for Preston with songs that were "insistently memorable without being terribly good" (Traubner 1995). John Kenrick's website *Musicals101.com*, unsparing in its review title "Flops on CD: *Ben Franklin in Paris*," joined the chorus of postmortem lamentations that the show "deserved a better fate" than to fall to *Fiddler on the Roof* and the rest of that season's legendary line-up. Kenrick lauds the original cast recording for exquisitely preserving the melodic score which, while not a masterpiece, "offers lots of fun moments" (Kenrick 2000). Gerard Alessandrini's *castalbumreviews.com* expressed great fondness for the score, chalking up all its misfortunes to the happenstance of having opened amidst a Broadway season for the ages: "the right musical at the wrong time." Alessandrini declares the score to be melodic, the lyrics "literate," and the entire concept "a winsome foray into the mind of Franklin." He also acknowledges that the more successful *1776* eventually relegated Preston's Franklin to the status of a "precursor" to Howard Da Silva's Ben Franklin in the later show. Nevertheless, Alessandrini insists that *Ben Franklin in Paris* is "a gem of a lost Broadway musical" (Alessandrini n.d.).

Historical accuracy and context

Franklin's mission to France

The historical setting and circumstances portrayed in *Ben Franklin in Paris* are fundamentally accurate. The musical covers the critical first fifteen months of Franklin's nine-year sojourn in France on behalf of the newly declared independent American colonies. Shortly after the signing of the *Declaration of Independence* in 1776, Franklin set sail to France with the blessings of the Continental Congress. His mission was to solicit from France diplomatic recognition for America as a sovereign nation and procure France's military and financial assistance in America's ongoing struggle—now a war for independence—against the British Empire. Franklin arrived in France in December 1776 with two of his young grandchildren in tow. At the time, Franklin was, by far, the most famous American among Europeans if not the world. For decades, he had been well known and admired—even idolized—by the French for his scientific experiments (especially in electricity), his inventions, and general writings, many of which had been widely read in France prior to his arrival in 1776.

In many respects the musical presents Franklin quite accurately. On stage and in real life he was a self-aware celebrity in Paris, joyously calculating and skillful at applying his charm and fame in service of his diplomatic goals. At the same time, *Ben Franklin in Paris* conveys appropriately the seriousness of Franklin's mission. There was a high probability that he could fail in attaining support from France. Moreover, with the signing of the *Declaration of Independence* he was now traveling in Europe as a traitor to the Crown of Great Britain and conceivably subject to execution if seized by British authorities. The musical conveys all of this quite clearly.

Diplomacy and the political inner circle in Paris

Some additional characters and sub-plots are also credibly represented in the musical, even if some Franklin quotes or events drawn from his life occurred prior to or after the brief timeline covered by the show. Arguably, the most intriguing and accurately drawn of these historical figures, apart from Franklin himself, is Lord David Stormont, the British ambassador to France. Franklin's principal nemesis, Stormont scrupulously maintains the protocols of diplomacy and civility when in conversation with Franklin at court. But the British ambassador has no illusions about the dangers Franklin's presence in Paris poses to Britain. In the play, Stormont wages his own propaganda campaign to offset Franklin's inflated accounts of how well American forces are doing against the British—a tendency toward self-serving misrepresentation that the real Franklin did, in fact, employ on occasion. Late in the play, when Stormont invites Franklin to come to London so that the "colonies" and the Crown can settle their differences peaceably, Franklin suspects the invitation is a pretext to have him imprisoned and/or executed while he is in London—an aspiration the real Ambassador Stormont had apparently confided to associates upon discovering that Franklin had arrived in Paris.

Another historic character in the show, Pierre-Augustin Caron de Beaumarchais (Beaumarchais), was a French journalist, playwright, and arms dealer as well as one of many intellectuals and aristocrats in King Louis' circle who supported America's defiance of Britain. Such support for the American colonies, while not unanimous, was fairly widespread among King Louis' inner circle and Parisian intellectuals. French sympathizers' motivations for supporting the "American cause" ranged from seizing a strategic advantage against age-old rival England/Britain, to individual profiteering opportunities in arms trading, to intellectual affinity for Enlightenment ideas embraced by the rebellious American colonies, and to fan fascination with Franklin as a symbol of the enigmatic "new American" emerging on the international scene. Portrayed in the musical as a confidant and close companion to Franklin, the real Beaumarchais, although a self-declared supporter of the American cause, was apparently not the intimate associate of Franklin that the musical presents.

However, Beaumarchais' actions creditably stand in for other well-placed powerbrokers at Versailles who were predisposed towards America in its fight with England. Likely examples would include two of King Louis' official advisors: Compte Charles Gravier Vergennes and Antoine de Sartine. Vergennes appears briefly in the musical; Sartine does not appear at all. While Vergennes, France's Minister of Foreign Affairs, quarreled occasionally with Franklin over details of how to implement France's support for America, he is credited with finalizing the Treaty of Alliance between France and America in 1778. Sartine, France's Minister of the Navy, was so enthusiastic in his support for America (and his antipathy for Britain) that his budget overruns and breaches of diplomatic protocols eventually became liabilities for the French court. He was removed from office in 1780.

Other brushstrokes of historical accuracy in the show include the incorporation of direct quotes and close adaptations from Franklin's vast writings into the dialog and lyrics. The show also makes clear that Franklin faced criticism from some American leaders back home who were openly skeptical of his loyalty to America in light of his undisguised affinity for the French and the celebrity status they accorded him. The musical also presents a brief if instructive insight into Franklin's estrangement from his son William, the governor of New Jersey, who opposed the revolution and supported British rule of the American colonies.

Author Michaels claims with some justice that the musical has important history lessons to teach about Franklin, an essential historical figure whose popular mythology, he believes, has left an oversimplified portrait in the minds of many Americans. Nevertheless, here the demands of putting on a Broadway show chafe against historical fact in a number of ways. Not the least among them is that the seventy-year-old lead "boy" and his forty-ish lead "girl" engage in a clichéd, on-and-off courtship whose fate holds the key to America winning France's support and gaining full independence from Britain. While Franklin recognized and excelled at the diplomatic skill of charming and engaging the leaders of his host country, he neither flirted nor romanced his way to political influence at the French court. Here, the musical side-steps complex diplomatic negotiations and maneuvers that characterized the real Ben Franklin's mission to Paris for the sake of the love story at the center of the show.

The hot air balloon ride

A Broadway director faced with the nightly challenge of one-upping a fiddler on a roof in a competing theater might be forgiven for airlifting a Founding Father and his love interest in the gondola of the first known "manned" hot air balloon flight. However, this historically fictitious moment, apart from being untrue and more than a little gimmicky, gave the show a beneath-the-surface relevance that ultimately honored the historical significance of Franklin's time in Paris, even if the scene misrepresented the event itself. The invention and public launch of the first recorded piloted hot air balloon in 1783 did, in fact, occur in Paris while Franklin was living there. In the 1780s, Franklin, a well-established and distinguished, if ailing, American diplomat, scientist, and "Renaissance Man" in Paris, was sought out by the French press for comment on the new invention. Franklin happily obliged, speaking glowingly of ballooning's implications for the future. But Franklin was almost seventy-eight years old at the launch of the first balloon and his health had been failing for some time. There is no record of him ever having taken a balloon ride, much less having commandeered the maiden voyage. The stirring fictitious scene, in which he woos Diane and touts the glories of the American Revolution while commanding the airborne balloon, certainly underscores Franklin's star status as a scientist and diplomat. But the scene itself is pure fiction.

The Dianes of Paris

The musical takes a significant, even distracting, liberty with historical accuracy with respect to the fictitious principal female character, Diane (Madame La Comtesse Diane de Vobrillac). In the musical she is close advisor and confidant to King Louis XVI at Versailles. The musical strongly implies that Diane is *the* power behind the throne, whose approval is necessary and sufficient for securing King Louis' support. She is also Franklin's single, all-consuming love interest during his first year in Paris—a handy coincidence for a genuine "politics makes strange bedfellows" story. But this character is unvarnished fiction. There is no single woman in Franklin's life or, for that matter, in all of France in the late 1770s who readily fits either description, much less both.

Michaels claims Diane's character is based on a composite of a number of women whom Franklin knew in France, but offers no details about their identities beyond stating unequivocally that Marie Antoinette is not among them. Perhaps the most obvious historical inspiration for Diane is Comtesse Diane de Polignac, who, apart from the similarity in name, was a lady in waiting for one of King Louis XVI's sisters. Caught up in Paris' celebrity fanfare over Ben Franklin, her constant praise for Franklin apparently bored and annoyed King Louis. But she had no significant political influence at court and no consequential relationship with Franklin.

While in Paris, Franklin did pursue an emotionally intimate relationship with a neighbor, Anne-Louise Brillon. She was unhappily married, thirty-seven years Franklin's junior, and one of the premiere concert harpsichordists in Paris. A frequent guest in her home, Franklin delighted in her company, her music, her erudition, and her cleverness. Brillon, in turn, was moved by Franklin's attention and cherished his friendship. Their mutual affection grew steadily during Franklin's first few years in Paris. Perhaps more than any other woman he met in France, Brillon held the depth of Franklin's affections, including romantic interest on Franklin's part and some flirtatious behavior on hers. But Brillon, who ultimately thought of Franklin more as a father figure than a lover, was not directly involved in high-level international diplomacy.

Franklin also sought the company of Anne-Catherine Helveticus, a wealthy widow who, like Brillon, lived near him. He eagerly joined her social circle of artists, philosophers, and intellectuals. He proposed marriage to her on several occasions, but she apparently lacked a commensurate level of enthusiasm for a formal commitment.

Quite apart from the fact that Ben Franklin did pursue relationships with elegant, well-placed, aristocratic women when he was in Paris, the musical invents out of whole cloth its inescapable inference that Franklin flirted, slept, kissed, embraced, charmed, and/or ballooned his way into King Louis' good graces. But for a novelty scene in which Franklin plies the Spanish ambassador to France with liquor to coax an arms shipment to America out of him, the musical shows very little of Franklin exercising his diplomatic skills within the labyrinthine circuits of European diplomacy. Franklin did a lot more to persuade Louis than beguile the king's courtesans to win his confidence in the American cause. As for his part, King Louis saw a chance to gain an advantage against Britain and explore new commercial and military opportunities with an emerging ally across the ocean. Balloons and pillow talk make for better theater, but Louis XVI's decision to support America's war with Britain, as Franklin had hoped all along, was a decision based on multilateral politics and diplomacy.

Franklin's welcome and reputation in France

To their credit, the company of *Ben Franklin in Paris* makes it clear at the outset that, upon arriving in France in 1776, Franklin was following his reputation as a well-known scientist, inventor, author, and rebel in the American fight against age-old rival England/Britain. It is a cheerful, confidently famous Ben Franklin who disembarks from his vessel upon docking in France. He gloats as the ship's crew brings out his luggage as well as samples of his inventions to be distributed strategically as diplomatic or romantic gifts: printing press, stove, kite, and rocking chair. Everyday French people (boy, man, shopkeeper, wench, baker's boy, etc.) recognize him on sight and shout their greetings, so as to impress Franklin and, doubtless, bring the audience up to speed on France's profound interest in America and Franklin himself. ("Baker's Boy: Ah, Monsieur le Docteur, are you come for recognition?") Franklin responds with a certain coyness ("I've come for my health and the education of my grandchildren"), accurately reflecting the fact that, while his mission was clear, Franklin did have to worry about being too obvious or aggressive in his solicitations, lest he breach the complex protocols of European diplomacy and the uneasy truce that France and Britain historically maintain to prevent perpetual conflagration between them.

While Franklin's arrival in France caused a sensation eventually, it actually took some time for his presence to become known and his impact to be felt in Paris—a small historical fact the musical sacrifices to give the lead actor a grand entrance to open the show. In reality, however, Franklin's one-month voyage across the Atlantic was a horrendous experience. The weather was dreadful and his relatively small vessel rocked ceaselessly. He was ill for most of the trip and arrived in France struggling to walk. He could not eat many of the basic provisions on board because of stomach ailments and weak teeth. It would take some time before Franklin and grandsons were settled into their accommodations in a suburb of Paris and before the great man recuperated sufficiently to strike out into the diplomatic wilds of Paris.

Thomas A. Greenfield

Further reading

Alessandrini, Gerard. n.d. "Ben Franklin in Paris." *Castalbumreviews.com*, http:// castalbumreviews.com/ben-franklin-in-paris/.

Chapman, John. 1964. "Robert Preston Perfect Choice to Portray Ben Franklin in Paris." *New York Daily News*, October 29, 1964.

Franklin, Benjamin. 1987. *Franklin: Autobiography, Poor Richard, and Later Writings*. Edited by J. A. Leo Lamay. New York: The Library of America.

Gaver, Jack. 1964. "Robert Preston Hailed as 'Ben Franklin' Opens on Broadway." UPI to the *New York Daily News*, October 28, 1964.

Gilmore, Nicholas. 2018. "Forever the Music Man: Robert Preston's Legacy at 100 Years." *Saturday Evening Post*, June 8, 2018.

Isaacson, Walter. 2003. *Benjamin Franklin: An American Life*. New York: Simon and Schuster.

Kenrick, John. 2000. "Flops on CD: *Ben Franklin in Paris*." Revised edition 2002, https:// www.musicals101.com/flops1.htm#Ben.

Michaels, Sidney. 1963. *Ben Franklin in Paris*. New York: Samuel French.

Michaels, Sidney. 1965. *Ben Franklin in Paris: A Random House Play*. New York: Random House.

Millstein, Gilbert. 1964. "That Brassy Music Man Returns to Broadway as Poor Richard." *Saturday Evening Post*, October 17, 1964, 87–9.

Page, Tim. 1987. "Robert Preston, Actor, Is Dead at 68." *New York Times*, March 23, 1987, https://www.nytimes.com/1987/03/23/obituaries/robert-preston-actor-is-dead-at-68.html.

"Sad Week." *Newsweek*, November 9, 1964, 92.

Schiff, Stacy. 2006. *A Great Improvisation: Franklin, France, and the Birth of America*. New York: Holt Paperbacks.

Schwartzkopf, General H. Norman. 1992. *It Doesn't Take a Hero: The Autobiography*. New York: Bantam.

Taubman, Howard. 1964. "The Theater: *Ben Franklin in Paris*; Preston in Musical at the Lunt-Fontanne. " *New York Times*, October 28, 1964.

Traubner, Richard. 1995. *American Record Guide*. Washington, D.C.: American Record Guide.

Viagas, Robert. 2014. "Was 1964 Broadway's Greatest Year for Musicals: *Dolly*, *Fiddler*, *Funny Girl*, and Other Groundbreakers." *Playbill*, May 15, 2014.

CHAPTER FIVE
BLOODY BLOODY ANDREW JACKSON (2008)

Book by Alex Timbers (1978–)
Music and Lyrics by Michael Friedman (1975–2017)
World Professional Premiere: The Public Theater production at Kirk Douglas Theater, Los Angeles, January 20, 2008–February 17, 2008 Broadway: October 13, 2010–January 2, 2011

Songs

"Populism, Yea, Yea!"
"I'm Not That Guy"
"Illness as Metaphor"
"I'm So That Guy"
"Ten Little Indians"
"The Corrupt Bargain"
"Rock Star"
"The Great Compromise"
"Public Life"
"Crisis Averted"
"The Saddest Song"
"Second Nature"
"The Hunters of Kentucky"

Overview

Although *Bloody Bloody Andrew Jackson* (*BBAJ*) fits comfortably into the genre of original rock musical, the show, like its subject, has little patience with prevailing convention. This non-traditional biography of Andrew Jackson (1767–1845) advances the premise that—notwithstanding that he was almost fifty when he became a national hero at the Battle of New Orleans and sixty-one when he was elected president—his popularity emanated from a youthful, glam-rock sexual charisma, indie rock anti-establishmentarianism, and an ability to inspire rebellious anger and territorialism that resonated with many white frontier settlers in the early nineteenth century.

Bloody Bloody Andrew Jackson insists that an analogy between Jackson's rise from his youth on the rural frontier to the American presidency and the ascendance of angst-ridden, inwardly reflective punk music (emo rock) in modern pop culture is a valid, if unconventional, dramatic interpretation of Jackson's life. For all its casual profanity, slapstick pratfalls, sexual innuendo, and midnight rock club histrionics, the play self-consciously wraps itself in traditional timelines, terminology, and curriculum associated with Jackson studies. For example, composer/lyricist Michael Friedman's opening number, "Populism Yea Yea" (performed aggressively by Andrew Jackson and the company and the stripped down, four-piece punk band "orchestra"), repeats the phrase "the age of Jackson" nine times, a more than casual nod to Arthur Schlesinger, Jr.'s 1945 Pulitzer Prize-winning biography of the same name. Midway in the show, the ensemble renders an irreverent hip rundown of "the Corrupt Bargain of 1824," an historical event so obscure to the general public that as part of the song the ensemble hints that they can't quite follow it all themselves. The play closes with a coda that plants its flag in the citadel of academic legitimacy: a flashback recreation of President Andrew Jackson receiving an Honorary Doctorate of Laws from Harvard University in 1833—a true historical event. The finale accompanying the curtain call neither reprises an earlier song nor introduces an original one. Instead, the band cranks out a club rock arrangement of "The Hunters of Kentucky," a campaign song from Jackson's 1824 and 1828 presidential runs.

The play develops Jackson's biography on the premise that his lifelong vision for America was made manifest in the coerced—and, as "necessary," violent—displacement of American Indians and the seizure of millions of acres of their land. Yet, the authors intend that "the darker subject matter butt up against the comedy in a somewhat disturbing and emotionally complex way" (Timbers and Friedman 2017). Thus pratfalls, cartoon-esque Founding Fathers, and ludicrous anachronisms are never far from the action. In addition, Jackson sporadically erupts into obscenity-laced tantrums, breaking the mood as needed to invoke the erratic temperament of the rock star seventh president of the United States.

Composer/lyricist Michael Friedman described *BBAJ* as

> ... an Emo-rock Musical about Andrew Jackson ... Emo-rock is kind of post punk [characterized by] deeply emotional boys with guitars who are very upset about girls who did not go out with them in high school. This is a show about a deeply emotional boy [Jackson, from youth through death at age 78], the adolescence of a country, and the growing pains for both.
>
> *Friedman 2011*

Laying the emo foundation of the play from the start, Andrew Jackson and the company sing "Populism Yea Yea." The song likens the resentments of a spurned love-struck teenage boy to populist anger fomenting on the emerging American frontier. The unnamed schoolgirl who spurned the boy and the despicable "cool guys" she preferred serve as stand-ins for nineteenth-century-rural America and the loathsome British, French, Spaniards, elite Northern aristocrats, and Indians who command "her" attention. The song culminates in a pledge that Americans "like us who just don't think about things ... but make things happen" will save the country and take her back from her unworthy suitors. *BBAJ*'s Jackson subsumes the people's raging passion for lost love and country. It engenders within him a bellicose, anti-intellectual nativism that profoundly shapes his life and defines his presidency.

In as much as cultural conflict lies at the heart of *BBAJ*, the rock musical is an altogether appropriate vehicle for conveying its story. Rock musicals brought forth a generational reaction against the so-called "golden age of musicals," which held sway over American musical theater from the mid-1940s to the mid-1960s. The "golden age" is also known as the era of the Rodgers and Hammerstein "book musical" in honor of the composer/lyricist team that dominated the era with straightforward boy-meets-girl plot structures, "literary" scripts, and musical sensibilities grounded in turn-of-the-century European operetta such as *Oklahoma!*, *South Pacific*, and *The Sound of Music*.

The era of the "book musical" coincided with the birth of rock and roll, which took over American AM radio and remodeled the recording industry for a newly prosperous, predominantly white teen market. Rock and roll resettled the mainstream musical, relegating original cast albums and show tunes to secondary status in American popular music: distinctly not hip (i.e., square) entertainment for middle-aged parents and the occasional nerdy musical theater kid. Rock and roll and musical theater were twins that did not meet until 1967, when the first and, for many, the platonic ideal of the rock musical emerged in the form of *Hair: The American Tribal Love-Rock Musical* (familiarly *Hair*).

By the time *BBAJ* opened in Los Angeles in 2008, the rock musical, now more than forty years old, had diverged into two groupings commonly known as "rock" for edgier sub-genres and "pop" for softer work. The first rock musicals comprised original musical scores, and most new rock musicals still do. However, rock music has had an ingrown sense of nostalgia since the 1960s, when "golden oldies" and later "classic rock" assumed rock radio and recording format status. From that sentiment sprang the jukebox or catalog musical—musicals based on established rock or pop hit songs around which writers develop a storyline or other stageable narrative. *Mamma Mia* (2000), *Jersey Boys* (2005), and *Rock of Ages* (2009) are among the most successful of that genre. Jonathan Larson's original rock musical *Rent* (1996) "introduced mainstream commercial theater to Generation X or the MTV Generation: sophisticated young urbanites born after 1960 and presumptively acclimated to racial tolerance, homosexuality, bisexuality, and casual drug use as cultural norms" (Metzler 2010). With its emphasis on young adult angst, its in-your-face defiance of the Rodgers and Hammerstein book musical, and its astonishing twelve-year Broadway run to 2008 (the year of *BBAJ*'s first professional production), *Rent* provided a sturdy transition from *Hair* to the punk-influenced music (including emo) that inspired such hit shows as *Spring Awakening* (2006), *American Idiot* (2010), and *BBAJ* itself.

Emo is a descendant of British and American socially rebellious punk and other hardcore club bands of the 1970s and 1980s, such as the Ramones, the Clash, and the Sex Pistols. While maintaining punk's signature pounding electric guitar chord riffs (no virtuoso solos, please), assault rifle percussion, quick songs (some barely two-minutes' long or even less) and *de rigueur* profane lyrics in live performance, emo branched off from original punk in its lyrical style, gaining popularity in the 1990s and early 2000s by turning the singer's anger inward. The emotive power of the lead singer displaced punk-born anger against the status quo with "equally forceful vulnerability, interrogating his own emotions like a bad cop with a perp in a dark room" (Richman 2018). The lead singer's emotive expressions also opened the music to gentler influences of balladry and "soft rock" as counterweights to emo's heavier punk-rooted anthems. Emo chart hits include "I'm Not Okay (I Promise)" by My Chemical Romance (2004), "Sugar We're Going Down" by Fall Out Boy (2005), and "I Miss You" by Blink-182 (2003) (Jones 2016).

Friedman's score for *BBAJ* does justice to his claim that emo rock dominates the show's musical presentation and attitude. In addition to the opening number, "Populism Yea Yea," the paired confessional numbers early in the show, "I'm Not That Guy" and "I'm So That Guy," stay true to emo as the young adult Jackson explores his inner feelings to determine whether the role of a leader of a restless anarchistic white frontier suits his emotional constitution. (Spoiler. It does.) Musically the two songs, while still maintaining a driving punk rock beat, account for Jackson's emotional introspection by featuring an acoustic guitar in the rhythm section. The score returns to full-on emo punk form when Jackson considers a presidential run from the show's unique historical perspective in the song "Rock Star": "Washington acted like a rock star." And, indeed, Jackson aspires to follow in Washington's footsteps as "a celebrity of first rank." Later during his presidency Jackson deteriorates into self-absorbed despotism. "The Saddest Song" offers the score's most successful rendering of a man's personal self-destructive emotion overflowing its banks and flooding into the body politic: "we'll take back the country and we'll take, and we'll take, and we'll take."

However, the emo tracks find effective counterpoints in a handful of songs written and performed in other modes, some of which are arresting in their contrast with the dominant emo punk idiom. The oft-betrayed Rachel Donelson Jackson—adored by her husband but no match for politics and warfare as competition for his affection—makes her case against him in a powerful feminist manifesto, "The Great Compromise." Her deep bitterness is mercifully void of punk's irrational rage. Rachel's anger soars in exquisitely reasoned, sharply argued, irrefutable grievances—wholly adult and rational, but boiling over just the same: "You tell me not to compromise ... You give up nothing! I give up everything." The quietly powerful "Second Nature" is a serious-minded folk protest lament in the mode of Pete Seeger's 1960s classic "Where Have all the Flowers Gone?" or even the Eagles' "The Last Resort." The song removes some of the acrid residue of Jackson's "The Saddest Song." Delivered by a nameless troubadour, "Second Nature" stands outside the show's central action and holds the

Jackson legacy accountable for laying waste to America's indigenous peoples, seizing their lands, and decimating their way of life. At the same time, the song indicts the audience and, indeed, the show itself for shared complicity in Jackson's legacy: "We clear [the continent] out and make it in our image … it's second nature to us."

Plot synopsis

The play opens in a hypothetical time and place during Andrew Jackson's presidency. Jackson, in tight jeans, enters with the ensemble of "cowboys and prostitutes" in lead-vocalist-and-back-up-singers formation. He cues the punk band orchestra and the audience ("You ready?" "You ready?"). He introduces himself as "your president" and the company sings "Populism, Yea Yea."

A storyteller in a motorized wheelchair enters, bumping into people and furniture (a recurring comedic "bit"). She reads aloud from a child-level biography of Jackson. She gives the date and location of Jackson's birth and cues the show's first biographical scene: Jackson's one-room rural childhood home in the Carolinas. Jackson's family expresses their resentment of Indians, European invaders, and other interlopers upon "our land" in the frontier. Jackson's parents and brothers are all killed by Indians right before his eyes.

Alone, teenaged Jackson joins a militia unit and is taken prisoner by British troops. He is tortured but released eventually. The experience fuels his hatred for Indians, the British, and officials in Washington who show no interest in the people living on the American frontier. Jackson ponders how the disenfranchised frontier states will rectify these injustices ("I'm Not That Guy").

Jackson, now in his early twenties, frequents local taverns. To the delight of his drinking compatriots, his grievance-ridden tavern talk evolves into calls for direct action against the enemies of the frontier. Jackson basks in their adulation. He is injured in a bar fight with Spanish soldiers and meets a young woman named Rachel. She cares for him as he recovers from his injury, and they fall in love ("Illness as Metaphor"). They marry, even though she is still legally married to another man.

Circa 1812, a frontiersman informs Jackson and friends that Tecumseh, a Shawnee chief, is unifying Northern and southern Indian tribes against American settlements as well as soliciting aid from British and Spanish troops. The people of the frontier turn to Jackson for leadership, and he eagerly accepts *de facto* military and political command of the American frontier ("I'm So That Guy").

The bandleader announces that Jackson has led a frontier militia to a brutal victory over Creek Indians. Jackson negotiates surrender terms with Creek Chief Red Eagle, which includes forfeiture of all Creek lands. However, via messenger, Jackson is overruled by President James Monroe who allows the Creeks to keep their land. Jackson defies Monroe's orders and banishes the Creeks from their territory anyway. Jackson continues his self-authorized conquest of Indian tribes: seizing land, sabotaging tribes with smallpox-infected blankets, and coercing tribal leaders to ally with him as informants and enablers ("Ten Little Indians").

The scene shifts to Washington, D.C., and the second generation of Founding Fathers enters. They are aristocrats whom Jackson despises and who despise Jackson in return. President James Monroe and senators John Calhoun, Henry Clay, and Martin Van Buren individually and collectively are one-dimensional foppish clowns. President Monroe declares he will summon Jackson to the White House to explain his unauthorized conquests.

At the close of the Creek conflict, Jackson sees an Indian boy lying in a battlefield by his dead mother. He adopts him, names him Lyncoya, and sends him home to Rachel at their estate in Tennessee to be raised in their family. Later, Jackson learns that British troops plan to attack the city of New Orleans. Jackson mounts a counterattack on the British. He prevails in the Battle of New Orleans, despite overwhelming odds in favour of the British, and becomes a national hero.

Jackson returns home bloodied from battle. Rachel pleads with him to spend more time at home, revealing that she is tormented by "the stain of bigamy" that is ruining her reputation and dashing her hopes for a normal life. Rachel compels Jackson to choose between her and public life. He chooses Rachel but neither of them believes he will honor the pledge. Battlefield glory at New Orleans has whet Jackson's political ambitions. He runs for president in 1824 but loses to John Quincy Adams, even after having won the popular and electoral votes. The ensemble explains how the Washington establishment manipulated the election to secure the win for Adams against Jackson ("The Corrupt Bargain").

Jackson honors Monroe's summons to Washington, where Jackson is interrogated by the aforementioned leaders plus John Quincy Adams, all cartoonish fops as before. They rebuke him for leading unauthorized military actions, but Jackson intimidates them with his intelligence, self-confidence, and open disdain for their privileged lives. They meekly threaten to censure him. Jackson departs, avowing to topple them with a new democracy-based political movement.

The play advances to the presidential election of 1828 where Jackson announces his candidacy ("Rock Star") and creates the Democratic Party to support his presidential run. The 1828 campaign pushes Rachel beyond endurance, especially since the Jacksons' adulterous marriage has become a national scandal and fodder for Jackson's political opponents ("The Great Compromise"). Jackson wins the election, but Rachel dies of despair shortly thereafter, never having become First Lady. Jackson blames his political opponents for her suffering.

The play now focuses on Jackson's eight years as president and is set almost entirely in the Oval Office. Predictably, populist President Jackson gleefully disrupts the regular order of government, routinely bypassing Congress, cabinet secretaries, and the Supreme Court in favor "the people"—a hodge-podge of friends and gate crashers hanging out at the Oval Office in perpetual party mode. Eventually the responsibilities of the office erode Jackson's patience with "the people," who in turn become frustrated by unsolved problems, government bureaucracy, and Jackson himself. Jackson abandons his populist outreach to the common people, dismissing them as dolts who need an authoritarian leader to tell them what to do ("The Saddest Song").

Despairing over his political and personal failures, Jackson falls back on his most reliable source of public- and self-validation: dislocation of the Indian tribes. He summons Black Fox, a former Jackson ally who now coordinates several tribes that are attacking white settlements, to a meeting. Jackson offers Black Fox the "least bad solution" to their current conflict: sign over all tribal lands under his control and evacuate peacefully or suffer forced dislocation by the U.S. Army. Black Fox refuses to sign. The unspoken results will be the Trail of Tears, alluded to as a troubadour sings of loss and resignation ("Second Nature").

The storyteller announces the date of Jackson's death and, mentioning the Trail of Tears, sums up his disputed legacy: was he a great leader of America's common people or a racist murderer who left a national legacy of divisiveness? The action ends with a flashback scene of Jackson receiving an honorary doctorate at Harvard. In his speech to the graduates, he defends his legacy as a unifier and peacemaker. Curtain calls are taken as the company performs "The Hunters of Kentucky," a Jackson presidential campaign song.

Critical reception

Before opening on Broadway in 2010, *BBAJ* had an initial run at the Kirk Douglas Theatre in Los Angeles from January 20 to February 17, 2008. The producers then took the show to Off-Broadway in New York before transferring the production to the Bernard Jacobs Theatre on Broadway. Like many of the raucous rock club gigs that inspired the show, *BBAJ* is a star turn vehicle for an alpha male lead. Benjamin Walker starred as

Jackson in early workshop productions as well as the Los Angeles, Off-Broadway, and Broadway runs—a fact that figured prominently in the critical reception of the show.

The critical reception in Los Angeles was overall very enthusiastic—particularly for Walker's performance as Jackson—and framed much of the critical discussion that would follow the show into New York. For the Los Angeles run, *BBAJ's* glitzy celebrity bombast seemed right at home in the star-is-born capital of the world. Local critics were generally supportive, offering varying degrees of forgiveness for the show's deliberate overreach and forays into excess. Paul Hodgins writing in the *Orange County Register* sounded what would soon become a familiar refrain: hosannas for Walker as Jackson followed by general approval mitigated by negotiated settlements with everything else (Hodgins 2008). Frequently noted shortcomings included uneven performances from the supporting cast, lapses into amateurish skit comedy, and mishandling of historical facts and information. The *Los Angeles Times* was especially lavish in its praise of Walker's performance and saluted the show's merging of rock and political stardom: "Jackson can rouse a crowd with speeches as hypnotically as he can wield a microphone in concert." The *Times* also took the show's approach to history very seriously but faulted the writers for attempting an "encyclopedic completeness" that ultimately weighed down the show's pace (McNulty 2008).

By contrast, *LA Weekly's* Ben Kusler had little patience with claims for the play as a meaningful history lesson, but admired the show's serious exploration of Jackson's genocidal war against American Indians within the context of its freewheeling silliness. At first skeptical that any historical lessons could survive the show's battery of profane asides, slapstick humor, and incongruous modern pop culture references, Kusler found redeeming educational value in the more serious second half of the show (Kusler 2008).

Once in New York, *BBAJ* received its best reviews from the *New York Times'* chief theater critic Ben Brantley. Brantley lavished praise on Walker but, more significantly, conferred his blessings on the show's historical chops:

> Though the United States may have been founded on the rational principles of the Enlightenment … what really makes it run—then and now—is the crazy, mixed-up energy of enduring adolescence. Idealism, resentment, a short attention span, a fear of being perpetually misunderstood and a ravenous sense of entitlement are mixed together here in one big, gawky, sexually charged package: America, the eternal teenager.
>
> *Brantley 2010b*

Reviewing the Broadway production six months later, Brantley was still all in, praising *BBAJ* for offering the most insightful reflection of the current state of America of any show currently running in the city.

By and large, other reviews of the New York productions echoed the perspective of the Los Angeles critics, leaving Walker unscathed but often wanting better work around the edges. Peter Marks of the *Washington Post* felt that Walker nailed his star turn but that the ensemble and the production as a whole tended to cross the line from professionally staged raucousness to unpolished amateurism (Marks 2010). David Sheward, writing in *Backstage.com*, noted a similar imbalance among the cast in his generally enthusiastic review of the Broadway run. Sheward noted that Walker skillfully balanced the complexity of Jackson's character, "simultaneously playing him like a spoiled teenager, angry rock star, wily politician, and real human being." Sheward was one of a few New York critics who noted that the supporting cast had improved since the production moved from Off-Broadway to Broadway, but found that cast members still showed lingering signs of overacting and mugging (Sheward 2010).

Chris Jones of the *Chicago Tribune* followed suit, calling the show "fractured, intermittently juvenile [yet] wholly fearless and arresting" (Ng 2010). John Simon of *Bloomberg News*, a well-known Broadway traditionalist and notoriously hard sell, found the show "not grown up enough" for Broadway. More charitably, Elisabeth Vincentelli of the *New York Post* observed that the show had improved upon its shallower aspects when it transferred to Broadway from the Public Theater: "Playing to Broadway audiences, [the show] feels more subversive" (Vincentelli 2010).

Bloody Bloody Andrew Jackson closed on Broadway after only ninety-four shows (exclusive of previews), with disappointing ticket sales colliding with investment shortfalls. The Tony Awards, which tend to shed their grace upon money-makers, largely snubbed *BBAJ*, offering a single nomination (and no win) to Timbers for the book and, to the surprise of many, not even a nomination for Benjamin Walker.

Historical accuracy and context

The death of Andrew Jackson's parents and brothers

The deaths of Jackson's parents and brothers are not significant historical events in and of themselves. However, *BBAJ* suggests erroneously that Jackson's parents and two brothers all died at about the same time in young Andrew's presence following attacks by hostile Indians. None of this is true.

Jackson's father died in 1767 shortly before Andrew was born. His mother and two older brothers died in service to the colonies against the British during the Revolutionary War but at different times and in different locations. The oldest Jackson brother, Hugh, died of heat exhaustion near Sono Ferry, South Carolina, in 1779. The middle brother, Robert, having been imprisoned with Andrew by the British, died of cholera shortly after the brothers' release in 1781. His mother died of cholera later that year in Charleston, South Carolina, while tending to wounded and sick colonial troops.

The Corrupt Bargain of 1824

President James Monroe, future presidents John Quincy Adams and Martin van Buren, and senators John Calhoun and Henry Clay—all represented on stage as cartoonish bumbling fops and nincompoops—were, of course, serious-minded politically capable men. Their farcical portrayals underscore Jackson's disdain for the aristocratic leaders in Washington but add little historical value. Having initially appeared quaking in fear over Jackson's growing fame after the Battle of New Orleans, the group reconvenes to confront the "crisis" of Jackson's impressive showing in the 1824 presidential election.

The musical accurately represents that Jackson, despite being a late entry into the race, won more electoral and popular votes than any of his rivals: Adams (then Secretary of State), Clay (Speaker of the House), and Secretary of the Treasury William H. Crawford (not portrayed in the musical). Calhoun gave up an early presidential candidacy to secure the 1824 election vice presidency, a strategy that proved successful.

Although the musical mentions in passing that Jackson did not win a majority of the electoral votes, thus failing to win the presidency, the staging implicitly embraces a "populist" interpretation: namely, that the Constitutional necessity of having Congress determine the winner amounted to an *ipso facto* act of corruption. The history is more nuanced than that.

The musical neglects to mention that, prior to the vote of the electors, each of the four candidates was known to have a substantial constituency, and there had been widespread advanced speculation that no candidate would win a majority in the first vote. This proved to be the case (Jenkins and Sala 1998):

Electoral Vote: First Count		
Andrew Jackson	99 Electoral Votes	38%
John Quincy Adams	84 Electoral Votes	32%
William H. Crawford	41 Electoral Votes	16%
Henry Clay	37 Electoral Votes	14%

(Peters and Wooly n.d.)

In what Jackson's supporters took to be an unprincipled arrangement between Clay and Adams, Clay persuaded enough of his own supporters and other electors to switch their loyalty to Adams. The "Bargain" worked and John Quincy Adams became the sixth president of the United States, denying Jackson—Clay and Adams' mutual nemesis of long standing—the presidency. Jackson's outraged supporters dubbed the arrangement the "Corrupt Bargain." The term stuck and continues to appear in historical accounts of the 1824 election.

The War of 1812 and the Battle of New Orleans: Jackson wins "The Second Battle for American Independence"

The end of the Revolutionary War did not end conflicts between Britain and the new nation. The Treaty of Paris (1783), in which Britain acknowledged the United States as a sovereign nation, established American territory south of Canada (British territory), east of the Mississippi River, and north of the 31st parallel, leaving most of what is now Florida and Louisiana controlled by Spain.

Britain still sought some control of the new nation. English companies had business interests in U.S. territory and the British still held military installations along the U.S.-Canadian border. Furthermore, Britain disdained the new nation to whom it had granted independence, doubting that the uncultured peasant country could long function on its own or protect its massive territory. Assuming the United States would soon be ripe for economic capture, the British acted accordingly. They seized American ships trading with its European rival France, coercing U.S. sailors into British military service. They also conducted military campaigns against Washington, D.C. and other U.S. interests and communities.

The end of the Revolutionary War also exacerbated hostilities between some Indian tribes and white communities. No tribes were consulted when U.S. territorial borders were drawn up in the Treaty of Paris. Tribes hostile to the new nation now had common interests with Britain and Spain: countering U.S. expansion and destabilizing U.S. frontier settlements. By the 1810s, Britain was openly assisting some tribes in hostile actions against U.S. interests and settlements. "It became obvious to most of the warring [political] factions in Washington that only a military victory could convince the world … and convince America itself, that its independence had been fairly won" (Remini 1988).

When Congress declared war on Britain in June of 1812, Jackson was a general in the Tennessee militia, a colonel in the U.S. Army, and a lifetime foe of Britons and Native Americans living in white-dominated frontier territory. Among the numerous military encounters that comprised the War of 1812, Jackson had three compelling military victories. He led several strikes against the Creek Indians of Alabama and Florida who had been particularly hostile to U.S. military and civilian encroachment on Creek lands. Culminating in March 1814 in the Battle of Horseshoe Bend, Jackson's assault killed approximately 600 Creek warriors before the Creek surrendered. Jackson lost only forty-nine U.S. soldiers and about twelve Creek tribesmen allied with Jackson's army. Jackson coerced the defeated Creeks into signing a treaty whereby they surrendered 23 million acres of their land.

Jackson next drove allied British and Spanish forces out of Pensacola, Florida, which was controlled by Spain. Outnumbering his British and Spanish adversaries, Jackson extracted a quick surrender in November

1814. British troops quickly abandoned Pensacola and the small remaining Spanish garrison surrendered to spare the town from Jackson's wrath and bloodshed.

Shortly thereafter Jackson received word that the British were planning to attack New Orleans in the hope of gaining control of the Mississippi River ports and waterways. Jackson's garrison got there first. A U.S. Army colonel and a formidable authoritative force, Jackson imposed martial law in New Orleans. He ordered soldiers and civilians to build elevated walls and defensive posts from which his troops could shoot down at British soldiers advancing across open lowlands. On January 8, 1815, British forces obliged by attacking straight into Jackson's army's line of fire. Weighted down with heavy packs and lacking equipment to scale Jackson's newly erected embankments, the British were slaughtered. Within minutes there were not enough surviving British field officers or able-bodied foot soldiers to devise, much less implement, a new battle strategy. The British forces were crushed (1,500 casualties compared to approximately fifty American troops killed or injured), along with Britain's ambitions to re-establish control of the U.S. territory. (In the musical, Jackson announces that he won the Battle of New Orleans with only 300 men, but historians' estimates tend to place the number at over 1,000. Beyond dispute is that Jackson's triumphant forces were outnumbered.)

The young country's response to Jackson's victory at New Orleans came nearly as fast as the victory itself. Newspapers, politicians, churches, and everyday people sang Jackson's praises across the land. A mythic aura grew up around Jackson's public image and heroic persona characterized by his extraordinary cunning, charismatic command presence, unyielding will to conquer, the care he showed his troops, and the fierce loyalty he earned from them in return. Over time this mythic image of Jackson, rather than dissolve under the scrutiny of historical critique, has been largely validated as a generally accurate, if partial, representation of Jackson's transformational legacy. Jackson's victory at New Orleans convinced the young republic that it was worthy of its independence and that, henceforth, its sovereignty would be respected throughout the world.

The goodwill Jackson inspired as a result of his victory at New Orleans carried him to the presidency in 1828. For the first time a frontier politician born in near poverty came to Washington with a political constituency entirely of his own making. He was the first president born in a state other than Massachusetts or Virginia. Known more for ferocious passions than rarified erudition, Jackson brought a new rustic, rural populism to the American political landscape that would exert its influence on national politics long after Jackson's presidency had ended.

Rachel Donelson Jackson and presidential family "scandal"

Bloody Bloody Andrew Jackson presents an effective, subtle portrait of Rachel Donelson Jackson (1727–1868). *BBAJ's* Rachel is a creditable reflection of the real Rachel even with the omission of key biographical details.

Rachel Donelson was three years into an abusive marriage to Kentuckian Lewis Robards when she met Andrew Jackson at her mother's home in Nashville (then Nashboro) in 1788. They fell in love immediately. Rachel had recently fled Kentucky to escape Robards, arriving shortly after Jackson had rented boarding space on her mother's property. The musical suggests that Jackson was at first only passingly concerned with Rachel's marital status. However, Robards, having followed Rachel into Nashville to coerce his wife to stay with him, was wary of Jackson as a rival. In turn, the volatile Jackson was fully cognizant of Robards as a threat to the woman he adored: "Despite their later claims to the contrary [the Jacksons chose] to live in adultery in order to provoke a divorce from Robards" (Meacham 2010).

By all accounts Andrew and Rachel were deeply and passionately in love for the forty years they were together. *Bloody Bloody Andrew Jackson* makes full use of their fabled romance, notably by showing Andrew and Rachel erotically cutting and bleeding each other as they sing of their mutual adoration ("Illness as Metaphor"). As to whether they actually performed lovers' cutting rituals on one another, documentary support is questionable at best. The musical's cutting scenes are probably suggested by the fact that Jackson, chronically ill from the effects of youthful sickness and fighting, likely practiced traditional curative bleeding as self-medication. The bloody lovers scenes are almost certainly fantastical stage representations of Andrew and Rachel's shared passion and, for Rachel's part, perhaps symbolic of her sacrifices during her life with Jackson.

Rachel's first marriage complicated her life with Andrew. As a woman, Rachel could not initiate divorce proceedings and had to depend upon the highly undependable Robards to terminate the relationship legally. In about 1791, believing that Robards had done so, Rachel and Andrew eloped. Later they learned that Robards never finalized the divorce, making Rachel a bigamist via her marriage to Jackson. Robards finalized the divorce in 1793, noting Rachel's bigamy in his filing. The Jacksons held another wedding ceremony in 1794 to legalize their union, but the "stain" of Rachel's bigamous past (to use the musical's terminology) caused lasting harm, especially to Rachel.

Jackson had launched his political and military careers in the 1790s as the first whispers of Rachel's bigamy wove their way through Tennessee and North Carolina. The scandal would resurface periodically, mostly as social gossip. Unlike Andrew, Rachel loathed public attention, positive or negative. Preferring home life managing the Jacksons' Tennessee plantation-estate and caring for nieces, nephews, and orphans they took in over the years, Rachel had no substantive public accomplishments to offset scandalous talk and social snubs.

Rachel's misery over her first marriage peaked during Jackson's successful 1828 run for president. For the first time, a presidential candidate's opponents and the press openly raised a spouse's reputation as a campaign issue. Public criticism of Rachel's thirty-five-year-old bigamy was merciless: "Shall a degraded female … a convicted adulteress … be placed in the highest office of this free and Christian land?" (Brady 2011). As *BBAJ* correctly affirms, Jackson's victory offered Rachel no healing for the anguish she suffered during the campaign. On December 22, 1828, Rachel died of a heart attack, most assuredly hastened by the campaign attacks. As the musical points out, Jackson blamed her attackers for her death.

Jackson and Native Americans: prejudice and policy

Jackson's lifelong antipathy for Native Americans constitutes the musical's most powerful driving force. Jackson's military skills, charisma, and populist appeal to ("white") frontiersmen and women are always evident and keep the plot moving briskly. But at its core *BBAJ* is a comically grotesque exploration of Jackson's unselfconscious cruelty to Native Americans. In charting that cruelty, *BBAJ* toys frequently, and sometimes confusingly, with chronology and historical fact.

The first significant staged interaction centers on Jackson's victory in the aforementioned Creek War of 1813–14 and his decisive triumph in the war's final battle at Horseshoe Bend. Jackson dictates the terms of surrender to Creek Chief Red Eagle, a real historic figure who spent much of his adult life as a negotiator and go-between for Native Americans in their dealing with Jackson and other U.S. officials. Immediately after presenting the Creeks with a "final offer" to remain on their land if they obey the laws of the United States, Jackson launches into a racist rant: "You people … are savages. You're soulless. Godless." Reversing himself, Jackson seizes 23 million acres of Creek land and orders Red Eagle to remove his people.

The Creek surrender scene jarringly illustrates an important paradox in Jackson's attitudes toward Native Americans, one that historians debate to this day. Jackson often represented himself as a benevolent "Great Father" to Native Americans. Referring to them as "his children," he was capable of magnanimity and graciousness toward the victims of his "Indian policies." However, where government control of contested Native American territory was concerned, Jackson showed an easy predilection for rapacious violence, degrading mockery, massive land seizure, and brutal dislocation of thousands of Native Americans. Biographies of Jackson are replete with examples of his alternately sympathetic and ruthless attitudes toward Native Americans as well as his ability to reconcile these contradictory feelings in his own mind.

The Creek negotiation scene contains a peculiar historic inaccuracy. As Red Eagle agrees to Jackson's terms, a messenger informs Jackson that President Monroe [*sic*] has overruled Jackson's negotiated surrender; the Creeks may keep their land. This moment is entirely fictionalized. James Madison, not James Monroe, was president in 1814, and Madison ordered no such injunction against Jackson's seizure of Creek land.

The Creek surrender scene transitions quickly into the morbidly comic song "Ten Little Indians," a sardonic nod to Jackson's propensity for decimating Native Americans: "Ten little Indians ... Then there were nine ... were four ... were none." Between verses the musical disrupts its chronological narrative and stages a negotiation scene set during Jackson's presidency in the 1830s. Chief Keokuk, commander of the Sauk tribes of the Upper Great Lakes region, suddenly appears and signs over to Jackson millions of acres of land. The scene is most likely based on Keokuk's 1830 negotiated settlement with the federal government, a signing at which Jackson was not present. Indian Commissioner William Clark signed on behalf of the federal government. Moments later, Jackson converses with "sinister" Black Fox, a fictitious stand-in for any number of Native American leaders and go-betweens who cooperated with Jackson in getting Native Americans to sign over their territory and vacate their homelands cooperatively. Black Fox's dialogue locates the otherwise undated scene during Jackson's presidency after the 1830 Indian Removal Act was in force.

The remaining important engagements between Jackson and Native Americans occur in the Oval Office during Jackson's presidency (1828–37), staged at a sprinter's pace in the final thirty minutes of the show. A blur of real historical events flow in and out of Jackson's Oval Office via messengers and anachronistic phone calls, only to have Jackson dispatch them one by one like a baseball player at batting practice. He swats away in dizzying fashion the Cherokee Nation's Supreme Court challenge to the State of Georgia for passing laws restricting their rights (*Cherokee Nation v Georgia*, 1831), South Carolina's attempt to nullify his new tariffs (the Nullification Ordinance of 1832), and his veto of Congress's reauthorization of a national bank (the National Bank War of 1832).

However, the otherwise frenetically rushed staging takes care to explore Jackson's frame of mind in enforcing his Indian Removal Act of 1830. The musical renders a compelling representation of President Jackson's ambivalence and lack of self-awareness with respect to his Indian policies. Jackson reintroduces the fictitious but emblematic Black Fox, who has "betrayed several Indian tribes on our government's behalf and it doesn't bother him." Black Fox provides a knowing victim's-eye-view of Jackson's manic frustration over the fact that hostility between Native Americans and white settlers has metastasized rather than subsided under his Indian Removal Act and his other efforts to accommodate Native Americans during America's westward and southward expansion.

In the play's most compelling revelation, Jackson speaks truth to powerlessness. He lays out a stripped-down reality to Black Fox, all Native Americans, and, by implication, all resisters present and future of white dominion over the United States: "And yeah, you totally were here first, absolutely ... the day we arrived, we saw it, we wanted it, and frankly it was easier to believe it was ours ... [I promise,] you sign this treaty here tonight and, in thirty years, you and I are gonna look like ... heroes for uniting this country."

Of course, the audience understands that thirty years after 1830 the country, far from being united, will be in the throes of the Civil War. Jackson's last broken promise to finally unite Native Americans and white settlers through his Indian policies will haunt the nation, its politics, and its identity for a duration of time we now measure in centuries.

Thomas A. Greenfield

Further reading

Brady, Patricia. 2011. *A Being so Gentle: The Frontier Love Story of Rachel and Andrew Jackson.* New York: Palgrave Macmillan.

Brantley, Benjamin. 2010a. "Ideal President: A Rock Star Just Like Me." *New York Times*, October 14, 2010.

Brantley, Benjamin. 2010b. "Old Hickory, Rock Star President." *New York Times*, April 6, 2010.

Eder, Bruce. n.d. "*Jesus Christ Superstar* (Original Cast Recording): AllMusic Review." *AllMusic*, https://www.allmusic.com/album/jesus-christ-superstar-original-cast-recording-mw0000056121.

Friedman, Michael. 2010. "*Bloody Bloody Andrew Jackson*: Original Cast Recording." *STLyrics.com*, https://www.stlyrics.com/b/bloodybloodyandrewjackson.htm.

Friedman, Michael. 2011. "Behind the Music: *Bloody Bloody Andrew Jackson* Composer Michael Friedman." *Broadway.com*, March 10, 2011.

https://www.youtube.com/watch?v=9TSWlexev3w.

Hodgins, Paul. 2008. "Bloody Good Time at the Kirk Douglas Theatre." *Orange County Register*, January, 21, 2008.

Jenkins, Jeffrey A. and Brian R. Sala. 1998. "The Spatial Theory of Voting and the Presidential Election of 1824." *American Journal of Political Science* 42, no. 4 (October): 1157–79.

Jones, Luca. 2016. "What Are Some Characteristics of Punk Music?" *Quora.com*, December 7, 2016, https://www.quora.com/What-are-some-characteristics-of-punk-music.

Kusler, Ben. 2008. "Theater Reviews: *Bloody Bloody Andrew Jackson* and More." *LA Weekly*, January 23, 2008, http://www.laweekly.com/content/printView/215161.

Marks, Peter. 2010. "NYC Reviews: 'Bloody Bloody Andrew Jackson,' 'La Bête,' 'A Life in the Theatre.'" *Washington Post*, October 14, 2010.

McCall, Tulis. 2010. "Bloody Bloody Andrew Jackson." *New York Theatre Guide.com*, October 1, 2010, www.newyorktheatreguide.com/reviews/bloody-bloody-andrew-jackson.

McNulty, Charles. 2008. "'Bloody' Goofy Musical." *Los Angeles Times*, January 3, 2008.

Meacham, Jon. 2009. *American Lion: Andrew Jackson in the White House.* New York: Random House.

Meacham, Jon. 2010. "Rocking the Vote in the 1820s and Now." *New York Times*, October 21, 2010.

Metzler, Molly Smith. 2010. "Rent." In *Broadway: An Encyclopedia of Theater and American Culture*, Vol. II, edited by Thomas A. Greenfield, 543–5. Santa Barbara, CA: Greenwood/ABC-CLIO.

Miller, Scott. 2011. *Sex, Drugs, Rock & Roll, and Musicals.* Boston: Northeastern University Press.

Ng, David. 2010. "*Bloody Bloody Andrew Jackson* on Broadway: What Did the Critics Think?" *Culture Monster* (blog), *Los Angeles Times*, October 14, 2010.

Peters, Gerhard and John T. Woolley. n.d. "The Election of 1824." *The American Presidency Project*, http://www.presidency.ucsb.edu/showelection.php?year=1824.

Remini, Robert V. 1988. *The Legacy of Andrew Jackson.* Baton Rouge: Louisiana State University Press.

Remini, Robert V. 2001. *The Battle of New Orleans.* New York: Penguin Books.

Richman, Jesse. 2018. "What Is Emo, Anyway?" *AltPress*, January 24, 2018, www.altpress.com/features/entry/what_is_emo_history_definition.

Sheward, David. 2010. "Broadway Review: *Bloody Bloody Andrew Jackson.*" *Backstage*, October 13, 2010, https://www.backstage.com/review/ny-theater/broadway/bloody-bloody-andrew-jackson_3/.

Timbers, Alex and Michael Friedman. 2010. *Bloody Bloody Andrew Jackson.* DVD, Matt Cohen, Video director, filmed at The Public Theater, New York, May 10, 2010. Theater on Film and Tape Archives (TOFT), New York Public Library.

Timbers, Alex and Michael Friedman. 2017. *Bloody Bloody Andrew Jackson.* New York: Music Theatre International.

Vincentelli, Elisabeth. 2010. "Bloody Brighter." *New York Post*, October 14, 2010, https:// nypost.com/ /2010/10/14/bloody-brighter/.

CHAPTER 6
THE CIVIL WAR (1999)

Book by Frank Wildhorn (1959–) and Gregory Boyd (1951–) Music by Frank Wildhorn
Lyrics by Jack Murphy (NA)
World Premiere: Alley Theatre, Houston, Texas, September 16–November 1, 1998 Broadway: St. James Theatre, April 22–June 13, 1999

Songs

"A House Divide"
"Freedom's Chil"
"By the Sword/Sons of Dixie"
"Tell My Father"
"The Peculiar Institution"
"If Prayin' Were Horses"
"Greenback"
"Missing You (My Bill)"
"Judgment Day"
"Father, How Long?"
"Someday"
"I'll Never Pass This Way Again"
"How Many Devils?"
"Virginia"
"Candle in the Window"
"Oh! Be Joyful!"
"The Hospital"
"If Prayin' Were Horses" (Reprise)
"River Jordan"
"Sarah"
"The Honor of Your Name"
"Greenback" (Reprise)
"Northbound Train"
"Last Waltz for Dixie"
"The Glory"

**The Civil War* is a staged concept album. Published lists of songs may vary in name and order among scores, cast recording, and production programs.

Overview

The Civil War is a dramatic theatrical concert that celebrates a wide range of perspectives on the Civil War presented by everyday people—both historical figures and fictionalized stand-in characters—who lived through the war years, 1861–5. Utilizing selections from letters, journals, and other historical documents, the creators of *The Civil War* developed a cycle of songs and recitations that offer intimate emotional reflections on lives altered by the war: Union and Confederate soldiers, their wives and families, and African American men and women—enslaved and newly escaped or freed. Three brief appearances by African American abolitionist Frederick Douglass (1818–95) and a few familiar spoken words written by President Abraham Lincoln (1809–65) provide, by design, only passing reference to the major players on the larger stage. *The Civil War* is at its core a sentimental homage to the unheralded common men and women of the time.

The Civil War offers a broad anthology of more than thirty discrete personal, heartfelt reflections and viewpoints intermixed with a few spoken references to well-known historical writings. Each viewpoint is honored with its own moment in the spotlight, and each point of view is enshrined in its own authenticity. Producer and co-author Gregory Boyd proclaims that "[*The Civil War*] is not history, it is not historical narrative … it is a musical theater event that tries to express a sense of the character and the emotional landscape of an America that is struggling to define itself during a time of terrible and profound change" (Boyd et al. 1999b). Boyd's pronouncement notwithstanding, however, a country's struggle for self-definition in crisis falls squarely within the provenance of history. *The Civil War*, in spite of itself, frequently wanders into the realm of the very history it seeks to transcend or at least minimize—and does so with mixed results.

The Civil War assumes its audience already knows basic details and major themes associated with the Civil War and, in accordance with Boyd's stated approach, adds little to the audience's academic knowledge of the era. The show unfolds as a celebratory pageant that touches on broad, universal themes. According to Boyd, "What is Freedom? What is Faith? What is Country?" are the central questions that guided the development of musical from its inception. While one could argue, as many reviewers did, over how successfully the finished product met the grandeur of these larger themes, the show aspires to provide an uplifting, unifying tribute to the resilience and sacrifices of the people—Americans all—who lived during "the bloodiest conflict in American history" (Boyd et al. 1999b). However, in a somewhat incongruous effort to tiptoe around the very history it wades into, the show steers clear of addressing long-standing political and social tensions rooted in the Civil War's complex historical legacy: racism and racial inequality; federal authority versus state sovereignty; cultural rivalries between and among different regions of the country; and the still unsettled question of how the Civil War should be taught and remembered—in schools, at home, and in the public sphere. The show's near-total disregard for social comment, much less social consciousness, raised questions among audiences and critics as to whether a historical "musical theater event" about the Civil War could do justice to its creators' aspirations, much less its subject matter.

From the production's opening scenes, *The Civil War* foretells the coming of grand themes while hinting that an illuminating historical narrative is not in the offing. Early on, an ensemble of blue (Union) and grey (Confederate) uniformed soldiers enters singing call-and-response refrains in which they regale each other with their shared eagerness to join the fight and the righteousness of their respective causes. In service to the show's theme of unification, at the song's conclusion the two armies appear to meld into a single entity, united in all but the color of their respective uniforms.

The Civil War proceeds on an implicit assumption that, if emotions and feelings of Northerners and Southerners are universal and common to all, the core circumstances from which those feelings arise are essentially universal and common as well. Such an approach may well serve the theatrical demands of pageantry, but in so doing it sets aside the considerable body of unfinished constitutional and societal business that the nineteenth-century war left for future generations and future centuries. The show professes that the war, having engendered sacrifice, hope, fear, and triumph in the face of adversity within all involved, unifies all Americans in a common emotional national remembrance. Yet the approach actually works against Boyd's stated mission to illuminate America's "emotional landscape."

Among the musical's most serious misrepresentations of the mid-nineteenth-century American landscape, emotional or otherwise, is that the Union and Confederate armies were near-mirror images of each other. As is generally the case with organized fighting forces, each is drawn from the residents of a specific citizenry and embody many of the social, economic, and cultural attributes thereof. The Union and Confederate armies reflected many of the differences that led to war in the first place. Appropriately, *The Civil War* also interweaves a moving narrative thread about an enslaved married couple separated at auction and reunited later. However, little is made of how the pivotal question—"What is Freedom?"—might weigh differently upon their shoulders than, say, on a propertied Northern woman who teaches herself to chop down a tree when her husband goes off to war. Perhaps to avoid the potentially disunifying impact of framing slavery's legacy as a "live" and complicated contemporary social issue, the musical presents slavery, first and foremost, as a moving, ennobling human interest story. Even in 1998 one might have reasonably asked "whose landscape is that?"

Nevertheless, to its credit, *The Civil War* is so steeped in the historical narratives it presumably disavows that the show provides some genuinely incisive historical context to its presentation of the war, despite efforts to avoid doing so. The brief appearances of Frederick Douglass, whose voluminous writings have filled library shelves and archives, focus tightly upon the evolution of Douglass' political opinions about and personal relationship with Abraham Lincoln. Their relationship is a largely under-appreciated yet significant aspect of the Civil War years, and the musical presents Douglass' changing perspective on Lincoln in an efficient, pointed, genuinely illuminating manner. In addition, *The Civil War* makes generous use of women's diaries and letters, calling attention to one of the most important developments in Civil War research over the last thirty years: women as chroniclers of the Civil War era.

A bit of advice widely attributed to nineteenth-century Russian novelist Leo Tolstoy might have well-served the creators of *The Civil War:* "You may not be interested in history, but history is interested in you."

Prior to its run on Broadway, *The Civil War* was recorded as a concept album, with songs sung by popular musical acts of the 1990s, including Hootie and the Blowfish and Patti LaBelle. The roster of celebrities recording the spoken interludes included actor Danny Glover, country singer Trace Adkins, and poet-activist Dr. Maya Angelou. The songs (almost all originals) range in musical styles, including country, gospel, pop, folk, R&B, and rock "in an effort to work in the American vernacular—to use as many different styles of the American 'sound' as we coul" (Boyd et al. 1999b). The premiere production of the musical at Houston's Alley Theatre stayed true to the original intention of the piece: expressing the emotional sentiments and reflections of the people rather than offering up grand stagings of battles or excited crowds. However, when *The Civil War* moved to Broadway in April 1999, additional staged battles scenes, costumes, props, and lighting were added, superseding the creators' initial intention to maintain an intimate and personal tone for the show. Composer Wildhorn already had two successful shows running on Broadway (*Jekyll & Hyde* and *The Scarlet Pimpernel*, both staged as grand theatrical productions). Broadway observers assumed that expanded staging of the original show would increase *The Civil War*'s chances of a successful commercial run. However, the Broadway production faced several scathing opening-night reviews followed by a rapid decline in ticket sales. The production closed after only a seven-week run, incurring losses of several million dollars in the process.

Since the Broadway debacle, *The Civil War*'s creators have intermittently adapted and transformed the show, rearranging, adding, and removing songs and narrative snippets from the score and book. Following the Broadway production, at least two reincarnations of the musical have appeared. In 2006, under the title *For the Glory*, the Majestic Theatre near Gettysburg National Military Park in Pennsylvania produced a well-received stripped-down version of the show in conjunction with the park's Civil War museum. Additionally, in 2015 a live adaptation entitled *Freedom's Song: Abraham Lincoln and the Civil War* was produced at Ford's Theatre in Washington, D.C. for the 150th anniversary of the assassination of Abraham Lincoln. This revised version of *The Civil War* contained a newly adapted script by playwright Richard Hellesen and theater director Mark Ramont. Hellesen and Ramon brought a narrative structure to this new version of the musical, addressing one of the more common criticisms of earlier productions.

Wildhorn finds *The Civil War*'s adaptability to be its saving grace: "what is so unique about the musical is that it can be interpreted and adapted in so many different ways" (Boyd et al. 1999b). Much like history itself.

Plot synopsis

The musical opens on Captain Emmett Lochran of the Union Army as he provides background on the conflict between North and South. In voiceover, Abraham Lincoln speaks of a house divided against itself as the music shifts to brief lyrical expositions of characters and their troubles ("A House Divide"): conflicted brothers Sam and Nathaniel Taylor join opposing armies; Corporal William ("Bill") McEwen and wife Sarah McEwen are separated as Bill leaves to join the Union Army despite Sarah's pleas for him to stay; and Captain Billy Pierce singing emphatically pledges to defend his home state of Virginia against Union occupation. All characters join in unison as they hope for peace before the impending bloody war.

The action shifts to the formerly enslaved Fredrick Douglass, who became a statesman and abolitionist and believes the abolition of slavery to be the root of the conflict to preserve the Union. With his fellow abolitionists, Douglass demands an end to slavery and the granting of freedoms set forth in the *Declaration of Independence* to everyone in America ("Freedom's Chil").

Fresh out of boot camp and ready to begin battle, soldiers from both the North and South enter on either side of the stage, singing exultantly on the eve of the approaching conflict. Both sides trust they will be triumphant when they take the field ("By the Sword/Sons of Dixie"). Following the battle, Private Sam Taylor lies dying. His last wish is to assure his father he fought honorably, having lived a boy and died a man ("Tell My Father").

The scene changes to an auction of enslaved people as an auctioneer sells off a young Black man. Enslaved people sing of their experiences being sold and separated from loved ones, praying to God for an end to their continued suffering ("The Peculiar Institution"). An enslaved married couple, Clayton and Bessie Toler, on the verge of being sold to separate owners, share a final moment praying that they can stay together ("If Prayin' Were Horses").

Frederick Douglass appears again, leveling a scathing critique at President Lincoln: "After a year of the most incompetent prosecution of any war effort in military history we are no closer to victory." Douglass declares that the only people "winning" the war are "profiteers and thieves." Autolycus Fell, one such profiteer, enters and sings of his proclivity for accumulating wealth.

The action transitions to Sarah McEwen, the young wife of a Union soldier away at war. Seated at her family farmhouse, Sarah writes a letter to her husband, Bill. Struggling to provide for her family ("I learned to chop a tree today"), Sarah is lonely and hopes to be reunited with her husband soon ("Missing You [My Bill]"). On the battlefields, both sides have now incurred heavy losses and early feelings of war euphoria have dissipated. Captains from the two opposing armies, confronted with fears of sending more men to die in battle, wrestle with the consequences of the military decisions they must make going forward ("Judgement Day").

Following a battle, Clayton Toler, now a runaway enslaved person turned gravedigger for the Union, digs graves for soldiers and asks God how long the war and slavery must last ("Father, How Long?"). Toler appeals to Heaven for freedom as his wife Bessie, Harriet Jackson, and other enslaved women plead with the audience to consider them to be women equal to any other women. They all sing jubilantly of being free in the future thanks to the unwavering love of God ("Someday").

Elsewhere, Corporal Stewart, a Confederate soldier, passes by his hometown reminiscing about the ordinary days he spent there before the war. He wishes he had appreciated his old life more, knowing that he will most likely die and never return home ("I'll Never Pass This Way Again"). Union and Confederate foot soldiers from the opening ensemble number re-enter in a sustained march, wondering when the war will come to an end. Like the aforementioned military captains, they are no longer naively optimistic about a quick victorious end to the war, having now experienced war's bloody realities ("How Many Devils?").

Act Two opens on Captain Billy Pierce of the Confederate Army. In song he paints an idyllic picture of his home state of Virginia before the war and sings of his desire to help return Virginia to its antebellum splendor

("Virginia"). In Washington, D.C., Harriet Jackson, having escaped her owner, observes a candle in Abraham Lincoln's office window. She contemplates what President Lincoln is thinking and hopes that Lincoln is close to winning the fight ("Candle in the Window").

At a Union Army camp, soldiers merrily sing of the benefits of whiskey during the hard times of war ("Oh! Be Joyful!"). The energy swiftly shifts to a somber moment in which Mrs. Lydia Bixby, the mother of five boys in the Union Army, receives word that all five have died in battle ("Five Boys"). The action then shifts to a chaotic scene in a Union hospital in which a nurse and Mrs. Bixby are tending to wounded soldiers. When Clayton Toler walks in lost, the soldiers yell at him to leave, projecting on to Clayton the cause of their sorrow and pain ("The Hospital"). As Clayton leaves the hospital, his wife Bessie appears on stage (invisible to Clayton). Singing in parallel, Clayton and Bessie again pray to be reunited one day ("If Prayin' Were Horses [Reprise]"). Bessie resolves to join Benjamin Reynolds, a recruiter for the Underground Railroad, in hopes of finding her husband. Reynolds, recruiting a group of enslaved people in their quarters, leads them in a song of deliverance and freedom ("River Jordan").

At an army camp as yet another battle looms, Bill McEwen writes a letter in response to his wife Sarah, proclaiming his undying love for her ("Sarah"). Days later on their farm, Sarah learns that Bill has died in battle. She writes one last love letter to him, promising to honor him for the rest of her life ("The Honor of Your Name").

As a harbinger of the war's conclusion, the two armies seem to blend into one group, depleted and dispirited from years of conflict. Union Captain Lochran pulls out a letter from his wife, hanging onto the thought that soon he will be able to board a train to return home ("Northbound Train"). Elsewhere, Captain Pierce and Confederate soldiers gather to discuss their fate and imminent defeat ("Last Waltz for Dixie"). Awaiting the final phases of conflict, Captain Lochran calls for his men to give their utmost to win their remaining fights. Frederick Douglass, now decidedly more supportive of Lincoln, enters and provides narration for the major events that follow: the surrender of the Confederate Army and Lincoln's assassination.

Lincoln in voiceover speaks lines from his second Inaugural Address ("With malice toward none, With charity for all ..."). Union and Confederate troops sing of the righteousness of their respective years of struggle. In conclusion, an angel appears on the battlefield "to take the fallen home" ("The Glory").

Critical reception

The Civil War premiered at Houston's Alley Theatre in September 1998. Set as a song-cycle rather than a traditional book musical, many critics condemned the lack of narrative structure. Michael Barnes of the *Austin American-Statesman* considered the musical to have "no unified story, no character development and little sense of historical perspective" (Barnes 1998). Similarly, *Variety* noted that *The Civil War* "never achieves a sense of narrative momentum, and utterly fails at making the audience aware of the months and years passing between musical episodes" (Leydon 1998). Equally problematic to critics were many of the musical numbers. The *Houston Chronicle* acknowledged that, while much of the music was appealing, when "Wildhorn shifts gears to an up-tempo pop vein ... the songs fall short of the gravity and grandeur the theme demands" (Evans 1998). Leydon also praised many songs, including "Sarah," "The Honor of Your Name," and "River Jordan," but noted that different songs seem quite similar and begin to blend together (Leydon 1998). Notwithstanding the mixed reviews of the songs and narrative form, on the whole Houston's critics and audiences shared the belief that *The Civil War* "offers so much that is first-rate and undeniably heart-tugging that it warrants a salute" (Evans 1998). The buzz and box office in Houston were sufficient to attract backing for a Broadway run at the St. James Theatre in the spring of 1999.

During the stretch between its Houston premiere and Broadway opening, *The Civil War*'s creators shifted the list of musical numbers and made major revisions to the production. However, their efforts failed to generate a successful return on investment. Reviewers of the Broadway premiere were noticeably more harsh in their assessments than were their peers in Houston. Ben Brantley of the *New York Times* all but declared war on the production: "Why are we here? ... What is the point? ... Why would anyone stage a show that improbably drains the drama from what is still the most fraught and painful chapter in American history?" (Brantley 1999). Robert Feldberg in *The Record* piled on, calling the show a "simplistic musical that reduces that great conflict to a succession of clichés," dismissing it as a "paint-by-numbers historical documentary" (Feldberg 1999). Other critics, equally unimpressed, faulted the show for being a weak derivative of such Broadway forerunners as *1776* (1969) and *Big River* (1985). Moreover, reviewers from the *Philadelphia Inquirer* and *The Record* noted disconcerting similarities between Autolycus Fell, a war profiteer in *The Civil War*, and Thenardier, the brutish ill-tempered ne'er-do-well from *Les Misérables*, giving the former the worst of the bargain as "a second-rate knockoff" of the "Les Miz" figure and music (Ridley 1999).

Broadway critics were more divided over the score and songs than they were over the production as a whole. Georgette Gouveia of the *Journal News* fiercely defended *The Civil War*'s "soaring score ... which draws on an array of American pop music styles, including gospel, blues, country-western and rock," praising Wildhorn for writing "his deepest, most wide-ranging score to date" (Gouveia 1999). *Entertainment Weekly*, however, concurred with Brantley, berating the show's "two dozen unrelated contempo-country-pop songs" for being generic and repetitious (Harris 1999).

If the Broadway run had a redeeming feature for the critics, it was the performance of the acting ensemble. Harris in *Entertainment Weekly* admired the performers' "full-throated conviction" despite the repetitive song lyrics and styles (Harris 1999). The *Philadelphia Inquirer*'s Ridley agreed, saluting the "tight" ensemble that in a sense "is *The Civil War*'s only real character" (Ridley 1999). *The Record* praised the cast of thirty for singing well, but noted that, owing to the nature of the work, not much was required of the actors aside from singing. Even the otherwise appalled Brantley of the *Times* conceded that the cast sang "rousingly or prettily, as occasion demands" even if they did not manage to "grab our hearts."

The spate of negative reviews took their toll. *The Civil War* closed on Broadway after a run of only seven weeks (sixty-one performances plus thirty-five previews). However, the show fared somewhat better among its peers. *The Civil War* received two Tony nominations—Best Musical and Best Original Musical Score—but no wins. The show also picked up five Drama Desk nominations, including Outstanding Musical, Best Featured Actor, and Best Featured Actress.

Perhaps reasoning that New York City was not the most hospitable location to showcase a sentimentally tinged reflection on the War between the States, the producers found support to mount a U.S. touring production in 2000, which gave *The Civil War* an extended if slowly evolving post-Broadway life. In 2006, the creators restructured the show for a staging in the newly restored Majestic Theater in Gettysburg, Pennsylvania (retitling the show for this production only as *For the Glory*). The Gettysburg production was an outdoor concert intended to give the show the feel of a second world premiere.

And, in fact, more recent productions of *The Civil War* have tended to draw more positive reviews than did the Broadway run. In an unvarnished rave review of a 2014 production in New Jersey, Pati Buehler writing in *Broadway World* argued that had *The Civil War* opened after the 2001 terrorist attack of 9/11, New York reviewers and audiences would have embraced it: "clearly Broadway audiences of 1999 were more preoccupied with cheerful musicals than history." Buehler went on to hail the "ceremonial concert" as "glorious" and "a new exciting and revolutionary possibility of what a Broadway musical can be" (Buehler 2014).

Historical accuracy and context

A house divided ... but brother against brother?

Through the characters of brothers Sam and Nathaniel Taylor, choosing to fight for the Union and the Confederate armies respectively, *The Civil War* brings to life the common expression "brother against brother," which is often associated with descriptions of the Civil War. There were certainly numerous cases of intense family divisions in both the North and South over such issues as the South's secession, states' rights to own enslaved people, and the four-year armed conflict that exploded upon them all. However, while there were actual instances of brothers joining and fighting in the two respective opposing armies, such circumstances occurred rarely (Taylor 2009). The Union and Confederate armies were organized by state, making it difficult for brothers to join opposing militia, unless one had moved South while the other remained in the North (or vice versa), or possibly if they lived in one of the border states, such as Delaware, Kentucky, Maryland, or Missouri. (Border states did not support Abraham Lincoln in the 1860 election, but neither did they secede from the Union as had the states in the Confederacy.) The trope of "brother against brother" actually evolved as a metaphor for the nation's house divided against itself rather than a metric for tracking military enlistments or conscriptions.

Another popular idea referenced throughout the musical is that the Union and Confederate armies (the "blue and gray" as portrayed in the songs "A House Divide" and "By the Sword/Sons of Dixie") were interchangeable mirror images of one another, divided only by regional loyalty. However, in many important respects, the Union and Confederate armies were very different entities. The Union was comprised of twenty states that had a total population of approximately 22 million people while the Confederacy was comprised of eleven states with approximately 9 million people ("A War Begins" 2019). Initially the two armies were equal in strength, but by 1863 the North's population advantage produced a Union fighting force twice the size of the Confederate Army. In addition to their homegrown population, the Union Army recruited soldiers from the North's growing immigrant population as well as upwards of 200,000 free Black men and runaway enslaved people who joined the Union Army or navy (Gannon 2016). However, Union victory was by no means inevitable. The Civil War confronted the Union with more demanding tasks than it did the Confederacy. The Union had to destroy the rebellion. They had to defeat the Confederate armies and then use other armies to secure the conquered lands from counter attacks. By contrast, the Confederacy just needed to survive.

As the war progressed, both armies needed to maintain a serviceable level of troop numbers. In so doing, the North and the South employed different approaches to fortifying their ranks. Many Union states, with their superior financing and resources, incentivized enlistments by offering bounties to men for military service, sometimes upwards of 700 per man. The Confederacy tried offering incentives for volunteers to extend their enlistments, but these measures produced insufficient results. In 1862, the Confederate States Congress enacted the Conscription Act, which extended the terms of currently serving volunteers and subjected all white male citizens of a Confederate state between the ages of eighteen and thirty-five to a possible three-year tour of duty in the Confederate Army. The Union also enacted a draft law one year after the Confederates. Despite their lack of finances and resources, however, the Confederacy mobilized a much higher percentage of military-age white men.

Both armies fiercely promoted competing ideologies as incentives for enlisting in the military. The North invoked the spirit of the Founding Fathers and distributed patriotic effigies such as Lady Liberty to invoke the causes of keeping the nation together and defending the government in Washington, D.C. The largely agricultural South was motivated by different goals, such as defending home and family from invading Union forces as well as preserving the slavery system in the South.

Other socio-economic differences between the North and the South affected the morale of soldiers in battle. The Union's growing manufacturing and industrial economy provided its military with a sizable advantage in war supplies. Moreover, to a considerable degree, the major battles were taking place far from the homes of Union soldiers, reducing Northern soldiers' anxieties about the safety of their families and security of their property. Although Confederate leaders worked hard to inspire a sense of loyalty toward the new government of the South, over time many citizens of the Confederacy became embittered over the destruction of land and the Confederate government's practices of "impressment"—the seizing of supplies and other resources from individual households to support the war effort.

Abraham Lincoln and Frederick Douglass

Much of the narrative text and several lyrics from *The Civil War* are adapted or taken directly from the actual letters and diaries of real people. Some of them, such as Mrs. Lydia Bixby (an historic character in the musical who received a letter of condolence from President Lincoln on the loss of her five sons) and Sullivan Ballou (a Union officer whose writings form the basis of fictional character Corporal William McEwen's lines) are not widely known to the public. However, two prominent historical figures—Abraham Lincoln and African American abolitionist leader Frederick Douglass—also have relatively small speaking roles largely based on their own writings. The pairing of Lincoln and Frederick Douglass in the musical is historically appropriate inasmuch as the historical significance of their complex, evolving relationship is immeasurable. Lincoln "appears" in the musical only as an enigmatic off-stage voice but is nonetheless a looming presence throughout the show. He is referenced frequently and his words, when not spoken by his off-stage voice, are woven through onstage readings and song lyrics. Douglass, however, is a realized stage character. Although he only makes a few brief appearances, Douglass functions as a symbolic affirmation of the importance of slavery in understanding the Civil War. (Through his writings and decades of activism, Douglass was also an important shaper of that history, more so than the musical conveys.)

Douglass' brief stage appearances serve as markers for the evolution of his opinions about Lincoln—a transition from harsh critic to exultant supporter that, notwithstanding the brevity of Douglass' stage time, admirably conveys the essence of that historic relationship. Douglass reluctantly endorsed Lincoln in 1860, believing his anti-slavery attitudes to be "lacking" but better than what might come from the Democratic hopefuls at the time (Fling 2019). In the first years of the war, Douglass excoriated Lincoln for prioritizing restoration of the union over abolition as his primary war objective. Douglass and other African Americans were also incensed at Lincoln's apparent inaction and lack of outrage in response to Confederate torture, killing, and selling into slavery of captured Black Union troops. In Douglass' initial appearance in *The Civil War* he unleashes a bitter invective against Lincoln's marginalization of abolition. Although written by the musical's authors, his lines reflect accurately Douglass' sentiments at the time:

> Douglass in *The Civil War*: "You are fighting to restore a union we do not want … diseased with prejudice and slavery."
>
> Douglass in 1860: "Whoever live[s] through the next four years will see Mr. Lincoln and his Administration attacked more bitterly for their pro-slavery truckling."
>
> *Douglass 1860*

Douglass' sentiments toward Lincoln began to change following Lincoln's issue of the Emancipation Proclamation in January 1863 declaring that "all persons held as slaves" were free. No less important to the softening of Douglass' feelings were three personal meetings and several correspondences between the two men during the war years. The first such meeting in August 1863 was particularly significant. Arranged after Lincoln learned of Douglass' desire to meet with him, their first meeting ultimately came about at Lincoln's invitation—making Douglass the first African American to receive a presidential invitation for a personal meeting at the White House. Aware of the historical import of the meeting, Douglass took pains to record his experience in detail. His recollections included the "utmost respect" which he was accorded; Lincoln's honesty and humility; and, to Douglass' surprise, "a deeper moral conviction against slavery than I had ever seen before in anything spoken or written by him" (Douglass 1881). Douglass' final lines in the musical are taken directly from the laudatory address he made in honor of Lincoln at the unveiling of The Freedmen's Monument in Lincoln Park, Washington, D.C. in 1876. Staged as part of the musical's finale, the speech illustrates the magnitude of Douglass' changes of heart and mind about Lincoln: "infinite wisdom has seldom sent any man into the world better fitted for his mission than Abraham Lincoln" (Douglass 1876).

Women at home ... and at work

Although it is a male dominated musical, *The Civil War* presents a number of female characters who share their perspectives on the war. Sarah McEwen, the wife of a Union soldier, is left to fend for herself and family as her husband leaves for battle, writing to her soldier/husband: "I learned to chop a tree today." Taking on men's roles on the home front in addition to their traditional responsibilities became a common occurrence for women in the North and the South, as hundreds of thousands of men left home to join their respective fighting forces. The new obligations often confronted women with unfamiliar physical demands, job skills, and workplaces outside the home. However, region, race, and class influenced heavily which women were likely to take on work outside the home as well as the kind of work they would perform and the circumstances under which they would perform it (Wright 2015).

For propertied white women, the new work demands generally weighed more heavily upon women in the South than their counterparts in the North. In the years leading up to the Civil War, many Northern urban middle-class and wealthy women had already been acculturated to a role of ethical moral guardians of their families, providing stability for a growing cadre of working men whose income derived from "doing battle" in the contentious world of urban business, industry, finance, and politics: "This moral superiority [had already] encouraged white Northern middle-class women to leave the confines of their homes to pursue acts of benevolence and reform" (Campbell 2012). Thus, when the war generated new social expectations for women outside the home (such as treating wounded soldiers, collecting supplies for troops, and fundraising for the war effort), many Northern women had already adjusted to the challenges of working in public spheres while simultaneously tending to traditional domestic duties. Northern women's fundraising efforts, particularly through "sanitary fairs" (civilian-organized bazaars, many run by women, that raised funds for the U.S. Sanitary Commission) were among the North's most successful means of collecting private contributions in support of the war. Union sanitary fairs raised upwards of 25 million in cash and contributed services to help the Union Army combat disease and infection among its troops (Stille 1866).

Wealthy women in the South, especially those who owned enslaved people, not only had to provide for their families, but they also had to supervise and provide for their enslaved people or other workers in their properties and businesses. These challenges were exacerbated by the fact that, prior to the war, the South's class structure strongly discouraged women from assuming management responsibility over their families' estates. In the mid-nineteenth century, propertied Southern women were subject to a more patriarchal social structure than were Northern women—a plantation culture that extended beyond plantations and militated against wealthy Southern women engaging in socially and economically purposeful, time-consuming activity outside the home. Thus, when war broke out, wealthy Southern women had relatively little experience in public works and service: "planter women accepted their subordinate [i.e., domestic-bound] existence as part of a reciprocal agreement that ensured their privileged position" (Campbell 2012).

The Civil War can hardly be faulted for its surface presentation of Black women during the war era. Historical research has its own considerable catching up to do: "The Civil War claimed the lives of … Black women in larger numbers than white women … For African American women, much of their trauma [during the War] appears as an unspectacular disability and has been invisible in our scholarship" (Glymph 2019). *The Civil War* posits familiar images of enslaved women just prior to the announcement of the "Emancipation Proclamation" and "Freedom": a Black married couple, separated at auction, is reunited; an enslaved woman escapes her plantation and works with the "Underground Railroad." But the musical is scarcely the first portrayal of Black women during the Civil War to miss "the tenuousness of their freedom, [which was] circumscribed by gender conventions, economic hardship, and, of course, racism" in both the North and South (Marshall 2007).

In assuming new roles during the Civil War, women exerted new dimensions of influence and power over their own lives and the lives of those around them: as business managersa and single heads (and chief disciplinarians) of households; as strong physical laborers; and as social and civic organizers. A few even fought alongside male army troops and conducted spy missions. While many women were ultimately spent, dispirited, and harmed by the effects of war, others discovered hard-won satisfaction in their new work and responsibilities (Wright 2015). In the aftermath of the Civil War, the extensive role women played in the war effort in both the North and the South significantly expanded America's ideas of women's capabilities and "proper place."

The Civil War honors the generally under-recognized role of women in both the North and South as prolific chroniclers of American life during the war years. In the last thirty years, researching, curating, and making public thousands of women's letters, diaries, and other writings have constituted one of the most important avenues of advanced Civil War historical study. In songs like "Missing You (My Bill)," "Sarah," and "The Honor of Your Name," lyrics are taken or adapted from real letters of the Civil War era. These and other parts of *The Civil War*'s libretto provide brief but revealing glimpses into a broad range of women's responses to the war and its discontents: despair at losing loved ones; the iron will necessary to press onward in the face of fear and uncertainty; the strain of loneliness and endless waiting; and the strength required to maintain home and property under duress. Not really touched upon in the musical, but certainly present in numerous published writings of the Civil War, are women's political and social commentary on the war and the fate of the nation (or the two nations). Whether celebrating the assassination of Lincoln on "Good Friday" (Preston 1865) or frantically burying personal valuables upon news that thieving rebel forces were heading toward Gettysburg to engage in battle (Ashhurst 1863), women letter-writers and diarists offered invaluable, pointed commentary on the state of America at war with itself.

Thomas A. Greenfield and Christina M. Baurle

Further reading

Ashhurst, Mary Hazlehurst. 1863. "Diaries 1863–1864." In *Women during the Civil War*, edited by Kristen Leahy. Philadelphia: University of Pennsylvania Libraries, updated 2012, https://hsp.org/collections/catalogs-research-tools/subject-guides/women-during-the-civil-war.

Barnes, Michael. 1998. "Alley Theatre Pushes the Envelope with 'Civil War,' 'Drive.'" *Austin American-Statesman*, October 28, 1998.

Blaine Hudson, J. 2008. "Abraham Lincoln: An African American Perspective." *Register of the Kentucky Historical Society* 106, no. 3/4: 513–35.

Boyd, Gregory, Jack Murphy, and Frank Wildhorn. 1999a. *The Civil War*. New York: Music Theatre International.
Boyd, Gregory, Jack Murphy, and Frank Wildhorn. 1999b. "Liner Notes." *The Civil War, The Complete Work*. Atlantic Recording Corporation, CD.
Brantley, Ben. 1999. "Theatre Review; History Soldiering On." *New York Times*, April 23, 1999.
Buehler, Pati. 2014. "BWW Reviews: Eagle Theatre's THE CIVIL WAR Is Glorious." *Broadway World*, September 25, 2014.
Burns, Ken et al. 2004. *The Civil War*. Burbank, CA: PBS Home Video.
Campbell, Jacqueline G. 2012. "Gender & the Civil War." *Essential Civil War Curriculum*. Blacksburg: Virginia Center for Civil War Studies at Virginia Tech.
"Civil War." 2018. *History.com*. A&E Television Networks, August 21, 2018, https://www.history.com/topics/american-civil-war.
"The Civil War." n.d. National Parks Service, U.S. Department of the Interior, https:// www.nps.gov/civilwar/index.htm.
Coski, John. n.d. "Myths & Misunderstandings Black Confederates." *News from the American Civil War Museum*.
Douglass, Frederick. 1860. "The Late Election, *Douglass' Monthly*, December 1860." In *Frederick Douglass: Selected Speeches and Writings*, edited by Philip Foner and Yuval Taylor. Chicago: Lawrence Hill Books, 2000.
Douglass, Frederick. 1876. "Oration in Memory of Abraham Lincoln." *A Lincoln Anthology*, Florida Center for Instructional Technology (FCIT), University of South Florida, https://etc.usf.edu/lit2go/authors/194/fcit/.
Douglass, Frederick. 1881. "The Life and Times of Frederick Douglass." *Documenting the American South*. University of North Carolina at Chapel Hill, https://docsouth.unc.edu/neh/dougl92/menu.html.
Evans, Everett. 1998. "'Civil War' Musical Overcomes Obstacles." *Houston Chronicle*, September 24, 1998.
Feldberg, Robert. 1999. "Black, White, Blue, and Gray: The War, Once over Lightly." *The Record*, April 23, 1999.
Fling, Sara. 2019. "Frederick Douglass and Abraham Lincoln." The White House Historical Association, December 4, 2019.
"Frederick Douglass—Mrlincolnandfreedom.org." The Lehrman Institute.
Gannon, Barbara A. 2016. "African American Soldiers." *Essential Civil War Curriculum*, May 2014 and February 2016. Blacksburg: Virginia Technical University.
Gouveia, Georgette. 1999. "Blue, Gray, Gold." *The Journal News*, April 22, 1999.
Harris, Mark. 1999. "The Civil War." *Entertainment Weekly*, May 7, 1999.
Jones, Kenneth. 2006. "Gettysburg Welcomes Wildhorn's 'New' Civil War Musical, *For the Glory*." *Playbill*, June 15, 2006.
Leydon, Joe. 1998. "The Civil War." *Variety*, September 28, 1998.
Marshall, Anne E. 2007. "Review: The Essence of Liberty: Free Black Women during the Slave Era." *Civil War History* 53, no. 2 (June): 214–15.
Masur, Kate. 2010. "The African American Delegation to Abraham Lincoln: A Reappraisal." *Civil War History* 56, no. 2 (June): 117–44.
McGuire, W. and L. Wheeler. 2019. "Frederick Douglass." In *American History*, ABCCLIO, 2019, http://americanhistory.abc-clio.com/Search/Display/246702.
McPherson, James M. 2010. *For Cause and Comrades: Why Men Fought in the Civil War*. New York: Oxford University Press.
Preetha, Ramachandran. 2019. "Duke Professor Shines Light on Untold Stories of Black Women in Civil War." *The Duke Chronicle*. Duke University, September 2019. www.dukechronicle.com/article/2019/09/duke-university-thavolia-glymph-Black-women-civil-war.
Preston, Margaret. 1865. "April 14, 1865." *Women's Diaries during the War*. University of Maryland Libraries, www.lib.umd.edu/civilwarwomen/primary-source-evidence/diaries.
Ridley, Clifford A. 1999. "'War': What Is It Good For?" *Philadelphia Inquirer*, April 26, 1999.
Sheehan-Dean, Aaron. 2015. "Confederate Morale during the Civil War." *Encyclopedia Virginia*, October 27, 2015, https://www.encyclopediavirginia.org/Confederate_Morale_during_the_Civil_War.
Stille, Charles Janeway. 1866. *History of the United States Sanitary Commission, Being the General Report of Its Work during the War of the Rebellion*. Philadelphia:Lippincott, https://archive.org/details/historyofuniteds00stiluoft/page/490.
Taylor, Amy Murrell, 2009. *The Divided Family in Civil War America*. Chapel Hill: University of North Carolina Press.
"A War Begins." 2019. *American History*, ABC-CLIO, http://americanhistory.abc-clio.com/Topics/Display/1187662?cid=41&sid=1187662.
Wright, Catherine M. 2015. "Women during the Civil War." *Encyclopedia Virginia*, October 2015. www.encyclopediavirginia.org/Women_During_the_Civil_War.

CHAPTER 7
THE CRADLE WILL ROCK (1937)

Book, Music, and Lyrics by Marc Blitzstein (1905–64)
Originally Produced by the Federal Theatre Project for the Maxine Elliott's Theatre First Broadway Performances at The Venice Theatre, New York City, June 16, 1937 Official Opening at the Mercury Theatre December 5, 1937–April 2, 1938

Songs

"Moll's Song (I'm Checkin' Home Now)"	"Gus and Sadie Love Song"
"Moll and Gent"	"The Rich"
"Moll and Dick"	"Ask Us Again"
"Moll and Druggist"	"Art for Art's Sake"
"Oh, What a Filthy Night Court!"	"Nickel Under the Foot"
"Mrs. Mister and Reverend Salvation"	"Leaflets"
"Croon Spoon"	"The Cradle Will Rock"
"The Freedom of the Press"	"Faculty Room Scene"
"Let's Do Something"	"Doctor and Ella"
"Honolulu"	"Joe Worker"
"Drugstore Scene"	"Finale/The Cradle Will Rock" (Reprise)

Overview

The Cradle Will Rock (*Cradle*) was an unusual Broadway show. It did not have a typical Broadway premiere, opening, or run. With thematic and stylistic ties to 1930s avant-garde and radical protest theater movements, *Cradle* did not bring to Broadway conventional theater themes or composition style. Its operatic or cantata musical sing-through form, while more familiar today, leaned toward European musical theater traditions more than the emerging American musical styles of the 1920s and 1930s. It is generally regarded among the first, if not *the* first, Broadway productions to introduce radical, contemporary European theater techniques to mainstream commercial American theater. The show has the further distinction of being the only Broadway production ever shut down by order of the U.S. federal government, as armed guards padlocked the theater doors and stood post around the building on the night of the first preview performance.

In 1937, *Cradle*'s threadbare storyline of unscrupulous steel mill owner Mr. Mister's efforts to sabotage his workers' attempts to form a union was virtually unheard of in New York's commercial theater. Furthermore, the German influence reflected in *Cradle*'s episodic scene-by-scene structure, through which we see Mr. Mister corrupting one Steeltown community institution after another, was a Broadway musical rarity as well. However, New York theater enthusiasts at the time would have been acquainted with the now largely forgotten Workers

Theater Movement of the 1920s and 1930s for whom labor versus management-themed melodramas were common fare. While many theater artists and avid theatergoers moved easily and unselfconsciously between highly commercial and non-commercial projects, profit-conscious producers and theater owners were reluctant to embrace the ethos of radical theater, which, almost by definition, scares away large audiences and corporate support.

But flexibility and versatility were the bywords for the creative team behind *Cradle*, including their original producers. Author-composer-lyricist Marc Blitzstein; producers Samuel Grisman and Orson Welles; Federal Theatre Project Director Hallie Flanagan; and original lead cast members Will Gear (Mr. Mister) and Howard Da Silva (Larry Foreman) individually and collectively carved out careers comprising many theatrical formats—commercial and non-commercial—to say nothing of popular music, broadcasting, film, and eventually television.

Blitzstein and company fully understood the left-wing polemical advocacy message of Workers Theater Movement plays (sometimes referred to as agit/prop drama, a conflation of agitation and propaganda). *The Cradle Will Rock* embraces that advocacy full on. *The Cradle Will Rock*'s abstractly conceived Steeltown, USA, presents a plausibly sketched American "company town"—any one of over 2,000 communities since the mid-nineteenth century that depend on a single dominant local industry or employer for most of its jobs and almost all manner of civic life (Hirsch 2015). The scope of Mr. Mister's corruptive influence over virtually every aspect of town life (education, the justice system, the arts, neighborhood businesses, etc.) reflects an historically significant factor in major labor–management disputes as well as a noteworthy phenomenon in the history of American labor and manufacturing.

While sparse on details, *Cradle* reflects for its time significant developments in the American labor movement in general and the history of steelworker unions in particular. Set in "the present" (1937), *Cradle* opens with a knowing recognition that, notwithstanding passage of the 1935 National Labor Relations Act protecting workers' rights to unionize, even legal workplace union drives could be sources of danger, intimidation, and even lethal violence. We see this point play out immediately in *Cradle*'s opening scene, when a seemingly innocuous street corner disagreement over price between a sex worker and a prospective client is instantly swept up into the all-consuming turmoil of the union-organizing drive occurring inside Mr. Mister's steel mill. *Cradle* also builds upon the strategic and political disadvantage many industrial workers faced against management in the 1930s. Economic prosperity in the 1920s had slowed unionization efforts with the result that American labor entered the Depression Era of the 1930s with a loss of momentum owing to a paucity of experienced leaders and an overall reduction in union membership (Montgomery 1987).

Among America's heavy industries, the steel industry was an oddity in the first four decades of the twentieth century, having thwarted nearly all significant unionization efforts from the early 1890s until the late 1930s (Rees 1998). In 1937, U.S. Steel, the largest American steel company, became the first steel company in the twentieth century to recognize a steelworkers' union. Smaller rival steel companies, particularly in Ohio, defiantly sought to reverse unionizing activity in their own shops. Their actions touched off the notorious four-month Little Steel Strike of 1937, the bloodiest steelworker strike in American history with upward of sixteen violent deaths directly associated with the conflict (Lipold and Isaac 2019). Six weeks into the strike, with a national spotlight on the Little Steel Strike, *Cradle* officially opened on Broadway.

Composer, lyricist, and author Marc Blitzstein, who had never written a full musical, had been commissioned to write *Cradle* in 1936 by the short-lived Federal Theatre Project (hereinafter Federal Theatre). Federal Theatre was a controversial government program under the Works Progress Administration (WPA), which itself was part of President Franklin Roosevelt's New Deal plan to spur economic recovery during the Great Depression. During its Congressionally funded years, 1935–9, Federal Theatre supported numerous non-controversial mainstream classical, popular, and children's stage productions all over the country. However,

Federal Theatre's director, Hallie Flanagan, was an expert on emerging avant-garde theater styles and social protest drama, and she wanted Federal Theatre to embrace these progressive movements. Many Federal Theatre plays addressed the current plight of poor and working-class Americans. Frequently, these plays adopted agit/prop and other polemic staging approaches, offering unvarnished, sometimes simplistic, indictments of capitalist business leaders for their cruel and unfair treatment of workers. Along the way these plays also routinely thrust blame upon politicians, police officers, anti-union workers, and other citizens assumed to be complicit in corporate misdeeds. Businesses and politicians closely allied with corporate interests objected strenuously to Federal Theatre's use of public funds to support one-sided anti-business propaganda. Their objections against such productions (the stoppage of *Cradle*'s Broadway opening preview night most notable among them) eventually led to Congress suspending Federal Theatre's funding altogether.

The Cradle Will Rock emerged from the turbulent history of the 1930s as arguably the most noteworthy individual original production in Federal Theatre's storied legacy. Moreover, in the larger sphere of 1930s American social drama, *Cradle*'s fame among theater enthusiasts is rivaled only by that of Clifford Odets' 1935 drama *Waiting for Lefty*, produced by the Group Theatre (a radical New York theater collective that Blitzstein had joined in the 1930s).

The Cradle Will Rock was perhaps an unlikely candidate for distinction as a historically significant and influential work of American theater. In 1937, the impact of the more than ten-year-old labor theater movement was waning. Even in its heyday, it exerted little influence over the commercial side of New York popular theater. By the late 1930s, professional theater artists and theatergoers tended to look upon American labor plays as bringing a spirited political voice to the arts scene, providing an antidote to the banality of commercial theater, and according a welcome place for theater artists to pick-up extra work—underpaid or unpaid—as opportunities in commercial theater shrank during the Depression. But more than most, Blitzstein was a true (or truer) believer in the spirit of strike drama, and the show's rather improbable legacy owes much to his singular talent and artistic vision.

Marcus Samuel Blitzstein was born and raised in Philadelphia, the son of affluent parents who had strong socialist leanings. His prodigious musical talent was discovered early on and nurtured at Philadelphia's heralded Curtis Institute of Music. After making his professional debut at twenty-one, he spent most of his early and mid-twenties studying, composing, and performing in Europe. During this time he developed fortes in composition for ballet, song composition for plays, and formal piano concerts. His experience in Europe disabused him of his early aversion to socially relevant, political, and broadly popular music and theater, especially as epitomized by German composer Kurt Weil and playwright Bertolt Brecht. By his late twenties, Blitzstein had warmed to the idea of writing for broader audiences and came to admire the ideas and energy behind Europe's avant-garde political theater and music of the 1920s and 1930s. As he entered his thirties, Blitzstein became friends and sometime collaborators with both Weill and Brecht. At about this same time he also became interested in making money.

Blitzstein moved permanently to New York City in 1933, where he nurtured his paradoxical interests in creating left-wing social activist art and achieving commercial success. He wrote prodigiously and worked especially hard on writing songs that could be placed in other people's Broadway shows. Flourishing in both non-commercial and commercial theater circles, Blitzstein broke down a barrier between those two worlds. With *Cradle*, Blitzstein realized his ambition to write socially significant art in a commercial vein. He even enjoyed the surprise benefit of witnessing the extra boost in publicity and audience interest *Cradle* received from the government shutdown of his Broadway opening night. Each time it is performed, witnessed, or written about, *Cradle* further solidifies Blitzstein's artistic and historical legacy.

Plot synopsis

The Cradle Will Rock is set in various locations in fictional Steeltown, USA.

Scene 1, a Street Corner. Moll, a sex worker, laments her lack of work and empty belly. A Gent offers Moll 30 cents for her services; Moll and Gent argue over her price and hard times. Dick, a corrupt police officer, interrupts them, threatening to arrest Gent unless Gent surrenders all his money to Dick. Gent does so (it is more than 30 cents) and leaves. Dick explains to Moll that the streets are empty tonight because steelworkers are at industrialist Mr. Mister's steel factory conducting a union-organizing meeting. Dick was sent by Mr. Mister to disrupt the workers' meeting. Now alone with Moll, Dick pressures her for sex as reward for scaring off Gent. As they argue, members of the Liberty Committee enter. The committee is an anti-union group composed of prominent Steeltown citizens: a minister, a newspaper editor, an ex-pharmacist ("druggist"), a doctor, a professor, professional artists, and so on. Mistaking them for pro-union activists, Dick arrests them plus Moll.

Scene 2: Night Court. The Liberty Committee members, incensed over their arrest, demand their release and call for the arrest of the union organizer (the as yet unnamed and unseen Larry Foreman). The on-duty cop tells them that the "guy who made the speech" is being held and beaten in the next room. Moll seated on a bench talks to committee member Druggist, a former drugstore owner who is now a vagrant. Moll tells him that she has been arrested for prostitution. Druggist responds by saying the Liberty Committee members are all prostitutes in their own way.

Scene 3: Flashback to 1915 (and in rapid succession 1916 and 1917) at Reverend Salvation's Mission. Mrs. Mister, a major donor to the Reverend's ministry, offers Reverend a large donation to preach peace. A year later (1916), she gives him another large donation and urges him to preach peace but oppose Germany's warlike aggression. In 1917, after a profitable year of arms manufacturing for the Misters' steel company, she gives him a donation and tells him to preach war against Germany.

Scene 4: Lawn of Mr. Mister's Home. Mr. Mister and Editor Dailey enter upon the Misters' children, Junior and Sister, who are idly trying to stave off the day's boredom. Mr. Mister cajoles and bribes Editor Daily to slander Larry Foreman all in the name of Freedom of the Press. Mr. Mister now owns the paper and threatens to destroy Editor Daily if he refuses. Mr. Mister also orders Daily to hire Junior and assign him a beat in Honolulu. A reluctant Junior accepts on his father's dubious promise of lovely women waiting for him.

Scene 5: The Drugstore. From his night court conversation with Moll, Druggist reveals how he became "a drunk," having lost his son and his drugstore. Two mobsters had entered his store, which is located across the street from a union hall. They confirm with the Druggist that a customer named Gus Polock and his wife are due to enter soon. The mobsters inform the Druggist that when the couple leaves there will be a violent explosion on the street, but he is to say nothing. The Polocks enter, a couple very much in love; she is pregnant. They have sodas at the lunch counter and leave. Steve, the Druggist's son, rushes after them to warn them, but he is too late. An explosion goes off in the union hall, killing Steve, the Polocks, and their unborn child. It is implied that Mr. Mister is behind this explosion, and Druggist will lose his store if he interferes.

Scene 6: Hotel Lobby. Yasha, a violinist, runs into Dauber, a visual artist. Both enjoy the patronage of Mrs. Mister and they both tutor the daughter, Sister. Dauber and Yasha both complain about having to pander to the rich, but it is the rich who subsidize their livelihoods. Mrs. Mister enters and they immediately start pandering to her. At her behest they join the Liberty Committee, foreswearing that art exists for art's sake, and that artists cannot be bothered with politics or social injustice.

Scene 7: Night Court. Moll sings about bad luck because she found a nickel under her foot, which somehow disappeared—a musical parable of false hope, bittersweet and full of longing. The Cop enters with Larry Foreman. The Liberty Committee members are riled at seeing him since they have been mistakenly arrested for being his supporters. Foreman confirms he has been charged with inciting a riot, by making a speech and passing out leaflets. We learn that Mr. Mister is at home with the judge, ensuring punishment for Foreman and his supporters. Foreman tells Moll and all present that the Liberty Committee are "lackeys" to the tyranny of Mr. Mister and the cause of Freedom. Foreman then expresses his dream of unions springing up around the country to give voice and power to workers everywhere.

Scene 8: Faculty. Mr. Mister enters the university faculty room to tell President Prexy he wants to expand the college's military tactics course, which Mr. Mister funds. At Mister's behest the president auditions three professors for the job. Mister rejects a male professor for being too erudite and fires a second for his participation in 1915 Henry Ford's Peace Ship (an American citizens' peace envoy to Europe attempting to stop World War I). However, they hire a professor who extols the sex appeal of soldiers. Mister looks forward to hiring graduates as security guards and "law enforcement" officers to use against union activism.

Scene 9: Dr. Specialist's Office. Dr. Specialist, examining Mr. Mister, concludes that Mister suffers from "nerves." Specialist thanks Mr. Mister for making him chair of Mister's Liberty Committee whereupon Specialist says he wants research funding to advance professionally. Mister overhears that Ella Hammer, brother of pro-union steelworker Joe Worker who died in a suspicious accident in Mister's factory, is about to see Specialist about her brother's death. Upon leaving, Mister threatens Specialist, who will perform Joe's autopsy, with financial ruin if he does not announce the cause of death to be a precipitous fall likely caused by serious drunkenness, rather than the unexplained push it is rumored to be. Ella tries to convince Specialist to tell the truth, but Specialist follows Mister's instructions.

Scene 10: Night Court. Larry tells Moll that the Liberty Committee is a front group for Mister composed of people who prostituted their principles out of fear. She will probably go to jail but they will not. Mr. Mister enters and tells the night court clerk that he has the judge's authority to let the Liberty Committee go. Mister offers Larry Foreman money and freedom from prison if he ceases union action. Larry turns down Mister's offer as a loud commotion is heard off-stage. It is the workers of Steeltown—and countless more from across the nation—rising up to form unions and join the struggle for workers' rights and dignity.

Critical reception

As Broadway premieres go, *Cradle* had a unique publicity roll-out. Scheduled for its first preview in the prestigious Maxine Elliott Theatre on June 16, 1937, the show's first press notice came in the form of an unattributed *New York Times* article about the WPA, now under budgetary attack by Roosevelt's opponents in Washington, compelling the Federal Theatre to cease production of *Cradle* immediately. The directive arrived in New York during the later stages of rehearsal. The producers lobbied their Washington allies in an effort to stave off a forced shutdown, but to no avail. The company and ticketholders arrived on the scheduled preview opening night to find the Maxine Elliott Theatre closed and guarded by armed security, ostensibly there at the direction of the WPA to safeguard props, sets, and costumes—all government property.

In one of Broadway's most legendary opening night meta dramas, Blitzstein, the producers, and cast scrambled and found an available venue (the Venice Theatre) twenty blocks uptown. They dissolved the production's ties to the government on the spot, instantly converting the show to a commercial production, thereby freeing it from government regulation. To honor the provisions of union contracts—in force for commercial productions but generally waived for Federal Theatre—the cast performed their roles from the audience seats as Blitzstein, substituting for a full orchestra, accompanied the players on a piano for the approximately 100 audience members that stuck it out. For the most part, the *Times* reported the bizarre events objectively, while noticeably tipping its hat to the producers, cast, and audience for gamely salvaging the evening's performance: "Many gathered for [the] Preview charged censorship of [the] 'radical' plot" ("Steel Strike Opera ..." 1937).

The Cradle Will Rock officially opened at the Mercury Theatre on December 6, 1937, and, unlike the June premiere, was reviewed in a traditional manner. Brooks Atkinson, the *Times*' senior theater critic, was enthralled: "*The Cradle Will Rock* is a summons to battle and a cry of warning ... rocking many things, including the audience ... [which it] blew out of the theater with the thunder of the finale." Atkinson swooned over Blitzstein's artistry: "He can write anything from tribal chant to Tin Pan Alley balladry ... [he] generates current like a dynamo ... his music box roars with rage and his actors frighten the aged roof of the miniature Mercury Theatre" (Atkinson 1937). The opening night review in New York's *Herald Tribune* was similarly enthusiastic, calling *Cradle* "a savagely humorous social cartoon with music that hits hard and sardonically" (Miller 2001).

Writing for *The Nation,* Joseph Wood Krutch praised the production but was decidedly more measured in his assessment than was Atkinson. Finding himself distracted by *Cradle*'s cantata form (invoking a nineteenth-century dismissal of the cantata as "a corruption of the cheerful uses of the playhouse"), Krutch was nonetheless impressed: "The interest is held and the evening passes quickly." Writing a month after publication of Atkinson's celebratory review, Krutch, without mentioning Atkinson by name, feared that earlier reviews would unrealistically elevate viewers' expectations: "*The Cradle Will Rock* is sort of a musical cartoon, with no more shading than a cartoon is expected to have." Moreover, Krutch had some doubts if anyone other than those already committed to the show's unnuanced pro-labor, anti-capitalist point of view would be able to enjoy it fully: "Mr. Blitzstein's vehemence is continuous but his wit is intermittent" (Krutch 1938). In an essay for *Current History,* V. F. Calverton contrasted a vibrant New York commercial theater season with what to his mind were comparatively staid London offerings, finding America's contemporary socially-themed plays to be the winning factor for New York. While not letting *Cradle* off the hook for its wholesale abandonment of subtlety, Calverton found the energy emanating from the stage compelling: "*The Cradle Will Rock* suffers from a host of inadequacies: exaggerated contrasts, strained situations, and a pathetic plethora of the obvious." Nonetheless, Calverton, unlike Krutch, asserts that *Cradle* transcends its weaknesses with pointed satire "directed at our economic injustices, social inequalities, and political perfidies" as well as exuding "vigor and cogency that cannot be denie" (Calverton 1938). *The Literary Digest* also expressed pleasant surprise that *Cradle* transcended its roots in "irritating" labor drama via "Blitzstein's lilting music, caricature characters ... and the fervent spirit of the actors" (Theater: Labor and Left-Wingers ... 1938).

The only Broadway revival of *Cradle* opened in 1947, this time with a pit orchestra conducted by twenty-nine-year-old Leonard Bernstein, who had put on a production of the show when he was an undergraduate at Harvard. (Bernstein also took the role of the night court clerk in the revival.) Atkinson again reviewed the production for the *Times* and was as generous with his praise as he had been in 1937. Informing his readers almost matter-of-factly that *Cradle* is "the most vivid proletarian drama ever written in this country," Atkinson hailed the revival production as "blistering ... no less militant and exciting than it was a decade ago." Atkinson conceded that some of the language and situations from the 1930s seem dated. Nonetheless, Atkinson proclaims that no other musical he knows is "so candid, so original, so fresh in stage conception" (Atkinson 1947). By contrast, Cecil Smith of the *New Republic* was deeply disappointed in the performance. Smith, a music critic writing in the magazine's regular "Music" column, observed that this "concert revival" of *Cradle* was presented as part of the New York City Symphony's season. He acknowledged the production's importance as the first public presentation of Blitzstein's original orchestration for *Cradle.* (Ultimately, a lone pianist accompanied both the unofficial, disrupted June preview performance and the original Broadway run in 1937.) Nonetheless Smith found the show dated "in a particularly discouraging way." He was highly dismissive of Blitzstein's "neatly contrived anti-thesis of the naughty tycoon and high-minded laborer," finding the characters and situations devolving into "naive clichés" and "disquieting propaganda." Smith went so far as to enlist the first-night audience in support of his argument, surmising from their reaction that they, too, could not take the show's "crude" political message seriously: "the first night audience seemed to take it as more of a lark than a lesson" (Smith 1947).

Subsequent productions have included Off-Broadway revivals in 1964, 1983, and 2019. *Cradle* had a London production, with its West End premiere in 1984. *The Cradle Will Rock* still enjoys a strong following among theater buffs who celebrate the show's singular place in theater history, love the challenge of its demanding score, and find it profoundly relevant to twenty-first-century American economics and politics.

Historical accuracy and context

Company towns, USA

The Cradle Will Rock's Steeltown, USA—an American community of undetermined size and location—is a thinly sketched prototype of an American company town. Company towns first appeared in the United States in the early 1800s and grew in number and socio-economic influence over the next 150 years, becoming major factors in establishing the United States as the pre-eminent manufacturing economy in the world for much of that period.

Company towns (also referred to as mill towns, mining towns, manufacturing communities, and "one-industry towns") were residential communities developed by an individual business or a single industry to provide workers and their families with a hometown close to the company workplace. Most early company towns were established in remote, sparsely populated locations, often in proximity to vital resources for the company: coal, iron, and copper deposits; accessible woodlands; open waterways, and so on. By definition, a company town's founding business or industry was the single largest employer in the area, frequently owning in the early years most if not all other buildings, property, and business concerns in the community. Once established and flourishing, a company town's founding industry, such as Mr. Mister's steel company in *Cradle,* "dominated the city and its sense of identity," often wielding at its discretion influence if not outright control over virtually every significant civic and economic enterprise within its reach (Rhodes 2013). *The Cradle Will Rock*'s veritable shopping list of civic activities corrupted by company owner Mr. Mister's influence (law enforcement, local politics, local commerce, higher education, art, medical practice, etc.), for all its melodramatic simplicity, speaks pointedly to the historical reality in many company towns, especially prior to World War II.

Lowell, Massachusetts, is often cited as the first true company town in the United States. Lowell was established as an experimental community in the 1820s. Chartered officially in 1836, and named after Francis Cabot Lowell, founder of the town's (and arguably America's) first industrial textile factory, Lowell provided a model for future American company towns. Other textile companies moved to Lowell, drawn by nearby Pawtucket Falls (which provided hydro power for factory looms and other equipment) as well as Mr. Lowell's success. The Lowell factories recruited single women from surrounding rural regions to provide the factories' labor. They housed the women in company-owned on-site boarding houses. In addition to requiring the women to arrive at work by 5 a.m. every morning, the companies demanded that the women attend church and "lead a moral life," setting an early template for labor and management tensions over working conditions and workers' rights that roiled many companies and company towns over the next century (Hirsch 2015).

Depending upon the individual town, historical circumstances, and even one's political point of view, company towns were created in order to attract, maintain, shelter, educate, and enrich their workers. Or conversely, they were created to entrap, exploit, politically manipulate, and otherwise control the workers and the civic affairs of the town. Historians often discuss companies that dominate a company town on a spectrum of quality of life and treatment of their workers. The spectrum runs between extremes of the idyllic ("Industrial Edens") and brutish "Satanic Mills" (Green 2010). With some exceptions, mining towns and mill towns share a history of exploiting workers and townspeople, often inviting comparisons with prison camps and work farms. On the other hand, many light industries, such as the famous "chocolate capital," Hershey, Pennsylvania (established 1905), are more frequently associated with utopian planned communities that generally improved the quality life for workers and their families (Green 2010). Steel company towns prior to World War II, the sites of many labor–management struggles since the late 1800s, tended to fall toward the brutish end of the spectrum, although generally viewed as less harsh than the most austere mining towns. Blitzstein clearly envisioned *Cradle*'s Steeltown, USA, and factory owner, Mr. Mister, in this vein.

Company towns, by definition, lack a diversified economy. A single business downturn or factory closing can wreak economic havoc, resulting in serious labor–management conflict and long-term hardship for an entire region irrespective of management's high-minded intentions. Although American company town collapses are often associated with bust periods in boom-or-bust cycles from the mid-nineteenth century through the Great Depression of the 1930s, traditional company towns still exist in the United States and still depend for their survival upon the fortunes of their primary employer (See "The Town That Maytag Left Behin" 2007).

Steeltowns, USA

In the mid-1930s *Cradle's* composer/writer Marc Blitzstein would have had a number of self-proclaimed "Steeltown, USAs" on which to model his fictitious company town. In 1880, Steelton, Pennsylvania, incorporated itself with that name to honor and promote its own Pennsylvania Steel Company. (Bethlehem Steel, located ninety miles east in Bethlehem, Pennsylvania, eventually acquired Pennsylvania Steel but kept the mills in Steelton, where they remained in production well into the twenty-first century.) Morgan Park, Minnesota, established in 1915, was a planned community built by America's largest steel company, U.S. Steel, and named after J. P. Morgan, the New York financier who helped broker the merging of several steel companies to form U.S. Steel.

U.S. Steel eventually expanded to operate steel mills in Minnesota, Arkansas, Texas, Pennsylvania, Indiana, and Illinois. However, Pittsburgh, Pennsylvania, the largest of America's twentieth-century steel towns, claims U.S. Steel as its home base. Pittsburgh still proudly flaunts its steel-industry roots, "Steel City" nickname, and numerous steel-themed businesses (the National Football League's Pittsburgh Steelers perhaps most notable among them). At the same time, Pittsburgh's business and civic leaders are quick to note that the city has transcended its heavy industry past, cleaned up its steel factory-driven polluted air, and ascended to national distinction as leaders in clean industries such as cutting-edge technology and health care (Price-Williams 2017). Youngstown, Ohio's Republic Steel Company (established 1899) and Youngstown Iron Sheet and Tube Company (established 1900) were among the first of more than thirty steel companies that have called the Youngstown area home. As Youngstown Sheet and Tube became one of the largest steel producers in the world, residents of Youngstown adapted the nickname "Steeltown" (Mercier 2003).

The Little Steel Strike of 1937

There is no record of Blitzstein having a single steel mill town or labor action in mind as a model for *Cradle*'s union drive in Steeltown, USA's steel mill. However, when the show opened in 1937, Youngstown, Ohio, was well known to much of the nation because of the ongoing "Little Steel Strike" which began only weeks before *Cradle*'s opening.

The Little Steel Strike pitted factory owners against workers in several small steel companies (when compared to U.S. Steel), collectively known as "Little Steel." Hoping to take action for better wages and on-the-job treatment, the Little Steel steelworkers welcomed representation by the newly formed Congress of Industrial Organizations (CIO), a national organization whose primary mission was to represent and unionize unskilled workers in mass-production industries. (No such organization appears or is alluded to in *Cradle.*) In 1936, the CIO had won a significant victory in nearby Akron, Ohio, representing a newly formed tire industry workers' union during their strike for better wages and working conditions against the B.F. Goodrich and Firestone Tire companies. That successful strike energized the relatively small United Rubber Workers union, which garnered a strong reputation for effectiveness over the next six decades (Meyer 2002).

Although the Youngstown steelworkers were technically unionized under the CIO, Little Steel company owners took actions that seemed to pre-figure Mr. Mister's efforts to sabotage the union drive in *Cradle.* Beginning May of 1937, the respective owners of Youngstown Sheet & Tube, Republic, and Inland Steel, incensed that rival U.S. Steel had recognized the national steelworkers union earlier that year, sought to undermine the CIO's organizing efforts within their own plants. They hired their own security force to intimidate workers, and organized townspeople and citizens committees (similar to *Cradle*'s Liberty Committee) to publicly rebuke the strikers. Rising tensions and violence (with blame predictably hurled at both owners and workers from each respective side) reached several boiling points, requiring the governor of Ohio to send state troopers to break up the strike. By the end of the strike in August, sixteen people had died in strike-related violence, the most deaths in any single steel industry labor–management conflict in history (Lipold and Isaac 2019).

The Workers Theater Movement in the United States

Workers theater, also known as labor theater, in the United States is best known as a Depression-era movement that was, in its idealized mission and to some extent in reality, "a national effort organized at the local level to use working people's leisure hours as a terrain for political education" (Hyman 1997). Over time, upwards of 400 small theater groups—most of them independent, perpetually underfunded or unfunded, and short-lived—collectively established a national presence from the mid-1920s through the end of the 1930s (Chilcoat 1998).

With varying degrees of success, workers theater drew workers to their performances by staging productions at union meetings, educational gatherings, and social functions as well as drawing actors and playwrights from the ranks of the workers themselves. However, many of the movement's most important leaders were politically sympathetic intellectuals, theater artists, and working professionals rather than industry day laborers. In 1929, socialist playwright and art critic Michael Gold, for example, reported in the Marxist-inspired *New Masses* magazine that there were over fifty workers theater groups in the United States and that his own performance piece "Strike" (a "mass-recitation") had been performed in a dozen different venues "from Maine to California" (Gold 1929).

One of the primary agents driving the national reach of labor theater was the government-funded Federal Theatre Project (1935–9), which had a legislative mission to provide theatrical services throughout the country. Federal Theatre's director, Hallie Flanagan, insisted that controversial pro-worker/anti-capitalist agit-prop protest plays be incorporated into Federal Theatre offerings. Ironically, the broad reach and high-profile controversies surrounding Federal Theatre soon drew attention, support, and audiences away from the independent groups that had birthed the American Workers Theater Movement in the 1920s. And, indeed, the first signs of decline of leading labor theater organizations, publications, and overall public support of small labor theater groups became apparent beginning in 1936 and 1937 (Levine 1985). Perhaps more alarming to the movement was that, as the 1930s drew to a close and international tensions in Europe increasingly commanded the attention of socially-aware Americans, workers theater became watered down and "tame" (Levine 1985). Eventually, formerly supportive unions dropped workers theater performances from their organizational and educational programs entirely (Hyman 1997).

Apart from providing entertainment, workers theater productions had specific teaching objectives in mind for their audiences: emboldening oppressed workers to unionize and take strike actions; portraying pro-union workers as more empowered, virtuous, and even more "manly" than anti-union workers; alerting workers to various management schemes for sabotaging union drives and breaking up strikes; and staging stories heralding the ultimate triumph of workers taking militant stands against exploitative corporations.

Although *Cradle* is a landmark work of 1930s left-wing theater, some historians decline to call it a labor drama per se. *The Cradle Will Rock* was intended for a "mid-town" commercial theater audience, and at least in Blitzstein and company's original vision, it was to open with a full orchestra and high-priced staging worthy of a Broadway fanfare. In addition, by 1937, the strike drama had been both a staple and a "fading star" within the Workers Theater Movement for ten years. In many respects, *Cradle* is a musical homage to, or a loving treatment of, the labor strike play genre more than a model of the genre itself. Other historians credit the play as a landmark of "Popular Front" Art, left-wing socially relevant works of art that became widely known—even iconic—works and, at the same time, politically influential. In this respect, *Cradle* stands alongside John Steinbeck's Depression-Era novel *The Grapes of Wrath* (1939), Yip Harburg's song "Brother Can You Spare a Dime?" (1932), and Orson Welles' film *Citizen Kane* (1941). Nevertheless, *Cradle* embraced and honored many of the essential features of the labor theater, including exposing the sophisticated treachery of union-busting corporate executives through Mr. Mister's multiple schemes; presenting heroic portrayals of courageous strikers, such as the stalwart Larry Foreman; and, most importantly, foretelling a hard-won victory for organized labor as workers ("thousands of 'em," in the aisles, off-stage, and ideally in the streets of America's Steeltowns) unite to crush Mr. Mister and his network of enablers and flacks.

Thomas A. Greenfield and Carissa Cordes

Further reading

Alexandersen, Christian. 2019. "'Gotta Hope for the Best': Sale of Steelton Steel Mill Remains Uncertain." *Pennsylvania Real-Time News*, January 12, 2016; updated January 5, 2015, www.pennlive.com/news/2016/01/gotta_hope_for_the_best_sale_o.html.

Atkinson, Brooks. 1937. "Marc Blitzstein's *The Cradle Will Rock* Officially Opens." *New York Times*, December 6, 1937.

Atkinson, Brooks. 1947. "Blitzstein's *The Cradle Will Rock*, Vivid Proletarian Drama, Revived at Mansfield." *New York Times*, December 27, 1947.

Blitzstein, Marc. 2013. *The Cradle Will Rock*. Whitefish, MT: Literary Licensing.

Calverton, V. F. 1938. "Current History in the World of the Arts." *Current History* 48 (April): 53.

Chilcoat, George W. 1998. "Workers Theatre as an Inquiry Process for Exploring Social Issues of the 1930s." *Social Education* 62, no. 4 (April/May), http://www.socialstudies.org/sites/default/files/publications/se/6204/620401.html.

Flanagan, Hallie. 1940. *Arena: The Story of the Federal Theatre*. New York: Duell, Sloan & Pearce.

Gold, Michael. 1929. "A Letter to Workers, Art Groups 9." *New Masses*, September 1929.

Green, Hardy. 2010. *The Company Town: The Industrial Edens and Satanic Mills That Shaped the American Economy*. New York: Basic Books.

Hirsch, Michele Lent. 2015. "America's Company Towns, Then and Now." *Smithsonian Magazine*, September 4, 2015, https://www.smithsonianmag.com/travel/americas-company-towns-then-and-now-180956382/.

Hyman, Colette A. 1997. *Staging Strikes*. Philadelphia: Temple University Press.

Kazin, Michael. 2011. "This Land Is Our Land: the Popular Front and American Culture." *Humanities* 32, no. 3 (May/June): 30–3.

Krutch, Joseph Wood. 1938. "Musical Cartoon." *The Nation*, January 1938, 107.
Levine, Ira A. 1985. *Left-Wing Dramatic Theory in the American Theatre*. Ann Arbor, MI: UMI Research Press.
Lipold, Paul F. and Larry W. Isaac. 2019. "Striking Deaths: Lethal Contestation and the 'Exceptional' Character of the American Labor Movement, 1870–1970." *International Review of Social History* 54, no. 2 (August): 167–205.
Mercier, Laurie. 2003. "Review: Remembering and Re-defining Industrialized Youngstown." *American Quarterly* 55, no. 2 (June): 315–21.
Meyer, Bruce. 2002. *The Once and Future Union: The Rise and Fall of the United Rubber Workers, 1935–1995*. Akron, OH: University of Akron Press.
Miller, Scott. 2001. "Inside *The Cradle Will Rock*." *Newline Theatre.com*, http://www.newlinetheatre.com/cradle.html.
Montgomery, David. 1987. "Thinking About American Workers in the 1920s." *International Labor and Working-Class History* 32 (Fall): 4–24.
Pollack, Howard. 2012. *Marc Blitzstein: His Life, His Work, His World*. New York: Oxford University Press.
Price-Williams, Beth. 2017. "7 Nicknames for Pittsburgh That We All Use and Love." *Only In Your State: Pittsburgh*, www.onlyinyourstate.com/states/pennsylvania/pittsburgh/.
Rees, Jonathan. 1998. "Managing the Mills: Labor Policy in the American Steel Industry, 1892–1937." *Business and Economic History* 27, no. 1 (Fall): 23–8.
Rhodes, James. 2013. "Youngstown's 'Ghost'? Memory, Identity, and Deindustrialization." *International Labor and Working-Class History* 84 (Fall): 55–77.
Smith, Cecil. 1947. "When the Wind Blows." *New Republic*, December 22, 1947, 35.
"Steel Strike Opera Put Off by WPA." 1937. *New York Times*, June 17, 1937, https://archive.nytimes.com.
"Theater: Labor and Left-Wingers Stage Two Riotous Shows." 1938. *Literary Digest* 125 (January): 34–5.
"The Town That Maytag Left Behind." 2007. *CBS News*, www.cbsnews.com/news/the-town-maytag-left-behind/.

CHAPTER 8
DEAREST ENEMY (1925)

Composer: Richard Rodgers (1902–79) Lyricist: Lorenz Hart (1895–1943) Libretto: Herbert Fields (1897–1958)
World Premiere: Akron (Ohio) Colonial Theatre, July 20, 1920 Broadway: Knickerbocker Theater, September 18, 1925–May 22, 1926
286 performances

Songs

Act One	**Act Two**
"Heigh-Ho, Lackaday!"	"Gavotte"
"War Is War"	"I'd Like To Hide It"
"I Beg Your Pardon"	"Where the Hudson River Flows"
"Cheerio"	"Bye and Bye"
"Full Blown Roses"	"Enough to Love"
"The Hermits"	"Sweet Peter"
"Here in My Arms"	"Here's a Kiss"
"Tho' We've No Authentic Reason"	**Act Three**
	"Here in My Arms" (Reprise)

Overview

Richard Rodgers and Lorenz Hart's first full-length musical *Dearest Enemy* posits a mischievously exaggerated version of a very likely, although disputed, incident that purportedly occurred during the Revolutionary War on September 15, 1776. As reported at the time, the incident lasted approximately three hours. It took place in the parlor of a plush central Manhattan estate following British General William Howe's (1729–1814) stunning victory over colonial forces in New York City. Not a single shot was fired during the parlor incident in question. No one was killed, injured, or even inconvenienced against their will. Many historians believe that cake and wine were served as reported, but conjecture surrounding a flirtation between a married American socialite and the commanding general of British forces in America cannot be verified. From these seemingly innocuous fragments of information and rumor, a historical conundrum emerged.

What possessed British General William Howe, whose own forces were holding 3,500 American patriot troops isolated and at his mercy in lower Manhattan, to order his superior land forces to stand down at Inclenberg, the 30-acre estate of a pro-British shipping magnate in central Manhattan? If Howe had pursued the ensnared Americans immediately, his ground forces would have easily disabled the American unit—one of Washington's largest—preventing them from joining up with Washington's main army encamped eleven miles north in Harlem Heights.

Had Howe planned all along to savor his conquest of the city in leisure? Did a Manhattan socialite with secret allegiances to the American cause knowingly forestall the general with wine, cake, charm, and counterintelligence? What is known is that Howe rested his victorious troops outside the central Manhattan estate of Mrs. Mary Lindley Murray (1726–82). At the same time, American General Israel Putnam (1718–90) and his 3,500 soldiers escaped catastrophic losses by retreating unencumbered from lower Manhattan up to Harlem Heights.

Dearest Enemy accepts as historical fact the entirely plausible reports that Howe and his generals paid a social call on Mrs. Murray following his victorious campaign in New York City. From there, the musical inflates the narrative into an unapologetically fictionalized love story with absurd speculations about Mrs. Murray's ability to conduct counter-espionage for General Washington while hosting the British high command for afternoon snacks. Nevertheless, in constructing their tale, the show's creators explore some meaningful, even under-appreciated, aspects of Revolutionary War study: New York City residents' outsized affinity for the British cause (compared to the more pro-rebel populaces of Boston and Philadelphia); General Howe's curious pattern of giving colonial troops time to escape from traps he had set for them; and General Washington's woefully unsuccessful first battlefield performances immediately following the colonies' formal declaration of independence. What remains in dispute, perhaps never to be resolved, is whether American history can rightly account Mary Lindley Murray's actions that day as authentic deeds of patriotic heroism or must relegate her saga to mythology and local history boosterism.

In 1925, twenty-three-year-old struggling composer Richard Rodgers and his thirty-year-old lyricist partner Lorenz Hart, both native New Yorkers, were familiar with the Mary Lindley Murray story. They had been laboring for a few years as Tin Pan Alley tunesmiths, selling individual songs to New York vaudeville shows and "additional music" to other people's musicals. They scored their first wave of fame with a hit song "Manhattan," the featured number in their popular Broadway revue *Garrick's Gaieties of 1925* (*Gaieties*). "Manhattan" was a clever love ballad to Rodgers and Hart's hometown, strewn with local rhymes and references: "fancy" Delancey Street; "love conquers" in Yonkers; "modern men itch" in Greenwich. Herbert Fields, the *Gaieties*' twenty-eight-year-old stage manager and son of legendary vaudeville comic-turned-producer Lew M. Fields, befriended Rodgers and Hart during the production. The three formed a team as composer, lyricist, and librettist, respectively just as "Manhattan" and *Gaieties* became a hit.

The success of "Manhattan" and the *Gaieties* gave the trio leverage to secure a producer for their first full-length book musical centered on the Mrs. Murray–General Howe story. George Ford, husband of *Gaieties* star Helen Ford, agreed to produce the new musical at the urging of Helen, who loved the script and wanted to play female lead Betsy Burke (Mrs. Murray's beautiful clever niece and master spy).

Mrs. Murray's story played to the writers' creative strengths as well as to New Yorkers' local pride. The conquest of too-sure-of-themselves British officers at the hands of charming, quick-witted, pro-revolution New York women presented myriad romantic and comedic possibilities. The historic backstory for Howe's New York City campaign was a gift for Hart, whose lyrical point of view has been aptly described as songs written for five guys sitting at a Broadway bar. The two weeks preceding Howe's presumptive visit to the Murray estate found warring British and American troops running up and down Staten Island, Long Island, lower Brooklyn, Brooklyn Heights, Kips Bay, lower Manhattan, upper Manhattan, and the Murray estate at Inclenberg (a central Manhattan plot of land now known as the Murray Hill neighborhood after Mary's family). Hart and librettist Field reveled in the opportunity to show off their hometown to a Broadway audience largely comprising hometown fans. After brief tryouts in Akron, Ohio, and Baltimore as well as several rewrites, Rodgers and Hart debuted their first Broadway musical in September, 1925. *Dearest Enemy* was part history lesson, part operettic romance, part battle of the sexes, and part musical map of New York City. The musical had a number of "firsts" associated with its creation above and beyond launching the Broadway careers of

Rodgers and Hart. It was the first twentieth-century Broadway musical about the Revolutionary War. Moreover, unlike its more illustrious successors *Ben Franklin in Paris* (1964), *1776* (1969), or *Hamilton* (2015), *Dearest Enemy*'s principal characters are not Founding Fathers—or anybody's fathers. Mary Lindley Murray, her beautiful, courageous, flirtatious niece Betsy Burke, and lovely daughter Jane Murray (largely fictionalized charges of the Murray household) drive all the action. The women devise the main plot intrigue, execute the successful strategy that forestalls the British generals from attacking Putnam's forces, flirt and woo their British adversaries/suitors to distraction, improvise adroitly as nonsense plot twists threaten to expose their charade, and struggle with their conflicted feelings between love for their charming British foils and devotion to the American cause. In *Dearest Enemy*, the war for American independence is women's work from start to finish.

Rodgers, Hart, Fields, and producer Ford's gamble on *Dearest Enemy* paid off with a solid hit. The show ran for 286 performances over the course of eight months—an impressive, money-making run for its time. Helen Ford's featured love song "Here in My Arms" for Betsy became the show's biggest hit. Opening night reviewers were generally enthusiastic although not uncritical. Significantly, many reviewers made special note of this rare instance of a Broadway musical conveying an American rather than European sensibility toward plot and story. Moreover, *Dearest Enemy*'s American historical setting, a relatively rare occurrence for Broadway at the time, drew commentary about the show's "deglorification" of American girlhood, laudable use of history for bolstering New York City's image, and excitement at seeing George Washington "in person." Moreover, unlike some future theater critics, *Dearest Enemy*'s reviewers by and large were unconcerned about whether, if, or when the show's historical content steered on or off an accurate course.

Dearest Enemy has never been revived on Broadway. Despite its distinction as Rodgers and Hart's first hit show, it is probably the least well known of their musicals. A well-received one-year tour followed the Broadway run. A few local theaters picked up the show in the 1920s and 1930s when a trimmed down version became available for licensing. In 1955, NBC produced a compressed, rewritten version for live broadcast starring Cornelia Otis Skinner as Mary Lindley Murray and English theater legend Cyril Richard as Howe. *Dearest Enemy* also received a surprising revival of sorts in 2013 when the Orchestra of Ireland and conductor David Brophy recorded a critically acclaimed new version of the original score sung in-studio by a cast of professional Irish musical theater and opera singers.

The success of *Dearest Enemy* was more than sufficient to launch Rodgers and Hart into an immediate boom period. Before *Dearest Ene*my even closed in May of 1926, Rodgers, Hart, and Fields had opened *The Girl Friend*. That show ran even longer than *Dearest Enemy* and produced a bigger hit number, the Charleston-tempo title song. Over the next five Broadway seasons, Rodgers and Hart wrote thirteen additional musicals for New York and London, most of which were highly successful. Their prodigious, if at times dysfunctional, writing relationship lasted until Hart's death in 1943, after which Rodgers formed his historic partnership with lyricist Oscar Hammerstein II.

Plot synopsis

On the Murray estate in Manhattan, September 15, 1776, Mary Lindley Murray's daughters, nieces, and maids sew uniforms for their menfolk away at war. They sing a risqué song of loneliness without men ("Heigh-Ho Lackaday"). Mary enters and affectionately refocuses their attention on sewing.

Mary's daughter Jane enters after delivering supplies to colonial troops stationed in Manhattan. She reports that Washington, having recently evacuated troops from Brooklyn following the American defeat there, has moved his main forces and headquarters to northern Manhattan in Harlem Heights. Betsy Burke, Mary's Irish-born niece who accompanied Jane on her delivery, does not return with Jane. Apparently, she is swimming in nearby Kips Bay off the East River. With Howe's ships stationed in Kips Bay and Washington having moved his main forces north, Mary worries about Betsy's safety. Jane assures an unconvinced Mary that Betsy has "experience" with soldiers, having recently gone swimming in Philadelphia where a British officer retrieved her clothes from shore.

Mary's nephew Jimmy enters, announcing that the British are landing at Kips Bay and heading toward the estate. Terrified that Betsy and the girls might be murdered or "compromised," Mary warns them about lustful soldiers. She orders them to make themselves look repulsive before the British troops arrive. The girls, wishing "to be compromised," complain ("War Is War").

Having joined the colonial army, Jimmy leaves for Harlem Heights. Outside the house, British officer Harry Tryon, son of British General Tryon, scouts locations for the generals to take refreshment after their victory at the harbor. Jane flirts with him but is disappointed that he treats women respectfully ("I Beg Your Pardon"). British generals Howe, Clinton and Tryon greet Harry, who reports that, notwithstanding the Murrays' alleged Whig sympathies, they are "sufficiently civilize" to receive the generals graciously. Plus, the house is filled with women. As the generals proceed to the house, British Captain Sir John Copeland informs them that General Washington has retreated northward, leaving General Putnam's troops vulnerable in lower Manhattan. Howe wants to attack Putnam after a brief rest, but Clinton is war weary and Tryon wants to flirt with women. Howe overrules them and orders Sir John to ready the troops at Kips Bay for further battle after their brief visit ("Cheerio").

In the house, the young women, now unattractive per instructions, greet the generals who are, indeed, repulsed at the sight of them. Mary enters dressed elegantly for entertaining, diverting the men's attention from the young women as planned. Outside the house, Betsy enters wearing only a revealing wooden barrel. Sir John follows in pursuit carrying her clothing. He is the same soldier who retrieved her clothing in Philadelphia and has pined for her ever since. Betsy, with Irish disdain for the British crown, dismisses his affections sarcastically: "Dearest enemy." On seeing Betsy, Mary orders her inside.

General Washington has ordered Jimmy to have Mary delay the British so Putnam's troops can escape undetected to Harlem Heights. The request stuns Mary but she quickly plans a strategy: "Soldiers … beautiful girls …" Mary sends Jimmy to inform Putnam of Washington's plan. Jane and Mary offer wine to Howe, Clinton, Tryon, and Sir John. Mary informs Jane that they must delay the men longer. Betsy, unaware of the plot, enters and insults the king in the generals' presence. Angered, Howe demands to search the house. Scrambling to compensate for Betsy's invective, Mary guides the generals on the search. Alone with Betsy, Sir John professes sincere feelings for her to no avail. He exits as Jane informs Betsy of Washington's directive to detain the officers.

Betsy immediately plans to use John's affections for her to stall the generals. She seeks him out, apologizes, and professes her love. During the ruse she deliberately arouses his suspicion that she is an anti-British subversive. Feeling betrayed, Sir John suspects her motives and urges the generals to extend their stay. The generals re-enter as Betsy shouts more vitriol about the king. Howe, suspecting treasonous activity afoot, orders his entourage to remain at the house indefinitely. The officers and the women are pleased for different reasons and exit. Alone, Betsy is conflicted; she is falling for Sir John even as she betrays him.

Act Two opens after dinner. All dance convivially except Betsy, who taunts Sir John as part of her deception ("I'd Like to Hide It"). The generals lavish praise on Mary's dinner and hospitality. She entertains them by extolling the virtues of rustic New York over bustling urban Philadelphia ("Where the Hudson River Flows"). Sir John and Betsy cautiously acknowledge their growing mutual attraction but struggle with the political intrigue that ensnares them ("Bye and Bye").

Howe is suspicious of Mary's eagerness to host the officers and Betsy's hostility toward them. British troops enter with Jimmy, whom they seized *en route* to Putnam's camp. Suspecting that Jimmy is a spy, Howe interrogates him, but Jimmy reveals nothing. Howe orders Jimmy to be imprisoned upstairs and assigns Sir John to guard him. Fearing that Jimmy may have alerted Putnam to his troops' location, Howe orders his officers to prepare to rejoin their troops.

Mary learns that Howe wants to mobilize his troops and that Jimmy has been captured. Betsy plans to sneak out to inform Putnam that Howe intends to mobilize against him, promising her worried aunt that she will be fine: "[just] keep them here." Howe and his generals are practically out the door when Mary persuades them to have one parting drink. Gentleman all, they agree to one. Then another … then a toast to the king … (Stage directions: "*happy and careless*"). With the drinking party in full swing, Betsy leaves for Putnam's encampment.

At Putnam's encampment, the general instructs Betsy to have Mary keep the British overnight. Once they are asleep, Betsy must light a signal lantern in a window for ten seconds to signal Putnam that it is safe to retreat. She agrees and exits. The generals, now drunk, agree to stay overnight against Howe's better judgment. Back at Inclenberg, Betsy seeks out Sir John. Fearing the unknown consequences of unfolding events, they assure each other of their love ("Here's a Kiss"). When the British soldiers are asleep, Betsy lights the signal. A gunshot breaks the window; it misses the lantern but wounds Betsy and awakens Sir John. Realizing that Betsy has signaled Putnam, Sir John shoots out the lantern, inadvertently completing the signal for Putnam to move his troops. The household is now astir and aware that Betsy has set Putnam's escape in motion. Howe threatens Mary with retribution as the generals storm out. Sir John rages at Betsy's additional betrayal. Betsy declares her love is true, but she cannot "sell her country for a kiss." She faints in his arms. Colonial troops enter and capture Sir John, the one redcoat in the house.

Act Three opens in 1783 after the war. At Inclenberg the women welcome their men home, including Jimmy. We learn that Betsy's bullet wound has healed, but she has pined for the missing Sir John for seven years. Harry Tryon and Jane, now newlyweds, ask for Mary's blessings. General George Washington makes a surprise visit to the house, thanking Mary personally for her loyalty and heroism. The enthralled household joyously escorts Washington as he leaves. A tearful Betsy sits alone inside the house when, in silence, Sir John enters. Mary stares in disbelief. They embrace. Curtain.

Critical reception

Favorable reviews and a respectable 286-show run produced a solid Broadway hit for its time and a sensation for Rodgers and Hart, newcomers to the world of full-length American book musicals. Among the most enthusiastic notices were Frank Vreeland's in the *Telegram* and unattributed reviews from the *New York Times* and the *Wall Street Journal*.

Fondly tongue-in-cheek, Vreeland's opening night review predicted (accurately) that Fields, Rodgers, and Hart would be "amply rewarde" for "deciding that all the American Revolution needed to make it famous was a musical comedy." Vreeland followed his off-handed remark with high praise for *Dearest Enemy*'s "enchantment" and "gracefulness," calling the show itself a commemoration of New York City worthy of the Murray legend. Despite "mishaps that bedeviled the performance" (apparently Sir John's effort to shoot out the lantern in Act Two hit a glitch), Vreeland reveled in the singing of leads Helen Ford and Charles Purcell as Betsy and Sir John, respectively (Vreeland 1925). The *New York Times* review lavished much of its praise upon Rodgers and Hart's score: "operetta with more than a chance flavor of Gilbert and Sullivan … Here we have duets, trios, and chorals that blend with the entire production. They are as uncommon as they are beautiful" (in Moore and O'Donoghue 2013).

The *Wall Street Journal* was particularly impressed with the "courage" required to produce a musical comedy on the basis of an incident in the Revolutionary War. Moreover, the reviewer asserted that the basic story was historically accurate, merely "distorted a bit for stage purposes" but handled "so skillfully and so respectfully as to make unusually valuable material for a libretto" ("General George Washington in Person" 1925).

Some opening night reviewers were less enthusiastic, although few if any dismissed the show outright. In his column for *The Graphic*, Walter Winchell complained that the action "sagged a bit" after the first act. Praising the lead actors (Ford and Purcell) and some of the tunes, Winchell told his readers that *Dearest Enemy* "is worth your attention," but did not think the show would thrive with the swells of the 1500-seat Knickerbocker Theatre. Writing in *The Eagle*, Arthur Pollock honored the score as "gracefully written" but sternly rebuked Fields for the libretto: "There is little or no humor in the [book], and what little noted was trivial, often out of place, and at times in decidedly bad taste" (Pollock 1925).

Unknown to opening night critics, of course, is that *Dearest Enemy* launched the careers of one the most important and prolific creative teams in Broadway history. As a result, Rodgers and Hart's more than twenty-five musicals receive new rounds of analysis in the ongoing assessment of their work. In the nearly 100 years since its premiere, *Dearest Enemy* has charted a course from the duo's successful maiden voyage to a disputed highpoint of their "early work" (roughly 1925 through 1931), to arguably the most obscure work by the legendary composer–lyricist team.

Although never revived on Broadway and rarely receiving a noteworthy American production since the NBC live television broadcast in 1955, *Dearest Enemy* now enjoys an improbable resurgence of critical interest, particularly in its score. In 2013, New World Records (a New York-based recording company dedicated to preserving important American music that is not otherwise available on commercial recording platforms) released a full cast, live in-studio recording of *Dearest Enemy*'s songs in original order. The recording was essentially a full in-studio performance of a newly reconstructed close-to-original score for which no prior recording or original manuscript existed. Perhaps to honor the Murrays' Irish heritage or to cut costs, or both, New World Records recorded the album in Dublin with the Orchestra of Ireland and a full cast of young, relatively unknown professional Irish musical theater performers. Highly enthusiastic reviews of the album shed new light on *Dearest Enemy*'s splendors. Reviewing the album for *Playbill*, Steven Suskin praised the recorded performance but dismissed the original musical as "a moderate success and the least interesting of Rodgers and Hart's musicals" (Suskin 2013). However, Darrel C. Karl, reviewing for the *Preserve Old Broadway* website, countered vigorously, calling *Dearest Enemy* "the best of the early Rodgers and Hart shows" (Carl 2013).

Many album reviews re-envisioned *Dearest Enemy* as important work beyond the context of Rodgers and Hart's early career. Kevin Clarke of the *Operetta Research Center* posited *Dearest Enemy* as a breakthrough piece on several levels: "*Dearest Enemy* went so far as to suggest that proper colonial women were interested in sex ... the mix of elements is fascinating, marking the important transition of American Operetta to modern musical comedy" (Clarke 2013). Bill White, reviewing the album for *Fanfare Archive*, places *Dearest Enemy* in a similar context:

> [It] is a truly transitional piece ... from old-world European style operetta to the new-world American style romantic Broadway musical. Gone are the gypsies, the Viennese waltzes, the old-world aristocrats (except for a stray British general or two) ... this little-known American musical by Broadway icons Rodgers and Hart deserves your attention.
>
> *White 2014*

Richard Barrios, long-time reviewer for the *Cast Album Recordings* website, found it inconceivable that anyone would dismiss the importance of the show: "To anyone wondering why it took nearly nine decades to come up with a complete *Dearest Enemy* ... A major work has been stirringly served here, as have Rodgers and Hart and, really, everyone who wants to know about the delights of 1920s musical theater" (Barrios 2013). Arguably the most remarkable reassessment in *Dearest Enemy*'s 2013 renaissance is Dominic Symonds' 2015 book on Rodgers and Hart's early work, *We'll Have Manhattan.* A twenty-two-page chapter devoted to *Dearest Enemy* views the show as Rodgers and Hart's platform for showing "their new approach to writing for the stage." Conceding heavy-handedness in Fields' script, Symonds cites key scenes in which Betsy's dialog with Sir John gives the female lead character "strength [and] dramatic depth … adding [heretofore unreachable] political clout to the events" she sets in motion. Symonds echoes the praise of recent critics who credit *Dearest Enemy* with freeing the American musical of its European operettic story traditions:

> *Dearest Enemy* is an enacted demonstration of Americanism in its presentation of a key historical moment [and] its characterization of key American figures [i.e., Mary Lindley Murray, George Washington, General Putnam] … It offered a chance for the cultural separation of American music from European to be symbolically staged.

Additionally, Symonds credits Rodgers and Hart among other tunesmiths of the 1920s with developing unique song forms for American musicals, specifically the "lyric binary chorus (AABA)," which is associated with the spontaneity between lovers. In *Dearest Enemy*, one of the first American musicals to adapt this form to the contours of its story, four such songs appear, including the show's biggest hit, "Here in My Arms." In so doing, according to Symonds, Rodgers and Hart help declare independence from Britain for the American showtune with *Dearest Enemy* leading the charge (Woods 2000 in Symonds 2015).

Historical accuracy and context

Howe's New York City campaign I: Staten Island, Brooklyn, and evacuation to Manhattan

General William Howe, Commander-in-Chief of British forces, had planned to seize New York City well before the colonies declared independence in early July, 1776. It is by coincidence that he arrived on Staten Island, five miles south of Manhattan, that very week to take up temporary residence near the city, plan the attack, and await the arrival of his full complement of soldiers and ships *en route* from New England.

Observing British troop and ship movements throughout the summer, General Washington knew in advance that Howe was preparing to attack New York City. Confident in the "agreeable spirit and willingness for action" among his men, Washington was nonetheless apprehensive about a strategy for defending Manhattan Island (Washington 1776). With an army of 20,000, Washington would have to secure Manhattan's twenty-three square miles of land, two long river shorelines, four smaller offshore islands, plus the region (now borough) of Brooklyn on southwestern Long Island, one mile across the East River (Procknow 2017).

Washington placed most of his troops throughout Manhattan, from the New York City center (then concentrated in lower Manhattan) up through the woodlands, manors, and farm areas of what are now midtown and upper Manhattan. He also stationed several thousand troops in two areas of Brooklyn: Gowanus Heights (now Prospect Heights) in South Brooklyn and a larger force headquartered in Brooklyn Heights, three miles north.

Howe had reasons to bide his time. He was assembling a presumably invincible amphibious and land attack: 30,000 troops, twelve warships (each with thirty or more ship-to-shore artillery guns), and 300 support vessels operated by a naval command of 10,000 men (Procknow 2017; McCullough 2005). Howe's patience was abetted by the disproportionate number of British loyalists living on Staten Island and throughout New York City (compared to decidedly more pro-rebellion Philadelphia and Boston). Loyalists often doted on British officials in the colonies, providing hospitality, supplies, and other amenities. Prosperous loyalists eagerly welcomed the British elite into their business and social circles, invitations General Howe was known to encourage enthusiastically. New York City was a loyalist hub.

Howe's military conquest of New York City unfolded in two major advances: the Battle of Brooklyn (August 27–29) and the invasion of Kips Bay (September 15) in Manhattan's East River shoreline—just south of where the United Nations building stands. In the pre-dawn darkness of August 27, Howe's columns attacked American troops at Gowanus Heights. Initially, American forces held their ground, but Howe sent a large force under General Henry Clinton (1730–90) to outflank the Americans, heavily outnumbering them and trapping them in a pincher movement. Learning of the attack, Washington brought reinforcements across the East River to Brooklyn but saw immediately that the British had routed his Gowanus forces. Washington ordered an immediate retreat of all Brooklyn troops northward to their headquarters at Brooklyn Heights.

The American casualty count on August 27 represented Washington's largest single-day defeat of the entire war: 300 troops killed, 800 wounded, and over 1,000 imprisoned or missing, compared to British losses of sixty-four killed, 293 wounded, and thirty-one imprisoned or missing ("Brooklyn [and] Long Islan" n.d.).

Howe immediately moved and stationed his land forces northward within a mile of Washington's Brooklyn Heights encampment, pinning the American forces against the East River. Sudden heavy rain and fog temporarily disabled British ships and may well have disincentivized Howe from launching a second, and likely fatal, land attack against the huddled Americans. Apparently, Howe was satisfied to keep Washington's troops entrapped for the time being. Having no way to retake Brooklyn, Washington planned a secret evacuation to Manhattan. After midnight on August 29, with fog obscuring their movements, American boats secretly evacuated all surviving colonial troops to Manhattan. By daybreak the "trappe" American forces at Brooklyn Heights had escaped.

Washington's successful evacuation of Brooklyn Heights, while a temporary salve to the spirits of his defeated army, could not offset the enormity of his casualty count. Moreover, Howe now had control of Brooklyn and the East River, leaving Manhattan more vulnerable than ever.

Howe's New York campaign II: Kips Bay, Midtown Manhattan, and Mrs. Murray's parlor

For two weeks following the Battle of Brooklyn, Washington and his generals, now headquartered eleven miles north of lower Manhattan in Harlem Heights, debated whether to abandon New York City altogether or defend it against Howe's imminent attack. Preparing for battle, Washington spread his thin forces throughout Manhattan, stationing 3,500–4,000 troops under General Putnam to guard the urban center in lower Manhattan and distributing his remaining forces throughout middle and upper Manhattan (Gabriel 2012). Now in a considerably strong position, Howe met with delegates from the Continental Congress on September 11 (including Benjamin Franklin and John Adams). He urged them to cease their violent rebellion and abandon their pursuit of independence, a proposal the delegates rejected.

On the morning of September 15, Howe launched an attack at Kips Bay, located between Putnam's troops in lower Manhattan and Washington's Harlem Heights headquarters. Before daybreak, Howe had positioned five warships broadside in Kips Bay just offshore, artillery guns aimed directly at American makeshift defenses. American troops awoke to find themselves staring down the barrels of 100 artillery guns ominously pointed right at them. By mid-morning, eighty British flatboats carrying 4,000 British troops and Hessian mercenary forces sailed quietly into Kips Bay among the warships. At approximately 11:00 a.m., Howe shattered the eerie silence at Kips Bay with a thunderous hour-long artillery bombardment of the shoreline (McCullough 2005).

The massive artillery assault destroyed the small American military encampment on shore, blasting bodies and fortifications in violent bursts of gun shells and beach dirt. Reportedly, American forces did not fire a single shot of any consequence and fled in panic. Under General Clinton, British troops and Hessian mercenaries swept into Manhattan, meeting no resistance. On Howe's orders, they marched half a mile inland from Kips Bay and encamped at the 30-acre estate of Robert and Mary Lindley Murray at Inclenberg (near today's intersection of 37th Street and Park Avenue).

Washington heard the Kips Bay assault from Harlem Heights and rode on horseback to the scene. As one historian noted: "It was everything he had feared and worse" (McCullough 2005). Washington's troops were swept up in a contagion of panic, abandoning positions, and frantically retreating north toward headquarters upon seeing enemy soldiers or just watching their own terrorized compatriots retreating past them. At his aides' insistence, Washington also returned to Harlem Heights once Manhattan was lost—a realization self-evident within three hours of Howe's first artillery shots.

Despite objections from General Clinton, Howe held his newly-landed Manhattan troops in stasis near the Murray estate. Clinton wanted to capitalize immediately on the victory and attack Putnam's troops still languishing in lower Manhattan. A quick attack or even a fortified blockade of north–south land routes would permanently cut off Putnam from Washington's headquarters and deliver a crippling if not fatal blow to the American army. Howe said no and kept his land forces inactive from about 2:00 p.m. to 5:00 p.m. that afternoon. During the lull, Putnam began leading his troops north, safely bypassing resting British and Hessian forces, and rejoined Washington's main forces at Harlem Heights.

Howe's rationale for allowing Putnam time to escape certain defeat is a subject of historical debate to this day. It is widely believed, although not entirely settled, that during the late afternoon and early evening of September 15, General Howe and an entourage of British leaders were entertained by Mrs. Mary Lindley Murray at her home at Inclenberg. *Dearest Enemy* celebrates the farthest reaches of that legend, namely that quite beyond entertaining Howe and company, Mrs. Murray saved Putnam's troops by knowingly charming the British leaders into docility and inaction. The musical revels in the story's potential for romance, intrigue, and outlandish exaggeration.

Dearest Enemy *and Howe's visit to Mrs. Murray's estate: facts, speculation, and romantic license*

The setting, time, location, and overall battle history presented in *Dearest Enemy* are accurate in most respects. Set in Inclenberg on the afternoon of September 15, 1776, the show's timing of the British assault at Kips Bay is historically correct, as are the first act's references to the British victory in Brooklyn two weeks earlier. The scenes of women sewing uniforms for men away at war and delivering supplies to soldiers on the frontlines of battle also reflect realities of the war. The show's creators—lyricist Hart in particular—loved writing about New York City, and the show's numerous geographical references to what was then America's second most-populated city (Philadelphia was first), over and above their entertainment value, provide creditable information for geography buffs and local history enthusiasts.

Howe's decision to hold back his invading force at Inclenberg rather than attack Putnam's vulnerable troops encamped in lower Manhattan is entirely factual. However, Howe's motives for ordering his troops to hold back remain the subject of speculation beyond *Dearest Enemy's* conjecture that Howe fell victim to Mrs. Murray's wine service and devious charms. Historians further concur that Putnam successfully led his troops out of harm's way on the same day that Howe rested his troops. But the question of whether there exists a causal relationship among Howe's respite, Mrs. Murray's hospitality, and Putnam's escape elicits competing responses.

Although there are no known, reliable eyewitness accounts of Howe's stopover at Mrs. Murray's on September 15, the event enters historical discussion via American army physician James Thacher's well-regarded *An Army Doctor's American Revolution Journal 1775–83,* published in 1823. In the September 20 entry, Thacher, in a detailed and largely verified account of Howe's invasion, reports learning from field troops that Howe's generals, "seeing no prospect of engaging our troops halted their own and repaired to the home of a Mr. Robert Murray … Mrs. Murray treated them with cake and wine and they were induced to tarry two hours or more." Thacher offers some details of the party and observes that it is "almost a common saying among our officers that Mrs. Murray saved [Putnam's] army" (Thacher 2019).

Notwithstanding the regard Thacher's *Medical Journal* has earned as a valuable primary source, some historians view his report of the social gathering as undocumented anecdotes rather than an historical occurrence. Others accept Thacher's account on the strength of corroborated, if circumstantial, contextual evidence: Howe did order a cessation of fighting and directed his troops to settle near the Murray estate; and he was known to enjoy socializing with wealthy Americans, especially aristocratic women. Furthermore, Robert Murray was a prosperous shipping merchant who traded with Americans, British colonial officials, and European merchants. The Murrays were held in high regard by British officials in New York as well as pro-British Tory loyalists, who wielded considerable political power in the city. Moreover, a social call upon an influential local citizen, made on the heels of a violent takeover of their city, would constitute a sensible diplomatic gesture on Howe's part.

While confident that Mrs. Murray entertained Howe's leadership entourage that afternoon, many acknowledge that making the case for her as a spy for Washington is a challenge. Mrs. Murray may well have sympathized with the rebellion (as Thacher suggests), but British officials in America were accustomed to engaging civilly with political adversaries and commonly socialized with well-heeled aristocrats with pro-rebel sympathies—a point the musical makes clear. Far less likely is the legend that proffers Mrs. Murray knowingly subverting Howe's military strategy with liquor and charm, improvising her ruse as relatives and servants pick up intelligence about Putnam's vulnerability from loose-lipped guests and bored British troops hanging around the estate with nothing to do. It is a remotely possible scenario but unverifiable and a considerable stretch.

Very likely, Howe took his rest at Mrs. Murray's parlor, having no intention of further engaging in battle that day. He had fulfilled his objective to secure the city, doing so in short order with little human or material cost to his command. He had no incentive to further endanger or tire his men. Awaiting an additional several thousand troops to come ashore, he might reasonably have chosen to rest his troops for the beginning of what would become Britain's seven-year occupation of the city.

The creators of *Dearest Enemy* hardly let historical fact stand in the way of the story, and some noteworthy historical information "died in battle" during the show. The musical expands Howe's afternoon social call to a full night's sleepover, so Putnam's troops could escape in darkness. During the party, generals Washington and Putnam, encamped approximately seven miles north and four south, respectively, of the Murray estate, miraculously communicate via signals and messages relayed by Mrs. Murray, her fictitious niece Betsy, and other household couriers. While devious flirting between an elegant British general and a charming American wife and mother held narrative appeal, on September 15, 1776, Mary Lindley was fifty years old, the mother of twelve children, and—as she had been all her life—three years older than General Howe. Bowing to chronology, *Dearest Enemy* relegates Howe and Mrs. Murray to polite exchanges and some mild woman-versus-man political repartee. By default, the musical's principal love story unfolds as a classic "forbidden" love affair between Mary's Irish-born, fervent revolutionist youthful niece Betsy Burke and the equally fictitious twenty-something Captain Sir John Copeland, a member of Howe's entourage.

Minor but notable departures from reality also include the dispositions of General Howe and General Clinton. In the musical, General Howe is the Brits' taskmaster, fearful of socializing too long and eager to get back to soldiering, while General Clinton complains of battle fatigue and cajoles Howe into prolonging their stay at Mrs. Murray's. In fact, General Clinton advised Howe to follow up with an attack on Putnam, while Howe insisted on ceasing military action for the afternoon. Furthermore, there is no record of George Washington ever having made a personal visit to thank Mrs. Murray or, for that matter, ever having written her a thank you letter.

On the question of whether the party ever occurred at all, Mary Lindley Murray gets something akin to the last word. In 1903, a New York City chapter of the Daughters of the American Revolution dedicated a plaque honoring Mary Lindley Murray for "services rendered her country" entertaining General Howe at her home and allowing General Putnam to escape. The plaque rests in a traffic island at the intersection of 37th Street and Park Avenue, "her home at this site" ("Mary Lindley Murray" n.d.).

Thomas A. Greenfield

Further reading

Ashworth, Margaret. 2019. "The Melody Makers 4: Rodgers and Hart," https://conservative woman.co.uk/the-melody-makers-4-rodgers-and-hart-part-i/.

Barrios, Richard. 2013. "*Dearest Enemy*, Studio Cast, 2013." *Cast Album Reviews*. 2013, http://castalbumreviews.com/category/reviews-by-show-name/d-f/.

"Brooklyn [and] Long Island." n.d. *American Battlefield Trust*, Washington, D.C., https:// www.battlefields.org/learn/revolutionary-war/battles/brooklyn.

Carl, Darrel C. 2013. "Dearest Enemy." *Preserve Old Broadway*, November 6, 2013, www.preserveoldbroadway.org/richard-rodgersdearestenemy-new-world-records-80749-2/.

Clarke, Kevin. 2013. "Rodgers & Hart's 'Native Operetta': A New 'Dearest Enemy' Cast Album." Operetta Research Center, October 27, 2013, http://operetta-research-center.org/rodgers-harts-native-operetta-dearest-enemy/.

Cohen, Steven. n.d. "Rodgers and Hart Reconsidered or 'Taken to Hart.'" *The Cultural Critic*, https://theculturalcritic.com/rodgers-hart-reconsidered/.

Fields, Herbert, Lorenz Hart, and Richard Rodgers. 1925. *Dearest Enemy*. Archived Typed Script. New York: New York Public Library at Lincoln Center.

Gabriel, Michael. 2012. "Battle of Kip's Bay." In *The Digital Encyclopedia of George Washington*, edited by James P. Ambuske. Mount Vernon, VA: Mount Vernon Ladies' Association. https://www.mountvernon.org/library/digitalhistory/digital-encyclopedia/article/battle-of-kips-bay/.

"General George Washington in Person." 1925. *Wall Street Journal*, September 21, 1925.

Hurwitz, Noah. 2016. "Legend of Murray Hill Tea Party Persists 240 Years After Battle of Brooklyn," www.dnainfo.com/new-york/20160826/murray-hill/legend-of-murray-hill-tea-party-persists-240-years-after-battle-of-brooklyn.

"Mary Lindley Murray." n.d. *NYC Parks*, www.nycgovparks.org/parks/park-avenue-malls-m060a/monuments/1076.

McCullough, David. 2005. *1776*. New York: Simon & Schuster.

Moore, Larry and Sean O'Donoghue. 2013. *Dearest Enemy: An American Musical Comedy*. Cast Recording Prod. By Judith Sherman. New World Records. October 8, 2013. CD.

Pollock, Arthur. 1925 (2019). "Plays and Things." In *The Complete Book of 1920s Broadway Musicals*, edited by Dan Dietz, 272–3. Lanham, MD: Rowman & Littlefield.

Procknow, Gene. 2017. "Did Generals Mismanage the Battle of Brooklyn?" *Journal of the American Revolution*, April 20, 2017, https://allthingsliberty.com/2017/04/generals-mismanage-battle-brooklyn/.

Rutkow, I. M. 2001. "James Thacher and His Military Journal during the American Revolutionary War." *Archives of Surgery* 136, no. 7: 837, doi:10.1001/archsurg.136.7.837.

Suskin, Steven. 2013. "On the Record: Rodgers and Hart's Early Musical *Dearest Enemy*." *Playbill*, October 27, 2013, www.playbill.com/article/on-the-record-rodgers-and-harts-early-musical-dearest-enemy-com-211111.

Symonds, Dominic. 2015. *We'll Have Manhattan: The Early Work of Rodgers and Hammerstein*. New York: Oxford University Press.

Thacher, James. 2019. *An Army Doctor's American Revolution Journal 1775–83*. Mineola, NY: Dover Publications.

Vreeland, Frank. 1925. "Dearest Enemy: Improving the American Revolution with a Charming Musical Comedy." *New York Telegram*, September 19, 2015.

Washington, George. 1776. "Letter from George Washington to John Hancock, July 3, 1776." *National Archives: Founders Online*, https://founders.archives.gov/documents/Washington/03-05-02-012.

White, Bill. 2014. "*Fanfare (Archive)*—Review by Bill White." In "Richard Rodgers, *Dearest Enemy*, New World Records 80749-2." *Preserve Old Broadway*, https:// www.preserveoldbroadway.org/richard-rodgers-dearest-enemy-new-world-records-80749-2/.

Winchell, Walter. 1925. "Dearest Enemy Arrives at the Knickerbocker Theater." *The Graphic*, September 19, 1925.

Wood, Graham. 2000. "The Development of Song Forms in the Broadway and Hollywood Musicals of Richard Rodgers, 1919–1943." Doctoral dissertation, University of Minnesota.

CHAPTER 9
FALSETTOS (1992)

Music and Lyrics by William Finn (1952–)
Book by William Finn and James Lapine (1949–)
World Premiere: *March of the Falsettos* (one-act musical), May 20–September 26, 1981
Falsettoland (one-act musical), June 28–August 12, 1990. Playwrights Horizons, Off-Broadway, New York City
Broadway Premiere: *Falsettos* (combined two-act musical), April 29, 1992–June 27, 1993. John Golden Theatre

Songs

Act One (*March of the Falsettos*)
"Four Jews in a Room Bitching"
"A Tight-Knit Family"
"Love Is Blin"
"Thrill of First Love"
"Marvin at the Psychiatrist"
"My Father's a Homo"
"Everyone Tells Jason to See a Psychiatrist"
"This Had Better Come to a Stop"
"I'm Breaking Down"
"Please Come to Our House"
"Jason's Therapy"
"A Marriage Proposal"
"A Tight-Knit Family" (Reprise)
"Trina's Song"
"March of the Falsettos"
"Trina's Song" (Reprise)
"The Chess Game"
"Making a Home"
"The Games I Play"
"Marvin Hits Trina"
"I Never Wanted to Love You"
"Father to Son"

Act Two (*Falsettoland*)
"Falsettolan"
"The Year of the Child"
"Miracle of Judaism"
"The Baseball Game"
"A Day in Falsettolan"
"Racquetball"
"The Fight"
"Everyone Hates His Parents"
"What More Can I Say?"
"Something Bad Is Happening"
"Second Racquetball"
"Holding to the Ground"
"Days Like This"
"Canceling the Bar Mitzvah"
"Unlikely Lovers"
"Another Miracle of Judaism"
"Something Bad Is Happening" (Reprise)
"You Gotta Die Sometime"
"Jason's Bar Mitzvah"
"What Would I Do?"
"Falsettolan" (Reprise)

Overview

Falsettos (1992) is a Broadway musical comprising the second and third installments of the "Marvin trilogy" of one-acts (or "Marvin plays") written by William Finn (book, music, lyrics) and directed by James Lapine, who also co-wrote the book. Set in 1979, *March of the Falsettos* (1981) explores the domestic adventures of a middle-aged Jewish man in New York City named Marvin, his ex-wife Trina, son Jason, lover Whizzer Brown, and psychiatrist Mendel. The brood expands in *Falsettoland* (1990), set in 1981–2, to include Marvin's lesbian neighbors, Dr. Charlotte, an internist, and Cordelia, a chef. The combined musical *Falsettos* focuses on character attitudes and relationships rather than politics, and specific cultural references are few. By dramatizing the effect of societal shifts through individual lives, each part reveals the emotional authenticity of its historical moment, especially concerning aspects of homosexuality and social norms, heretofore largely unexplored in American popular culture in general, much less on Broadway.

By the end of the 1970s, pop-culture psychoanalysis was ubiquitous. Finn was intimately familiar with its effect on secular, middle-class, New York City Jewish culture, which he mined for comedy by employing and upending familiar tropes. The first Marvin play, *In Trousers*, depicted the mid-1970s quest of a wealthy, professional, Jewish man for self-discovery and sexual awakening with both women and men. The four principal male characters begin *March of the Falsettos*, setting a knowing tone for the neuroses on full display for the audience's entertainment.

The musical notably presents homosexuality as normal rather than a source of shame or conflict typical of many previous gay-themed plays. Finn chose to depict an idealized social environment for his gay characters, one that fully embraced the significant strides for gay and lesbian rights and recognition during the decade since transgender women and others took a stand against police harassment at the Stonewall Inn in New York's Greenwich Village in 1969. In the wake of Stonewall, gay rights groups multiplied and began exerting pressure on political and business leaders to end discrimination in housing, employment, and public accommodation. Gay men, lesbians, and other queer people made their presence known not just in New York and San Francisco—cities with well-known, self-identified queer communities—but also in Chicago, Boston, and even smaller communities across the country.

By the mid-1970s, homosexuality had secured a prominent, though often controversial, place in mainstream American popular culture and political discourse. Fully dimensional gay and lesbian characters started appearing in movies, novels, and television, along with real lesbian and gay guests on talk shows, which brought homosexuality out of the shadows and into public discussion. Perhaps the most significant event of the decade for gay rights occurred in 1973, when the American Psychological Association removed homosexuality from its list of disorders in the *Diagnostic and Statistical Manual* (DSM). Amid persistent societal resistance to queer people, often fueled by religious conservatives who considered homosexuality sinful, the medical establishment had recognized queer sexualities as normal.

Rather than engage the swirling political debate about homosexuality, Finn chose to dramatize its normalcy, and the normal problems that come with it. Marvin's narcissistic want of it all ultimately drives everyone away from him, save his son Jason, with whom he reconciles in the final number of *March of the Falsettos*. After the one-act musical's 1981 Off-Broadway premiere launched Finn into theater celebrity, he reflected that he and Marvin were similar only in certain respects, like being "very Jewish," but what fascinated Finn about the character enough to write a second musical was: "By trying to be nice, he is stepping over everyone, dodging and bumping into the world" (Blau 1981).

It would be nearly a decade after collaborating on *March of the Falsettos* that Finn and Lapine would revisit Marvin's world in *Falsettoland*. The liberated exuberance that characterized gay life in New York City during the 1970s within a few years had given way to the devastation of AIDS that dominated gay life and politics through the 1980s. This next Marvin play could not avoid that grim reality. Finn wanted to weave a bar mitzvah and a death into the story, while Lapine was focused on tone, keeping the material light without undermining the seriousness of the moment or overindulging sentimentality. He told the *New York Times*, "The world is a darker, much more serious place than it was a decade ago. The downside of writing about AIDS is that everyone has an opinion of what you're supposed to say. This show [*Falsettoland*] is not out to educate an audience about AIDS, it's out to educate an audience about people" (Harris 1990).

Unlike *March of the Falsettos*, which was an exploration of contemporary life in New York City, *Falsettoland* would be a period piece, beginning two years later, in 1981. Ronald Reagan is the newly elected president of the United States. Marvin lives alone and has not seen Whizzer in two years, but the two reconcile during the play. Marvin divides custody of Jason, now twelve years old, with Trina and Mendel, who are now married. The source of dramatic conflict in this play is Jason's forthcoming bar mitzvah, about which everyone has a different opinion. But the play's historical context is rooted in Dr. Charlotte's observation that "something bad" is happening to gay men in New York City. They do not get better and no one knows why, including the physicians treating them. When Whizzer falls fatally ill with this disease, every member of the audience and no character in the play understands it to be AIDS.

It is precisely the contrast between the audience's foreknowledge and the characters' naivete of the forces at work upon them that gives *Falsettoland* its didactic power. Theatergoers in 1990 and beyond, entered armed with knowledge of the massive numbers of AIDS-related deaths in the United States (over 400,000 by 2001 ["20 Years of AIDS" 2001]), a pervasive cultural stigmatizing of AIDS victims, and years of political conflict over whether federal and local governments should even consider AIDS a public health issue, much less support research into it.

The premiere of *Falsettoland* in 1990, reunited at Playwrights Horizons the actors who originated Marvin (Michael Rupert), Whizzer (Stephen Bogardus), and Mendel (Chip Zien) after "a sobering nine years," according to Rupert. "How often, in musical theater, do you get a chance to deal with material like this that has so many levels, and how often do you get wonderful music like this? I think it's a show that needs to be seen. And I don't think I ever felt that about a show before" (Collins 1990). Off-Broadway audiences and critics responded similarly. The 1980s had delivered a dramatic reversal of attitude and fortune for the gay community from the decade before. *Falsettoland* offered audiences an opportunity to remember the light-hearted neuroses, mourn the loss of innocence, and find solidarity to continue fighting.

March of the Falsettos and *Falsettoland* were first presented in a single evening at Connecticut's Hartford Stage in the fall of 1991 in a production directed by Graciela Daniele. The only alteration of the shows' original text was the addition of the song "I'm Breaking Down" from *In Trousers*, which framed Trina with a more rueful presence than the resilient comedian of past versions.

The following year, with Lapine back at the helm and further trims to the material, the two-act musical now called *Falsettos* premiered on Broadway at the John Golden Theatre. Positive reviews and warm public reception led to seven 1992 Tony Award nominations and wins for Book of a Musical and Original Musical Score, cementing the place of *Falsettos* in the musical theater canon.

Although honest depictions of contemporary gay male life had been introduced to Broadway a decade earlier via the Tony Award-winning writing of Harvey Fierstein in *Torch Song Trilogy* (1982) and *La Cage aux Folles* (1983), *Falsettos* was the first Broadway show to depict AIDS. In the 1990s, the subject would come to prominence on Broadway with two ensuing landmark productions: Tony Kushner's two-part play *Angels in America* (1993) and Jonathan Larson's musical *Rent* (1996).

Nearly a quarter-century after its Broadway premiere, *Falsettos* was revived in 2016 at the Walter Kerr Theatre by its original producer at Playwrights Horizons, André Bishop, who was now running the non-profit Lincoln Center Theatre. James Lapine returned to direct a brand-new show and cast. Although the events of

1979 and 1981–2 were by then even further in the past, the human truths explored in *Falsettos* found enduring appeal for critics and audiences.

Plot synopsis

Act I: *March of the Falsettos*

1979. The four male characters—protagonist Marvin, his ten-year-old son Jason, psychiatrist Mendel, and Marvin's boyfriend Whizzer—are introduced amid an argument ("Four Jews in a Room Bitching"). Despite resistance from the others, Marvin espouses incorporating Whizzer into a new stasis of domestic bliss with his ex-wife Trina and Jason ("A Tight-Knit Family"). When Trina crumbles under the feelings of failure, Marvin encourages her to visit Mendel, his psychiatrist, who instantly falls in love with her ("Love Is Blin"). Meanwhile, Marvin and Whizzer worry about what will sustain their relationship when the physical attraction wanes ("Thrill of First Love").

Emceed by Whizzer, the interlude "Marvin at the Psychiatrist: A Three-Part Mini-Opera" depicts Marvin's frustration with Whizzer, Mendel's interest in Trina, and the growing distance between Marvin and his son. As Jason withdraws with the anxiety that he may inherit Marvin's sexuality ("My Father's a Homo"), Marvin and Trina agree that Jason should see Mendel for therapy, which he resists until consulting Whizzer ("Everyone Tells Jason to See a Psychiatrist"). When Whizzer reluctantly becomes more prominent at home and marginalizes Trina, pent-up frustrations explode toward Marvin ("This Had Better Come to a Stop"). Trina continues to dissemble despite attempts to maintain normalcy and corral Jason's behavior ("I'm Breaking Down"). In desperation, she invites Mendel over for dinner and therapy ("Please Come to Our House"). Mendel's presence woos Trina and appeases Jason ("Jason's Therapy"). The unorthodox arrangement becomes a pattern, and Mendel asks Trina to marry him ("A Marriage Proposal"). With family and psychiatrist slipping from his control, Marvin panics ("A TightKnit Family" Reprise). Although she realizes that Mendel is no less flawed than Marvin and that she is exhausted living in a man's world, Mendel's devotion fulfills her need to be needed. The four male characters sing an anthem to the varieties of masculinity ("March of the Falsettos").

Marvin attempts to teach Whizzer how to play chess, but underlying resentment boils over ("The Chess Game"). Trina and Mendel move in together ("Making a Home"). As Whizzer packs to move out, he contemplates his life with Marvin ("The Games I Play"). Trina and Mendel's wedding announcement sends Marvin over the edge. He confronts Trina, blames her for ruining their family, and slaps her ("Marvin Hits Trina"). Shocked by the physical assault into stillness, Trina then gathers her strength and dignity to let Marvin go as everyone reflects on the risk of pain and loss that comes with loving ("I Never Wanted to Love You"). His relationships with Whizzer and Trina tattered, Marvin finds solace in Jason's relief in his attraction to girls and shares his unwavering love and support for the boy ("Father to Son").

Act II: *Falsettoland*

Mendel welcomes the audience back. The setting is 1981, two years later. The cast of characters now includes lesbian neighbors: internist Dr. Charlotte and chef Cordelia. Marvin, who now splits custody of Jason with Trina and Mendel, still longs for Whizzer but realizes that he needs to move on. Trina arrives to pick up Jason and announces that it is time to start planning his bar mitzvah, likely the last pleasant thing this ex-couple will do. Amid their instant bickering, Mendel suggests a simple celebration, which they, along with Cordelia, reject in favor of a big affair ("The Year of the Child").

At his Jewish Little League baseball game, Jason contemplates which girls to invite to his bar mitzvah ("Miracle of Judaism"). Secretly invited by Jason, Whizzer appears in the stands to Trina's dismay and Marvin's pleasant surprise. Whizzer coaches Jason on batting while Marvin musters the courage to ask him out ("The Baseball Game").

A three-part interlude ("A Day in Falsettolan") depicts Mendel listening to a yuppie patient blather about upper-middle-class problems; Trina jazzercizing while contemplating why Marvin and Whizzer getting back together upsets her; and Cordelia discussing "nouvelle bar mitzvah cuisine" with Dr. Charlotte, who is relieved by the rare day of someone not dying at the hospital. Meanwhile, Whizzer beats Marvin soundly at sports ("Racquetball"). It's a day when life is wonderful. The conflict quickly resumes as Marvin and Trina argue about the bar mitzvah ("The Fight"), which makes Jason want to call it off. Mendel consoles him by pointing out that his feelings are normal ("Everyone Hates His Parents"). Watching Whizzer sleep, Marvin is overcome by feelings of love. Dr. Charlotte reports that gay men are coming to the hospital with an unknown illness ("Something Bad Is Happening"). Whizzer collapses during a game ("Second Racquetball").

Trina finds herself surprisingly upset by Whizzer's condition ("Holding to the Groun"). In the hospital room, with everyone gathered to cheer up Whizzer, Jason is the only one who tells the truth about how bad he looks ("Days Like This"). Amid the reality of Whizzer's worsening condition, Mendel and Trina give Jason an option ("Canceling the Bar Mitzvah") and he storms off, upset. Marvin, Cordelia, and Dr. Charlotte gather by Whizzer's bed and affirm their commitment to one another ("Unlikely Lovers"). Jason promises God that if Whizzer gets better, he will follow through with the bar mitzvah ("Another Miracle of Judaism"). Dr. Charlotte warns Marvin about his own health risk ("Something Bad Is Happening" Reprise). Whizzer accepts his terminal illness with dignity ("You Gotta Die Sometime").

Jason decides to celebrate his big event in Whizzer's hospital room ("Jason's Bar Mitzvah" Reprise). At its conclusion, Whizzer collapses and is rushed out, followed by everyone but Marvin. Alone, he wonders what life would be like if he had not loved Whizzer. Appearing in memory as he did at the top of the show, Whizzer asks if Marvin has regrets. Marvin responds that he would do it all over again ("What Would I Do?"). Whizzer fades, Marvin's family and friends enter, and he collapses in grief in their arms. Mendel steps forward and declares that we must take a stand ("Falsettolan" Reprise).

Critical reception

The 1981 Off-Broadway premiere of *March of the Falsettos* was widely praised by critics, sparking a flood of inquiries from commercial producers eager to transfer the show to Broadway. The *New York Times*'s chief theater critic Frank Rich—who would become a champion of the Marvin plays in the decade to come, as well as one of the LGBT community's most outspoken straight allies—was ebullient about twenty-nine-year-old Finn's compositional talent: "The songs are so fresh that the show is only a few bars old before one feels the unmistakable, revivifying charge of pure talent … with original, unpredictable melodies that run from melancholy ballads to eccentric comic riffs" (Rich 1981). The *New Yorker*'s John Simon said the show "augurs well for its sole author, William Finn" and lauded "the extremely clever staging of James Lapine" (Simon 1981). Despite this recognition, Finn was skeptical about *March of the Falsettos*'s success, believing it to be inferior to his earlier unheralded works. Finn was depressed by invitations to write new shows based on rave reviews, telling one critic inquiring about more musicals about Marvin, "I've had it with him for a while" (Blau 1981).

When *Falsettoland* finally premiered Off-Broadway in 1990, the *New York Times* was somewhat less exuberant about this musical than its predecessor, a shift in critical reception that reflected both content and context: "While Mr. Finn is blissfully back in full voice after several projects of esthetic drift, that voice has inevitably been tempered by time; some of his ethnic humor seems a bit strained even as his sentiments about romance in hard times are more deeply felt" (Rich 1990). At least one scholar has argued that while the New York reviews fell evenly into positive, mixed, and negative categories, critics generally failed to see beyond the surface of stereotypes to the underlying human condition Finn and Lapine were attempting to reveal (Smart 1996). Despite this, the *Chicago Tribune* declared *Falsettoland* "one of the highlights of the New York season … a skillful and provocative work, its story filled with life in the midst of dying and its sadness pierced with the quick tempos and bright lyrics of Finn's songs" (Christiansen 1990).

The following year, when director Graciela Daniele first combined *March of the Falsettos* and *Falsettoland* in one evening, Rich's enthusiasm for the project returned in full force, now with more historical perspective. His *New York Times* review opens as follows:

> It is not news that the history of American musicals in the 1980s begins and ends Off Broadway at Playwrights Horizons, with a pair of startling one-act musicals by William Finn that bracketed the decade, "March of the Falsettos" (1981) and "Falsettolan" (1990). But it was a secret, until now, that the two 'Falsetto' shows, fused together on a single bill, form a whole that is not only larger than the sum of its parts but is also more powerful than any other American musical of its day.
>
> *Rich 1991*

Fueled by the *New York Times* stamp of approval in Hartford, *Falsettos* gathered momentum and investment to greet audiences on Broadway the following spring, directed once again by James Lapine and reuniting much of the original Off-Broadway cast. The final show to open in the 1991–2 season, *Falsettos* provided a welcome breath of fresh air for theater critics. *USA Today* raved that the combination of one-act musicals was "much more than the sum of their parts … The characters have a three-dimensional quality that musicals rarely achieve … All told, this is a musical and Broadway landmark" (Stearns 1992). The *New York Post* observed: "[T]o label this a musical about gay life in modern times is to shortchange its tremendous appeal as a masterly feat of comic storytelling and as a visionary musical theater work" (Gerard 1992).

Amid the expected kudos from the *New York Times*, Rich's review of the Broadway production brought attention to the role of historical context in meaning-making and the musical's origination eleven years earlier, when "nothing so bad was happening … the high spirits of that moment pump through Act I of 'Falsettos' as if pouring out of a time capsule. Act II plays out in another key, as lovers 'no longer come and go' but 'live and die fortissimo",' (Rich 1992). *New York Newsday* observed both craft evolution and historical perspective: "As one might expect, the first act doesn't have the lyrical maturity or rich sadness of Finn's later writing, but somehow, the early part—a time capsule of lusty innocence and luxurious narcissism—resonates through what we know today" (Winer 1992).

The Broadway reviews were not all raves, however, as some critics who were not taken by the show's message or historical importance took shots at Finn's writing and a cynical approach to the whole endeavor. *New York* magazine saw the work as pandering and lacking in craft: "With music that is largely Sondheim derivative, lyrics that are barely serviceable, and drama that consists of pushing the right buttons, *Falsettos*—with the added virtue of being relatively cheap to mount—is a triumph of packaging and salesmanship not to be confused with art" (Simon 1992). The *Daily News* asserted: "Finn's chattering, clattering score 'could drive a person crazy,' to quote a Sondheim lyric 'Falsettos,' too sweet and sugary by far, rings false" (Watt 1992).

Still other reviews, neither raves nor pans, criticized the musical's depiction of female characters and gender roles. The *Wall Street Journal* buttoned its mostly complimentary assessment of the show and cast with, "That the women come off less well may be due in part to the fact that their roles are not as well rounde" (Wilson

1992). *Newsday* pointed out an unsatisfying—and perhaps not fully examined—heteronormativity amid the homosexuality in *Falsettos*: "Finn and Lapine have a disconcerting '50s idea of couples; straight or gay, there's always one decorative wifey-poo who cooks and nests" (Winer 1992).

When *Falsettos* was revived on Broadway in 2016, the *Chicago Tribune* hailed the "musical that throbs with passion and compassion, a masterwork strong enough to bare formative comparison to the work of Stephen Sondheim, but a whole lot more cuddly of a show," but noted that the production "cannot quite lock down on the love, and the mutual dependency, that keeps everyone alive" (Jones 2016). The *Daily News* likewise recognized its enduring power: "While things get a bit heavy-handed as one man's life ends while another begins at a bar mitzvah, it's hard to grouse when you're being moved to tears" (Dziemianowicz 2016). The long-time *Newsday* theater critic, who had also reviewed *Falsettos*' Broadway premiere, noted: "The show remains brave and hilarious, a charming and deeply moving treasure" (Winer 2016). Although Frank Rich had long since left the *New York Times* theater desk, the publication maintained its enthusiasm:

> Today ... American families come in all shapes and sizes. "Falsettos" was eerily prescient in its presentation of one such family, well before it became almost—normal The plague of AIDS no longer claims lives in the numbers it did in the 1980s But "Falsettos" never feels like a singing time capsule. Its fundamental subject is that mysterious, maddening, uplifting, life-complicating emotion we refer to as love, which hasn't changed in 25 years.
>
> *Isherwood 2016*

Historical accuracy and context

Falsettos and queer normalcy

For much of U.S. history, queer people existed on the fringes of society. Designated as sinful by organized religion and disordered by the medical establishment, their intimate relationships were illegal in most jurisdictions, with virtually no government protection from discrimination or abuse. Even if queer individuals were privately accepted and validated, they were expected to remain publicly closeted. Many queer people became practiced at leading dual lives, passing for normal (but neutered) in the workplace and even among their families, who might otherwise reject them. They established a code for communicating their secret identity to other queer people and sought out havens, often in the shadows, where they could express themselves as both loving and sexual beings, finding moments of joy and freedom in lives often plagued by shame.

A distinguishing factor of *Falsettos* from other gay-themed American plays prior to 1990 is that sexual orientation is not the source of the dramatic conflict. Rather, it is asserted nonchalantly, taken for granted as a normal manifestation of human sexuality; shame is absent. Finn has asserted that *Falsettos* is about family, one that happens to include gay and lesbian as well as heterosexual people. Although textual historical references are minimal, political and cultural context played a significant role in *Falsettos*' reception. The New York City setting of the two acts—in 1979 and 1981–2, respectively—along with the significant nine-year gap separating the creation of the two parts, established a layered historical contrast that shaped the impact of *Falsettos* in 1992 and beyond. Whereas *March of the Falsettos* (1981) reflected the innocent optimism that culminated in 1970s gay liberation activism, *Falsettoland* (1990) foreshadowed the dread of the AIDS disease that dominated the 1980s. *Falsettos*, therefore, dramatized a historical hinge between eras of gay liberation and devastation.

Liberation and activism in the 1970s

The Marvin plays were conceived, written, and originally produced during the sexual revolution—roughly the 1960s through the 1980s in the United States—during which the established restrictive social and moral attitudes toward sex were challenged in favor of increased sexual freedom and experimentation. Same-sex liaisons, in particular, became increasingly visible to the public during this period. Set in 1979 New York City, *March of the Falsettos* is a character study of a man reconstructing his liberal, middle-class, Jewish family around his new sense of self, new romantic relationship, and new goals for life. Marvin epitomizes the era's personal liberation yet is seemingly detached from the public politics that had been engaging much of the gay community for a decade, historical context that would nonetheless inform the play's reception and legacy.

The Stonewall Inn uprising in 1969, in which queer patrons of a popular city bar resisted what was then a routine police raid on "gay hangouts," sparked a series of riots and demonstrations in New York's Greenwich Village. Collectively known as Stonewall, they soon inspired metropolitan gay men, lesbians, and other queer people across the United States to become more visible in public spheres and more political in advocating for their rights and representation. For many queer people, "the ancient conspiracy of cultural invisibility was finally over" (Kaiser 1997/2019). Within a few years, hundreds of new advocacy and support groups formed in New York City and around the globe. They represented a spectrum of political approaches, from the radical Gay Liberation Front to the more mainstream Gay Activist Alliance. Using varying tactics, their prime focus was to pressure politicians and business leaders to take positions on homosexuality and support protections from discrimination. In June 1970, the newly minted Gay Pride Week celebrated the first anniversary of Stonewall with numerous political actions and demonstrations throughout New York City. Pride would become an annual event there and in cities and towns around the world as the gay rights movement grew in the years and decades that followed.

Gay cultural representation and the Stonewall legacy

In the United States, gay characters were seldom represented in popular media, and representations that existed often portrayed queer people in a negative or dismissive way. But after Stonewall, the 1970s saw a burgeoning of gay characters in popular media that transcended limited stereotypes to represent fully dimensional and diverse human beings. One film from this era that broke new ground for gay representation was *Cabaret* (1972), based on gay writer Christopher Isherwood's *Berlin Stories* and directed by legendary Broadway director-choreographer Bob Fosse. *Cabaret* had been produced on Broadway in 1966, but even at that late date all the gay elements had been expunged for the stage. Set in 1930s Weimar Berlin, the film restored the gay aspects of Isherwood's original work while capturing the sexual milieu of 1970s America.

That decade's network television, then limited to a handful of channels, played a major role in exposing the public to the diversity of queer people and experience. Phil Donahue, a beloved heterosexual talk show host, began broadcasting nationally in 1970. He featured scores of gay and lesbian guests, providing many Americans with their first exposure to a previously invisible world. In 1972, Hal Holbrook and Martin Sheen starred in the first made-for-TV gay movie, *That Certain Summer*. The following year, public television aired a twelve-hour multipart documentary, *An American Family*, which gave viewers the most prolonged prime-time exposure to a gay character to date: teenager Lance Loud, who came out to his parents and the nation during one of the episodes. In a landmark essay about gay culture, Frank Rich called the televised presentation of Lance Loud living his best gay life with his family "one of the defining images of 'The Gay Decades",' (Rich 1987).

The battle for public opinion

The gay rights movement gained an unprecedented boost in December 1973 when, after much internal debate, the American Psychological Association (APA) removed the diagnosis of homosexuality from the second edition of the *Diagnostic and Statistical Manual* (DSM). This decision effectively recognized the spectrum of human sexual attraction, regardless of gender, as normal rather than disordered. Whereas "the Stonewall riot had served as the movement's *de facto* Declaration of Independence," within four years, "psychiatrists had become the wildly unlikely ratifiers of its Constitution" (Kaiser 1997/2019).

Despite the APA's watershed recognition, battles over public opinion about homosexuality played out in many forums, including the press. In September 1971, prominent academic Joseph Epstein wrote a lengthy diatribe for *Harper's* against the "insidious" spread of homosexuality amid a hedonistic culture. Epstein's widely read article prompted responses in other leading publications, establishing key critics and defenders of the gay cause in public discourse. *Washington Post* columnist and *60 Minutes* commentator Nicholas von Hoffman attacked NBC's *Tonight Show* for inviting members of the Gay Activists Alliance to air their opinions without refutation. Years later, von Hoffman decried the proliferation of attractive gay characters on network television shows. In 1978, Senator Robert Kennedy's former speechwriter Jeff Greenfield argued vehemently in the *Village Voice* against legislation to protect queer people from discrimination: "The cultural majority always sets the rules, and minorities have the choice of conforming, defying those rules, or finding a community where *they* are the cultural majority … it is not a denial of a fundamental right to be refused promotion because of your companions" (Greenfield 1978).

Perhaps the most spectacular display of anti-gay bigotry came from Anita Bryant: former Miss Oklahoma, popular singer, *Good Housekeeping* "Most Admired Woman in America," ambassador for the Florida Citrus Commission (orange growers), and outspoken opponent of gay rights. In 1977, she ran the Save Our Children campaign in Florida, which supported the repeal of a local ordinance prohibiting discrimination on the basis of sexual orientation. Bryant railed against the perceived threat of queer people's "recruitment" of children and child molestation. In that same year, Florida legislators approved a measure that would last three decades, prohibiting visibly queer people from adopting children. Galvanized by these legislative defeats, gay activists and prominent allies led a boycott of orange juice, which succeeded in damaging Bryant financially. Bryant remained defiant, publishing a book about her campaign and persisting as an emblem of bigotry and homophobia as the Marvin plays premiered. Although Finn generally avoided political references in *March of the Falsettos*, ten-year-old Jason's worry about his own sexual orientation ("What about chromosomes? / Will they carry? / Who's the homo now?"), his nascent attraction to girls, plus Marvin's passionate declaration of love for his son all served as counter-arguments to Bryant's unfounded claims of homosexual threats to children and of the unfitness of gay men to be parents.

Even against public backlash, the 1970s brought unprecedented freedom to millions of lesbians and gay men, with individuals and communities continuing to grow in number and visibility. Nonetheless, the stakes of coming out remained high, especially in work settings. In the absence of laws protecting them from employment discrimination, most queer people remained firmly inside the closet. For example, not a single gay reporter at any Manhattan daily newspaper was out of the closet in the 1970s. Only a very small proportion of gay men and lesbians became politically active. One of those was an openly gay community organizer Harvey Milk, who won a San Francisco Board of Supervisors seat and championed a bill banning discrimination of gay people. On November 27, 1978, he was assassinated along with Mayor George Moscone by a disgruntled former supervisor, Dan White. This devastating action made international news, propelling gay rights advocacy to a fever pitch by the end of the decade. It is within this historical and political context that *March of the Falsettos*' bold depiction of homosexuality as a given rather than a polemic was ahead of its time.

Conservatism and devastation in the 1980s

Whereas *March of the Falsettos* offered an optimistic contemporary snapshot of the LGBT movement's progress at the end of the 1970s, *Falsettoland* was a period piece. Written at the end of the following decade but set near its beginning, this one-act musical capped the Marvin plays with a foreshadowing of the deadly setbacks for gay men that the 1980s would bring. One of *Falsettos*' few historical references manifests during the presentational opening of Act Two, when the newly introduced lesbian neighbors sing: "Nancy Reagan, meanest and thinnest of the first ladies, / moves into the White House. It's the eighties." This lyric, coupled with the entire cast singing in unison to the audience as "Liberal Democrats," framed the show's political perspective. Those theatergoers who found themselves on the wrong theatrical flight were free to exit.

The landslide election of Republican candidate Ronald Reagan as president of the United States in 1980, coupled with the first Senate Republican majority in a quarter-century, launched an era of political and social conservatism. Previous political gains of marginalized groups including gays and lesbians, women, and people of color would be systematically eroded. From the perspective of many queer people, President George Herbert Walker Bush presided over a continuation of Ronald Reagan's policies (often referred to as an effective "third term of Reaganism") during the period from *Falsettoland*'s 1990 debut through *Falsettos*' 1992 Broadway premiere. With the more salutary Clinton administration and the "gay 1990s" lying ahead, the political and social landscape for gays and lesbians remained bleak.

Under public pressure from gay activists and allies, by 1980 over 120 of the country's largest companies along with forty towns and cities had adopted policies, laws, and ordinances prohibiting discrimination based on sexual orientation. In addition, twenty-two states had ended all prohibitions on sexual relations between consenting adults (Kaiser 1997/2019). Ironically, New York City, the setting for Finn's Marvin plays, had no such protective ordinance, largely due to vehement opposition from the city's powerful Catholic archdiocese and its outspoken lobbyist, closeted gay attorney Roy Cohn, who would become an influential friend of the Reagans and mentor to future President Donald Trump.

As Governor of California from 1967 to 1975, Reagan had a mixed record on gay rights. While Nancy Reagan's openly gay decorator was welcome in the White House, no openly gay person served in the upper levels of Reagan's presidential administration. In 1981, an applicant for Assistant White House counsel had his job offer rescinded upon disclosing his gay identity. The rescinded offer made national news, causing repercussions in gay circles. Fear that blatant workplace discrimination at the highest government level would trickle down to the rest of society caused many gay people to remain in the closet, especially those in public positions, such as journalism, government, broadcasting, education, and athletics. Trepidation turned to reality when in that same year tennis star and television commentator Billie Jean King was publicly identified as a lesbian and subsequently lost lucrative product endorsement deals.

Refreshingly, none of the four gay characters in *Falsettoland*—Marvin, Whizzer, Dr. Charlotte, or Cordelia—even acknowledge that a closet exists. In that respect, Finn presented an idealized social environment where sexual orientation is not an issue so that he could focus on family dynamics and other social questions, such as a sense of soulless consumerism and greed that later critics associated with Reagan's presidency under the looming AIDS epidemic.

AIDS and radical advocacy

While *March of the Falsettos* was thrilling audiences during the summer of 1981, physicians in Manhattan were becoming alarmed at the high rate at which relatively rare but serious opportunistic diseases—such as Pneumocystis pneumonia (PCP) and the skin cancer Kaposi's sarcoma (KS)—were afflicting gay men. This realization is dramatized in *Falsettoland* when Dr. Charlotte relays to Cordelia the events of her workplace: "Bachelors arrive sick and frightened / They leave weeks later, unenlightened / Rumors fly and tales abound." With transmission a mystery and cure out of reach, fear quickly spread. Initially called "gay cancer" or GRID (gay-related immune deficiency), the same opportunistic infections began to be documented in hemophiliacs and intravenous drug users. As nearly half the victims were not gay men, in August 1982 the Center for Disease Control (CDC) officially coined Acquired Immune Deficiency Syndrome (AIDS). In the following years, the virus causing the disease was identified by multiple researchers, and in 1986, the International Committee on Taxonomy of Viruses ruled on a new permanent name: Human Immunodeficiency Virus (HIV).

With no openly gay staffers inside the Reagan administration, virtually no one in the executive branch of the U.S. government would advocate to fund extensive AIDS-related research and services. Moreover, Reagan had campaigned on reducing non-military government spending and promptly targeted federal health services for cuts. Reagan's spending priorities and his administration's dismissiveness of the growing AIDS crisis reignited nationwide gay advocacy in the form of organizations like Act Up! and Gay Men's Health Crisis. During the early 1980s in New York—Finn's (and Marvin's) hometown—the city's leading gay activist, author Larry Kramer, famously lashed out at Mayor Ed Koch (an early advocate for gay rights when he had served in Congress) as well as the *New York Times* for not identifying AIDS as a serious problem. Even after transmission methods for the disease were identified, many federal and state agencies resisted efforts to educate the public. Well into the 1990s, some states and localities prohibited AIDS education in schools, sometimes yielding to pressure from religious groups who feared that such an undertaking would expose children to homosexuality. Finally, in 1986, Surgeon General C. Everett Koop issued a report calling for an end to the silence about AIDS and condemning the withholding of adequate education from the public, especially children. He urged frank discussion of sexual practices that would help people protect themselves from the AIDS virus, but obstacles persisted.

AIDS and HIV would have a greater impact on the gay community than the events of the previous four decades combined. Moreover, in the 1980s, a decade characterized by social conservatism, public acceptance of queer people, especially gay men, receded dramatically. With no cure—or even life-preserving treatment—widely available until the mid-1990s, a positive HIV test was for most people a death sentence. However, on November 7, 1991, just six months before *Falsettos* debuted on Broadway, public opinion about AIDS pivoted when the revered heterosexual basketball star of the Los Angeles Lakers, Earvin "Magic" Johnson, revealed that he had tested positive for HIV and announced his retirement. Subsequent research found that Johnson's announcement generated positive changes in public awareness, attitudes, and behaviors with respect to AIDS, its victims, and safe-sex practices (Kalichman 1994).

Kenneth J. Cerniglia

Further reading

"20 Years of AIDS: 400,000 Americans Dead, Over 1 Million Have Been Infected." *HIV/ AIDS News*, Centers for Disease Control and Prevention (CDC), May 31, 2001, aidsinfo.nih.gov/news/560/20-years-of-aids--450-000-americans-dead--over-1-million-have-been-infected.

Bádue, Alex. 2019. "Performing Gender, Sexuality, and Jewishness in the Songs of William Finn's Musical *Falsettoland* (1990)." *Studies in Jewish American Literature* 8, no. 2: 159–78.

Barnes, Clive. 1992. "'Falsettos' Doesn't Always Ring True." *New York Post*, April 30, 1992.

Beaufort, John. 1992. "'Falsettos' Mixes Humor and Pain." *Christian Science Monitor*, May 22, 1992.

Bishop, André. 1989. "Introduction to *The Marvin Songs: Falsettoland, March of the Falsettos*, and *In Trousers*." Fireside Theatre, 1989.

Blau, Eleanor. 1981. "For 'Falsettos' Author, Watchful Agonizing." *New York Times*, May 8, 1981.

Cerniglia, Kenneth James. 2010. "Gay Culture." In *Broadway: An Encyclopedia of Theater and American Culture*, edited by Thomas A. Greenfield. Santa Barbara, CA: Greenwood Press.

Christiansen, Richard. 1990. "'Falsettoland' Closes Trilogy on a Skillful, Provocative Note." *Chicago Tribune*, November 21, 1990.

Collins, Glenn. 1990. "Men of 'Falsettoland' as Their Old Selves but with New Fears." *New York Times*, July 23, 1990.

Dziemianowicz, Joe. 2016. "'Falsettos' Fills Broadway with Music, Laughter and Tears." *New York Daily News*, October 27, 2016.

Finn, William and James Lapine. 1992. *Falsettos*. Video Recording, at John Golden Theatre, Theatre on Film and Tape Archive, New York Public Library for the Performing Arts.

Finn, William and James Lapine. 1995. *Falsettos: Acting Edition*. New York: Samuel French.

Finn, William and James Lapine. 2016. *Falsettos: 2016 Broadway Cast Recording*. New York: Ghostlight Records.

Gerard, Jeremy. 1992. "'Falsettos.'" *Variety*, May 4, 1992.

Greenfield, Jeff. 1978. "Why Is Gay Rights Different from All Other Rights?" *Village Voice*.

Harris, William. 1990. "Back to 'Falsettoland' in the Age of AIDS." *New York Times*, June 24, 1980.

Hischak, Thomas S. 2003. "William Finn." In *Contemporary Gay American Poets and Playwrights: An A-to-Z Guide*, edited by Emmanuel S. Nelson. Westport, CT: Greenwood Press.

Isherwood, Charles. 2016. "'Falsettos,' A Perfect Musical, An Imperfect Family." *New York Times*, October 27, 2016.

Jones, Chris. 2016. "'Falsettos' Revival Rings True Despite a Few Flaws." *Chicago Tribune*, October 28, 2016.

Kaiser, Charles. (1997) 2019. *The Gay Metropolis: The Landmark History of Gay Life in America*. New York: Grove Press (updated with a New Introduction).

Kalichman, S. C. 1994. "Magic Johnson and Public Attitudes toward AIDS: A Review of Empirical Findings." *AIDS Education and Prevention* 6, no. 6 (December), https://www.ncbi.nlm.nih.gov/pubmed/7702965.

Kissel, Howard. 1992. "All Keyed Up for 'Falsettos.'" *Daily News*, April 30, 1992.

Pitman, Gayle E. 2019. *The Stonewall Riots: Coming Out in the Streets*. New York: Abrams.

Rich, Frank. 1981. "'March of the Falsettos,' A Musical Find." *New York Times*, April 10, 1981.

Rich, Frank. 1987. "The Gay Decades." *Esquire*, November 1, 1987.

Rich, Frank. 1990. "What Has AIDS Done to Land of 'Falsettos'?" *New York Times*, June 29, 1990.

Rich, Frank. 1991. "The 'Falsetto' Musicals Unite at Hartford Stage." *New York Times*, October 15, 1991.

Rich, Frank. 1992. "Broadway Boundary Falls Amid Reunions." *New York Times*, April 30, 1992.

Simon, John. 1981. "Unfinished Business." *New York*, April 27, 1981.

Simon, John. 1992. "Evasions and Manipulations." *New York*, May 25, 1992.

Smart, Jeffrey. 1996. "Labels Are Not Characters: Critical Misperceptions of *Falsettoland*." *Journal of Dramatic Theory and Criticism* X, no. 2 (Spring): 61–74.

Stearns, David Patrick. 1992. "'Falsettos' Rings Clear on Broadway." *USA Today*, April 30, 1992.

Watt, Doug. 1992. "'Falsettos.'" *Daily News*, May 8, 1992.

Wilson, Edwin. 1992. "End of Big Broadway Season." *Wall Street Journal*, May 6, 1992.

Winer, Linda. 1992. "'Falsettos': The Pain of Love and Lovers Lost." *Newsday*, April 30, 1992.

Winer, Linda. 2016. "'Falsettos' Review: Revival Still Powerful, Passionate, and Funny Too." *Newsday*, October 27, 2016.

CHAPTER 10
HAIR: THE AMERICAN TRIBAL LOVE-ROCK MUSICAL (1967)

Book and Lyrics by Gerome Ragni (1935–91) and James Rado (1932–) Music by Galt MacDermot (1928–2018)
World Premiere: Public Theatre, October 17, 1967, for eight-week run; transfer to Cheetah Disco, December 22, 1967
Broadway: Biltmore Theatre, April 29, 1968–July 1, 1972

Songs

"Aquarius"	"Don't Put It Down"
"Donna"	"Frank Mills"
"Hashish"	"Be-In"
"Sodomy"	"Where Do I Go?"
"Colored Spade"	"Electric Blues"
"Manchester"	"Black Boys"
"Ain't Got No"	"White Boys"
"I Believe in Love"	"Walking In Space"
"Air"	"Abie Baby"
"Initials"	"Three-Five-Zero-Zero"
"I Got Life"	"What a Piece of Work Is Man"
"Going Down"	"Good Morning, Starshine"
"Hair"	"The Be"
"My Conviction"	"The Flesh Failures
"Easy to Be Hard"	(Let the Sun Shine In)"

Note: The song list is from the Broadway opening night as documented by the Broadway League for the Internet Broadway Database.

Overview

Hair: The American Tribal Love-Rock Musical (familiarly *Hair*) owes its surprising success to an artful balance of outrageous youth-inspired defiance of convention and warm-spirited, catchy pop rock music. Generally acknowledged as the first Rock Musical, *Hair* bridged the gap between hippie counterculture and the very target of its social critiques: middle-aged, middle-class Broadway audiences. By introducing youth counterculture to mainstream commercial theater, *Hair* both celebrated and helped normalize many affronts to middle-class respectability of the 1950s and 1960s posed by hippies and other self-styled rebellious youth.

Politically, hippies were openly opposed to America's involvement in the Vietnam War years before such opposition became the prevailing sentiment of the country. In the process, hippies and other early participants in "the anti-war movement" were routinely castigated by critics as traitors, communist dupes, and cowards. Long hair was the visible marker adopted by hippie men. Their "freak flag" was labeled effeminate by mainstream culture and marked them as unfit to assume the masculine duties of protecting women, children, and the nation. Hippies supported the more widely accepted belief in racial equality, but they also championed interracial co-habitation and sexual intimacy—taboos among many middle-class integrationists and a topic that major civil rights organizations generally avoided. Sociologically, hippie philosophy disdained traditional education, careerism, and bourgeois individual pursuit of financial success. Employers took to heart the anti-authority messages conveyed by young men's long hair. It would be years before long-haired men were routinely seen holding traditional jobs in public schools, government, law, hospitality, and customer service. In defiance of conventions of American middle-class morality and etiquette, hippies and *Hair* embraced casual conversational profanity, public nudity, same-sex relationships, and communal rather than couples-based romantic and sexual relationships.

With the exception of the anti-war movement, the Hippies' most significant act of social rebellion took the form of their embrace of hallucinogenic drugs—a phenomenon that, unlike war, joblessness, and sex, was disturbingly unfamiliar to middle-class American adults. Long-standing cultural associations of marijuana and cocaine with street crime and insanity, combined with the alien new world of hallucinogens, genuinely alarmed middle-age adults. Parents recoiled as they witnessed their college-age and even high-school-age children embrace the drug culture that sprang up in the mid- to late 1960s. Young people distinguished sharply between psychedelic drugs that opened their minds to new perceptions and ways of thinking, and "drugs" that deadened perception, such as alcohol, which they associated with conformist, materialistic values of their parents' generation. *Hair* played an important role in demonstrating that, even if the behavior was new, the young people themselves were healthy, smart, sometimes confused, and caring. *Hair* conveyed their passion for experiencing life fully and participating in American democracy, even if their modes of expressing their values were decidedly different from those of their parents' generation.

Over and above presenting important, timely social commentary to mainstream Broadway audiences, *Hair* made significant contributions to American popular culture, particularly in the realms of rock music and musical theater history. Broadway had resisted adopting rock and roll music into its shows since the beginning of the rock and roll era (*c.* 1950) except as an occasional target of musical satire (e.g., fictional rock and roll singer Conrad Birdie's songs in *Bye, Bye, Birdie* [1958] were intentionally written to be puerile). With rock and roll's takeover of AM radio and record sales, by the late 1960s songs from Broadway shows, long a reliable source of hit records, gradually ceased to be an important part of the youth-driven pop music industry.

By the late 1960s, rock and roll (by then commonly "rock"), and particularly psychedelic rock, had become a powerful socializing, community-building force among counterculture youth. For precisely that reason, composer Galt MacDermot chose rock as the musical style for *Hair*. *Hair*'s score completely overwhelms its book, which centers on a hippie musical gathering rather than a conventional plot. To create the feel of a rock concert, the orchestra (rock band) was placed on stage and actors sang into visible microphones (uncommon on Broadway at the time). MacDermott's score reflects important changes to rock music of the late 1960s, including now familiar electronic sound amplification and distortion. The contemporary pop and rock music styles that MacDermott adapted for his score include 1960s protest song-oriented folk rock ("Frank Mills"); psychedelic rock ("Walking in Space," "Be-In"); variations on 12 bar blues ("Aquarius," "Let the Sun Shine In"); and nods to rockabilly, Motown, and pre-adolescent bubble gum pop.

Hair's music was phenomenally successful. The show's music, cultural critiques, and outlandish reputation spread from New York out to living rooms across the country. The original cast album won the Grammy for Best Score from an Original Cast Show and then topped the *Billboard* record charts for thirteen weeks in 1968. It spawned four covers in 1969 that reached the top five on the charts: "Aquarius/Let the Sun Shine In" by The

5th Dimension; "Hair" by the Cowsills; "Good Morning Starshine" by Oliver; and "Easy to Be Hard" by Three Dog Night. Many more artists recorded these and other tunes from *Hair*, and it became the most covered Broadway show score in history. The extraordinary success of the original cast recording and popularity of the music in cover versions demonstrate how effectively librettists Ragni and Rado and composer MacDermot had packaged hippie values and practices for middle-class America to embrace.

In order to capture the 1960s counterculture on stage, *Hair* also broke with many theatrical conventions of the Broadway musical. Director Tom O'Horgan cut his teeth in downtown Off-Broadway and emerging Off-Off-Broadway theater groups, such as La MaMa ETC (Experimental Theatre Club). *Hair* marked his Broadway debut along with the introduction of many downtown staging techniques to mainstream theater. These include breaking the fourth wall (intentional performer-initiated speech or action directed at the theater audience), placing the band visibly on stage, improvisational development of script, casual swearing, and public nudity. O'Horgan's novel approach to *Hair* was to imagine that the hippie "tribe" (the cast) lived in the theater and the audience was joining them for an event or Happening. Thus, the cast wanders through the theater greeting audience members as they enter. Actors interact with the audience throughout the performance, and the audience is invited to dance on stage with the cast as a part of the finale "Let the Sun Shine In." The loose plot of *Hair*, in which Claude gets drafted into the army, is discovered, as if by chance, while the celebratory Happening scene unfolds and the singing cast protests the Vietnam War and conventional parental behavior.

This suppression of plot in service to the theatrical experience is similar to conceptual art and has been dubbed a concept musical. In fact, many theater historians point to *Hair* as the original concept musical—a now common approach to theater in which a controlling idea or theme, rather than narrative plot, frames the work. Much of *Hair*'s original choreography and cultural satire were the result of O'Horgan's improvisational collaborations with his cast. Results of such collaborations became part of the actual production, including choreography that appears to be improvisational and the three sets of mothers and fathers who berate Claude for his hippie appearance. Typical of hippie youth but not a Broadway libretto, the cast also swore casually. *Hair*'s most controversial Off-Broadway practice, never before seen in a Broadway musical, was the inclusion of a nude scene. O'Horgan included the nude scene at the end of Act One to viscerally convey that young people's bodies are at stake in the Vietnam War, and to juxtapose the hippie tribe's celebration of life with their fear of death in war. The nude scene also served *Hair*'s commercial interests, as advance publicity for the show often raised the larger issue of nudity on Broadway. The artistic novelties in *Hair*'s staging that were developed Off-Broadway sharply contrasted with conventional Broadway practices. The now familiar concept approach in *Hair*'s libretto departed radically from the integrated book musical as established with *Oklahoma!* (1943), which was still standard practice when *Hair* opened on Broadway.

Notable in the history of theater in New York City, *Hair*'s initial Off-Broadway run inaugurated Joseph Papp's Public Theatre. Papp, who began producing free Shakespeare in innovative stagings downtown in 1954, eventually moved his location to the lawns of Central Park. When the New York Parks Commission informed him that he'd have to pay for destroying the grass, he raised money to build the Delacorte Theatre, which continues to present free Shakespeare in the Park productions to this day. Papp returned to his downtown roots to build a venue for the development of innovative projects. He purchased the elegant but abandoned Astor Library on Lafayette Street, dubbed it The Public Theatre, and remodeled it to house three theater venues. *Hair* was The Public's very first production, and with its wildly successful Broadway transfer, set a pattern for many future Public successes. Today, The Public enjoys an international reputation for developing important new plays and musicals. *A Chorus Line*, *for colored girls*, *The Normal Heart*, *Fun Home*, and *Hamilton* are among the major works that premiered at The Public. The theater has earned a remarkable fifty-four Tony Awards and five Pulitzer Prizes. *Hair*'s success on Broadway was a surprise to the industry for many reasons. It flouted traditional subject matter, musical style, primacy of plot, and standard staging conventions. It satirized and mocked the cultural conservatism of its core audience. Yet, *Hair* ran for four years and spawned nine national satellite and touring companies as well as nineteen international productions and tours. It has also enjoyed three Broadway revivals. Clive Barnes' prophetic opening night review in the *New York Times* caught the sense of theater history in the making: "it has the authentic voice of today rather than the day before yesterday" (Barnes 1968).

Plot synopsis

Actors comprising a hippie tribe wander in as the audience takes their seats. The tribe takes over the theater and interacts with the audience as if the members of the tribe are living out their daily lives in front of them. George Berger, a tribe leader, ritualistically cuts a lock of hair from his best friend Claude Bukowski's head and burns it. Ronny, another tribe member, leads the whole tribe in singing an astrological paean to peace and love ("Aquarius"), as if the song itself were the climax of the ritual.

The main characters introduce themselves in direct address to the audience, singing of their wants and ambitions. Berger sings of searching for love ("Donna"), Woof Donovan lists sexual acts ("Sodomy"); without explicitly stating his sexuality Woof signifies that he is a queer character. The only African American tribe leader, Hud, sings "Colored Spade," confronting the audience with a tsunami of obscene anti-Black derogatory terms and insults. Claude, who has received a draft notice from the army at a time when new draftees were likely to be sent to the warfront in Vietnam, proclaims his fantasies of escapism in the song "Manchester" ("it's groovy / to hide in a movie / [pretending I'm] Fellini"). Sheila, an NYU student in love with Berger, sings "I Believe in Love." Jeannie, who is pregnant, sings of her environmentalist sensibilities in the comically satiric "Air" ("Welcome sulfur dioxide / Hello carbon monoxide").

The tribe performs a sequence, parodying and rejecting bourgeois values. Three moms and three dads, played by tribe members, berate Claude for his hair, dress, jewelry, lack of a job, and incessant mooching for money. They tell him to join the army, clean up after himself, and conform. Claude, prior to leaving the stage to take his draft physical, responds in joyful affirmation of his bohemian body-conscious existence: "Ain't got no clothes, no job … / I got my back, I got my sex" ("Ain't Got No" and "I Got Life"). Berger, who was kicked out of high school, re-enacts his expulsion as tribe members grotesquely portray his authoritarian principal. Berger satirically responds, "Lucifer and Me … banished forever" ("Going Down") while clearly embracing the counterculture of dropouts.

Claude reappears having passed his physical exam for the army. Intensely opposed to the Vietnam War, as are all members of the tribe, Claude feigns burning his draft card to the pleasure of his friends. However, ambivalent about violating strict draft laws, Claude has actually burned his library card.

Margaret Mead and Hubert, a pleasant older couple from the audience, ascend the stage and question the tribe about their long hair, which fascinates the couple. Claude and Berger lead the tribe's response, which takes the form of a bursting celebratory ensemble song, "Hair" ("ain't no words for the beauty, the splendor, the wonder of my hair, hair, hair …"). Margaret Mead responds by singing "My Conviction," in which she observes knowledgably that among several members of the animal kingdom the male is showier than the female, such as peacocks. As they head back to the audience, the couple reveals that they are actors, too.

A brief scene explores a love triangle among three principal characters. Claude loves Sheila, but Sheila is "hung up" on Berger, who treats her poorly ("Easy to Be Har"). The tribe distributes invitations among the audience to a ritualistic tribal "Be-In." The Be-In unfolds under dimly colored and patterned lighting, which both enhances and obscures the tribe's sexualized dancing. Claude questions the meaning of his life and possible death in "Where Do I Go?" as the tribe disrobes under a parachute, emerging nude to join him in the final chorus. As house lights come up for the intermission, police officers pretend to arrest audience members for watching a "lewd, obscene show."

Act Two opens with a few members of the tribe singing "Electric Blues," which comments on the use of amplified vocals and electric instruments versus "old-fashioned melody." The song culminates with the power in the theater momentarily seeming to have been cut. Claude returns again from the draft board. Resigned to entering the army, he gives farewell gifts to the tribe. Out of the tribe's goodbyes comes a trio of white women who sing "Black Boys" followed by three Black women singing "White Boys," both groups extolling interracial dating and love. Berger passes out marijuana cigarettes to the tribe as they sing in celebration of getting high ("Walking in Space"). A trippy fantasy sequence follows, which enfolds Claude's nightmarish anxieties about entering the army. At first, he imagines himself jumping out of a helicopter in Vietnam and then envisions a montage of wars in American history—all enacted bizarrely and comically by the tribe. The fantasy sequence spirals to a serious ending when, after a final strobe-lit killing sequence, the whole tribe lies "dea" on the ground. Ronny and Walter sing "What a Piece of Work Is Man," a simple setting of Shakespeare's text from *Hamlet* II:2, extolling what humans should be, but fail to be.

The tribe plans to spend one last night together before Claude leaves, with Sheila planning an "Exorcism of the Khaki" at the induction center where he has been ordered to report. Claude says his farewells and, in a reprise of "Ain't Got No," he reacts as if he is hit by bullets. The tribe gathers for an anti-war protest. Claude appears in uniform, but the others can't see him. The tribe sings the finale, "Let the Sun Shine In," and we realize that in their minds Claude is dead. During the curtain call, the audience is encouraged to dance with the cast in a final gesture to bring the audience into the tribe.

Critical reception

Hair's first press notice appeared in a preview story by the *New York Times*' Dan Sullivan. Reporting on small shows Joseph Papp planned to produce in his newly rehabilitated public theater venue in lower Manhattan, Sullivan concluded with a prophetic quote from Papp: "[Our plays] are scheduled to run for eight weeks. What if we have a hit? Where do we put it?" (Sullivan 1967).

Papp's Off-Broadway production of *Hair* was, indeed, a hit and made an historic transfer to Broadway shortly after its Off-Broadway run. Clive Barnes of the *New York Times* gave the Off-Broadway production a lukewarm review, stating that while well-intentioned, *Hair* was good but not great. Barnes praised the score and the cast's energetic honesty (Barnes 1967). Other reviewers considered *Hair* Off-Broadway an artistic success. Richard P. Cooke in the *Wall Street Journal* praised the ensemble numbers and "unsophisticated but appealing" music (Cooke 1967). The *New York Post* hailed the "stunning effects of stagecraft and comment in *Hair*" and praised the musical's overall conception as representing the best of the protest shows springing up in small theaters at the time (1967). Several reviews were generally positive with reservations, including *Newsweek*, *Variety*, and *Dance Magazine*. Edith Oliver of the *New Yorker* expressed "mixed feelings" about *Hair* but noted "it does catch … one of the many moods and aspects of life in this city in 1967" (Oliver 1967). The show's photographic set, faithful costuming, on-stage rock band/orchestra, and bold use of lighting earned strong notices as well.

Hair Off-Broadway also had detractors. The *Daily News* dismissed *Hair* as cliché-ridden generation gap sociology set to unexceptional songs and dance numbers (1967). Michael Smith's review in the *Village Voice* was singularly hostile: "I loathed and despised it … it's all phony" (Smith 1967). He disparaged *Hair*'s adoption of hippie beliefs for profit, shallow presentation of the Vietnam War, and insipid racial politics. Robert Brustein in a mixed review for the *New Republic* observed insightfully that the production's Broadway-style direction was incongruous with the open theater Public venue and noted a fundamental antithesis between the bubbly bouncy *Hair* ensemble and authentic hippie cool (Brustein 1967).

Hair transferred to Broadway's Biltmore Theatre on April 29, 1968, with revised staging, a rewritten book, new designs, new choreography, an expanded score from twenty to thirty-one musical numbers, and many new cast members. An especially noteworthy change in the Broadway production was the introduction of the nude scene at the end of the Be-In at the close of Act One. The show sold out to capacity for months in advance and the press gushed. *Times* critic Clive Barnes now effusively praised the improved thematic structure of the book, "sweet and subtle" lyrics, "masterly" visuals, and a "sheer fun" experience. Saving his best notes for the music, Barnes hailed MacDermot's songs as broadly appealing to audiences by balancing "pop-rock, with strong, soothing overtones of Broadway melody" (Barnes 1968). Len Harris on CBS-TV spoke for many about the transition from a small Off-Broadway thrust stage to a large proscenium Broadway house: "The staging … which I feared would suffer in the transition … is better now … because it has been moved into the realm of controlled anarchy" (Harris 1968). Even reviewers who did not love the musical style or subject matter admitted to being charmed by it. The *New York Post*'s Richard Watts Jr. wrote, "it has a surprising if perhaps unintentional charm, its high spirits are contagious, and its young zestfulness make it difficult to resist" (Watts 1968).

Many reviewers predicted correctly that *Hair* would open up new directions for attracting a younger generation of theater artists and audiences to Broadway musicals. These critics homed in on *Hair*'s potential to revitalize Broadway by embracing controversial socio-political content, inspiring new forms of the musical itself, and opening the all-important Broadway score to youth-centered rock music. The *Christian Science Monitor*'s Alan N. Bunce wrote that "in the spirit of a fraternity prank, the company lashes out at pollution, patriotism, religion, war, and uptight middle-aged bigotry" (Bunce 1968). John J. O'Connor of the *Wall Street Journal* hailed the arrival on Broadway of New York's legacy of independent theater: "the happier results of Off-Off-Broadway experimentation." Additionally, O'Connor correctly anticipated that the fluid, semi-episodic form of *Hair* "will be important to the history of the American musical" (O'Connor 1968)—a prediction borne out by the emergence of new musical genres, such as "concept musicals" and "rock musicals." Michael Smith of the *Village Voice*, who disliked the Off-Broadway show, changed his tune about the Broadway production: "*Hair* is now a direct freak-out. [Director] O'Horgan has blown up Broadway" (Smith 1968).

Dissenting voices were in the minority. *Variety* decried a world in which *Hair* could succeed at the expense of Rodgers and Hammerstein-style book musicals (1968). The *New York Daily News* bemoaned *Hair*'s paucity of "pretty girls," a glaringly sexist observation that would seem to validate *Hair*'s countercultural politics (1968). Later reviews seeking to explain the show's success agreed with *Rolling Stone*: "*Hair* has an unbeatable combination of ingredients, guaranteed to shock and reassure [a theoretical elderly audience member from Dubuque] at the same time" (1968).

Hair was a hit, running for four years and 1,750 performances. It earned only two Tony nominations (Best Musical, Best Direction of a Musical) and no wins, but national tours, three Broadway revivals, and a stream of school and community productions have given *Hair* remarkable staying power. The original cast album (1968) was extremely successful in its own right, winning the 1969 Grammy for Best Score from an Original Cast Show Album, and reaching No. 1 on the *Billboard* album charts. In 2019, the Library of Congress inducted the album into the National Recording Registry for its "historic and aesthetic importance to the nation's sound heritage" (Culwell-Block 2019).

Significantly, for the first time since the start of the 1950s rock era, cover versions of songs from a Broadway show became hit singles on AM rock and roll radio. Single recordings of "Aquarius/Let the Sun Shine In," "Hair," "Good Morning Starshine," and "Easy to Be Hard," performed by different artists, all reached the top five on *Billboard*'s Top 200.

Theater historians credit *Hair* with renewing the long-broken connection between showtunes and mainstream popular music. A major source of popular hit "singles" since the Tin Pan Alley era of the 1920s, showtunes lost ground after the early 1950s when youth-oriented rock and roll took over the popular recording and radio music industries. Until *Hair* arrived on Broadway, original cast albums and rock and roll records occupied altogether different spheres in commercial music. *Hair* bridged that separation, spawning new rock and roll-inspired musical genres and Broadway shows that heretofore would have been inconceivable, such as *Jesus Christ Superstar* (1970), *Rent* (1996), *Rock of Ages* (2005), and *Hamilton* (2015).

Historical accuracy and context

Hair *and the origins of the hippie movement*

Hair is both an homage and an instructional guide to hippie culture, which began in the early to mid-1960s in Northern California near San Francisco and the University of California, Berkeley. The word "hippie" evolved in the 1960s as a likely derivation of "hipster," a term widely associated with the Beatniks of New York City, who created an influential counterculture movement after World War II. The new West Coast hippie movement was comprised of young self-declared social "dropouts," mostly from comfortable or prosperous white middle-class backgrounds, opposed to America's involvement in the Vietnam War but also dismissive of school, career paths, and other middle-class social conventions. As hippiedom grew larger, it landed in the Haight-Ashbury district of San Francisco, with as many as 75,000 young people (Love 2017) arriving in the mid-1960s to foster, as several journalists proclaimed, an "alternative lifestyle" (Albert 1996).

The hippie movement spread rapidly across the country, nesting primarily in cities as well as smaller communities with college student populations. When the movement spread to New York City, hippies settled primarily in lower Manhattan's Greenwich Village, which is the setting for *Hair*. On Easter Sunday, 1967, hippies staged a Be-In in Central Park that attracted 10,000 people, providing inspiration for the Be-In staged in *Hair* at the end of Act One (Holson 2019).

Hippie lifestyle espoused several anti-conformist values, many of which are celebrated in *Hair*: tribal and communal living; unfettered use of psychedelic drugs; opposition to the Vietnam War and the draft (mandatory military service registration for males age eighteen to twenty-six); equality of all races; frank sexuality; non-judgmental celebration of the body (including, notably, hair); and psychedelic music. *Hair* is the first successful pop culture phenomenon to try to capture the communal and tribal lifestyle hippies embraced and to do so almost entirely through rock music, assisted only minimally by plot and dialogue.

The Vietnam War, the draft, and the protesters

Claude's anxiety about being drafted by the army to fight in Vietnam, a major plotline in the Off-Broadway production of *Hair*, is downplayed somewhat in the Broadway show. However, the political realities of the late 1960s—especially regular news coverage of anti-Vietnam War protests, often characterized as led by "long-haired hippies"—elevated the relevance of Claude's storyline.

In 1954, having just liberated itself from seventy years of French colonization, the Southeast Asian country of Vietnam was divided by treaty into two separate governments: a North Vietnamese government sympathetic to Soviet (i.e., Russian) communism and a pro-Western government in South Vietnam. Diplomatic efforts to unify the North and South failed, setting off armed conflict between the two. Eager to establish alliances with anti-communist governments, President Dwight Eisenhower supported South Vietnam with financial and military aid, including a few hundred non-combatant U.S. troops stationed in Vietnam. Nevertheless, armed conflicts between North and South Vietnam persisted. By 1962, President John F. Kennedy had stationed 9,000 troops in Vietnam, but to no avail.

In 1964, North Vietnamese torpedo boats attacked U.S. military ships in the Gulf of Tonkin off the Vietnamese coast. In response, President Lyndon Johnson, with support from Congress and the public, "redouble" America's "full commitment" to South Vietnam (1964). The Selective Service System modified procedures to recruit more volunteer and conscripted (drafted) soldiers. By 1965, 85,000 American troops were fighting in Vietnam. When *Hair* opened on Broadway in 1968, that number had swelled to over 500,000, with no end to the war in sight. A formerly supportive American public, especially draft-age youth, was losing patience and faith in the war effort.

Youth-driven protests against the Vietnam War began in 1964. Anti-war protesters were inspired by Civil Rights Era demonstrations from the 1950s and early 1960s, as were Women's Rights activists at the time. As all three movements gained momentum in the late 1960s, some large-scale demonstrations coalesced around multiple issues—the war, Civil Rights, Women's Rights, and others—creating a loose but increasingly visible coalition of protest movements.

When anti-war protesters were asked by reporters why they demonstrated, some merely echoed their protest chants ("Make love, not war" or, as Sheila shouts during the *Hair* Peace Rally, "Hell no, we won't go"). Others expressed thoughtful considerations of other nations' rights to self-determination or skepticism over the government's claim that a small communist-leaning country 8,000 miles away posed a threat to America's security. However, the impact of the war on many young people was not intellectual, but sensory and visual.

For the first time in history, television film crews embedded with combat troops provided the primary means by which America received news from a warfront. The carnage those nightly news reports broadcast was often horrific and shocking. (Some of Claude's visions of wartime combat in Act Two invoke the impact of Vietnam news coverage.) War protests themselves presented inviting visual images for broadcasters. As staged in *Hair*, some men publicly, if sometimes symbolically, burned their military registration cards (draft cards). College students occupied campus buildings, disrupting business-as-usual. Crowds protested at military recruiting stations and buildings owned by companies associated with the war. (Dow Chemical, manufacturer of the defoliation agent Napalm, was a conspicuous target for protesters ["Two Days" 2005].)

President Johnson's troop escalations in 1965 fostered dynamic changes in the anti-war movement. That year saw a proliferation of campus teach-ins and sit-ins against the war, capped by a March on Washington that drew over 20,000 participants (Hall 2004). "Summer of Love" gatherings in San Francisco (1966) and New York (1967) spawned interest in tribal social structures from which sprang the Be-In, a playful twist on the sit-in and teach-in demonstrations that originated in the Civil Rights Era.

The first Be-In, held in San Francisco in January 1967, drew upwards of 30,000 people (Hartlaub and Whiting 2017). Be-Ins galvanized a next-phase image and social agenda for Hippies: anti-war protest overlaid with incantations of utopian tribal life, sexual freedom, and psychedelic drugs, with rock music drawing together large groups in public parks. San Francisco and New York emerged as the cultural hubs for larger hippie gatherings. San Francisco hippiedom, whose symbolic leader was psychedelic drug researcher Dr. Timothy Leary, emphasized countercultural lifestyle more so than political action, while New York hippiedom was more focused on the anti-war movement. However, East and West Coast hippie cultures were highly compatible. Their shared beliefs, political views, and music profoundly influenced the lives of countless young people across the country and American society as a whole.

Psychedelic drug use

Taking drugs to create a psychedelic effect (mind expansion) formed an essential part of 1960s hippie culture. Hippies took psychedelics in order to trip: open the mind to the beauty of the world, shun bourgeois society, and celebrate life-affirming values. Hippies believed their parents' generation's indulgences of alcohol and depressant drugs such as Valium deadened rather than affirmed life, thus providing an implicit validation of psychedelic drug culture. Preferred psychedelic drugs included marijuana, LSD (lysergic acid diethylamide or "aci"), peyote, and certain groups of mushrooms. *Hair*'s numerous references to drugs speak to the broader history of how 1960s youth counterculture and psychedelic drugs discovered each other.

The hippies' guru of drug use was Dr. Timothy Leary (1920–96), directly referenced in *Hair* via Claude's song "Manchester": "Answer my weary query / Timothy Leary dearie." A clinical psychologist at Harvard from 1959 to 1963, Leary conducted research on Psilocybin, a hallucinogenic compound present in many mushroom varieties. Iconic beatnik poet Allen Ginsberg heard about Leary's research and joined Leary in his work extolling the spiritual benefits of psychedelic drug trips.

From 1963 through 1967, Leary conducted his most famous research on an estate in Millbrook, New York, where he expanded his explorations into Eastern religions. He professed that Eastern mystic beliefs combined with widened consciousness experienced through drugs yielded a new paganism: an approach to life valuing peace, love, and natural connections among all people and other beings. In 1966, the U.S. Senate convened hearings to consider criminalizing hallucinogenic drugs. Leary's widely publicized testimony before the Senate advocated legalized, regulated, safe manufacture and sale of hallucinogens to adults. Despite Leary's efforts, California made LSD illegal in October 1966. Many states followed suit, as did the federal government. In 1967, Leary was invited to speak at the San Francisco Human Be-In, where his mantra "tune in, turn on, drop out" became a motto of the hippie movement. The Be-In appearance permanently cemented Leary's identification with the legacy of hippie drug culture, particularly LSD.

Unlike LSD, marijuana (commonly weed, grass, or hashish) had a long cultural and legislative history in the United States. Unregulated sale and ingestion of dried or extracted Cannabis plant tips, the hallucinogenic in marijuana, date to at least the late 1800s and early 1900s. The 1920s saw a rise in recreational marijuana associated with an influx of Mexican immigrants after 1910. Economic downturns in the late 1920s fueled resentment against Mexican immigrants and fostered hostility among many white Americans to "foreign" Mexican culture, including speaking Spanish and smoking marijuana. In 1930, the government established the Federal Bureau of Narcotics, initiating a history of marijuana-related legislation and law enforcement fraught with dubious practices. These practices included racially discriminatory enforcement in marijuana-related searches, arrests, and sentencing—a pressing issue in law enforcement to this day. Moreover, throughout the twentieth century government officials and popular media promulgated false or exaggerated claims about the physiological and morally adverse effects of marijuana (Stringer and Maggard 2016; Schlosser 2003).

In addition to Claude's salute to Timothy Leary in "Manchester," *Hair* is replete with drug references that present psychedelic drug use as normalized behavior within the hippie tribe. The opening song "Aquarius" alludes to "mystic crystals," shorthand for LSD dripped onto sugar cubes for easy swallowing. Lyrics for "Hashish" offer a shopping list of drugs culminating in "sex and you." "Ain't Got No," another listing of needs, announces: "Ain't got no grass / Can't take no trip / Ain't got no acid." And that's just Act One.

Much of Act Two draws on Claude's drug trip that occurs after Berger distributes marijuana cigarettes (joints) to celebrate Claude's last day before reporting to the military. Visual projections of Claude's trip images imply that his joint is laced with LSD. The next song, "Walking in Space," alludes to Timothy Leary's teachings: "My soul is in orbit with God, face to face / Floating, flipping, flying, tripping." Notwithstanding documented health and safety risks associated with illegal psychedelic drug use, *Hair* all but ignores the negative effects of drug use in keeping with hippie views of psychedelic experiences. While Claude has nightmarish visions during his trip, his experience is isolated and contextualized by his decision to "drop back in" (return to society) and report for military duty. At the end, the *Hair* tribe tacitly mourns Claude's disappearance, but their larger message is that tripping lets the sunshine in.

Anti-bourgeois values and culture

Underpinning the anti-war and pro-psychedelic drugs stance of the hippie movement was a rejection of consumer capitalism that their parent's generation eagerly embraced following World War II. Supported by the GI Bill (1944), which subsidized college tuition and low-interest mortgages for veterans, millions of young adults furthered their education, married, became homeowners, pursued careers, and looked forward to guiding their children toward a similarly secure, materially-grounded life. Black veterans, however, rarely received benefits from the GI Bill because of local and national discriminatory practices. As a result, the children of GI beneficiaries tended to be white and grew up in new, federally subsidized suburbs. In rebellion against their own upward social mobility, hippies chose a contrarian, anti-establishment path that impacted mainstream American culture and politics for decades.

In the late 1960s, the hippie movement took root in the Haight-Ashbury district of San Francisco and New York City's East Village. Groups of young people—most aged between eighteen and twenty-five—tried to live together communally in shared crash pads or on the streets. Many created food co-ops and shared or bartered possessions to minimize their own consumerism. Free medical and social services sprang up supported by professional and community volunteers. To the consternation of their parents' generation, hippies spoke committedly of love, peace, and the decadence of material success. They spoke dismissively, if at all, of educational achievement, careerism, military service, and wealth. Their unapologetic focus on experiencing the moment through psychedelic drugs rebuked their parents' Great Depression Era ethos of youthful self-denial to ensure future financial security.

Hair joyously scorns establishment and materialistic ideology throughout. The song "Aquarius" promises no more establishment "falsehoods or derisions." In "Ain't Got No," three tribe members take turns describing what hippies don't possess, while other tribe members mock the "straight world's" likely reaction:

WOOF	TRIBE
Ain't got no home	so
Ain't got no shoes	poor ...

Rebuke of parental authority figures bred generational solidarity among hippies, and *Hair* approached that theme head-on as well. In Act One, Claude is confronted by his disapproving mom and dad, Berger recreates his expulsion from high school by his school principal, and the tribe merges parental rejection with the prevailing visual image of the day: "My hair like Jesus wore it ... Mary loved her son / Why don't my mother love me?" ("Hair").

With some justification, hippies were criticized for fashioning anti-materialistic beliefs from narrow, simplistic conceptions of Native American spiritualism, Eastern mysticism, and utopian philosophy. However, hippiedom also embraced serious writers, including Henry David Thoreau, Rachel Carson, J. D. Salinger, and Aldous Huxley, and Beat writers such as Jack Kerouac and William Burroughs. Over time, hippie literature added intellectual weight to the movement's impact on society.

Race relations in Hair *and hippiedom*

Appearing toward the end of a decade that saw passage of the 1964 Civil Rights Act and other significant advances for African Americans, *Hair* sought to demonstrate hippie culture's embrace of the Civil Rights Movement's integrationist values: racial equality, acceptance, and mutual respect in all legal and social spheres. While hippies espoused the ideal of racial integration, and producers of the musical view interracial harmony as fundamental to the show's legacy, history suggests strongly that young people of color generally kept their distance from hippie tribal culture.

From its earliest productions to this day, *Hair* requires racially integrated casting, although specific gender and racial cast composition can vary with each production. Black cast members are featured in three songs that countermand entrenched patterns of American racism: sanctions against interracial friendships, sexual intimacy, and marriage ("Black Boys/White Boys"); verbal assaults with racist epithets ("Colored Spade"); and harassment and suspicion Blacks encounter going about their normal lives ("Dead En"). With every new production of *Hair*, each cast names its tribe and confronts the history of racism invoked in "Colored Spade," "Dead End," and other aspects of the show. The on-stage connectivity among racially diverse tribes is a manifestation of the show's permanent commitment to the ideal of racial inclusivity.

However, notwithstanding *Hair*'s linking of hippie culture and the struggle for racial equality, hippiedom as a movement was overwhelmingly white (approximately 97 percent) and largely unappealing to people of color (Lemke-Santangelo 2009). The 1960s Civil Rights Movement championed access for Blacks to education, jobs, and upward mobility that hippies dismissed as plastic and corrupt. Few African Americans identified with white dropouts who wanted to "build a new ghetto and lock themselves in it" (Moretta 2017). Furthermore, hippies' appropriation of Native American culture was widely viewed—including by some Native Americans—as artificial and self-serving: "an attempt to align themselves with Native Americans ... to express an imagined sense of shared otherness" (Hahn 2014).

Greenwich Village, the setting for *Hair*, was more likely than most communities to foster integrated hippie tribes. "The Village" had a long history of integrated neighborhoods and social integration. The Village hosted the first public meeting of the NAACP (1909) and the first integrated nightclub in New York City (1938). The racially integrated *Hair* tribe might have reflected Greenwich Village's reality in the 1960s, but the concept of a nationwide racially-integrated hippie movement was, at best, an aspiration rather than an historical outcome.

Melanie Blood

Further reading

Albert, Stew. 1996. "Death of a Salesman: Remembering Timothy Leary." *Tikkun*, 11, no. 5 (September/October): 48–51.

Barnes, Clive. 1967. "HAIR, a Love-Rock Musical, Inaugurates Shakespeare Festival's Anspacher Playhouse; Contemporary Youth Depicted in Play." *New York Times*, October 30, 1967.

Barnes, Clive. 1968. "Theater: 'Hair:' It's Fresh and Frank; Likable Rock Musical Moves to Broadway." *New York Times*, April 30, 1968.

Barnes, Clive. 1971. "Hair." *Saturday Evening Post* 241, no. 16 (August 18): 66–9.

Bender, Marilyn. 1968. "'Hair' Topless and No Bottoms Either." *New York Times*, April 28, 1968.

Brustein, Robert. 1967. "From Hair to Hamlet." *The New Republic*, November 18, 1967.

Bunce, Alan N. 1968. "Hair Arrives on Broadway." *Christian Science Monitor*, May 3, 1968.

Chapman, John. 1968. "*Hair* Is Itchy, Twitchy, and Dirty: The Company Dances with Zest." *New York Daily News*, May 1, 1968.

Cooke, Richard P. 1967. "The Theater: Protesters but Likeable." *The Wall Street Journal*, October 31, 1967.

Culwell-Block, Logan. 2019. "*Hair* Original Broadway Cast Album Inducted into Library of Congress' National Recording Registry." *Playbill*, March 29, 2019.

Davis, James. 1967. "Hippie Hair Cliché Show." *New York Daily News*, October 31, 1967.

Davis, Lorrie and Rachel Gallagher. 1974. *Letting Down My Hair*. New York: Harper Collins.

Grode, Eric. 2018. "'Hair' 50 Years Later: Readers Tell Us When They Let the Sunshine In." *New York Times*, April 29, 2018.

Hahn, Miriam. 2014. "Playing Hippies and Indians: Acts of Cultural Colonization in the Theatre of the American Counterculture." Theatre Ph.D. dissertations, https:// scholarworks.bgsu.edu/theatre_diss/5.

"*Hair:* The American Tribal Love-Rock Musical." n.d. http://hairthemusical.com/.

Hall, Mitchell K. 2004. "The Vietnam Era Antiwar Movement." *Magazine of History* 18, no. 5 (October): 13–17.
Harris, Len. 1968. "Broadway Review." *CBS Television*, April 29, 1968.
Hartlaub, Peter and Sam Whiting. 2017. "Reliving the Human Be-In 50 Years Later." *San Francisco Chronicle*, January 13, 2017; revised March 11, 2017.
Holson, Laura M. 2019. "When a Be-In in Central Park Was Front-Page News." *New York Times*, March 25, 2019.
Horne, Barbara Lee. 1991. *The Age of Hair: Evolution and Impact of Broadway's First Rock Musical.* Westport, CT: Greenwood Press.
Johnson, Lyndon Baines. 1964. "August 4, 1964: Report on the Gulf of Tonkin Incident." Presidential Speeches of the Archive of the Miller Center of the University of Virginia: Speeches of Lyndon B. Johnson, millercenter.org/the-presidency/presidential-speeches/august-4-1964-report-gulf-tonkin-incident.
Knapp, Raymond. 2005. *The American Musical and the Formation of National Identity.* Princeton, NJ: Princeton University Press.
Lemke-Santangelo, Gretchen. 2009. *Daughters of Aquarius.* Lawrence: University Press of Kansas.
Libbey, Peter. 2018. "When 'Hair' Opened on Broadway, It Courted Controversy from the Start." *New York Times*, April 19, 2018.
Love, Robert. 2017. "50 Years Ago a Tiny Part of the Boomer Generation Tried to Change the World. Did They Succeed?" *AARP*, August/September 2017.
Making Sense of the Sixties. 1991. PBS documentary miniseries, 6 episodes. 1991.
Miller, Scott. 2003. *Let the Sun Shine In: The Genius of HAIR.* Portsmouth, NH: Heinemann Drama.
Moretta, Anthony J. 2017. *The Hippies: A 1960s History.* Jefferson, NC: McFarland.
O'Connell, Jack. 1968. *The Hippie Revolution.* Documentary film. Updated edition 1986, www.youtube.com/watch?v=zv3_caG7S5c&t=81s.
O'Connor, John J. 1968. "The Theater: Hair." *Wall Street Journal*, May 1, 1968.
Oliver, Edith. 1967. "Theater Reviews." *New Yorker*, November 11, 1967.
Philipps, Tom. 1968. "Rock Musicals: The Hippies Are from Time Magazine." *Rolling Stone Magazine*, July 20, 1968.
Schlosser, Eric. 2013. *Reefer Madness: Sex, Drugs, and Cheap Labor in the American Black Market.* Boston: Houghton Mifflin.
Smith, Michael. 1967. "Hair—Off Broadway Review." *Village Voice*, November 2, 1967.
Smith, Michael. 1968. "Theatre Journal: *Hair.*" *Village Voice*, May 2, 1968.
Stringer, Richard J. and Scott R. Maggard. 2016. "Reefer Madness to Marijuana Legalization." *Journal of Drug Issues* 46, no. 4 (October), doi:10.1177/0022042616659762.
Sullivan, Dan. 1967. "Papp Is a Love Person." *New York Times*, October 15, 1967.
"Supreme Court Clears 'Hair' for Boston Run." 1970. *New York Times*, May 23, 1970.
Tallmer, Jerry. 1967. "They Say No." *New York Post*, October 30, 1967.
"Two Days in October: Napalm and the Dow Chemical Company." 2005. *American Experience*, PBS, Aired October 2005, www.pbs.org/wgbh/americanexperience/features/two-days-in-october-dow-chemical-and-use-napalm.
Walsh, David and Len Platt. 2003. *Musical Theater and American Culture.* Westport, CT: Praeger.
Watts, Richard, Jr. 1968. "Two on the Aisle—Broadway Theater Review Music of the American Tribe." *New York Post*, April 30, 1968.
Wollman, Elizabeth L. 2009. *The Theater Will Rock: A History of the Rock Musical from Hair to Hedwig.* Ann Arbor: University of Michigan Press.

CHAPTER 11
HAMILTON: AN AMERICAN MUSICAL (2015)

Book, Music, and Lyrics by Lin-Manuel Miranda (1980–)
World Premiere: The Public Theater, New York City, February 17, 2015
Broadway Run: August 6, 2015–Present

Songs

Act One	**Act Two**
“Alexander Hamilton”	“What’d I Miss?”
	“Cabinet Battle #1”*
“Aaron Burr, Sir”*	
	“Take a Break”
“My Shot”	“Say No to This”
“The Story of Tonight”	“The Room Where It Happens”
“The Schuyler Sisters”	“Schuyler Defeated”
	“Cabinet Battle #2”*
“Farmer Refuted”	“Washington on Your Side”
“You’ll Be Back”	“One Last Time”
“Right Hand Man”	“I Know Him”*
“A Winter’s Ball”*	“The Adams Administration”
“Helpless”	“We Know”*
“Satisfied”	“Hurricane”
“The Story of Tonight” (Reprise)*	“The Reynolds Pamphlet”
“Wait for It”	“Burn”
“Stay Alive”	“Blow Us All Away”
“Ten Duel Commandments”	“Stay Alive” (Reprise)*
“Meet Me Inside”*	“It’s Quiet Uptown”
“That Would Be Enough”	“The Election of 1800”
“Guns and Ships”*	“Your Obedient Servant”
“History Has Its Eyes on You”	“Best of Wives and Best of Women”*
“Yorktown (The World Turned Upside Down)”	“The World Was Wide Enough”
“What Comes Next”*	
“Dear Theodosia”	
“Non-Stop”	“Finale (Who Lives, Who Dies, Who Tells Your Story)”

*Songs on the Original Cast Recording that were not listed as “Musical Numbers” in the opening night Broadway *Playbill*.

Overview

Hamilton: An American Musical (alternately *Hamilton*) recounts the life of Alexander Hamilton (*c.* 1757–1804), "Founding Father" and America's first Secretary of the Treasury. Lin-Manuel Miranda wrote the lyrics, music, and book after reading Ron Chernow's biography *Alexander Hamilton* (2004) during a vacation. The musical traces Hamilton's life, beginning with his arrival as an orphaned youth in New York City from his native West Indies, through his triumphs and setbacks in the founding of America, until his death after a duel with his long-time rival Aaron Burr (1756–1836). The tempestuous Hamilton–Burr feud frames the entire story of the musical and corresponds to their historic feud in many important ways. Most notable is that their ultimately fatal association—which saw conflicts arising from political philosophies, career jealousy, and personal animosity—begins during the Revolutionary War and metastasizes over more than twenty-five years.

The musical renders a creditable, if at times disjointed, representation of Hamilton's life and the pivotal roles he played in the founding of the United States. Divided into two acts (the Revolutionary War and the founding of the government, respectively), *Hamilton* firmly establishes its hero's imposing, occasionally reckless, verbally aggressive personality—a profile borne out by Hamilton biographies. A Caribbean-born orphan who migrated to New York, Hamilton is unique among the Founding Fathers who otherwise were sons of prosperous "in-country" families. *Hamilton* underscores its hero's immigrant status by making itself, in part, a celebration of American immigration throughout history. *Hamilton* also highlights the pivotal friendship between Hamilton and George Washington, twenty-five years Hamilton's senior and a mentor to Hamilton from their military service in the Revolutionary War until Washington's death in 1799. Additionally, the show notes Hamilton's quick ascent from newly arrived youth to "establishment" husband and in-law to a wealthy New York family—a status change that accelerated Hamilton's rise to power in real life.

As President Washington's Secretary of Treasury, Hamilton developed a comprehensive financial plan to stabilize the new nation. Hamilton hoped to alleviate the country's burdensome war debt and prepare America to assume a formidable economic presence on the world stage. Hamilton introduced his plan in 1790 and 1791, calling for the federal government to consolidate all remaining war debt; levy tariffs and domestic taxes to retire the debt; and charter a national bank to manage future government credit and taxation. Hamilton, by then a wealthy New York attorney and businessman, favored policies that prioritized emerging Northern manufacturing over traditional Southern agrarian economics. His plan also reflected his long-standing Federalist political philosophy, extolling the primacy of central government authority over states' rights. Equally predictable was Southern opposition, led by Thomas Jefferson: Secretary of State, states rights' advocate, and wealthy Virginia plantation slaveholder. Jefferson and his allies had the votes to block the plan in Congress, so Hamilton negotiated with Southern leaders to move the nation's capital from New York City to Washington, D.C. in return for their support of the financial plan. The deal was struck and Congress approved Hamilton's plan in 1791.

In the same year, Aaron Burr won a New York Senate seat, unseating incumbent Philip Schuyler, Hamilton's father-in-law. Hamilton's resulting resentment accelerated the two men's collision course of personal antagonism and political rivalry that lasted through the elections of 1792, 1796, and 1800, ending in their fatal duel in 1804. Along the way, Hamilton became embroiled in a scandalous romantic affair; the humiliating publicity ended his presidential hopes and nearly destroyed his marriage to Eliza Schuyler.

Although *Hamilton* is replete with humor and clever wordplay, Miranda wanted *Hamilton*'s historical content to be "taken seriously." He hired biographer Ron Chernow as historical consultant on the project. Miranda continuously questioned Chernow on the minutiae of Hamilton's life and solicited Chernow's fact-checking scrutiny of the script. While dutifully attentive to Chernow's factchecking, Miranda was not bound by its constraints. For example, Chernow questioned a meeting set in 1776 with Hamilton and friends the

Marquis de Lafayette, Hercules Mulligan, and John Laurens. Chernow noted that Hamilton did not meet Lafayette until much later, but Miranda wanted to establish a narrative trajectory for the four friends and thus the scene remained.

Miranda also marched his musical into discussions over historical process, specifically the tension between objectivity and subjectivity in historical narratives. Normally "shop talk" among historians and history teachers, questions surrounding historical objectivity and subjectivity increasingly fascinated Miranda as he engaged with Chernow about Hamilton and his times. Of these exchanges, Miranda declared: "Ron [Chernow] tells you a story, and he's the star of the story. I tell you a story and I'm the star of the story" (Miranda and McCarter 2016). Significantly, Miranda's doctrine of the storytellers' ownership of history figures prominently in the musical. The power of writing and speaking is itself a recurring theme in the show. Moreover, the character of Aaron Burr, functioning as both principal narrator and antagonist within the play, literally bring history's storyteller center-stage, as does the show's finale: "Who Lives, Who Dies, Who Tells Your Story?"

Another significant aspect of historical representation made its presence known when Miranda introduced Chernow to the original cast. Chernow expressed surprise upon discovering that Miranda had selected African American and Latinx actors to portray Washington, Jefferson, Burr, and other figures whose ethnic identities were indisputably Anglo-European. In addition to sending a message that diversity and inclusion were American founding principles, if not founding realities, Miranda wanted his actors/singers to represent the cultural source of the show's dominant modes of music, which were African American and Latinx urban-based rap and hip hop. Miranda has said of the show's casting, "[*Hamilton*] is the story of America then told by America now" (Miranda and McCarter 2016). Chernow concurred, dismissing racial considerations in casting as irrelevant to historical accuracy. When *Hamilton* premiered, the casting drew largely favorable support along with some fervent rebukes. Over time, audiences and educators overwhelmingly embraced the show's casting as a positive element in the musical's approach to inclusion, diversity, and American history itself.

Miranda and *Hamilton* broke with other theater traditions as well. The production history of *Hamilton* expanded the ways in which America reads, writes, and learns about American theater. Typically, even successful Broadway shows struggle for national attention. Theater press coverage and books are perpetually overshadowed by writings on other popular arts. A Broadway musical sold out for three years will be seen by fewer than half the viewers of one 30-minute episode of a low-rated network television comedy. As such, American musicals occupy a relatively small space in the national landscape of artistic information. However, Miranda, *Hamilton*'s chief publicist and painstaking documentarian on top of everything else, turned standard audience development strategies upside down for his show.

In May 2009, auspiciously and doubtless opportunistically, Miranda announced his in-progress concept mixtape of songs about Alexander Hamilton while performing at the White House in front of President and First Lady Barack and Michelle Obama. Appearing at a White House poetry jam, Miranda had completed only one song for the mixtape and had never performed it professionally. He told the amused, skeptical presidential party that Treasury Secretary Hamilton's life was an inspiring American immigrant hip hop story. Miranda promptly launched into a stunning performance of the song "Alexander Hamilton," which, six years later, would become the opening number of *Hamilton* (A *YouTube* video of that performance had been viewed over 7,300,000 times by late 2020. That same video had over 10 million views in late 2025, and *Youtube* is now filled with original and cover versions of the song.). As a public relations rollout for a show that had no script, no cast, and one completed song, Miranda's White House performance of "Alexander Hamilton" stands as a one-of-a-kind musical theater promotional phenomenon.

Miranda eventually developed new songs about Hamilton. He had been particularly moved by Hamilton's early life: an outsider, mixed race, orphaned, impoverished. Once educated in New York, Hamilton forged his brilliance and brashness into a quintessential American immigrant success story: famous lawyer-politician, war hero, and aide to General George Washington while in his twenties; Secretary of the Treasury at thirty-two. Twenty-eight-year-old Miranda, a descendent of Puerto Rican immigrants, had recently made a leap from an obscure unsigned rap artist to rising Broadway star. He could relate to Hamilton and did. Amid other projects, more songs about Hamilton and an elaborate storyline emerged. Ultimately, Miranda realized he was writing a musical and not just a collection of Hamilton songs.

As his *Hamilton* musical neared completion, Miranda secured backing from The Public Theater, New York's premiere Off-Broadway venue. *Hamilton* opened at The Public on February 17, 2015, to a sell-out run and rave reviews. The show transferred to Broadway, opening on August 6, 2015, at the Richard Rodgers Theatre—home of his previous debut musical, *In the Heights*. Eight months later, Miranda published *Hamilton: The Revolution*, an exquisitely designed, annotated coffee-table edition of the libretto. Unprecedented for a commercial Broadway book in its scholarly yet accessible depth of content, *Hamilton: The Revolution* became an award-winning, bestselling book.

As the musical demonstrates, Hamilton was a prodigious writer, and *Hamilton: An American Musical* honors that quality. The musical tells a story about Hamilton and his times, but it also tells a story of how history is told and recreated in the telling. Miranda's creative process reveals how musicals are made as well as how they evolve. *Hamilton* invokes the Miranda family's immigrant journey even as it celebrates America's epical immigrant tradition. Like its namesake, *Hamilton: An American Musical* sought an elevated place for itself in the world. With its tenth Broadway anniversary behind it, the 4,000th performance a presumptive certainty for 2026, and national touring productions selling well ten years after its Tony Awards near-sweep, *Hamilton* has certainly found one.

Plot synopsis

The musical opens in New York City, 1776. Twenty-year-old Alexander Hamilton, an orphan from the West Indies sent as a teenager to the mainland, is an ambitious college graduate eager to make his mark in the War for Independence. He meets Aaron Burr, assistant to General George Washington, whose career advice to deferentially "talk less" offends the self-assertive Hamilton. Hamilton befriends three young revolutionaries: the Marquis de Lafayette, John Laurens, and Hercules Mulligan, who bond over their shared vision of an independent nation led by themselves ("My Shot," "The Story of Tonight"). The Schuyler Sisters—Eliza, Angelica, and Peggy—sing in celebration of New York City, imminent American independence, and future equality for women ("The Schuyler Sisters"). In London, King George III warns his rebellious American subjects to accept his authority or face destruction ("You'll Be Back").

In New York the war effort falters as the British have surrounded the city. A beleaguered General Washington appoints Hamilton as his chief aide, passing over Burr ("Right Hand Man"). Hamilton hopes that his appointment will earn him a military command. A jealous Burr ponders the meteoric rise of his rival, acknowledging Hamilton's prodigious writing skills and ambition ("A Winter's Ball" and "Wait for It"). Both Angelica and Eliza Schuyler have fallen for Hamilton, but he marries Eliza. Eliza fears her sister's designs on him as Angelica privately confesses her feelings for Hamilton. Resignedly, Angelica offers best wishes to Eliza and her groom ("Helpless," "Satisfied").

George Washington exhorts Hamilton to invigorate the lethargic colonial war effort. Hamilton asks Washington for a military command but is denied. We learn that Hamilton has now been passed over twice for a command, first losing out to Charles Lee whom Washington subsequently replaced with Lafayette. Offended by his demotion, Lee openly criticizes Washington. An incensed Laurens engages Lee in a pistol duel; Hamilton and Burr second Laurens and Lee, respectively. Washington enters, thanks the wounded Lee for his service and chastises Laurens, Hamilton, and Burr for abetting a fight among officers. In a private meeting, Washington sends Hamilton home, where Eliza reveals that she is pregnant. Eliza and Hamilton discuss the tension between his commitment to the revolution and his obligations as husband and father ("That Would Be Enough").

Lafayette proclaims his successes in battle and in securing armaments from France for the Americans' war effort. Lafayette and Washington plan a final attack at Yorktown, realizing they need Hamilton to ensure their success. Washington summons Hamilton and assigns him a command. Confiding that he failed in his first command, Washington cautions Hamilton about the perils of leadership ("History Has Its Eyes on You").

The ensemble celebrates Washington's victory and Britain's surrender at Yorktown. They hail American independence while singing the praises of Hamilton, Lafayette, and Mulligan ("Yorktown: The World Turned Upside Down"). King George, acknowledging defeat, oozes confidence that the burdens of self-governing will overwhelm the fledgling country ("What Comes Next?"). New fathers Burr and Hamilton sing in parallel of the responsibility of fatherhood ("Dear Theodosia").

Laurens, fatally shot by British soldiers, enters as a spirit, warning that the dream of a free America will go unrealized unless slavery is abolished. Burr and Hamilton return to New York and open separate law practices. Burr is awestruck by Hamilton's prodigious legal practice and writing ability. Burr declines Hamilton's request to help write what would become the *Federalist Papers*. Working with John Jay and James Madison, Hamilton writes fifty-one of the eighty-five documents. George Washington is elected President and selects Hamilton as Secretary of the Treasury ("Non Stop").

Act Two

After the war, Burr worries that Secretary of the Treasury Hamilton will divide the colonies with his Federalist economic proposals. Thomas Jefferson returns home after serving as Ambassador to France to become Secretary of State ("What'd I Miss?"). Jefferson protests against Hamilton's financial plan in cabinet, castigating Hamilton's proposed national bank as a self-serving encroachment on individual freedom and states' rights. Hamilton denounces Jefferson's position as a shameless defense of slavery in the South ("Cabinet Battle #1").

Eliza gives nine-year-old son Philip a birthday piano lesson, beckoning Hamilton to cease writing and join their celebration ("Take a Break"). Hamilton is secretly exchanging amorous letters with Angelica, who will soon visit America from London. Angelica arrives and both sisters plead with Hamilton to join them in upstate New York for a Schuyler family vacation. Hamilton declines, citing work responsibilities. He meets Maria Reynolds who, claiming abandonment by her husband, seeks Hamilton's assistance. They begin an affair, which Maria's husband discovers. He proceeds to blackmail Hamilton to maintain his silence about the affair ("Say No to This").

Burr expresses frustration over his exclusion from a meeting wherein Hamilton, Madison, and Jefferson negotiate moving the nation's capital to Washington, D.C. in return for Southerners' support for his financial plan ("The Room Where It Happens"). Burr wins a New York Senate seat from incumbent Philip Schuyler, Hamilton's father-in-law, thus exacerbating the long-simmering Hamilton–Burr feud ("Schuyler Defeated"). In Cabinet, Hamilton and Jefferson debate whether Washington should send military assistance to France during the French Revolution. Jefferson argues for intervention in consideration of France's support in the American Revolution. Hamilton, arguing for neutrality, prevails with President Washington ("Cabinet Battle #2").

Burr aligns himself with Jefferson and Madison in their shared resentment of Hamilton's influence over the President ("Washington on Your Side"). Washington confides to Hamilton that he will step down as President, noting that Jefferson has resigned his Cabinet position to run for the presidency himself ("One Last Time").

Adams defeats Jefferson for the 1796 presidency. King George re-enters, disparaging Adams as an incapable leader ("I Know Him").

President Adams removes Hamilton as Treasury Secretary. Jefferson, Madison, and Burr accuse Hamilton of improper use of federal funds (speculation) when he made blackmail payments to James Reynolds regarding his affair with Maria Reynolds ("The Adams Administration," "We Know"). Jarred by these setbacks, Hamilton turns to his strength: writing his way out of trouble. He pens a legal defense of his conduct, confessing his affair in the process ("The Reynolds Pamphlet"). Eliza is heartbroken. Philip Hamilton, now ninteen, is shot fatally in a duel with George Eacker, a New York lawyer who had slandered Alexander Hamilton in a public speech ("Blow Us All Away," "Stay Alive"). The cumulative misfortunes render Hamilton grief-stricken. Eliza silently takes Hamilton's hand in forgiveness ("It's Quiet Uptown").

With Hamilton politically weakened, Jefferson and Madison assess Jefferson's chances against Burr in the upcoming 1800 presidential election. The vote results in an electoral dead heat. Prior to the Congress' tie-breaking vote, Hamilton endorses Jefferson, preferring Jefferson's odious political philosophy to Burr's lack of principles ("The Election of 1800"). Believing that Hamilton's endorsement swayed the election toward Jefferson, an enraged Burr exchanges angry letters with Hamilton and challenges him to a duel ("Your Obedient Servant"). Burr and Hamilton duel. Hamilton is shot fatally and delivers a meditation as he dies. Burr acknowledges his moral failing in killing Hamilton ("The World Was Wide Enough"). Washington, Jefferson, and others pay tribute to Hamilton. Eliza addresses the audience on her lifelong effort to proclaim Hamilton's legacy and tell his story ("Who Lives, Who Dies, Who Tells Your Story?").

Critical reception

Advance publicity surrounding *Hamilton* was so overwhelming that the hype itself became part of the show's critical reception. Prior to opening on Broadway, *Hamilton* had made national news on several fronts: Miranda's White House appearance; the controversial race-conscious casting of the Founding Fathers; box office (not scalped) ticket prices as high as $1,000 (Lawrence 2017); and advance ticket purchases that sold out the show eight months ahead of the opening night. Some critics even spoke of "*Hamilton* fatigue" in advance of reviewing it.

Critics fearing that *Hamilton*'s Broadway opening might fall short of its soaring expectations ultimately acknowledged the superb innovative theater experience that unfolded before them. "Yes, it's that good," wrote Ben Brantley in the *New York Times*, noting that the advance publicity made the show a tempting target for disparagement (Brantley 2015). Linda Winer of *Newsday* also wondered if the "delirious" advance praise would deflate the Broadway production but found the show masterfully "nuanced, cohesive, and effective" (Winer 2015). Dan Aucoin of the *Boston Globe* observed that *Hamilton*, having arrived on Broadway "under the burden of expectation," triumphed by forging "the storytelling power of hip-hop . . . with the revolutionary passions of a new nation heaving itself into existence" (Aucoin 2015). Terry Teachout in the *Wall Street Journal* wrote that initial misgivings about the show were swept aside by Miranda's "vaulting score" that powered this "most important musical" of the decade (Teachout 2015). *Hamilton's* opening night reception more than justified its advance reputation and established Miranda as a superb promoter among his other talents.

Many reviewers perceived *Hamilton* not simply as an excellent show in its own right, but a milestone in the evolution of the American musical. Brantley proclaimed "*Hamilton* is making its own resonant history by changing the language of musicals . . . insisting that rap, hip-hop, [and] R&B ballads have both the narrative force and the emotional interiority to propel a hefty musical about long-dead white men" (Brantley 2015). Jesse Green of the cultural website *Vulture* embraced Miranda's self-conscious mirroring of the Founding

Fathers' revolutionary experiments with forms of government and the author's own innovations with forms of musical theater: "*Hamilton* not only incorporates newish-to-Broadway song forms; it . . . advances them . . . opening up new territory for exploitation. It's the musical theater, not just American history, that gets refurbished" (Green 2015). Chris Jones of the *Chicago Tribune* straightforwardly anointed *Hamilton* "the most entertaining, provocative and moving civics lesson in Broadway history" (Jones 2015). Some reviewers even went so far as to assert that the thirty-five-year-old Miranda, with this and one other hit show under his belt (*In the Heights*, 2007), had already secured a place of distinction in the history of American musical theater.

Among Broadway opening night critics, *Hamilton* had virtually no genuine detractors, although the *New York Post*'s Elisabeth Vincentelli found claims for the show's "revolutionary" achievements overstated: "Truly radical art is divisive, and under its brash exterior, *Hamilton* is warmly reassuring" (Vincentelli 2015). She also found the show's "history-with-a-capital-H-stuff" diluted and relatively ineffective.

Within three months of *Hamilton*'s opening night, the "history-with-a-capital-H stuff" took on a surprising and unprecedented role in the critical reception of a Broadway show. As part of a philanthropic initiative to make $10 *Hamilton* tickets available to groups of New York public school students, a not-for-profit organization developed online and classroom curriculum materials on *Hamilton* and the Revolutionary War era. The high-profile educational initiative generated a surge of commentary by historians on *Hamilton* as a vehicle for studying American history in schools. For the most part, professional historians found *Hamilton* to be an excellent educational resource with much to admire and enlarge upon. However, the issue of casting the Founding Fathers with performers of color, which generated no controversy among the traditional opening night reviews, surfaced in several writings on *Hamilton* and the history of slavery. Some writers took strong exception to Miranda's and Chernow's assertion that the show's casting offers a positive message of inclusion and diversity. Poet and critic Ishmael Reed posited the show's casting as a Halloween-like grotesque of racial history that distracts from Hamilton's personal family history of involvement with slavery and slave trading. Historian Lyra Monteiro noted that the conspicuous representation of white aristocratic slaveholders as people of color "erases" racial identity, undercutting Miranda's own argument that the identity of the storyteller ("who tells your story") is a fundamental tenet of historical truthtelling. However, the heated debate over *Hamilton*'s casting, while resurfacing periodically, has had a negligible impact on the show's overall enthusiastic critical and audience reception.

As a magnet for musical theater awards and accolades, the Broadway production of *Hamilton: An American Musical* is in a class by itself. It received the most Tony nominations (sixteen) in the sixty-nine-year history of the awards. With eleven Tony Award wins, it is second only to Mel Brooks' *The Producers* (2001), which won twelve. *Hamilton* won the Grammy Award for Best Musical Theater Album as well as the Pulitzer Prize in Drama. Largely on the strength of *Hamilton*, Miranda was awarded a 2015 MacArthur Fellowship (the prestigious "Genius Grants") for "expanding the conventions of musical theater . . . that reflect the diverse cultural panorama of the American urban experience" ("Lin-Manuel Miranda: Class of 2015" 2015). Former First Lady Michelle Obama has proclaimed *Hamilton* "The best piece of art I have ever seen in my life" (Obama 2016). In 2018, the Kennedy Center Honors, which recognizes *lifetime* achievements in the arts (emphasis added), created a special award just for *Hamilton* and presented it to Miranda and his youthful collaborators in the televised ceremony along with the other honorees: singers Cher and Reba McEntire, jazz musician Wayne Shorter, and composer Philip Glass, all of whom had been established artists since before Miranda was born.

Miranda left the Broadway cast after one year. Two U.S. tours in 2017 and 2018 brought "Miranda-less" productions to locations far and wide. Yet, even without Miranda starring on stage or relentlessly promoting the show in the media, *Hamilton* sustained its original appeal and mystique (at somewhat reduced ticket prices) well beyond its seismic Broadway opening.

Historical accuracy and context

Hamilton's financial plan: who borrows, who pays, who borrows later?

Parts of Hamilton's legacy as Secretary of the Treasury do not lend themselves readily to theatrical expression. Most notable is Hamilton's arcane, trenchantly detailed financial plan he proposed to President Washington's Cabinet and to Congress in 1790 and 1791. Hamilton's financial plan contained several key points:

- consolidating the federal and states' Revolutionary War debts into a single national debt;
- replacing individual state currencies with a single national currency;
- establishing a national bank to collect federal taxes and regulate borrowing and lending practices;
- levying excise taxes on certain goods made in America and levying tariffs on imports to strengthen American manufacturing ("Hamilton and the Public Debt" 2019).

Hamilton was the target of the plan's many critics. Principal among them was Thomas Jefferson, Secretary of State, a strong voice for anti-Federalist policies (i.e., states' rights) and a leading politician among the Southern states. *Hamilton: An American Musical* effectively presents Hamilton as a visionary thinker among his peers. In addition, the musical accurately represents Hamilton's contentious debating style via Miranda's rap-battle lyrics and cadences, especially as they appear in the two Cabinet battles. Cabinet Battle #1 concerns itself specifically with Hamilton's financial plan, credibly recounting Jefferson's major objections to Hamilton's proposals. By 1790, Virginia and other Southern states had little or no outstanding war debts. Jefferson argued that forcing states like Virginia to overpay in order to bail out debt-ridden states like New York unfairly disadvantaged the debt-free states. Moreover, Jefferson protested that a national debt managed by a national bank conferred powers upon the federal government not explicitly mentioned in the Constitution.

While Jefferson's objections in Cabinet Battle #1 are faithful to Jefferson's historic positions, Hamilton's on-stage counter-arguments drift away from Hamilton's actual rationale for his proposals. Hamilton's on-stage rebuttal to Jefferson assumes an historically dislocated sensibility, delivering a profanity-laden *ad hominem* rebuke of Jefferson. He dismisses Jefferson's opposition to the national bank as the morally convenient hypocrisy of a Southern slaveholder and elitist privilege of an aristocrat who did not fight in the Revolutionary War. Apart from the fact that in 1790, slavery was still legal, heavily supported, and practiced widely in the state of New York, Hamilton's actual defense of his financial plan was grounded in straightforward, decidedly unentertaining economic theory: "In countries in which the national debt is . . . an object of established confidence, it answers most of the purposes of money . . . A National Bank is an Institution of primary importance to the prosperous administration of the Finances [and] Public Credit" (Hamilton 1790).

Hamilton *and Burr rivalry part I: 1776–1800*

Notwithstanding its sprawling plot, *Hamilton* is held together by the nearly thirty-year rivalry between Hamilton and Aaron Burr, which ended in 1804 when Burr fatally shot Hamilton in a duel. The musical honors the fact that the Hamilton–Burr feud developed over decades. The two men continuously crossed paths as military and career rivals, philosophical and political adversaries, and personal antagonists. Burr, the first character to speak in *Hamilton,* frames the entire musical as an investigation into his rival's improbable life: "How does a bastard, orphan, son of a whore . . . Grow up to be a hero . . .?"

Historians cannot document a date-specific first meeting between the two, but it certainly had occurred by the early stages of the Revolutionary War. Hamilton and Burr's meeting scene in Act One is a fictionalized conjecture ("Aaron Burr, Sir"), in which Miranda's inventive word volleys foreshadow the lifelong clashes between the deliberative Burr and the confrontational, expressive Hamilton.

The historical significance of the Hamilton–Burr feud rests largely in the two men's contrasting political ideologies. Lead author of the *Federalist Papers*, Hamilton's advocacy for a strong centralized government frequently conflicted with Burr's general preference to leave most governing power to individual states. In so doing, Burr often aligned himself with fellow Hamilton rival Thomas Jefferson.

Although it abridges a number of details and reorders some sequences of events, the musical sensibly represents the regularity with which Hamilton and Burr found themselves in conflict. The show recounts accurately that Burr fell out of favor with Washington during the Revolutionary War while Hamilton, a superb officer and administrator, won Washington's admiration. In 1777, Washington promoted Hamilton over Burr into a senior staff position. Burr never regained Washington's favor and his subsequent jealousy of Hamilton serves as an energizing force throughout the show. Burr's 1791 victory in a New York Senate election against incumbent Philip Schuyler, Hamilton's father-in-law, not only satisfied Burr's political ambitions but also infuriated Hamilton—a sequence highlighted within the show. Hamilton and Burr's rivalry grew increasingly fierce as both men became influential in national politics. In the presidential elections of 1792, 1796, and 1800, Burr and Hamilton often worked in direct opposition to the other's political interests and allies.

Hamilton and Burr rivalry part II: 1800–4

The musical's staging of the political backstory surrounding the election of 1800 is as well presented as any historical information in the show. The election of 1800 resulted in an electoral tie between Thomas Jefferson, immediate past Secretary of State, and fellow Democratic-Republican Aaron Burr, former senator from New York. Notwithstanding Hamilton's antagonism for both men, Jefferson and Burr each solicited Hamilton's endorsement for the tie-breaking vote among the electors. Hamilton endorsed Jefferson with faint praise for Jefferson's "pretensions to character," but dismissing Burr as "[morally] bankrupt beyond redemption" (Hamilton 1800). Jefferson won a close tie-breaking electoral runoff. An embittered Burr became Vice President in accordance with prevailing election rules.

The rivalry drives the musical's climax. Vice President Burr fell out of favor with Jefferson and realized he would not win re-election as Vice President in 1804. Burr runs for Governor of New York in 1804 but is confronted by Hamilton's disparaging remarks about him in a letter circulating among New York's social and political elite. Burr lost the gubernatorial race to State Attorney General Morgan Lewis. The musical accurately presents Burr's gubernatorial defeat as precipitating an angry exchange of letters between Hamilton and Burr ("Your Obedient Servant"), plausibly suggesting that this feud is, in part, a carryover from previous grievances. The hostile exchange culminated in Burr challenging Hamilton to a duel, which occurred on July 11, 1804. The musical suggests that Hamilton shot first, deliberately firing above Burr's head, but historical accounts are not conclusive on that point. Burr's bullet struck Hamilton in the waist causing multiple injuries. Hamilton died the following day. In the aftermath (not staged in the musical) Burr was prosecuted for his role in the duel. Although later acquitted of criminal charges, Burr's political career was ruined beyond recovery.

Hamilton successfully captures the broad sweep of the Hamilton–Burr rivalry as well as the prominent role that the weaponized written word played along the way. However, some of its representations of the Hamilton–Burr feud are glaringly false. *Hamilton* presents Burr as a face-to-face accuser of Hamilton in the "Reynolds Pamphlet" scandals. Burr likely knew many details in advance of the Pamphlet's publication, but he was not, as portrayed, among the men who initially confronted Hamilton with the letter. Some observers argue that *Hamilton* exaggerates the Hamilton–Burr feud in their early years. While at one point in the show, they refer to each other passingly as friends, apparently during their years as young lawyers in New York they readily set political differences aside, worked cooperatively on legal matters, and socialized. As their respective political ambitions and influence grew in the 1790s, however, the earlier friendship and pleasantries indisputably fell by the wayside.

The Reynolds Pamphlet: America's first political "hush money" scandal

One way in which *Hamilton* distinguishes itself as a history-oriented musical is its attentiveness to a wide range of Revolution-era documents over and above foundational works like the *Declaration of Independence* or the *Constitution*. A case in point is the obscure but impactful "Reynolds Pamphlet," whose actual title was "Observations on Certain Documents Contained in No. V & VI of 'The History of the United States for the Year 1796,' In Which the Charge of Speculation Against Alexander Hamilton, Late Secretary of the Treasury, is Fully Refuted. Written by Himself." As the musical demonstrates in an abridged recreation of key events, the "Reynolds Pamphlet" permanently altered Hamilton's political fortunes.

In 1792, Hamilton, then Secretary of the Treasury under Washington, was confronted by three Congressmen with evidence that Hamilton had misused government funds while making unauthorized payments (improper speculation) to one James Reynolds. What the Congressmen had actually discovered was that Hamilton had used his own money legally to dissuade Reynolds from exposing Hamilton's affair with his wife, Maria Reynolds. While not embezzlement, Hamilton knew that public disclosure of the illicit affair and scandalous blackmail payments would destroy his political future. Hamilton persuaded the Congressmen to let the matter drop, and the Reynolds' affair remained undisclosed for nearly five years.

The accusations resurfaced in 1797 as presidential hopefuls were positioning themselves for the 1800 presidential election to determine John Adams' successor. Potential candidates included Jefferson, Burr, and Madison, each of whom had reasons for viewing Hamilton as a political threat. Journalist James Callender, unmentioned in the musical, advertised his forthcoming exposé purportedly detailing multiple transgressions on Hamilton's part, some true and some false. Hamilton pre-empted Callender's exposé by producing the aforementioned painstakingly documented counterattack on his accusers. Informally known as the "Reynolds Pamphlet," Hamilton's decree included a legalistic refutation of the financial charges against him and a cringeworthy confession of his affair with Maria Reynolds.

With the "Reynolds Pamphlet," Hamilton sought to write his way to personal vindication and public acclaim, but he woefully misjudged its impact. The "Reynolds Pamphlet" was widely mocked for its outsized self-indulgence and unsettling account of the love affair. Hamilton lost any chance he had to earn the presidency in what turned out to be the relatively short remainder of his life. Although historical consensus holds that publishing the "Reynolds Pamphlet" represented the greatest political error of Hamilton's career, his ambition and close ties to President Washington allowed him to maintain considerable political influence in the years that followed.

But for abridging the timeline, the musical gives a remarkably accurate and informative account of the "Reynolds Pamphlet" incident. Miranda compresses Hamilton's two separate phases of the surfacing scandal (1792 and 1797) into a single encounter in 1797. Thus, events leading up to the scandal, the writing of the pamphlet, and the aftermath of publication occur on stage in rapid succession even though they were actually spread out over several years. Moreover, Miranda has Jefferson, Madison, and Burr confront Hamilton with the first appearance of evidence—doubtless an intentional inaccuracy intended to exacerbate hostilities between Burr and Hamilton for dramatic effect.

The four-song "Reynolds Pamphlet" sequence ("We Know," "Hurricane", "The Reynolds Pamphlet,""and "Burn") lasts barely ten minutes but adroitly conveys critical elements of the entire incident: rising animosities between Hamilton and both Burr and Jefferson; plausible representations of Hamilton's self-destructive impulses; the demise of Hamilton's presidential ambitions (the phrase "never gon' be President now" is repeated sixteen times); and Eliza's despair over the scandal.

Hamilton and Hamilton *on slavery*

Miranda's balance of historical detail and creative license has excited audiences and, for the most part, impressed educators. Not surprisingly, the main controversies arising from the musical's historical representation, apart from issues concerning race and casting, concern slavery itself. Scholars and educators have never reached a consensus on how best to conceptualize and teach the legacy of American slavery. A single musical theater production was hardly going to settle matters.

Miranda's *Hamilton* viscerally denounces slavery on both human rights and economic grounds. In the song "Alexander Hamilton," Miranda opens the show asserting that Hamilton's opposition to slavery was formed during his childhood in the Caribbean and remained with him throughout his life. Miranda owes much of this view to Chernow's biography, which draws the inference that Hamilton observed the brutality of slavery as a child in the Caribbean, recoiled in disgust, and carried that sensibility into adulthood. Some historians have challenged not only the assertion in Miranda's song but also Chernow's hypothesis directly as undocumented and speculative.

Hamilton accurately positions New Yorker Hamilton and Virginian Jefferson as principal adversaries in debates over Hamilton's financial plan. However, in so doing, the musical expands the two men's well-documented differences on economics into a highly fictionalized morality play-within-a-play, wherein righteous Northern egalitarianism triumphs over plantation slave-economy corruption. However, Hamilton's opposition to slavery is not nearly as clear-cut as the musical suggests.

Hamilton expressed anti-slavery beliefs in several writings. In addition, he was a member of the New York Manumission society, a group that helped fund education for freed African Americans, and he lobbied for emancipation laws in New York. However, the musical ignores the relevant fact that Hamilton's wealthy in-laws, the Schuylers, owned slaves. As the family lawyer, Hamilton often assisted the family in financial matters to his own and their benefit, apparently without protesting or withdrawing from the family's lifelong involvement in slavery. Pertinent as well is the musical's first-act celebration of late eighteenth-century New York City as a hotbed of new ideas ("the greatest city in the world"), which foregrounds Hamilton's anti-slavery rebuke of Jefferson in "Cabinet Battle #1." The musical strongly implies that Hamilton confronts Jefferson in Cabinet from the moral high ground of anti-slavery New York state shaming a Southern slave state. However, through the late eighteenth and into the nineteenth century, New York City and state maintained strong connections to the slave trade. New York was one of the last Northern states to outlaw slavery, only passing a "gradual emancipation" law in 1799, eight years after the presumptive date of Cabinet Battle #1, and it did not pass an abolition law until 1817, thirteen years after Hamilton's death. During Hamilton's time, as one historian notes, "slavery could produce great wealth, as was true for George Washington, Thomas Jefferson, and Alexander Hamilton, all of whom married into families made rich by slaves" (Harris 2018). Hamilton actually adopts a common pro-Northern rhetorical maneuver of invoking Jefferson's massive slaveholdings to obscure the North's 200-year complicity in America's slave trade.

Additional factual inaccuracies and misrepresentations

While initially an exercise in academic fact-checking, identifying errors in *Hamilton* expanded over time into a niche trivia game played by *Hamilton* fans in social settings or online. Miranda himself has been known to participate in fact-checking chats, famously on the website *Genius.com* ("Hamilton . . . Inaccuracies" n.d.). Documented historical inaccuracies in the text of *Hamilton* include the following:

Alterations of time sequences

- Miranda acknowledges altering details of Laurens' travels just before his death to abet the dramatic timing of his posthumous challenge to the celebrants at Yorktown: "Black and white soldiers wonder alike if this really means freedom."
- In the musical, John Adams, upon becoming President, removes Hamilton as Secretary of the Treasury. However, Hamilton had resigned in 1795, two years before Adams was inaugurated as President.
- Angelica Schuyler, Hamilton's sister-in-law and a woman whom Hamilton found very attractive, was married when Hamilton first met her. She is single when Hamilton meets her in the play. Perhaps, Miranda felt that Hamilton's simultaneous attraction to two unmarried sisters worked well dramatically.
- Hamilton's oldest son Philip was killed in a duel in 1801. However, for the musical, Miranda moves Phillip's death back to around 1797, intensifying the anguish that Alexander and Eliza face in the aftermath of the "Reynolds Pamphlet" scandal.
- *Hamilton* alludes briefly to (Levi) Weeks' court case, sometimes heralded as the country's first "celebrity murder trial," setting it in the 1780s. The Weeks trial actually occurred in 1800. Hamilton and Burr were Weeks' co-counsel, as noted in the show.

Head counts, attendance, and absences

- While Alexander and Eliza's son Phillip appears in the musical, the Hamiltons had eight children; none of the others appear on stage. (Miranda did not want child characters drawing attention from Hamilton's public ventures.)
- Angelica Schuyler states in "Satisfied" that her father has no sons—only three daughters. However, Philip Schuyler was father to fifteen children, eight of whom survived to adulthood, including two sons.
- Foreshadowing the Hamilton–Burr duel, the musical recounts a duel between Laurens and General Charles Lee, in which Lee was wounded. On stage, Hamilton and Burr serve as seconds to Laurens and Lee, respectively. Although Burr was an ally of Lee's, he did not participate in this duel in any respect.

Thomas A. Greenfield

Further reading

Aucoin, Dan. 2015. "Hip-Hop and History Collide in Broadway's Dynamic *Hamilton*." *Boston Globe*, August 6, 2015.

Brandt, Anthony. 2014. "Rye Whiskey, Rye Whiskey." *American History* 49, no. 3: 40–7.

Brantley, Ben. 2015. "Review: *Hamilton*, Young Rebels Changing History and Theater." *New York Times*, August 6, 2015.

Chernow, Ron. 2003. *Alexander Hamilton*. New York: Penguin.

Freeman, Joanne B. 2018. "Can We Get Back to Politics? Please?: Hamilton's Missing Politics in *Hamilton*." In *Historians on Hamilton*, edited by Renee C. Romano and Claire Bond Potter, 2–57. New Brunswick, NJ: Rutgers University Press.

Green, Jesse. 2015. "Theater Review: Is *Hamilton* Even Better Than It Was?" *Vulture*, August 6, 2015, https://www.vulture.com/2015/08/theater-review-hamilton.html.

Hamilton, Alexander. 1790. "Final Version of the Second Report on the Further Provision Necessary for Establishing Public Credit (Report on a National Bank), 13 December 1790." *Founders Online: Alexander Hamilton Papers*. Washington, DC: National Archives, https://founders.archives.gov/documents/Hamilton/01-07-02-0229-0003.

Hamilton, Alexander. 1800. "Letter to Senator Harrison Gray Otis." *Digital History: Alexander Hamilton and the Election of 1800*. Houston: University of Houston, 2016, http://www.digitalhistory.uh.edu/disp_textbook_print.cfm?smtid=3&psid=169.

"Hamilton and the Public Debt." 2019. In *American History*, ABC-CLIO, https://americanhistory.abc-clio.com/Topics/Display/1183580?cid=41&sid=1183580.

"Hamilton: Lin-Manuel Miranda on the Play's Historical Inaccuracies." n.d. Video Interview, *Genius.com*, https://www.youtube.com/watch?v=YRJEOsyCfvQ.

Harris, Leslie M. 2018. "The Greatest City in the World: Slavery in New York in the Age of Hamilton." In *Historians on Hamilton*, edited by Renee C. Romano and Claire Bond Potter, 71–93. New Brunswick, NJ: Rutgers University Press.

Hogeland, William. 2018. "From Ron Chernow's *Alexander Hamilton* to *Hamilton*." In *Historians on Hamilton*, edited by Renee C. Romano and Claire Bond Potter, 17–41. New Brunswick, NJ: Rutgers University Press.

Jones, Chris. 2015. "*Hamilton*: Hip-Hop and Founding Fathers in Dazzling Broadway Musical." *Chicago Tribune*, August 6, 2015.

Lawrence, Jesse. 2017. "*Hamilton* Is Broadway's Most Expensive—Ever." *Daily Beast*, May 3, 2016. Updated July 12, 2017, www.thedailybeast.com/hamilton-is-broadways-most-expensive-showever.

"Letter from Charles D. Cooper to Philip Schuyler (April 23, 1804)." 2019. In *American History*, ABC-CLIO, https://americanhistory.abc-clio.com/Search/Display/2120934.

"Lin-Manuel Miranda: Class of 2015." 2015. *MacArthur Foundation*, https://www.macfound.org/fellows/941//.

Miranda, Lin-Manuel. 2009. "Lin-Manuel Miranda Performs at the White House Poetry Jam." *YouTube* video, November 2, 2009, https://www.youtube.com/watch?v= WNFf7nMIGnE.

Miranda, Lin-Manuel, and Jeremy McCarter. 2016. *Hamilton: The Revolution*. New York: Grand Central Publishing.

Montiero, Lyra D. 2018. "Race-Conscious Casting and the Erasure of the Black Past in *Hamilton*." In *Historians on Hamilton*, edited by Renee C. Romano and Claire Bond Potter, 58–70. New Brunswick, NJ: Rutgers University Press.

Obama, Michelle. 2016. "Remarks by The First Lady at 'Hamilton at The White House' Student Workshop." *The White House*, March 14, 2016.

O'Brien, Steven G. 2019. "Alexander Hamilton." 2019. In *American History*, ABC-CLIO, https://americanhistory.abc-clio.com/Search/Display/246962.

Reed, Ishmael. 2015. "*Hamilton: The Musical* [*sic*]: Black Actors Dress Up Like Slave Traders . . . and It's Not Halloween." *Counterpunch*, August 21, 2015, https://www.counterpunch.org/2015/08/21/hamilton-the-musical-black-actors-dress-up-like-slave-tradersand-its-not-halloween/.

Smith, Jada F. 2016. "*Hamilton* Takes a Road Trip to the White House." *New York Times*, March 14, 2016.

Teachout, Terry. 2015. "*Hamilton* Review: The Revolution Moves Uptown." *Wall Street Journal*, August 6, 2015.

"Thomas Jefferson: Constitutionality of a National Bank (1791), Excerpt." 2019. In *American History*, ABC-CLIO, https://americanhistory.abc-clio.com/Search/Display/254499.

Vincentelli, Elizabeth. 2015. "*Hamilton* Isn't Quite Revolutionary." *New York Post*, August 6, 2015.

Winer, Linda. 2015. "*Hamilton* Review. Even Better on Broadway." *Newsday*, August 6, 2015.

CHAPTER 12
I'D RATHER BE RIGHT (1937)

Book by George S. Kaufman and Moss Hart Music by Richard Rodgers
Lyrics by Lorenz Hart
World Premiere: Boston, Colonial Theatre, October 11, 1937
Broadway Run: Alvin Theatre, November 2, 1937–July 9, 1938

Songs

"A Homogeneous Cabinet"
"Have You Met Miss Jones?"
"Take and Take and Take"
"Spring in Vienna" (changed to "Spring in Milwaukee" during run)
"A Little Bit of Constitutional Fun"
"Sweet Sixty-Five"
"We're Going to Balance the Budget"
"American Couple"
"Labor Is the Thing"
"I'd Rather Be Right"
"Off the Record"
"A Baby Bond"

Overview

Set in New York City on Independence Day 1937, *I'd Rather Be Right* is the story of a young couple, Phil Barker and Peggy Jones, who wish to marry but are stymied by a setback in Phil's career. His employers refuse to grant him a promotion due to the uncertainty of current business conditions, a familiar scenario in American households in the later years of the Great Depression. But Phil and Peggy's situation is merely a pretext to bring on the show's central figure: President Franklin D. Roosevelt (FDR). The couple have come to Central Park to attend a Fourth of July concert and are startled to see FDR strolling down a path. Moreover, they are all the more surprised when he befriends them, promising to solve Phil's job predicament and bring about their marriage. Only in the play's final moments is it revealed that Phil actually had fallen asleep in the park, and thus the singing and dancing FDR that he and Peggy had met was only part of a dream.

This elaborate dream premise granted *I'd Rather Be Right*'s creators the latitude to concoct an audacious political satire: a lampoon of FDR's administration and New Deal policies as well as a broader cultural critique of contemporary issues. Along the way the show touches on matters such as the labor–capital relationship of the Depression era, the nascent mass communications revolution, and FDR's heated feud with the Supreme Court.

The idea for the show came about in the early summer of 1937, when the playwriting team of George S. Kaufman (1889–1961) and Moss Hart (1904–61) met to consider a follow-up to their enormous success *You Can't Take It With You*, winner of the 1937 Pulitzer Prize for Drama. They began work on a musical about psychoanalysis and contacted the renowned composer-lyricist team Richard Rodgers (1902–79) and Lorenz "Larry" Hart (1895–1943) to write the score. But when this project stalled, the playwrights conceived an entirely new idea, a musical spoof of the Roosevelt administration. Initially given the working title *Hold on to Your Hats, Boys!*, the play was granted its official title at the suggestion of Rodgers' wife Dorothy, who recalled the phrase uttered by nineteenth-century Kentucky Senator Henry Clay. In a speech on the Senate floor in 1838, Clay said, "I'd rather be right than President" (Rodgers 1975).

Kaufman, Rodgers, Larry Hart, and Moss Hart, all had previous experience with political satire. Kaufman had written the caustic libretto for the 1927 anti-war musical *Strike Up the Band* and had co-authored *Of Thee I Sing*, the first musical ever to win the Pulitzer Prize for Drama (1932). Moss Hart had written the libretto for Irving Berlin's 1933 revue *As Thousands Cheer*, which satirized current events and featured parodies of several prominent personages of the day, including former president Herbert Hoover. The songwriting team of Rodgers & Hart had also contributed tunes to the 1925 *Garrick Gaieties*, another lampoon on modern mores, which included a sketch poking fun at President Calvin Coolidge. Kaufman's previous political librettos had been populated with fictional characters, while Hart's send-up of Hoover and the *Gaieties* jab at Coolidge had been comprised of little more than brief comedy skits. This new project, however, would be a full-length, up-to-the-minute satire aimed at the nation's current leadership: a musical comedy built entirely around the larger-than-life personality of President Franklin Roosevelt. Rodgers & Hart wrote nineteen songs for *I'd Rather Be Right*, seven of which were dropped during the preview period. Oddly, for a project built around FDR, the chief executive would ultimately have only two solos to perform. Phil and Peggy have three numbers between them; their duet "Have You Met Miss Jones?" became the show's lone hit tune. All other songs are choral pieces for the supporting players, such as the Supreme Court justices or Cabinet members. The paucity of songs for FDR is especially surprising in light of the decision to cast legendary Broadway pioneer George M. Cohan (1878–1942) in the role. Cohan, who had been performing on stage from childhood in the 1880s, was a veteran playwright, director, producer, and a prolific songwriter himself. But his first solo for *I'd Rather be Right*, "We're Going to Balance the Budget," does not arrive until the finale of Act One, while his second and final song, "Off the Record," serves as the show's "11 o'clock number" toward the end of the second act. (The phrase "11 o'clock number" commonly refers to a major, showstopping song sung by the protagonist in or approaching the final act to build audience anticipation for the show's climax.)

Hardly a plot-driven show, *I'd Rather Be Right* is a loosely assembled series of comic set-pieces. The songs serve their purpose within these sequences, but only a handful express the show's overarching historical themes, such as optimism in the face of adversity, the banality of political corruption, and the increasingly blurred line between politics and show business. In the first number, "A Homogenous Cabinet," the members of FDR's administration arrive for a meeting and several introduce themselves with rhymed couplets. For instance, FDR's political advisor Postmaster General James Farley declares that he provides jobs for Democratic Party operatives' family members, in dubious if not outright corrupt fashion: "I give a job for every vote, and how the votes increase! / Some guys are such good voters they get twenty jobs apiece!" Secretary of Labor Frances Perkins and Treasury Secretary Henry Morgenthau are also caricatured. While this show portrays FDR as an essentially decent, ethical public servant, his associates are more crudely drawn.

Because quarrels between the President and the Supreme Court dominated the news in 1937, one might expect a song devoted to that conflict. Instead, the composers openly mock the justices—who Roosevelt himself had denounced as "nine old men"—with a surprisingly risqué number entitled "A Little Constitutional Fun." Here nine scantily clad young women appear in the park, link arms with the jurists, and imply in song that the "constitutional fun" which awaits them is carnal in nature. In "Sweet Sixty-Five," more poignantly, Phil and Peggy look toward the day, forty years in the future, when the promised Social Security checks will fulfill their needs. "Labor Is the Thing" plays upon the common criticism that New Deal job programs such as the

Public Works Administration (PWA) were soft, cushy jobs, which encouraged or at least tolerated laziness among workers in New Deal programs.

Finally, in the second act closer "Off the Record," FDR has the floor. The song portrays him conducting a press conference, in which he repeatedly reveals more than he intended. Catching his errors, Roosevelt tells his listeners that what he has just said is "off the record" and, thus not intended for publication or broadcast. However, in keeping with the lighthearted spirit of the show, FDR's unintended gaffes during the song pose no threat to the economy or national security. We learn he's not troubled about his post-presidential life, as he imagines his well-connected sons will take care of him. He boasts about his radio fame. He even complains about the cuisine at the White House, adding "If Eleanor would stay at home I'd get a decent meal." This, incidentally, is the only reference to the First Lady, who is not a character in the play. The song, a *tour-de-force*, was Cohan's guaranteed show-stopper, but he and the songwriters would clash over it bitterly.

Cohan was an extraordinary choice to play the key role of FDR. By 1937 he had been a star for decades and a jack-of-all-trades, having penned a number of standards, including "Give My Regards to Broadway" and "Over There" for his own productions. But therein lurked a problem. Cohan was a notorious *prima donna* who seldom acted in others' plays, rarely took direction with equanimity, and generally avoided singing songs he did not write himself. Upon making inquiries, however, the playwrights learned that when Cohan acted in Eugene O'Neill's comedy *Ah, Wilderness!* four years earlier, he had been thoroughly cooperative with all concerned. Furthermore, the producer of this new project would be Sam Harris, Cohan's former business partner and close friend.

As rehearsals proceeded with Cohan in the starring role, an awkward conflict became clear to the creative team. Although their show was a spoof of Roosevelt, all four of the authors admired FDR and supported him politically; Cohan did not. According to biographer John McCabe, Cohan was a lifelong Democrat but a conservative one. He initially supported Roosevelt and had even penned a pro-FDR song, but soon soured on him and by the mid-30s hated him outright. The star's antipathy to the character he portrayed would become public knowledge during the production's tryout tour prior to the Broadway opening.

Plot synopsis

I'd Rather Be Right opens at dusk in New York City's Central Park, present day, on the Fourth of July. A crowd is gathering to hear a concert. Phil Barker and Peggy Jones, a young engaged couple in their mid-twenties, enter the scene. Phil is troubled and reveals that he won't be getting an anticipated promotion, since his firm has canceled the opening of a new branch. As a result, he and Peggy must postpone their wedding. Phil's employers blame the change in plans on the uncertainty over Roosevelt's fiscal policy, or, as Phil complains: "We can't get married until they balance the budget. It doesn't make sense, but it's true." Phil and Peggy recline under a tree. Moments later an "impressive-looking man" in a frock coat comes along. Phil and Peggy are startled to realize that he is President Roosevelt, walking to his Manhattan residence to compose the speech he is to deliver that evening in the park. He chats with the couple, who tell him about Phil's job situation. FDR promises he will do what he can to balance the budget. At that moment the members of his Cabinet assemble—right there in the park—singing "A Homogeneous Cabinet." The President introduces Phil and Peggy to his Cabinet officials and invites the couple to tell their story. Phil sings "Have You Met Miss Jones?" and Peggy takes up the refrain. Moved by the performance, the officials agree to balance the budget. As they consider new tax possibilities, Peggy mentions that she has read that American women annually spend $3 billion on beauty products. FDR decides to ask women to give up their beauty products for one year and send their unspent money to the government. He thereupon broadcasts a radio "fireside chat" from the park, and asks the women of America to send the government money they would otherwise spend on cosmetics. Immediately he is assailed by a chorus of indignant women who sing "Take and Take and Take," an angry refusal of this request.

A balloon vendor enters. Phil is startled when he realizes that it is Mr. Maxwell, his former boss. Maxwell explains he has taken this modest job because FDR's tax policies have made his wholesale furniture business unprofitable. Maxwell uses balloons to demonstrate the impact of taxation on his previous year's gross profits, popping one at a time as he itemizes each tax he must pay. When he finishes, no balloons remain and he storms out. Next, a theatrical troupe enters. Their director asks if the players can stage a show on the spot. He explains that they are with the Federal Theatre Project (a New Deal program that supported theater artists) and are required to stage a show whenever they encounter a group of at least three people. Without further preamble the troupe performs the ode "Spring in Vienna," then departs.

Franklin D. Roosevelt decides on a new strategy: if he can persuade the Supreme Court to declare the budget balanced, the matter would be settled. He summons them, but the justices refuse to comply. The Chief Justice explains that they were offended by his rebuke of them as "nine old men." To demonstrate their virility, they summon nine young women who sing "A Little Constitutional Fun." At the number's conclusion the justices vanish into the shrubbery with the women. FDR is downhearted. His mother happens to come along. Phil and Peggy are shocked to realize that Mrs. Roosevelt's butler Landon is in fact Kansas Governor Alfred "Alf" Landon, FDR's defeated opponent in the 1936 presidential election. As Phil and Peggy absorb this jolt, another man approaches and hands them their Social Security cards, informing them that these cards will be valuable when they are sixty-five years old. Phil and Peggy muse on this notion in a duet, "Sweet Sixty-Five."

Franklin D. Roosevelt re-enters with the Cabinet. Morgenthau declares the officials have concocted a new plan; extract billions of dollars' worth of gold currently held at Fort Knox, bring it to Washington, D.C., and use it to pay off the national debt. Franklin D. Roosevelt approves the idea, and everyone celebrates with a rendition of "We're Going to Balance the Budget." But no sooner has this plan been approved than newsboys rush into the park, hawking 'extra' editions of the evening papers announcing that the stock market has crashed. This calamity was a direct result of the news about gold, which had reached Wall Street with surreal speed. The plan is abandoned. Phil and Peggy sadly conclude that they will never marry. The President "consoles" them by reaffirming his pledge to balance the federal budget as the curtain falls on the first act."

The second act curtain rises on FDR, Phil, and Peggy, still in the park. Peggy is asleep. When FDR wonders what she might be dreaming about, Phil speculates she's dreaming of their future together. Her dream is enacted in a dance, "American Couple," which dramatizes their wedding, parenthood, and old age, at which point Peggy awakens. A group of Public Works Administration workers enters. Mr. Maxwell, the former balloon vendor, is among them. Mr. Maxwell and the workers sing "Labor Is the Thing," expressing their glee at collecting a government paycheck in return for doing little work. After they depart, two of FDR's grandchildren arrive, upset because they were turned away from Central Park's merry-go-round. Joe and Tony, respectively the owner and operator of the merrygo-round, enter arguing. Joe has ordered Tony to speed up the ride to maximize profits, but in return Tony demands a raise in his wages. Joe refuses. FDR acts as mediator in their dispute but to no avail. Neither Joe nor Tony will budge from his position. FDR consults the Wagner Act (the National Labor Relations Act of 1935) and determines that the government must assume ownership of the merry-go-round. Joe and Tony depart, both delighted at the prospect of collecting federal funds.

Afterwards, FDR discloses that despite everything, he enjoys being President. He reveals other facts about himself in "Off the Record." But when his Cabinet officers return and admit they cannot balance the budget, he decides the only solution is to grant himself more time in office and seek a third term. In order to sell the American people on the idea he goes on the radio again. But as soon as the broadcast is over, he is informed by the Chief Justice that a third term would be unconstitutional. When Phil tells the President of his hopes for the future, FDR's faith in himself is restored. Whereupon the President delivers his Independence Day address and urges his listeners to believe in themselves. After the speech, FDR encourages Phil and Peggy to go ahead and get married, whether the budget is balanced or not. Franklin D. Roosevelt departs with a cheery wave. Moments later, the lights come up slowly on Peggy and Phil under the tree, as they were before FDR arrived on the scene. The park concert is coming to a close in the distance. As Phil awakens from his slumber, the audience realizes that what they have just seen has been an enactment of Phil's dream. Phil suggests to Peggy that they get married right away, a proposal she happily accepts.

Critical reception

The production's pre-Broadway tour opened at Boston's Colonial Theatre on October 11, 1937. This event generated substantial excitement among theatergoers, largely because of the subject matter but also because ten years had passed since Cohan had appeared in a musical. The premiere was well attended by celebrities and thoroughly covered by the press. In an interview published in the *Boston Globe* three days before the opening, Cohan surmised that President Roosevelt himself would probably enjoy the show "because it doesn't really stab at anyone very deeply and it's a farcical fantasy more than a satire" ("Cohan Cast as President" 1937). When asked about his own political views, Cohan politely declined to share them, but suggested ambiguously that since the show did not change his own vote he did not believe it would change anyone else's.

On opening night, however, a more outspoken Cohan intensified audience excitement considerably when he committed a severe breach of professional ethics. In the middle of his number "Off the Record" he omitted a verse written by Larry Hart and interpolated lines of his own. It appears Cohan's exact wording was not recorded, but a subsequent news story in the *Los Angeles Times* reported that in the inserted verse he alluded to the brown shirt worn by Adolf Hitler and the black shirt worn by Benito Mussolini, then speculated about what color shirt he, FDR, might choose to wear in the future. To make matters worse, Cohan compounded his offense when he stepped out of character and joked that he would probably be fired for dropping this verse into the song.

Larry Hart, watching from the back of the house, was livid. Backstage afterwards he threatened to quit and pull his lyrics from the show. Rodgers backed him up, and the entire brouhaha was covered in national newspapers the following day. Under the headline "Cohan Refuses to Sing Lyric About Al Smith," the New York *Herald Tribune* relayed Cohan's claim that he had balked at singing a lyric that disparaged former New York Governor Al Smith, a close friend. Yet in the same article Larry Hart maintained that the offending lines had already been cut while the show was in rehearsal (Nolan 1994). Hart went on to assert that writers must take a firm stand and not permit performers to alter their material. Kaufman, who in addition to co-authoring the book also directed the show, assured the press that all was "smooth and lovely" among members of the show's creative team, and added wryly that he hoped Cohan liked to work with him as much as he liked to work with Cohan. But behind the scenes, Kaufman confronted the star in tandem with producer Sam Harris and exacted a promise that this misbehavior would not be repeated. Thereafter, Cohan stuck to the script.

After a second preview run in Baltimore, *I'd Rather Be Right* opened at the Alvin Theatre (now the Neil Simon Theatre) in New York on November 2, 1937. When Rodgers wrote later that this was the most eagerly awaited musical of all time, he may have been exaggerating only slightly (Rodgers 1975). Advance sales ran to nearly a quarter of a million dollars, which, adjusted for inflation, would be almost $5.6 million in 2025 currency (CPI n.d.). This was welcome news for the show's backers. Production costs to stage the show ran at a higher-than-average $150,000 ($3.3 million today), mainly because the show's sole Central Park set was designed for a smaller theater and had to be rebuilt on a larger scale for the Alvin (Goldstein 1979).

Critics were generally supportive of the Broadway run. Cohan received some of the best notices of his long career—even Rodgers conceded that he fully deserved them. Still, the high expectations generated during the show's out-of-town run resulted in a distinct hint of disappointment in the reviews. "Although advance reports seemed to indicate that *I'd Rather Be Right* might discharge a lampoon at the follies of current politics," wrote Brooks Atkinson in the *New York Times*, "it turns out to be a pleasant-spoken musical comedy that leisurely ambles away the evening." Atkinson also suggested that President Roosevelt need not worry about his depiction in the show, as the playwrights plainly liked him.

Several critics likened the show to harmless comic sketches performed at the Gridiron Club's annual dinners, often attended by the President, where current political figures would be spoofed. Critics also compared *I'd Rather Be Right* to Kaufman's earlier political satire *Of Thee I Sing*, albeit unfavorably where the new opus was concerned. Richard Lockridge of the *New York Sun* observed that the playwrights "laugh at their President, but always with the thought that he is a good guy in a bad spot." It was widely accepted that the tone of the show was amicable toward FDR. However, Howard Teichmann, friend and biographer of Kaufman, reported that some of the playwright's liberal friends were displeased at his handling of the subject matter. One confronted him, demanding to know how he could disparage Roosevelt, the champion of the Democratic Party. Kaufman replied: "There's nothing funny about a dead elephant" (Teichmann 1972).

If a common thread could be found in virtually all reviews of *I'd Rather Be Right*, it was the view that this show could only be produced—and would only be permitted—in America. The author of an unsigned editorial in the *Philadelphia Inquirer* bluntly concluded that Stalin, Hitler, or Mussolini would have the authors killed. Richard Watts spoke for the community of critics when he wrote that "the impudence of the proceeding is the healthiest possible demonstration of our freedom" (Watts 1937).

Beyond the critical response, there was keen public interest in how the First Family and administration figures would respond to the production. President Roosevelt himself did not see the show, either in New York or later in Washington, D.C., when it played there. According to one account he did read the libretto; unfortunately, his response was not recorded for posterity. Franklin D. Roosevelt's friend Admiral Cary Grayson attended on the President's behalf while the show was in previews. Grayson admitted afterward that he found it offensive at first, but came to feel that Cohan's affable portrayal softened any harsh elements in the script.

Franklin D. Roosevelt's son Franklin D. Roosevelt Jr. saw the Broadway production and laughed heartily throughout. He went backstage at intermission to meet Cohan, whom he addressed as "Pop." Franklin D. Roosevelt's oldest son, John, was decidedly less amused and told the press he found the script "pretty rough in places." According to the show's *ingénue* Joy Hodges, who watched him from the stage, Postmaster General James Farley was "embarrassed to the color of a beet at some of the [wisecracks] in the second act." Treasury Secretary Henry Morgenthau attended one evening and remarked, in reference to his part in the show, "I'd love to play that role myself" (Chapman 1938).

There was particular curiosity about the First Lady's response. Eleanor Roosevelt addressed the subject of *I'd Rather Be Right* in her daily newspaper column a month after the show opened in New York. She noted that she'd intended to go but had decided against it in the belief that her presence might cause undue commotion. Instead, she relied on the reports of friends. She reported that most people she knew who saw the show observed that it illustrated the freedom we take for granted in the United States, where such a play could be produced without government interference (which, again, was the observation made by many critics). "I would add fervently," she concluded, "Thank God for a nation with a sense of humor!"

A confirmed hit, *I'd Rather Be Right* settled in at the Alvin for a respectable run of 290 performances, running well into 1938. In March of that year came a grim reminder of how topical satire can be affected by current events. Following the Anschluss, the annexation of Austria by Nazi Germany, the show's number

"Spring in Vienna" could no longer be used in a comic context, so it became "Spring in Milwaukee." After the Broadway run ended in July the show traveled to Washington, D.C., Chicago, Des Moines, Providence, R.I. (George M. Cohan's hometown), and finally Wilmington, Delaware, where it closed in February 1939. Wilmington, it would seem, was the end of the line for *I'd Rather Be Right* in every sense of the phrase. Before the year was out the retirements of two Supreme Court justices and the death of a third enabled FDR to nominate three men of his own choosing to the bench, which consigned the "court packing" controversy—and the show's related jokes—to the past. Moreover, in September of that year Germany invaded Poland, leading to all-out European war, at which point almost all political commentary predating the invasion was instantly irrelevant.

Historical accuracy and context

Roosevelt and the Supreme Court

Franklin D. Roosevelt's heated public feud with the Supreme Court provided the musical's creators with an abundance of farcical material, which they used throughout the show. At issue was Roosevelt's proposal to appoint additional justices, ostensibly to improve efficiency. The controversy, which caused a sharp decline in Roosevelt's popularity, occurred shortly after his 1936 landslide re-election and, coincidentally, just as Kaufman, Hart, and company were developing *I'd Rather Be Right.*

Frustrated during his first term by Supreme Court (Court) rulings that struck down or otherwise weakened several New Deal programs on constitutional grounds, Roosevelt introduced a plan to increase the number of Court justices. In the Judicial Procedures Reform Bill of 1937, Roosevelt proposed to appoint a new Court justice for every current member who was over seventy years and six months of age and had served for at least a decade. He defended his position by asserting that older justices required on-the-job assistance owing to a decline in "mental or physical vigor [that] leads men to avoid an examination of complicated and changed conditions."

The proposal's outlandish stereotyping of elderly men combined with the fact that six of the nine justices then on the Court were already past the proposed age limit provoked an uproar. Obviously, the bill would have permitted Roosevelt to "pack" the Court with six new justices sympathetic to his policies. Virtually all Republicans opposed the bill, but so too did many Democrats. Public opinion was mixed, but a majority of major newspaper editorial boards criticized the proposal in print, even those that usually supported Roosevelt. Numerous editorials blasted the bill as a blatant grab for power, and some went so far as to compare the President's scheme to that of a European dictator. In an extraordinary step, Chief Justice Charles Evans Hughes insisted in a letter to Congress that the Court's workload was not excessive and, in any case, he and his fellow jurists had their tasks well under control. Congress defeated the bill in July of 1937.

By the time *I'd Rather Be Right* opened in November 1937, Roosevelt's Court plan was dead, but the President's battle with the Court remained fresh in public memory. The inflammatory nature of the feud and its attendant backlash lent itself to farcical representation, and the show's creators responded accordingly. When FDR wants to summon the jurists he simply announces, "I am going to pass a law—" and they appear from behind the Central Park rocks and bushes, ready to thwart him. Chief Justice Hughes, the Court spokesperson, indignantly cites the real President Roosevelt's actual statement about the aging jurists' declining "mental or physical vigor." And in response, the justices cavort with a chorus line of young women who sing "A Little Constitutional Fun." Ridiculous, lustful old men are familiar comic stage types dating back to ancient Greek comedy, and this portrayal of the Court honors that tradition. While ludicrous, the scene conveys Chief

Justice Hughes' rebuke of Roosevelt's challenge to the fitness and abilities of the Supreme Court Justices in suitably comic fashion.

Roosevelt's public persona and popularity

Roosevelt's temporary decline in popularity in 1937 is noticeable in his stage characterization. Generally regarded as a highly confident, self-assured figure, the FDR of *I'd Rather Be Right* is often hapless and defensive, befitting his recent embarrassing political defeat in the Supreme Court battle. He complains petulantly that newspaper columnists say mean things about him, and he is given to remarks such as "The trouble with this country is that I don't know what the trouble with the country *is*." Had the show been conceived a few years earlier when the Depression was at its nadir, and FDR was endeavoring to reassure a traumatized people that all they had to fear was fear itself, or a few years later when the nation was at war and FDR was commander in chief, such a satiric depiction of the President would not likely have been accepted by the public.

Postmaster General James Farley

The playwrights were fairly lenient in their depiction of FDR, but harsher treatment was reserved for some of his Cabinet members, most notably Postmaster General James Farley (1888–1976). A lifelong New York City area politician and a well-known public figure in New York since the 1910s, Farley was also Chairman of the Democratic National Committee while serving as Roosevelt's Postmaster General. Widely considered to be a political "kingmaker," Farley was instrumental in Roosevelt's political career as his campaign manager, first when he ran for Governor of New York and subsequently when he won the presidency. Farley also controlled federal patronage. Although never formally charged with any illegal political activity, he was not infrequently accused of corruption by the administration's critics. In the show, Farley is ruthless in securing positions for "deserving" Democrats and amusingly cavalier in other respects. For example, when FDR insists on balancing the budget, Farley asks: "Isn't there anything we could sell? Do we need Baltimore?" When the plan to remove gold from Fort Knox causes a market crash, Farley tells the President: "Frank, we can't fool around with Wall Street. To hell with the country!" This last remark is genuinely startling even now. No wonder the real Farley was said to be "embarrassed to the color of a beet" when he attended the show.

The New Deal

In *I'd Rather Be Right* the administration's New Deal programs are subject to sharp criticism. This is particularly apparent in the sequence where Phil's former employer Mr. Maxwell turns up as a balloon vendor and complains bitterly about excessive taxation. Maxwell offers the show's most dramatic political jab as he itemizes taxes he must pay (excess profits tax, Social Security tax, etc.) and illustrates his point by popping a balloon for each one. Here Maxwell voices the resentment of the upper classes, who viewed the administration's annual tax hikes as "soak-the-rich" measures. Roosevelt himself had said as much in 1935, when he denounced affluent Americans for avoiding their fair tax burden. The Revenue Act of 1936, which Roosevelt promoted, imposed a new tax on undistributed corporate profits, specifically to redress the imbalance. Because his own family was wealthy, some called Roosevelt a "traitor to his class." Although this phrase—which quickly became a cliché—is not used in the show, Maxwell speaks for those (not yet called "one-percenters") who felt this way about the president.

Social Security, arguably the most significant and enduring New Deal program, came into being when President Roosevelt signed the Social Security Act of 1935 into law. While the program has been greatly expanded and much amended since its inception, the central provision of the original act extended financial benefits to retirees over the age of sixty-five based on each individual's lifetime payroll tax contributions. (Unemployment insurance and health insurance for those still in the workforce were also important components of the Social Security Act from the beginning.) Registration for the new program began in November 1936. Eligible workers were obliged to fill out an application form, and, in return, each received a national identity card complete with a unique nine-digit identification number.

The Social Security system was barely a year old, highly controversial, and a fresh topic for satire when *I'd Rather Be Right* premiered in November 1937. So, at an opportune moment in the first act, an officious man with a bulging briefcase approaches Phil and Peggy. After confirming their identities, the man reaches into his satchel, hands the couple their new Social Security cards, congratulates them, and assures them the cards will be valuable when they are sixty-five years old. This gesture cues the young couple's ode to the joys of aging, "Sweet Sixty-Five." The irony in this song is compounded by its placement immediately following the Supreme Court's number "A Little Constitutional Fun," in which the senescent justices have lustily demonstrated their youthful virility. Phil and Peggy, in touching contrast, look forward to a benign old age of financial security promised by Social Security disbursements.

A more barbed attack on the New Deal agenda follows in Act Two when Maxwell, now employed by the Public Works Administration (PWA), returns with a group of fellow PWA workers, all of whom are corporate chiefs. Unlike the similarly named Works Progress Administration (WPA), the PWA handled large-scale construction projects carried out by private firms, who then hired skilled laborers as needed. This scene implies that Maxwell and his cohorts, who presumably represent the private firms contracted to execute PWA projects, are taking advantage of the arrangement. They wear silk overalls and boast that, as government employees, all they care about is getting paid: "We work all day / for the P.W.A. / Let the market crash, we collect our cash!" ("Labor Is the Thing"). Moreover, during their song, the man at one end of the group picks up a twig, which is then passed from man to man until it is delicately dropped just a few feet from its original spot on the ground. The satire in this sight gag is more in line with common criticism of the WPA than the PWA. The WPA generally handled small-scale projects and hired unemployed unskilled workers. Conservative politicians and journalists frequently assailed the WPA for encouraging poor work habits and rewarding laziness in its workers. The PWA and the WPA, often confused with one another in their own era and ever since, seem to have been conflated by the playwrights in this sequence.

One of the ventures sponsored by the WPA was the Federal Theatre Project (FTP), formed in 1935. The FTP's mandate required the program to hire unemployed theater workers and bring quality productions to audiences across the country. Federally funded and administered, the FTP was not intended to operate at a profit; the majority of its shows were presented to the public free of charge. Performances took place in theaters, schools, churches, factories, hospitals, and, significantly where *I'd Rather Be Right* is concerned, in parks. Naturally, in a stage show poking fun at New Deal programs, Kaufman and Hart took aim at this organization.

The FTP was widely criticized for presenting shows with a left-wing bias (i.e., works critical of corporate greed, business mistreatment of labor, etc.), although they staged many apolitical plays as well. Such criticism would ultimately serve as a rationale for Congress to terminate the entire project in 1939 by cutting off its federal funding. Rather than attacking the FTP on political grounds, the playwrights found humor in its sheer ubiquity. At an odd moment a troupe of players arrives and puts on a performance because that is what they feel they must do. Their director remarks: "It's pretty hard to go anyplace these days without tripping over the Federal Theatre. Went into my own bathroom the other day, and there they were!" He explains that the actors were performing the eighteenth-century English comedy *She Stoops to Conquer* for his wife, who watched from the bathtub. The troupe's number "Spring in Vienna" was intended as an innocuous parody of Teutonic operetta but fell victim to real-world political events when Nazi Germany annexed Austria during the run, forcing a change in the song's title and its lyrics.

Labor relations

The park merry-go-round sequence, in which FDR attempts to negotiate a settlement between Joe (the ride's owner) and Tony (the striking operator), is staged in the show's prevailing farcical style. But in this sequence, the librettists assume a mock-naïve tone unlike other segments of *I'd Rather Be Right*, a tone that feels disconcertingly off-point as historical satire. The ostensibly zany vaudeville-like exchanges between the three men belie the violent real-world clashes taking place around the country between striking workers and strikebreakers, police and/or National Guard troops. Such confrontations had increasingly been in the news since the stock market crash of 1929 and worsened as the Great Depression itself deepened in the early 1930s. The show's audiences would likely have recalled calamities such as the California cotton workers strike of 1933, which resulted in the deaths of four strikers at the hands of strikebreakers and the police, or the Southern textile workers' strike of 1934, which spread across the South and led to the death of a Georgia man. Most attendees would also have recalled recent news coverage of a sit-down strike in January 1937 at a Michigan General Motors plant. The confrontation deteriorated into a gun battle between workers and the police in which fourteen men were wounded.

In light of the highly publicized bloodshed surrounding so many recent strike actions, the conflict between Joe and Tony seems incongruously puerile in tone. Both men are presented as dim-witted. They speak in coarse, Chico Marx-style Italian dialect ("You no pay me more money, I quitta' the job"). Franklin D. Roosevelt fares no better in his failed attempt to mediate their dispute by explaining the process of collective bargaining. Ultimately, Tony and Joe angrily refuse to settle the dispute and cease negotiating. With reluctance the President takes over operation of the merry-go-round on behalf of the government. In a slick comedic reversal (if, in fact, a moment of ahistorical nonsense), Joe and Tony express their pleasure with this turn of events and depart exclaiming: "We worka for the Government! That meansa we're rich!" Notwithstanding the superficial manner in which the librettists touch on this most serious of contemporary labor issues, a number of critics lauded the sequence as a comic highlight of the show.

The President as media celebrity

From a contemporary perspective, it is intriguing that the playwrights find incongruity in the notion of a president who is also a radio star. In 1937, the very existence of electronic mass communications media was a novelty and its application in politics was still evolving. Several jokes in the show suggest that Americans of the day had not entirely adjusted to hearing the President's voice in their own homes as only one portion of a daily audio soundscape that might include comedy shows, sports coverage, soap operas, jazz, and commercials. That this remained an unsettling idea for many is implied in the sequence when *I'd Rather Be Right*'s FDR decides to broadcast a special "Fireside Chat." Postmaster General Farley, who had recommended that the President give his listeners an extra helping of razzle-dazzle, introduces the program with the then-current slang phrase "Yowsah, Yowsah." Opening acts for the presidential speech include a stand-up comic, a Bing Crosby-style crooner, a gossip columnist, and a "Hillbilly Swing Band." After his speech, the President is required to deliver a plug for the sponsor, Lady Esther's Face Powder, and does so with obvious discomfort. For those raised on *Saturday Night Live* and *The Daily Show*, this sort of shtick may seem quaint, but for theatergoers of the time, the sequence must have conveyed a sense of cognitive dissonance many shared in hearing a presidential address over the airwaves at home. In any event, at the play's climax FDR is granted a final, dignified oration more in keeping with traditional presidential decorum.

Roosevelt's disability

Perhaps the most remarkable aspect of *I'd Rather Be Right* is that it offers a Franklin D. Roosevelt who *dances.* In reality, due to paralysis from polio which had struck him at age thirty-nine, Roosevelt could not walk without assistance. At home he used a wheelchair or crutches and sometimes wore steel braces on his legs. In public he eschewed the wheelchair but relied on assistants to get from place to place. Public knowledge of the President's physical condition was paradoxical. It was certainly no secret, and yet there is much anecdotal evidence to suggest that people who met the President for the first time, or saw him at public appearances, were shocked by the extent of his disability. For the FDR of *I'd Rather Be Right*, however, mobility is not an issue. One of his first lines, spoken when Phil and Peggy recognize him walking along a path in Central Park, is "I was just taking a little stroll." Thereafter he stands, sits, or walks as the occasion demands but always under his own power. Towards the end of Act One, as Peggy loses hope that she and Phil can wed and starts to cry, FDR tells her: "Everything will come out all right. I'm not unhappy. I'm not sad. Look." So saying, he goes into a dance that inspires observers to sing a spirited refrain and wave flags as the curtain falls. The librettists finessed the matter by making the play's Roosevelt a dream figure, therefore capable of anything, but the degree to which playgoers of the day were even conscious of Roosevelt's disability remains an open question.

William Charles Morrow

Further reading

Atkinson, Brooks. 1937. "THE PLAY; George M. Cohan as the United States President in 'I'd Rather Be Right.'" *New York Times*, November 3, 1937.

Bach, Steven. 2001. *Dazzler: The Life and Times of Moss Hart.* New York: Alfred A. Knopf.

Chapman, John. 1938. "Mainly about Manhattan." *New York Daily News*, February 13, 1938.

"Cohan Cast as President Has Never Met Roosevelt." 1937. *Boston Globe*, October 1937.

"CPI Inflation Calculator." n.d. *U.S. Bureau of Labor Statistics*, Washington, D. C., https://www.bls.gov/data/inflation_calculator.htm.

Goldstein, Malcom. 1979. *George S. Kaufman: His Life, His Theater.* New York: Oxford University Press.

Kaufman, George S., with Moss Hart, lyrics by Lorenz Hart. 1937. *I'd Rather Be Right: A Musical Revue.* New York: Random House.

Lockridge, Richard. 1937. "'I'd Rather Be Right' Arrives; Musical Satire on Roosevelt, New Deal and Supreme Court Opens at Alvin." New York *Sun*, November 3, 1937.

Marmorstein, Gary. 2012. *A Ship Without a Sail: The Life of Lorenz Hart.* New York: Simon & Schuster.

McCabe, John. 1973. *George M. Cohan: The Man Who Owned Broadway.* Boston: DaCapo.

Meredith, Scott. 1974. *George S. Kaufman and His Friends.* Garden City, NY: Doubleday.

Morehouse, Ward M. 1943. *George M. Cohan: Prince of the American Theater.* Philadelphia: J. B. Lippincott Company.

Nolan, Frederick. 1994. *Lorenz Hart: A Poet on Broadway.* New York: Oxford University Press.

Rodgers, Richard. 1975. *Musical Stages: An Autobiography.* New York: Random House.

Secrest, Meryle. 2001. *Somewhere for Me: A Biography of Richard Rodgers.* New York: Alfred A. Knopf.

Teichmann, Howard. 1972. *George S. Kaufman: An Intimate Portrait.* New York: Atheneum.

Watts, Richard, Jr. 1937. "THE THEATERS; *I'd Rather Be Right.*" *Herald Tribune*, November 3, 1937.

CHAPTER 13
NEWSIES (2011)

Book by Harvey Fierstein (1954–)
Music by Alan Menken (1949–)
Lyrics by Jack Feldman (NA)
World Premiere: Paper Mill Playhouse, Millburn, New Jersey, September 25–October 16, 2011
Broadway: March 29, 2012–August 24, 2014

Songs

"Santa Fe" (Prologue)	"Santa Fe"
"Carrying the Banner"	"King of New York"
"The Bottom Line"	"Letter from the Refuge"*
"Carrying the Banner" (Reprise)	"Watch What Happens" (Reprise)
"That's Rich"	"The Bottom Line" (Reprise)
"I Never Planned on You/Don't Come a-Knocking"	"Brooklyn's Here"
	"Something to Believe In"
"The World Will Know"	"Seize the Day" (Reprise)
"The World Will Know" (Reprise)	"Once and for All"
"Watch What Happens"	"Seize the Day" (Reprise)
"Seize the Day"	"Finale"

*Song was added for the North American Tour (debuted October 11, 2014) after the Broadway production.

Overview

Newsies is loosely based on the Newsboys Strike of 1899 in New York City. Following the Spanish-American War (1898), circulation of American newspapers generally declined. Most New York City newspaper publishers rolled back their wholesale price the newsboys paid for papers from 60 cents per hundred to 50 cents, but two major publications refused to do so—Joseph Pulitzer's *New York World* and William Randolph Hearst's *New York Morning Journal*. The higher wholesale price angered the "newsies," teenage and pre-adolescent boys who sold papers every day on the streets of New York. The newsies were, technically, independent businessmen working to support themselves and their families. Newsies would buy newspapers from the publishers by the hundred-pack to sell on the streets for one cent per paper, hoping to earn double what they paid for them.

However, the loss of sales due to the postwar decline in circulation and the price increase of the Pulitzer and Hearst publications cut into the newsies' income. Inspired by strikes in other industries occurring all around the city, the newsies took action. On July 20, 1899, the New York City newsboys formed a union and went on strike for the next two weeks. On August 1, Pulitzer and Hearst agreed to buy back unsold papers in the form of credit to the newsies, who were satisfied with the compromise and ended their strike. The Newsies Strike was one of the first times in American history that working children successfully fought for their rights. Their efforts helped start a revolution in attitudes and legislation regarding child labor in America. The strike also brought new levels of public attention to such social justice issues as child poverty and conditions in juvenile detention facilities.

Adapted from a 1992 Walt Disney Company movie of the same name, *Newsies* is a traditional "book musical" with a narrative that drives the music and characters. The musical's central conflict is a "David and Goliath" tale, pitting ostensibly weak underdogs (the newsboys) against strong power-hungry publishing giants, Pulitzer and Hearst. In addition to the presence of named historical figures Joseph Pulitzer, his business manager and successor (Donald C.) Seitz, and Governor of New York Theodore Roosevelt, some of the fictionalized characters in *Newsies* are inspired by specific people from the time period. Medda, a theater owner and performer, and Katherine, a reporter, are modeled after dancer and producer Aida Overton Walker and journalist Nellie Bly, respectively. Jack Kelly, the musical's strike leader, is an amalgam of the two principal leaders of the real strike, Louis Ballat (Kid Blink) and Morris Cohen.

Jack Kelly and *Newsies* adhere closely to the traditions of "coming of age" literature: innocent (often parentless) youth, left to fend for themselves in a corrupt adult world, triumph in pursuit of a dream, justice, community, or love. The Harry Potter novels by J. K. Rowling are collectively the most widely known coming-of-age tale in recent literature. American novels *The Adventures of Huckleberry Finn* by Mark Twain and *A Catcher in the Rye* by J. D. Salinger follow that tradition as well. And, of course, the charm, grit, idealism, and honesty of American youth have been at the center of Walt Disney Company productions for almost a century.

Like other lucrative Disney theater productions, *Newsies* was adapted from a musical film to the stage. However, the live-action film *Newsies* was a relatively rare Disney financial flop at the box office. Despite its poor showing in theaters, *Newsies* soon built an audience through its release on television and home video, becoming a cult classic with a fervent, youthful following. Schools and theater companies persistently sought from Disney a licensed version of *Newsies* that they could perform, and the show soon became Disney Theatrical Productions' most sought after title. Seizing on the demand, the company put a stage version into development. Original film composers Alan Menken and Jack Feldman stayed on the project, but Tony-Award winning writer-actor Harvey Fierstein was brought on to adapt a book from Rob Tzudiker and Noni White's original screenplay. Seven new songs were added (plus "Letter from the Refuge" for the first National Tour) to the already popular score and song list.

In translating the film to the stage, the producers kept the film's core original songs, including "Carrying the Banner," "The World Will Know," "Seize the Day," "King of New York," and "Once and for All," all of which enhance the sense of camaraderie and exuberance that bond the newsboys together as they face their hardships and battle their foes. The film also maintained Menken and Feldman's original repetitive call-and-response design of the score. The boys' forceful, dynamic call-and-response performances mimic the feeling of war cries and invoke their urgent on-the-job shouts, as up until the strike, they hawked the latest news about the Spanish-American War on the city streets. The boys trumpet this feeling of war multiple times in their songs, such as in "The World Will Know": "Either they gives us our rights or we gives them a war [*sic*]."

Although the plot of both the film and the stage version of *Newsies* centers on the strike, Fierstein and company made three significant changes to the stage version. They fleshed-out the key antagonist characters, particularly Joseph Pulitzer, whom they endowed with a greedier, more corrupt persona and a new corporate villain's song, "The Bottom Line." They expanded the character of Jack's best friend, Crutchie, a newsie with "a bum leg" with whom Jack has bonded as a big brother figure. Through Crutchie, the musical more pointedly tests Jack's loyalty to his newsboy family when he realizes that his ultimate ambition is to seek his fortune out west ("Santa Fe"); if pursued, Jack would leave them all behind. Predictably, the writers introduced a love interest for Jack. The character of Katherine, a young reporter struggling for recognition in the male-dominated field of journalism, makes a statement for women's rights in the context of the labor struggle at the center of the story.

Plot synopsis

The play opens to a rooftop in lower Manhattan before dawn. Newsboys Jack Kelly and Crutchie awaken and head down to the streets. Jack shares his dreams of a better future out west ("Santa Fe—Prologue"). The prologue transitions to the Newsboys' lodging house where more newsboys prepare for another day of selling "papes." They sing of their independent life as newsboys ("Carrying the Banner") as they head to Newsies Square to purchase their daily copies of Pulitzer's the *New York World*. Newcomers Davey and Les, brothers earning money to support their family, join the newsies line. Jack makes a deal to partner with the brothers and teach them all he knows.

The action shifts to Joseph Pulitzer's corporate office. Fuming at the recent decline in sales since the end of the Spanish-American War, Pulitzer and his executives decide to increase the wholesale cost of the papers from 50 cents to 60 cents per hundred, forcing newsboys to pay the company more money upfront ("The Bottom Line").

Back on the city streets, Jack, Les, and Davey finish selling their papers for the day. The brothers start to leave, and Jack is surprised to learn that, unlike the other newsboys, Les and Davey have a home and family. But before the boys disperse, Snyder, the manager of the Refuge (a juvenile detention center), chases after them. The boys escape into a Bowery vaudeville theater owned by Jack's friend, Medda Larkin, a successful dancer. Jack reveals that he is an escapee from Snyder's Refuge as well as a talented painter who earns extra money painting sets for Medda's productions. Medda invites the boys to stay and watch her perform ("That's Rich"). During Medda's song, Jack notices Katherine, a young reporter observing the action from the box seats. Jack had noticed her earlier on the street and is captivated by her. He climbs up to the box and tries unsuccessfully to woo her.

The next day, newsies gather at the distribution window and discover that every newspaper in the city has upped the price of papers by 10 cents per hundred. As they contemplate what to do, Jack suggests forming a union and striking ("The World Will Know"). The boys concur and gather at Jacobi's Deli, where they appoint Jack as their leader and plan their next steps. Jack assigns the newsboys to spread the word of the union around the boroughs and convince other newsboys to join them. Katherine appears in the deli, requesting permission to write an exclusive about the strike for the *Sun*, a paper unaffiliated with Pulitzer or Hearst. As Katherine begins writing, she struggles with the pressure of being a young, unestablished woman in the male-dominated newspaper business ("Watch What Happens").

The following morning, only a few newsies assemble for the strike. Davey and Jack encourage the frightened boys to stand in solidarity with all of the city's exploited children and continue to fight ("Seize the Day"). Katherine and a photographer arrive to snap a victorious photo moment before the boys are surrounded by Snyder and several other thugs ("goons" in the musical) hired by Pulitzer as security guards. The newsies and Pulitzer's goons fight as the police arrive and chase the boys. Crutchie is struck down in the melee and carried off to the Refuge. Jack escapes with Snyder in pursuit. Jack safely reaches his rooftop, feeling guilty about having just led the boys into harm's way. He longs for an escape from the city and his desperate existence ("Santa Fe").

In dire straits after the confrontation, the newsies again gather at Jacobi's Deli, but this time without Jack. They despair over their present circumstances and worry about Jack's fate. Katherine enters excitedly displaying her strike article, which makes the *Sun*'s front page. The boys rejoice and celebrate their fame ("King of New York"). In the Refuge, Crutchie writes to Jack about the terrible conditions of his incarceration, begging him to encourage the boys to stay strong and stick together.

Jack leaves his rooftop, still discouraged by his initial failure to organize his union. Returning to Medda's theater, he paints backdrops, hoping to save money and escape the city. Davey finds him and tries to convince him to return to the fight. Jack refuses, overwhelmed by the odds against defeating Pulitzer. Katherine and Les appear, joining Davey in persuading Jack that they really do stand a chance of winning. Consoled and buoyed by their faith in him, Jack rejoins the cause, and the four of them plan a rally.

Later, Jack shows up in Pulitzer's office and invites the furious publisher to the rally. Pulitzer threatens to have Jack and the other newsies locked up in the Refuge. Pulitzer also reveals that Katherine is his daughter. Having put Jack on the defensive with this revelation, Pulitzer offers Jack a choice: renounce the strike and leave New York with enough money to start a new life elsewhere or get locked up again in the Refuge. To give Jack time to contemplate his options, Pulitzer temporarily confines Jack to a cellar storage room that houses old printing press equipment. That evening, Spot Conlon (leader of the Brooklyn newsies) joins the rally at Medda's theater with newsies from the five city boroughs. Davey gives a speech to rile up the boys when suddenly Jack appears. Having bowed to Pulitzer's threat, Jack tells the newsboys to return to work and abandon the fight against Pulitzer.

Back on his rooftop, Jack finds Katherine waiting for him. She is looking through drawings he had made of the horrible conditions in the Refuge during his internment. They argue until she kisses him, and they express their love for one another. Katherine shares her plan to write an article entitled "The Children's Crusade," calling for a city-wide strike of all working children and distribute it independently. She suggests using her writing and his drawings. Jack tells her that there is an old printing press in Pulitzer's cellar and joins forces with Katherine. Gathering reinforcements, Katherine, Jack, and the boys spend all night printing their newsletter in Pulitzer's cellar and distributing it throughout the city ("Once and for All").

That morning, Pulitzer's office is flooded with angry calls from people outraged over the injustices of child labor and juvenile detention that they had just read about in Jack and Katherine's newsletter. Jack, Davey, and Spot enter Pulitzer's office proposing a compromise to settle the strike, but Pulitzer refuses. Suddenly, Governor Teddy Roosevelt appears along with Katherine. Disgusted by what he has learned about juvenile detention centers from the newsletter, Roosevelt demands that Pulitzer resolve the strike. Chastened by the Governor, Pulitzer meets privately with Jack and they negotiate a final agreement: the price increase will remain, but the publishers will buy back unsold papers at the end of each day. The two shake hands and the strike ends.

Outside in Newsies Square, Jack announces the end of the strike. Crutchie appears with a handcuffed Snyder, who is led off to jail by police. Despite his dreams of heading out west, Jack accepts a job offer as an artist at the *World*, realizing that he cannot bring himself to leave Katherine and his newsies family.

Critical reception

The initial staged version of Disney's *Newsies* premiered at New Jersey's Paper Mill Playhouse in September 2011. Intended only as a pilot before opening for licensing to theater groups, the production was given a limited Broadway engagement in March 2012 owing to enthusiastic audience response and reviews at Paper

Mill, especially from David Rooney of the *New York Times*: "[With an] irrepressible scrappy band of ragamuffins *Newsies* . . . has a stirring, old-school sincerity that is hard to resist" (Rooney 2011). Due to strong ticket sales the limited-run was extended, eventually persuading Disney that there was sufficient demand for the show to justify a full, open-ended Broadway run.

While the Broadway show earned widespread critical praise for the younger actors in the cast, particularly for actor Jeremy Jordan as Jack Kelly, reviewers were generally less impressed with the show than had been the critics of the Paper Mill production. Ben Brantley, the *Times*' lead critic, found the show to be hyper-energized while lacking originality and discipline: "a supertabloid . . . [with] nothing but headlines, all set in extra-large type, all goal-posted with exclamation points and all proclaiming essentially the same thing" (Brantley 2012). Several reviewers echoed these comments. *TIME* found it to be "as disposable as yesterday's paper . . . a lot of motion but too little wit, or grit" (Zoglin 2012). Similarly, the *San Diego Union-Tribune* compared the story to exactly what the newsies were selling on stage: "the overall story, like newsprint, is black and white" (Kennedy 2012). David Rooney, reviewing the Broadway production for the *Hollywood Reporter*, agreed that the show was "brashly formulaic, sentimental or simplistic" but knowingly observed that, as a Disney production, *Newsies* maintained the "time-honored Disney tradition of inspirational storytelling in the best possible sense" (Rooney 2012). The show generally fared better in reviews that focused on the stage adaptation's improvements over the film, which never outlived its dismal critical notices. *Entertainment Weekly* felt that Disney had "polished this hardscrabble gem from a notorious big-screen dud," citing "several smart additions" such as the character of Katherine as a love interest as well as her featured song, the "delightful, doubletalking 'Watch What Happens'" (Geier 2012). The *NY Daily News* also touted the Jack and Katherine love story as one of Fierstein's smart enhancements to the original narrative. However, critics did not respond well to efforts to more fully actualize the adult characters from the stage version. *Variety* was altogether dismissive of Joseph Pulitzer's character, stating that he was saddled with "subpar scenes and a weak song." *Entertainment Weekly* felt that virtually all of the adult characters were upstaged by the youthful cast and lacked substance, while the *NY Daily News* proclaimed that the show "flies" whenever the newsies are on stage, but "sinks when the [carboard cutout] adults appear" (Dziemianowicz 2012).

Overall, the performances of the young newsboys, led by twenty-seven-year-old Jeremy Jordan as teenaged Jack Kelly, provided the saving grace in *Newsies*' critical notices. The online cultural journal *Vulture*, highlighting the younger performers, proclaimed that "the cast is uniformly strong, down to the rank and file." The *NY Post* applauded Jordan's performance as hitting "a good balance of sexiness and humor" (Vincentelli 2012), while *Entertainment Weekly* called him "an explosive presence on stage" and felt he conveyed "a rare combination of masculine swagger and vulnerability" (Geier 2012). The *NY Daily News* credited Jordan with carrying the whole show, hailing him as "a Page 1 headline" who "announces himself as a powerhouse talent" (Dziemianowicz 2012). The *Hollywood Reporter* praised Jordan for bringing "effortless charisma to the role and an ideal blend of wise-guy attitude, innate leadership and romantic wistfulness" (Rooney 2012).

Doubtless, the show's best friend among the critics was *Vulture*'s Scott Brown, whose review practically rises to a consecration of the special experience awaiting the young people flocking to see *Newsies* on Broadway: "There's enormous magnetism in this show, both for children and the grownups who brought them . . . *Newsies* will be many young fans' first Broadway experience. They'll emerge knowing they're not alone, and that there's not just strength in numbers, but rhythm and harmony, too" (Brown 2012).

Newsies had a longer-than-average run of 1,004 performances over nine months and quickly turned a profit in ticket-sales against its relatively modest $5 million production costs. Notably, *Newsies* had a stronger than anticipated showing in the major theater awards competitions, receiving eight Tony nominations (including one for Best Musical) and winning in two major categories: Best Original Score Written for the Theatre and Best Choreography. *Newsies* also won two Drama Desk awards, one each for music and choreography.

Shortly after closing on Broadway, *Newsies* began a highly successful national tour that would last nearly two years (October 11, 2014 to October 2, 2016). In September 2016, Fathom Events, producer of special filmed projects for single- and two-day international distribution to movie theaters, partnered with Disney Theatrical Productions to bring many original *Newsies* Broadway stars together in Los Angeles to film a performance of the production. Fathom's successful one-day release of *Disney's Newsies: The Broadway Musical* in early 2017 led to an additional two-day encore showing, earning $3.47 million at the box office. Due to popular demand, the Fathom–Disney filmed stage version was released for streaming on Netflix later that year. As the *Chicago Tribune* mused, marveling at the over-achieving musical's unlikely string of successes, "Sometimes less-than-great musicals just find their audience and work" (Jones 2016).

Historical accuracy and context

Newsies *and child labor*

Overall, *Newsies* provides an accurate representation of social issues surrounding child labor laws and practices in the urban northeast toward the end of the nineteenth century. Children working to support their families or themselves had been commonplace in American agriculture and guild craft apprenticeships since before the American Revolution. However, child labor as a social justice issue developed in the late nineteenth century as an outgrowth of the Industrial Revolution and the consequent rise of organized labor in America. With its rapid expansion of factories, mills, sweatshops, and refineries, the Industrial Revolution had a particularly powerful impact on people living and working in Northern cities and, as such, literally set the stage for *Newsies*.

By 1899, when the action of *Newsies* occurs, New York had already seen over fifty years of massive industrial expansion within its city limits and surrounding areas. The corresponding growth of manufacturing and heavy industry generated a decades-long demand for low and unskilled labor in factories, mills, plants, refineries, and sweatshops. Low-wage, often dangerous jobs combined with impoverished living conditions for workers and a paucity of regulations governing child welfare provided an incentive for employers to take on large numbers of child workers. The 1870 U.S. Census calculated that one in eight American children was in the workforce, not counting the children working in illegal forms of employment. Most children worked to supplement or even replace the wages of adults in their own households, a reality represented in *Newsies* by brothers Les and Davey who are their family's breadwinners. However, some child workers were runaways or orphans living on the streets or in various institutions for juveniles. *Newsies* represents their condition via scenes in Jack Kelly's rooftop hideaway and the Newsies lodging house.

Widespread and commonplace, mistreatment of child workers eventually aroused the ire of labor leaders and social reformers. Principal among them was Mary Harris Jones ("Mother Jones," *c.* 1830–1930), a long-time strike organizer and labor activist who in the early 1900s would become America's best-known advocate for the rights of child workers. The combined publicity surrounding the successful newsies' strike in 1899 followed by Mother Jones' high-profile advocacy for child workers were pivotal in bringing about public awareness and genuine reform on behalf of America's working children.

Newsies embraces a self-conscious awareness of the future of child labor, "predicting" social changes that we now know to be historical fact. Katherine entitles her article about the strike "The Children's Crusade," a term that would come to be associated with Mother Jones' 1903 labor march on behalf of child workers in Philadelphia textile mills. Additionally, when Katherine convinces Jack to return to the strike, she shares her vision that this first-ever organized children's labor action will have repercussions beyond the newsboys' moment in history: "[For] all the kids in every sweatshop, factory, and slaughterhouse ... You challenged [your] whole generation to stand up and demand a place at the table."

Although *Newsies* does a commendable job of presenting the environment in which the striking newsboys found themselves, the show takes liberties with some details. Notably, the show "ages" the newsies. With the exception of Davey's little brother, Les, the newsies onstage are portrayed in their late teenage years, perhaps sixteen or seventeen years old. However, at the time of the strike most newsies were between ten and fifteen years old. As a practical matter, the ages of the actors cast as newsies for the Broadway production, many in their mid- to late twenties, militated against a portrayal of pre-adolescent boys. *Newsies* also implicitly overstates the relative number of newsies who resided in institutions or lived on the streets rather than in more traditional family households. Notwithstanding the hardships they faced, working newsboys had a daily income and by and large lived, slept, and ate meals at home. On a related issue, by 1899 many newsies attended school and worked part-time selling afternoon and evening editions, an historical circumstance *Newsies* omits altogether.

The world will know: the strike of 1899

Considering the challenge of compressing the myriad details of a two-week strike (July 20 to August 1, 1899) into a two-and-a-half-hour musical, *Newsies* admirably portrays key events surrounding the strike. However, the creative team exercises some license along the way, especially in its portrayal of the well-known historical characters.

The dispute between the newsboys and New York's two biggest publishers, Joseph Pulitzer (*New York World*) and William Randolph Hearst (*New York Evening Journal*), erupted in the months following the end of the Spanish-American War in August 1898. For the most part, the musical is faithful to the complicated strike backstory. During the war, newspaper circulation saw astonishing increases owing to a steady stream of sensational breaking news stories emanating from the warfront. Publishers wanted to capitalize on the increase of wartime paper sales and hiked the wholesale price the newsboys paid from 50 to 60 cents per hundred while the war was in progress. Once the war ended, newspaper sales in general dropped back to pre-war levels. Correspondingly, most publishers returned the wholesale price to the pre-war level of 50 cents. However, Pulitzer and Hearst chose not to lower the wholesale price, igniting the conflict between the newsboys and themselves.

The show's creators chose to compress the timeline between the price changes, so they moved up the timing of the 50-to-60-cent price hike from during the war (when the real price hike occurred) to immediately after the war. This historically inaccurate change in timing, unnoticeable to anyone without detailed knowledge of the strike, enhanced the musical's narrative in two ways: it eliminated a potentially confusing point of exposition without disturbing the narrative thread; and it made the publishers appear all the more heartless by gratuitously placing the financial burden of the postwar sales downturn on the backs of the newsies. Either way, both the stage newsboys and the real newsboys were outraged and, thus, all the more motivated to organize and strike against the publishers.

As the turn of the century approached, numerous strikes had broken out in American cities, and nowhere more so than in New York. Considered the "Greatest Strike City in America," New York was beset by over 3,000 different strikes and labor actions in the course of little more than a decade. Strikes are newsworthy and, of course, newsboys knew about major strikes reported in the papers they sold. These street heralds of growing worker dissatisfaction were inspired by the stories they were selling. As the musical accurately reflects, in late July 1899 thousands of newsies from all five boroughs, along with sympathetic politicians and other supporters, gathered for a rally in the Lower Eastside of Manhattan to bolster their new union and gain publicity for their cause.

The musical also points out that striking children were not immune from the violence that had arisen in many labor actions taken by adult workers. In a dramatic fight scene, striking newsboys are attacked by "goons" working for the Pulitzer company. *Newsies* also recognizes the historical reality that striking newsboys were capable of instigating violence and vandalism on their own, such as attacking non-union "scabs" who sold papers during the strike and damaging private property. *Newsies* generally alludes to such action in dialogue and lyrics, rather than fully staging them, so as not to undermine the audience's sympathy for the newsies' righteous struggle. But the show does, in fact, raise the issue.

In order to provide Jack Kelly and the newsies with a stage-worthy villain, *Newsies* caricatures its portrayal of Joseph Pulitzer beyond recognition. The musical implies that Pulitzer somehow ordered a city-wide blackout of all news coverage of the strike. However, newspapers not owned or controlled by Pulitzer published whatever they wanted, including coverage of the newsies' strike against Pulitzer and Hearst. Moreover, Joseph Pulitzer had far less involvement with the strike than the musical would have its audience believe. In 1899, Pulitzer had been long-retired as managing editor of his paper and had moved out of New York well before the strike. The functional head of Pulitzer's news operations during the Spanish-American War and the strike was Don C. Seitz, represented in the musical by the minor character Seitz. Actions staged in the musical that correspond with real actions taken by the Pulitzer company were operationalized by Don C. Seitz, including instigating police mobilization against the newsies and hiring company "goons" (or security guards) to confront the strikers. Although *Newsies*' villainizes Pulitzer, Hearst was directly involved in the strike, meeting with union leaders and resisting their demands. Although mentioned frequently, Hearst does not appear in the musical at any time.

The success of the Newsies Strike exacerbated problems for the *World* and *Journal*, already suffering from the postwar dip in sales and corresponding losses of advertising revenue. Hearst and Pulitzer's management agreed to a compromise with the newsboys after only two weeks: the price of the newspapers would remain at 60 cents per hundred, but the publishers would give a financial credit to the newsboys for any unsold papers. However, *Newsies* fictionalizes some of the terms of the agreement. In the musical's version of the settlement the newspapers drop the wholesale price to 55 cents per hundred and the publishers agree to buy back all unsold papers in cash, and not, as the real terms dictated, extend a comparable credit to the newsies.

The musical's most flagrant departure from history occurs when New York Governor Theodore Roosevelt, functioning as a *deus ex machina* plot device, arrives in Pulitzer's office to chastise Pulitzer and set things right. This confrontation never occurred. Roosevelt had no active role in the dispute and certainly did not engineer its resolution. The historic victory truly belonged to the newsies, not the grown-ups.

Turn-of-the-century women

Although maintaining the story's focus on the newsboys, the stage adaptation of *Newsies* features women characters more heavily than did the original film. Moreover, unlike the film, the musical seeks to convey that the American labor movement at the turn of century intersected with a concurrent struggle for women's rights. The musical's portrayal of women corresponds to the musical's core narrative: a story about work outside the home. Thus, the two principal female characters are a journalist (Katherine Plumber) and a theater owner/performer (Medda Larkin) supported by a secretary and an ensemble of nuns and vaudeville-era professional dancers. *Newsies* has little to say about the domestic life of women, men, or children. However, challenging gender norms in work, education, the arts, and politics was a hallmark of "the New Woman," a term associated with the rise of feminist activism and social change in the American Progressive Era (1880–1920). Katherine Plumber and Medda Larkin, each in her own way, offer plausible representations of the Progressive Era's New Woman within the limitations of a musical starring working boys. Although in *Newsies*

Katherine is the daughter of Joseph Pulitzer, her character is a fictionalized Nellie Bly (née Elizabeth Cochrane, 1864–1922), a female reporter who pioneered American investigative journalism. Generally restricted to writing pieces for the society pages or other light features, female journalists of the time were rarely given straightforward news assignments. However, Bly, a writer for Pulitzer's *New York World*, famously cracked that barrier, writing investigative exposés on such topics as the horrendous conditions in psychiatric institutions and mistreatment of young girls laboring in a box-making factory. Katherine's solo song "Watch What Happens" tells of her yearning for a career-making breakout story, her wariness about hostile male editors, and, ultimately, her awe at investigative journalism's power to transform the world by giving "the little guy some ink."

The character of Medda Larkin, inspired by dancer, choreographer, and director Aida Overton Walker (1880–1914), expands *Newsies*' message of the intersectionality of social movements by presenting an independent African American career woman as a friend and philanthropic supporter of the strike and its leaders. Reflecting the "New Negro" movement of the Harlem Renaissance (1920–30) among the leading social forces of the time, Medda Larkin's artistry, like Aida Overton Walker's, defied stereotypical, debasing stage routines white audiences often demanded of Black entertainers. Significantly, Larkin also shares with Walker revolutionary hard-earned, self-made wealth, of which Medda boasts with a pride tempered by knowledge that money alone cannot conquer racism: "I live in a mansion on Long Island Sound . . . But you [*sic*] telling me you don't want me around." If glancingly, *Newsies* makes the point that accomplished influential professional women like Katherine and Medda, while rarities in their own time, were harbingers of many more to come.

Yellow Journalism

Although *Newsies* focuses on the newsboys' strike, at the forefront of their story is the media war between Joseph Pulitzer and William Randolph Hearst. With the expanded market for newspapers during the 1890s, and particularly during the Spanish-American War, came advances in technology that enabled well-financed publishers to print more daily editions in larger volume and in more elaborate formats than ever before. The increase in productivity to satisfy the expanding news-reading market spawned a new level of competition between the rival publishing giants, as they both sought to profit from the increasing demand for news.

Hearst, whose family publishing interests had originated in California, acquired the *New York Morning Journal* in November 1895, igniting a circulation war with Pulitzer's *New York World*. The Pulitzer–Hearst rivalry soon brought to the fore what came to be known as Yellow Journalism: sensationalized news stories with "screaming headlines" designed to shock people into quick, impulse purchases of newspapers. Although originally identified specifically with the Pulitzer–Hearst rivalry, Yellow Journalism evolved into a term of art for journalism characterized by sensationalism, profuse exaggeration or falsification of facts, and melodramatic human-interest stories involving both celebrities and everyday citizens.

The "Yellow" name originated in a popular comic strip, "Hogan's Alley," that appeared regularly in Pulitzer's *New York World* and featured a yellow-dressed character named the "Yellow Kid." Hearst lured the creator of the comic away from Pulitzer and ran the strip in his *New York Morning Journal*. Enraged, Pulitzer found an artist to create a competing "yellow kid," sending the two publishers into a fierce, if somewhat ridiculous, battle over the "yellow kid comic." The yellow kid dispute became both a symbol and a source of mockery for Pulitzer and Hearst's intensely serious competition for dominance in newspaper sales and profits. Many other newspapers in New York and elsewhere criticized both Pulitzer and Hearst for their sensationalist news reporting, often deriding their feud with insults about "yellow kid journalism." In time, the Pulitzer/Hearst imbroglio faded from public memory, but the related term "Yellow Journalism" outlived them. While somewhat dated now, the term still holds currency as a descriptor for sensational, scandal-prone, factually-dubious reporting whether in print, broadcast media, or on the web.

The musical does not substantively address the issue of the role the Pulitzer–Hearst rivalry likely played in hastening, or even inciting, the Spanish-America War after the mysterious sinking of the American battleship USS *Maine* in Havana Harbor on February 15, 1898. Historians identify Hearst's *Journal* in particular as having made a calculated rush to judgment that the sinking was an act of sabotage by Spain, an accusation Spain denied. Fueled by the Hearst and Pulitzer newspapers' heated coverage of the sinking of the *Maine*, diplomatic relations between Spain and America deteriorated so rapidly that the two countries entered into war by April of that year. The war, widely believed to be the outcome Hearst sought with his paper's inflammatory coverage of the USS *Maine*, generated a spike in demand for news. In response, the *World* and the *Journal* produced a steady stream of compelling headlines to be shouted in the streets by newsies heralding bloody victories, bloodier defeats, murder, mayhem, and disasters. The market value of such headlines assumes center stage in *Newsies*. Early in the show newsboys sing of how shouting sensational headlines generates sales: "Give us an earthquake or a war" and "a pistol-packin' floozy." Predictably, the lead newsie, Jack Kelly, has his "Extra! Extra!" street moment: "Terrified Flight from Burning Inferno!" Even the intrepid reporter Katherine concedes that to attract readers and move them to action "a little hyperbole never hurt anyone."

As Pulitzer and Hearst continued to compete against each other, both companies eventually began to lose money on their extra editions and splashy front pages. Unlike papers that avoided the media war, the *World* and the *Journal* actually drained their resources over the course of their competition. Improbably, it was the newsies' strike that finally brought the two publishing giants together as they jointly negotiated to keep the higher wholesale price of their papers but extend credit to the newsies for unsold copies.

Thomas A. Greenfield and Christina M. Baurle

Further reading

Brantley, Ben. 2012. "Urchins with Punctuation 'Newsies the Musical,' by Alan Menken and Harvey Fierstein." *New York Times*, March 29, 2012.

Brown, Scott. 2012. "Theater Review: Newsies and the Pleasures of the Gateway Musical." *Vulture*, March 29, 2012.

Calhoun, Jeff and Brett Sullivan. 2017. *Disney's Newsies the Broadway Musical*. Video Recording, September 11, 2016 at Pantages Theatre, 149 minutes. *Netflix.com*.

Chadwick, Bruce. 2011. "'Extra! Extra! Read All about It': Newsies Makes Media History Soar." *History News Network*, September 26, 2011.

Dziemianowicz, Joe. 2012. "Theater Review: Disney's 'Newsies' Opens on Broadway." *New York Daily News*, March 29, 2012.

Feldman, Jack, Harvey Fierstein, and Alan Menken. 2018. *Disney's Newsies the Broadway Musical*. New York: Music Theatre International.

Feldman, Jack, Susan Haskins, Alan Menken, and Michael Riedel. 2012. "Theater Talk: Alan Menken & Harvey Fierstein on 'Newsies.'" *YouTube.com*, 26:46, May 4, 2012.

Geier, Thom. 2012. "Newsies." *Entertainment Weekly*, March 29, 2012.

Haverkate, Julie. n.d. *Disney's Newsies Production Handbook*. New York: Musical Theatre International.

Jones, Chris. 2016. "Disney's 'Newsies' Still Delivers a Good Time." *Chicago Tribune*, August 1, 2016.

Kennedy, Mark. 2012. "Review: Musical 'Newsies' Is Relentlessly Cheery." *San Diego Union-Tribune*, March 29, 2012.

Nasaw, David. 1985. *Children of the City: At Work and at Play*. Garden City, NY: Anchor Press/Doubleday.

Rabinovitch-Fox, Einav. 2017. "New Women in Early 20th-Century America." *Oxford Research Encyclopedia of American History*, August 2017.

Riis, Jacob A. 1890. *How the Other Half Lives: Studies among the Tenements of New York*. New York: Charles Scribner's Sons.

Rooney, David. 2011. "Newsboys Strike? Sing All About It." *New York Times*, September 27, 2011.
Rooney, David. 2012. "Newsies: Theater Review." *Hollywood Reporter*, March 29, 2012.
Schuman, Michael. 2017. "History of Child Labor in the United States—Part 1: Little Children Working." *Monthly Labor Review*, January 2017.
Seitz, Don C. 1899. "Memo for Mr. Pulitzer on the Newsboys' Strike." World Papers Columbia University, Rare Book & Manuscript Library, July 22, 1899.
Simonson, Robert. 2012. "ASK PLAYBILL.COM: Joseph Pulitzer, the 'Villain' of Newsies, Illuminated." *Playbill*, March 29, 2012.
Suskin, Steven. 2012. "Newsies: The Musical." *Variety*, March 29, 2012.
Valis Hill, Constance. 2010. "Ada Overton Walker [biography]." In *Tap Dancing America, A Cultural History*. Oxford: Oxford University Press.
Vincentelli, Elisabeth. 2012. "Striking Ensemble Is on Tap." *New York Post*, March 30, 2012.
Zoglin, Richard. 2012. "Newsboys Striking, Garland Freaking: Broadway's Newsies and End of the Rainbow." *TIME*, April 3, 2012.

CHAPTER 14
PARADE (1998)

Librettist: Alfred Uhry (1935–)
Composer and Lyricist: Jason Robert Brown (1970–)
Co-Conceived by Harold Prince (1928–2019)
World Professional Premiere: December 17, 1998, Vivian Beaumont Theater at Lincoln Center

Songs

"Prologue: The Old Red Hills of Home"
"Anthem: The Dream of Atlanta"
"How Can I Call This Home?"
"The Picture Show"
"Leo at Work/What Am I Waiting For?"
"Interrogation: I Am Trying to Remember . . ."
"Big News!"
"Funeral: There Is a Fountain/It Don't Make Sense"
"Watson's Lullaby"
"Somethin' Ain't Right"
"Real Big News"
"You Don't Know This Man"
"People of Atlanta"
"Twenty Miles from Marietta"
"Frankie's Testimony"
"The Factory Girls/Come Up to My Office"
"Newt Lee's Testimony"
"My Child Will Forgive Me"
"That's What He Said"
"Leo's Statement: It's Hard to Speak My Heart"
"Closing Statements and Verdict"
"A Rumblin' and a Rollin'"
"Do It Alone"
"Pretty Music"
"Letter to the Governor"
"This Is Not Over Yet"
"Factory Girls" (Reprise)
"Newt Lee's" (Reprise)
"Blues: Feel the Rain Fall"
"Where Will You Stand When the Flood Comes?"
"All the Wasted Time"
"Sh'ma"
"Finale: The Old Red Hills of Home"

Overview

Parade defies expectations of musical theater with its highly controversial subject matter and unrelenting pessimism. The musical takes on the chilling events surrounding the 1913 killing of thirteen-year-old Mary Phagan in Atlanta, Georgia, at the National Pencil factory, and the trial, conviction, and mob lynching of the likely innocent Jewish factory supervisor, Leo Frank. In musicalizing this very unmusical story, *Parade* presents the overall facts of the case fairly accurately. However, the case itself acts as a crucible for many familiar, persistent tensions in American history. Principal among them are the intersection of antisemitism, racism, and hatred of the Other, as well as the legacy of slavery and the Civil War. However, the show also confronts flaws and injustice in the American judicial system, child labor, violence against women, and social class tensions brought on by American industrialization. The creative team's strong point of view regarding the historical events, particularly their unflinching belief in Frank's innocence and in the complicity of the culture and social structures of the South in the miscarriage of justice Frank suffered, framed the manner in which the events and principal figures of the case were presented on stage eighty-five years after the fact.

The Leo Frank–Mary Phagan case is a fascinating, dark episode of our history whose impact still reverberates today. A teenage girl's murder and the subsequent lynching of an innocent man are unlikely fare for a Broadway musical. However, Alfred Uhry (author of the play and film *Driving Miss Daisy* and the play *The Last Night of Ballyhoo*, also about Jews in the American South) had personal ties to the Frank case. His great-uncle owned the National Pencil Factory where the events took place and his grandmother knew Lucille Frank, Leo Frank's wife. Uhry relates: "When I was growing up in Atlanta in the '40s and '50s, Leo Frank was mentioned only in hushed tones. I remember people getting up and walking out of the room if anyone talked about the case" (Schechter 2015).

Once he began looking into the events surrounding the case, Uhry knew he wanted to dramatize it. He broached the idea to Hal Prince, an acclaimed producer of Broadway musicals. Intrigued by the idea and the difficulties inherent in dramatizing this historical material, Prince joined Uhry in developing the story as a musical. To that end, he enlisted the young, promising composer Jason Robert Brown to write the songs and lyrics.

The creative team wanted *Parade* to take an unequivocal point of view towards their understanding of the crime, its aftermath, and the root causes of the calamitous fate of Leo Frank. Prince understood that, even in the late 1990s, some people still believed in Frank's guilt. However, upon researching the case independently, Prince came to believe that Frank was completely innocent. Moreover, Prince was no less certain as to whom the show would blame for the miscarriage of justice: "Nuance and ambivalence would be thematic luxuries the musical would have no time for . . . It would therefore become the show's responsibility to present [Frank] as the victim of a Dixie-based strain of virulent antisemitism" (Hirsch 2005).

The final musical did, indeed, embody firm and clear loyalties to the innocence of Leo Frank and worked towards making him as sympathetic a hero as possible. In so doing, *Parade* emphasizes antisemitism as the central thematic concern of the plot. While antisemitism was clearly responsible for the way the actual case unfolded, modern demands of historical accuracy—even for a musical—challenged *Parade*'s creative team to explore, even minimally, internal motivations or other contexts for the actions of Frank's tormentors and accusers. However, the show was criticized for oversimplifying virtually all of its characters other than the Franks, and particularly faulted for presenting white Southerners as uniformly one-dimensional ignorant bigots. That criticism seemed to register since, some years after the initial run, the creative team revised the show for a less strident revival in 2007.

In addition to struggling with the portrayal of Frank's white tormentors, *Parade* marginalizes African American characters and experiences connected to the history of the case. Some African Americans who were involved in the series of events that ultimately brought Leo to his death exist only along the edges of *Parade*. Two African American men in particular—Jim Conley, who many believe was the true culprit, and Newt Lee, who found Mary Phagan's dead body—are represented in the musical, but are not substantively drawn characters. Even allowing for poetic license, glossing over the role and presence of African Americans in a narrative involving race relations in the South clearly works against *Parade*'s aspirations to fully portray an important event in American history.

Beyond gauging their overall point of view about the historical events before them, *Parade*'s creative team had to wrestle with the shear bulk of detail connected with the murder, Frank's trial, and its aftermath. Much of this material was not only difficult to present in sequence but pointedly non-theatrical in nature: hearings, appeals, waiting periods (in jail) between court actions, and so on. The complexity of the basic information about the case required judicious editing and strategic presentation. To make the details of the events comprehensible and as appealing to an audience as possible, Prince felt that the musical required a love story to humanize Leo Frank, whom Uhry's script presented as sorely lacking in charisma. Thus, an enlarged role for Frank's wife Lucille both humanized Frank as a common man figure and rendered the central crisis of the play—Frank's futile struggle to assert his innocence—a shared struggle between husband and wife, Leo and Lucille.

To make the court material musically appealing despite its darkness, Prince and Brown presented the trial scenes as an extended series of interconnected songs, with an individual musical moment assigned to many of the most important figures in the sequence of events. This miniature popular opera within the musical made the historical trial content relatively accessible via conceptually unified melody, lyrics, and dialog. Prince's staging of this sequence and other aspects of the show, inspired by the American political dramas of the Living Newspapers of the 1930s, gave the show a cinematic, film noir inspired look, which included an ominous lynching tree hanging over the set throughout.

The Broadway production opened December 17, 1998, at Lincoln Center's Vivian Beaumont Theater. It ran for a disappointing thirty-nine previews and eighty-five performances, later closing on February 28, 1999. Notwithstanding admiring responses from the theater community (including Tony wins for Uhry's book and Brown's score), the show did not find an audience. Mixed and some outright negative reviews, plus the bankruptcy of co-producer Garth Drabinsky's production company Livent Inc. during the Broadway run, caused the ultimate demise of the show. A fall 2000 touring production took *Parade* to several cities with composer Jason Robert Brown conducting a number of performances during the tour.

The Donmar Warehouse theater in London opened a limited-run production of *Parade* on September 24, 2007. After two months in London, the production closed up and then reopened at the Mark Taper Forum in Los Angeles in October 2009, with Rob Ashford as director. Ashford, the assistant choreographer and dance captain of the original production, made judicious cuts and staging choices which brought this later production far more success with critics and audiences than the original had received.

Assessing *Parade*'s level of historical accuracy is complicated by the nature of the events themselves. Someone committed a crime, and a person was found guilty in a court of law for that crime. However, it is widely agreed among historians and other serious-minded students of the case that the conviction was wrongful. Nonetheless, the Leo Frank trial remains controversial to this day as its invocations of racism, antisemitism, and violence against women resonate all too powerfully in contemporary life. Notwithstanding a preponderance of research supporting Frank's innocence, anger and conspiracy theories reasserting Frank's guilt continue to circulate, particularly online.

The musical was not a commercial success in its first production but it has since attained cult-classic status in the musical theater community, largely through the growing reputation of composer/lyricist Jason Robert Brown in the years following *Parade*'s Broadway run. A 2023 revival fared only slightly better despite garnering strong reviews and winning Tony Awards for Best Revival of a Musical and Best Direction of a Musical. It closed after only 169 performances.

Plot synopsis

Parade opens in 1862 with a young Confederate soldier in Marietta, Georgia, singing praises of his homeland as he prepares to join the battle at hand ("The Old Red Hills of Home"). The action jumps ahead fifty-one years to Atlanta on April 26, 1913, Confederate Memorial Day, and this same solider, now elderly and missing a leg, finishes the song as part of the parade referenced in the title ("Anthem: The Dream of Atlanta"). At his Atlanta home, Leo Frank, a Brooklyn-raised Jewish man, sings of his distaste and confusion over the alien Southern world where he has lived for the past five years ("How Can I Call This Home?").

On a streetcar heading towards the National Pencil Factory where she works and where Leo Frank is superintendent, Mary Phagan, thirteen, is met by her young friend Frankie Epps who wants her to go with him later to the movies ("The Picture Show"). At the factory, Leo balances the books while, at home, his wife Lucille reminisces and longs for something more from their relationship ("Leo at Work/What Am I Waiting For?"). Mary Phagan enters Leo's office to collect her pay. In the middle of that night, two policemen come to the Franks' house and take Leo to the factory. Newt Lee, the African American night watchman, tells the police about finding Mary Phagan's body. Leo reacts nervously at the sight of the body, and the police appear to be suspicious of him ("Interrogation"). Britt Craig, a frustrated local reporter, drunkenly laments the lack of a big story in backwater Atlanta ("Big News!"), but then hears of Mary's murder from Hugh Dorsey, the District Attorney. Governor John Slaton of Georgia, worried about inflaming public ire over the controversial issue of child labor, puts pressure on Dorsey to convict a suspect quickly.

At Mary's funeral, Frankie Epps angrily swears revenge and Tom Watson, editor of the right-wing newspaper the *Jeffersonian*, warns the Governor that the culprit must "face his maker" ("There Is a Fountain/It Don't Make Sense"). While questioning Newt Lee, to the background of Watson singing a lullaby to Phagan ("Watson's Lullaby"), District Attorney Dorsey decides that Leo Frank must be the real culprit ("Somethin' Ain't Right"). Craig and other reporters encourage bystanders to share rumors about Frank, and Dorsey pushes Conley to implicate Frank. Finally, Leo is indicted and Lucille is surrounded by reporters ("Real Big News"). She angrily sings to Craig ("You Don't Know This Man").

In a nine-part mini opera within the play, Leo's trial unfolds. Outside the courtroom, country singer Fiddlin' John sings a ballad about Mary while Watson riles up the people of Atlanta ("The Trial: Part I, It Is Time Now"). Judge Leonard Roan, elderly and in a wheelchair, opens the proceedings and Dorsey sets the scene ("The Trial: Part II, Twenty Miles from Marietta"). Frankie Epps testifies and we see his altered version of his meeting with Mary, who reveals to him that she is uneasy because Leo "looks at me" ("The Trial: Part III, Frankie's Testimony"). Other girls from the factory testify and echo Mary's story that Leo watched them strangely, or came too close. Suddenly we see the version of Leo the young girls are describing come to life and, in that persona, Leo sings a disturbing plea for them to "Come up to my office" ("The Trial: Part IV, The Factory Girls"). Newt Lee testifies that he saw Leo by the doorway when the girls were changing ("The Trial: Part V, Newt Lee's Testimony"), and Mrs. Phagan, Mary's mother, sings a ballad of forgiveness ("The Trial: Part VI, My Child Will Forgive Me"), which she concludes with an angry burst of antisemitic invective. Conley testifies that Frank killed Mary by mistake and sought Conley's help to be a look-out at the door. Conley further alleges that after killing Mary, Frank had him take her body to the basement ("The Trial: Part VII, That's What He Said"). With the crowd angered and bloodthirsty, Leo's lawyer Luther Rosser puts an unprepared Leo on the stand to make a statement, strategizing that since Leo is innocent, his honesty will convince the crowd. Leo struggles as he makes his plea to the courtroom ("The Trial: Part VIII, It's Hard to Speak My Heart"). During the closing statements the jury reads out their guilty verdict as ascending sounds of a dissonant cakewalk and bell tolling overtake the scene. Crowds outside the courtroom dance wildly ("The Trial: Part IX, Closing Statements/Cakewalk").

Act Two opens on Confederate Memorial Day one year later. Judge Roan rejects Leo's appeals and sentences him to hang. Craig tells us that in the North, Frank's defenders are mobilizing. Riley and Angela, the Franks' African American servants, join Newt Lee and Jim Conley to sing about the ironies surrounding Northern whites coming to Frank's defense ("A Rumblin' and a Rollin'"). In prison, Leo fires his lawyer and tries to rebuff Lucille's offer to help. To his surprise, she responds angrily ("Do It Alone"). At a formal dance in the Governor's mansion, Governor Slaton sings a carefree song about dancing ("Pretty Music"). Last in line to dance with him is Lucille Frank. She pushes him to reopen the case, but he turns her down.

Judge Roan, close to death, dictates in song a "Letter to the Governor." The judge now regrets the way the trial was handled and declares that it's up to Governor Slaton to correct that mistake. In jail, Leo gets a message that the Governor is going to re-examine the trial. Frank jubilantly sings a duet with Lucille ("This Is Not Over Yet"). The Governor, with Lucille, questions the factory girls ("Factory Girls [Reprise]") and Newt Lee, whose testimony falls apart. In the next scene, Slaton interrogates Conley, who is on a prison chain gang serving a one-year sentence as an accomplice to Leo. Slaton pokes holes in Conley's testimony while Conley sings ("Blues: Feel the Rain Fall"). Governor Slaton announces he is commuting Leo's death sentence while Watson whips up an angry mob in response ("Where Will You Stand When the Flood Comes?").

Leo is transferred to a farm-like prison near Marietta, Georgia. Lucille brings a picnic to his new cell. The jail disappears as they imagine themselves out in the countryside, and they sing a love duet about their regrets ("All the Wasted Time"). In the middle of the night, three men break into Leo's cell and drag him out. He is brought to a tree in Marietta. Leo asks his abductors to send his wedding ring to his wife and cover him as he is in a nightshirt. Leo sings a Hebrew prayer ("Sh'ma") before he is lynched. Weeks later, on yet another Confederate Memorial Day, Craig returns the ring to Lucille, and she sings that Leo is "finally free." Lucille puts on her ring as Frankie leads the citizens of Atlanta in a final reprise of the opening number ("The Old Red Hills of Home").

Critical reception

Parade received a mixed critical reaction to its original production, with the harshest reviews largely credited for the early demise of the Broadway run. *Parade* did, however, win Tony Awards for Best Book and Best Original Score (out of a very impressive nine Tony nominations) and was nominated for thirteen Drama Desk Awards, winning six, including Outstanding Musical of the year. Despite some favorable notices from the Associated Press, Long Island's *Newsday*, and the *American Reporter* among others, Ben Brantley's devastating review in the *New York Times* seemed to be the critical response that forced the show to close early. Brantley found the show distancing, laboriously unnuanced, and too focused on being a civics lesson: "Leo is as flat and iconic as a bleeding saint in a religious mural . . . the result is often more podium-thumping screed than compelling story." Brantley felt the material necessitated an emotional connection and an appeal to tears, however "for those tears to flow, we have to get to know Leo Frank as a man, not a symbol. *Parade* forbids our ever approaching such knowledge." Brantley also found Brown's score complicit in the show's failure to make an emotional connection with the audience: "while artfully shading classic hymn and march forms with dark dissonance, [the songs] also keep you at an intellectual remove" (Brantley 1998). Writing for *Variety*, Charles Isherwood concurred that the emotional impact of the musical faltered: "while nothing about this production is less than accomplished, *Parade* might still be called the feel-bad musical of the year . . . Even at its most musically lively, *Parade* is dramatically inert." Isherwood also protested that Southern white characters were portrayed one-dimensionally as racist antisemitic bigots willing to do anything to get their guilty verdict: "it's hard to take unalloyed pleasure in a score that so thoroughly depicts human mendacity, stupidity, opportunism and cruelty" (Isherwood 1998).

Brantley and Isherwood's verdict on the Broadway run was hardly unanimous. Linda Winer of *Newsday* hailed the show as "Powerful . . . about two-thirds of the way through the first handsome act of *Parade* . . . something happens that makes us stop merely admiring the show and start connecting deeply to it" (Winer 1998). Writing in the *American Reporter*, Lucy Komisar called *Parade* a "brilliant musical" in her headline. Unlike Isherwood, who disparaged *Parade*'s oversimplified view of Southern history, Komisar argued that

Parade's historical content was well handled and valuable: "it is a broad look into the social history of the South—its child labor, provincialism, political opportunism and corruption, yellow journalism, racism, antisemitism, and also its moments of political and personal courage" (Komisar 1998). David Patrick Stearns in *USA Today*, while faulting a slow-moving first act and some inexplicable gaps in the narrative, hailed the show's "daringly gradual dramatic crescendo" as Lucille Frank attempts to free her husband, yielding a musical that is "pointedly in step with its time" (Stearns 1998). However, in the minds of the creative team, there was no overcoming the impact of the *Times* opening night review. As Hal Prince recalled to his biographer, "If Brantley hadn't slaughtered the show, it would have run over a year and then gone on the road to the major cities . . . With a show like *Parade* the *Times* had better like it" (Hirsch 2005). The *Times* clearly did not.

In 2000, the touring production of *Parade* faced a curtailed schedule owing to lingering controversies over the musical that surfaced in prospective tour locations. Nevertheless, the tour was generally well received by audiences and local critics who saw it. The most well-reviewed production of *Parade* thus far has been the 2007 Donmar Warehouse production in London, directed by Rob Ashford, which transferred to the Mark Taper Forum in Los Angeles two years later. For this production the creative team trimmed the original book and made cuts to the original Broadway score. In addition, the reduced cast of fifteen actors instead of the original cast's thirty-seven gave the show a more accessible staging. Reviewing the 2009 Los Angeles production a decade after he panned the original Broadway production, Isherwood again expressed doubts that the subject matter truly suited a musical presentation. However, he liked this production more than the original:

> On the vast Vivian Beaumont stage [on Broadway], *Parade* was dark and solemn—as it is here—but also somewhat bloated with self-importance. Scaled down to a more intimate size here, it speaks in a quieter voice and seems less strident in its depiction of the power of antisemitism, bigotry and venality in the South of the early 20th century.
>
> *Isherwood 2009*

On the whole, British critics were very positive toward the London production. Paul Taylor in the *Independent* pointed out a trend with respect to British audiences appreciating challenging American works that were not understood or fully appreciated in the States: "Donmar Warehouse once again vibrantly vindicates an American musical cold-shouldered by its homeland in this immensely impressive production . . . It establishes *Parade* as an admirably ambitious, musically daring piece that deserves praise for attempting to intertwine the political and the personal" (Taylor 2007). David Benedict in *Variety* also praised the revival for "proving again that the best things come in small packages; [this] pared-down, blistering production is, in every possible sense, a thriller" (Benedict 2007).

Over time, *Parade* picked up something of a cult audience as interest in Jason Robert Brown's work as a composer and songwriter grew with later musical theater successes such as *The Last Five Years* (2002), *13* (2007), and *The Bridges of Madison County* (2013).

Historical accuracy and context

Leo, Lucille, and the crime

Parade's portrayal of Leo as being nervous and uptight corroborates biographical information about him. Frank was described by contemporaries as "nervous and apparently high-strung" and having a "nervous, bilious," unattractive temperament (Dinnerstein 1987). Frank's sense of alienation from Georgia and the South prior to Mary Phagan's death, a point emphasized in Frank's first appearance on stage, also rings true to the tenor of the times. Frank was born and educated in New York. He moved to Atlanta to manage the pencil company in 1908, a time when Atlanta's many white gentiles and established Jewish communities were distrustful of newly arriving Jewish merchants and businesspeople.

In Atlanta, Frank met Lucille Selig who was from a well-connected, prosperous Atlanta Jewish family; they married in 1910. *Parade*'s staging of their marriage as a redeeming love story is perhaps overly romanticized for the sake of musicalization. However, we do know that after Frank was arrested, Lucille rushed to the station, told a reporter that "My husband is absolutely innocent," and petitioned officials on her husband's behalf while he was jailed (Dinnerstein 1987). Lucille stayed in Atlanta after Leo's lynching. She retained Frank as her surname and never remarried.

Parade does not portray the actual murder on stage but rather takes Frank's perspective, posited unequivocally as that of an innocent man tormented by the seeming inexplicability of his perilous legal situation. Mary Phagan was, as staged, killed on Confederate Memorial Day, April 26, 1913, and was thirteen years old at the time. For the most part documented facts of the case are presented faithfully in the musical. Like many young girls, Mary worked at a factory to help her struggling family survive. She came to the pencil factory on April 13 at around noon to collect wages from Frank for her most recent shift ($1.20 for twelve hours, or about $2.60 per hour today, CPI [Consumer Price Index] n.d.). At approximately 3:00 a.m. Newt Lee, the night watchman, found her body in the factory basement and called the police. The police found Mary's clothes ripped, bloodstained and dirty; she was bruised, and a cord had been wrapped around her neck (*Parade* does not represent on stage the gruesome condition of Mary's corpse).

There is no single undisputed authoritative account of events that occurred in the hours between the time Mary arrived at the factory and the time the police were notified about her death, and disputes surrounding basic facts of the crime persist to this day. For example, the police found near Mary's body two notes presumably providing evidence of Frank's guilt: a purported admission that he (Frank) accidentally killed her and instructions for Conley to help Frank escape. Conley ultimately claimed that Frank dictated the notes to him, an assertion Frank maintained was entirely false. There is some speculation that Conley wrote the notes to frame Newt Lee, the night watchman, and, indeed, debates about the notes' origins and meaning still proliferate.

At the location, police did not treat the crime scene properly. For example, footprints where the body was likely dragged along the floor in the basement were trampled over before police secured the area—a detail not represented on stage. However, the musical does indicate clearly that soon after the investigation commenced the police and District Attorney Hugh Dorsey felt pressure from the public to quickly identify and prosecute a culprit. The police summoned Frank to the scene for questioning; he seemed nervous but was temporarily released. Frank was arrested on April 29. (The musical conflates Frank's initial interrogation and the arrest into one scene.) Conley was arrested on May 1 as an accomplice.

The trial

The musical portrays the events of the trial in an elaborate nine-part cinematic montage. Nevertheless, *Parade* excludes a large amount of the trial's massive detail. The musical largely skips over the two months between Frank's Grand Jury indictment and the beginning of his trial (May 24 through July 28). Also underplayed is the large crowd that gathered outside the courtroom throughout the proceedings, chanting angrily against Frank near the courtroom's open windows. On the other hand, the musical does convey that the press played a large role in distributing misinformation and fomenting antisemitism throughout the trial. Tom Watson, a populist radical agrarian leader who published two magazines, the *Jeffersonian* and *Watson's Magazine*, was particularly aggressive in promoting an antisemitic backlash against Frank and is shown doing so in the musical.

The musical presents a solitary, inept defense by Leo's attorney Luther Rosser, who is portrayed as doing little more than encouraging a spur-of-the-moment cry from his client's heart. However, in reality a defense team of eight lawyers represented Frank at his trial. They argued that Jim Conley was the murderer in a robbery gone wrong, put forth substantial incriminating evidence against Conley, and presented a detailed timeline about Frank's whereabouts on the night of the murder that appeared to clear Frank of the crime.

Jim Conley was the star witness for the prosecution: the first case in the post-Civil War South wherein testimony from an African American was instrumental in finding a white defendant guilty (Melnick 2000). Conley's testimony against Frank is presented in powerful, largely accurate detail during the *Parade* trial scene. Conley testified that Frank frequently had women in his office for lewd and lascivious acts. He testified further that, on the night of Mary's death, Frank had called him into his office after he had killed her, asked Conley to help him move the body, and then dictated the incriminating notes police found near her body. During later scenes, the musical reveals inconsistent and contradictory information in Conley's testimony. However, in the musical as in the real events, the impugning of Conley's truthfulness and integrity occurred outside the view of the judge, the jury, and the press.

During the trial Frank was not allowed to testify on his own behalf but did make an uncontested speech, in which he spoke for several hours on the financial workings of the factory. Although he concluded in an emotional tone, the vast majority of Frank's turgid courtroom speech is barely recognizable on stage in the moving three-minute song from the heart Jason Robert Brown wrote for Frank's courtroom statement ("It's Hard to Speak My Heart").

Following what became the longest and hardest-fought trial in Georgia's history to that point, the jury found Frank guilty after less than four hours of deliberation. In between the trial and the subsequent commutation by the Governor, public tensions only grew and arguments about Frank's guilt or innocence became more polarized.

The appeals process and the lynching

Parade tightly compresses the details of Frank's lengthy, multi-phased appeals against his conviction, although the musical clearly conveys Leo and Lucille's anguish over delays and waiting periods associated with the appeals process. Eventually, Frank's attorneys successfully brought Frank's case to the Supreme Court. On April 19, 1915, over a year and a half after Frank's conviction at trial, the Supreme Court denied his appeal, by a majority verdict of 7–2. Although an additional court appeal for commutation of his death sentence was rejected, Governor Slaton finally agreed to review Frank's case. The musical somewhat overemphasizes the Governor's involvement in Frank's case, but Slaton did, in fact, commute Frank's sentence from the death penalty to life in prison based on his own doubts about Frank's guilt.

The musical's portrayal of Leo Frank's lynching diverges considerably from the historical record. In *Parade* a group of five men, many of whom we have met before in the libretto, lynch Frank. In reality, the plan to lynch Frank was large scale, detailed, and intricate. It involved a large group of prominent Marietta men, including a former Governor of Georgia, the Mayor of Marietta, various sheriffs, and others, organized into the "Knights of Mary Phagan." On August 16, 1915, a large group kidnapped Frank from jail and transported him over two hours to Marietta. They cut telephone wires, drained the gas from the police cars, and handcuffed the prison warden. They posted lookouts along the route back to Marietta. After they hung Frank from a large tree facing Mary Phagan's house, a riled crowd that reached 3,000 in number arrived on the scene, celebrating the execution, taking pictures near the body, and cutting away parts of Frank's shirt for souvenirs. Photographs of people posing beside the body were made into postcards.

Although a grand jury was formed to indict the lynchers, none were ever formally identified or punished. However, the identities of the lynchers remained a fairly open secret in parts of Georgia for eighty-five years. Various individual efforts to publish the names of those involved in the lynching conspiracy persist, including a 2015 public statement at a conference on the Frank case by a descendent of two of the lynchers. The man publicly defended the lynching as a lawful act on the part of his father, uncle, and their allies (Jacobs 2015). There have been several attempts to pardon Leo Frank posthumously, owing to a growing body of historical evidence that Frank was innocent of the crime and a victim of prosecutorial malfeasance. However, Frank's conviction at trial still officially stands as rendered in 1913.

Antisemitism in Parade

The Leo Frank case is considered a defining event in the history of American antisemitism. The outcome of the case certainly reflected complicated social tensions that accompanied urban industrialization in the South at the turn of the century. Turn-of-the-century expansion of American road and rail transportation broadened the pattern of Jewish migration in America. New Jewish communities developed in Southern and Midwestern cities. Moreover, long-established Southern Jewish communities found themselves facing an influx of new migrants and immigrants, many of whom were merchants and factory managers who emerged as conspicuous economic forces within those communities. These circumstances made a recently arrived Jewish employer like Leo Frank a likely default scapegoat for a heinous murder with the other leading suspect in the case, an African American employee, Jim Conley.

Changes in migration patterns among non-Jewish whites also impacted the history of antisemitism in the South, especially as rural whites sought factory work in growing Southern cities. The old guard of the Atlanta Jewish community were wealthy German Jews, long established in the city, who prided themselves on their Southernness. They felt secure and well accepted within the broader Atlanta population owing to their long-standing participation in local philanthropy and civic life. However, established German Jews who had spent generations in Atlanta were surprised by the changes that occurred when Southern rural whites moved to Atlanta in search of industrial work, bringing with them prejudices and antisemitic beliefs exploited by rabble rousers like Tom Watson, editor of the *Jeffersonian*.

In addition, tensions arose between wealthy, established German Jews and newer Jewish immigrants, most of whom had ethnic origins in Eastern Europe, not Germany. Some members of Atlanta's established Jewish community went so far as to blame the new Jewish arrivals for creating the social climate that ultimately led to Frank's arrest and conviction. After the Frank case, the Atlanta Jewish community took years to recover from the realization that they, too, were now vulnerable to antisemitism and that their prior assimilation had been temporary if it had ever been more than illusory in the first place.

The antisemitism surrounding the Frank case also took on a sexual specificity. It was widely rumored, though never proved, that Mary Phagan was raped before being murdered. The prosecution enfolded intimations of sexual perversion on Frank's part into their case. Rumors of Frank's sexual criminality combined with public dissemination of familiar, hyper-sexualized antisemitic images made Frank a likely villain. In the types of propaganda circulated by Watson's *Jeffersonian*, Leo Frank became the perfect embodiment of this set of vicious stereotypes. Antisemitic criminality and sexual perversity became a way to reconstitute a traditional vision of white Southern masculinity: guardians of white female purity whose social prominence faced challenges from twentieth-century urbanization, gender and ethnic diversification in the workforce, and the growth of Jewish and African American middle-class communities in the South.

To this day even casual mention of the Leo Frank case invokes feelings of anger, antisemitism, racism, and fear. The case's inflammatory afterlife has influenced the reaction to *Parade* as well, particularly online. As historian Jefferey Melnick points out: "It's not the case itself so much but how successfully Jews and Jewish interests organized around it that confirms to white supremacists that all the conspiracies about Jewish control of the media are true" (Melnick 2000). And, in fact, a simple Google search about the Frank case reveals its currency among white nationalists.

African Americans and Parade

Parade's potential to stoke controversy today is exacerbated by the musical's failure to explore its African American characters in depth, including and especially Jim Conley, whom the musical strongly implicates as Phagan's true murderer. Some critics believe that *Parade*'s author Uhry reduced the presence of African American characters in order to force the centrality of Leo and Lucille. In so doing, *Parade* relegates the contextualization of significant and relevant historical tensions between African Americans and Jews—as played out in the direct conflict between Conley and Frank—to the status of insignificant subplot.

The generally superficial portrayal of *Parade*'s two main African American characters opens the musical to criticism that their representations rely on toxic racist stereotypes: an Uncle Tom type for Newt Lee, the night watchman, and Jim Conley as a conniving jailbird. Conley's central song, sung on the chain gang where he is serving a one-year sentence as Frank's accomplice in Phagan's murder, is "Feel the Rain Fall," a haunting, ominous, angry blues piece. The song clearly posits the show's thesis that Conley is the real murderer, even if his guilt is never explicitly stated, much less contextualized or explored, in the musical.

Even though Conley and Lee are not meant to speak for the African American experience as a whole, producer Hal Prince understood that their status as secondary characters (and in Conley's case, an antagonist) made the show vulnerable to charges of racism. Prince's proposed solution was to add a song from the perspective of the Black experience. In "A Rumblin' and a Rollin'," Lee and Conley and two female African American servants, Riley and Angela, sing about the hypocrisy of Northern defenders of Leo Frank: "They comin' . . . Cause a white man gonna get hung, you see / There's a black man swingin' in ev'ry tree." The singers note that the Northerners don't pay the same attention to Black victims, and that no one would be filling Atlanta hotels if it was a Black girl who had gotten killed instead of a white girl. The cutting lyrics make vivid the African American characters' justifiable cynicism about Leo Frank's martyrdom among Northerners. The song clearly attempts to peremptorily address criticism that *Parade* minimizes relevant Black experiences and perspectives on the Frank case. Prince had asserted that the song is the most important in the score, as if one song offsets the racial imbalance of the dominant narrative through-line.

Prince's defense of *Parade*'s approach to African American perspectives on the Frank case, however well intentioned, struggles with its own historical realities. During the year Frank was lynched, twenty-one other men were lynched in Georgia. All but Frank were Black, but Frank's death alone became a front-page national news story—or a Broadway musical. In the years since *Parade* premiered, audiences and critics have become increasingly skeptical of white savior tropes, wherein white artists presume to champion racial justice on behalf of marginalized or muted African American voices. Prince's case for the "A Rumblin' and a Rollin'" scene is itself a product of the fluidity of historical perspective *Parade* so ambitiously embraces.

Jessica Hillman-McCord

Further reading

Benedict, David. 2007. "Parade." *Variety*, September 25, 2007, https://variety.com/2007/legit/reviews/parade-6-1200555924.

Billington, Michael. 2007. "Parade." *Guardian*, September 25, 2007, https://www.theguardian.com/stage/2007/sep/25/theatre.musicals.

Bogage, Jacob. 2017. "Leo Frank Was Lynched for a Murder He Didn't Commit. Now Neo-Nazis Are Trying to Rewrite History." *Washington Post*, May 22, 2017.

Brantley, Ben. 1998. "Theater Review; Martyr's Requiem Invokes Justice." *New York Times*, December 18, 1998.

"CPI (Consumer Price Index) Inflation Calculator." n.d. *Bureau of Labor Statistics*, https://data.bls.gov/cgi-bin/cpicalc.pl.

Dinnerstein, Leonard. 1987. *The Leo Frank Case*. Athens: University of Georgia Press.

Hausam, Wiley. 2003. *The New American Musical: An Anthology from the End of the Century*. New York: Theatre Communications Group.

Hirsch, Foster. 2005. *Harold Prince and the American Musical Theatre: Expanded Edition*. New York: Applause Theatre and Cinema Books.

Isherwood, Charles. 1998. "Parade." *Variety*, December 17, 1998, https://variety.com/1998/legit/reviews/parade-1200456199/.

Isherwood, Charles. 2009. "Sorrow Over an Anti-Semitic Miscarriage of Justice, Rendered in Sotto Voce." *New York Times*, October 13, 2009.

Jacobs, Michael. 2015. "Lyncher's Son Defends Frank's Hanging." *Atlanta Jewish Times*, September 21, 2015, https://atlantajewishtimes.timesofisrael.com/frank-lynchers-son-defends-hanging/.

Komisar, Lucy. 1998. "*Parade* Recounts the Lynching of Leo Frank in Brilliant Musical." *American Reporter*, December 26, 1998, http://theatre_chick.tripod.com/parade13.htm.

Lindemann, Albert S. 1991. *The Jew Accused: Three Anti-Semitic Affairs (Dreyfus, Beilis, Frank) 1894–1915*. Cambridge: Cambridge University Press (Google Books abridged version).

MacLean, Nancy. 1991. "The Leo Frank Case Reconsidered: Gender and Sexual Politics in the Making of Reactionary Populism." *Journal of American History* 78, no. 3: 917–48, doi:10.2307/2078796.

Melnick, Jeffrey Paul. 2000. *Black–Jewish Relations on Trial: Leo Frank and Jim Conley in the New South*. Jackson: University Press of Mississippi (Google Books version).

Oney, Steve. 2003. *And the Dead Shall Rise: The Murder of Mary Phagan and the Lynching of Leo Frank*. New York: Pantheon Books.

"Profile: Lynching of Leo Frank and the List of Lynchers Responsible Has Been Published on Web Site." 2000. *Weekend Edition Sunday*, July 2, 2000.

Schechter, Dave. 2015. "Struggling with Leo Frank's Lynching a Century Later." *Atlanta Jewish Times*, August 12, 2015, https://atlantajewishtimes.timesofisrael.com/struggling-with-leo-franks-lynching-a-century-later/.

Stearns, David Patrick. 1998. "*Parade* Pointedly in Step with Today." *USA Today*, December 18, 1998, http://jasonrobertbrown.com/reviews/parade-pointedly-in-step-with-today/.

Taylor, Paul. 2007. "Daring and Ambitious Musical Vindicated." *The Independent*, September 25, 2007, www.independent.co.uk/arts-entertainment/theatre-dance/reviews/parade-donmar-warehouse-london-464651.html.

Winer, Linda. 1998. "Murder-Trial 'Parade' Is a Powerful Musical." *Newsday*, December 18, 1998, Jasonrobertbrown.com/reviews/murder-trial-parade-is-a-powerful-musical/.

CHAPTER 15
RAGTIME (1996)

Book by Terrence McNally (1938–2020)
Based on the novel by E. L. Doctorow (1931–2015)
Music by Stephen Flaherty (1960–)
Lyrics by Lynn Ahrens (1948–)
World Premiere: Apotex Theatre, Ford Centre for the Performing Arts, North York, Toronto, December 8, 1996
Broadway Premier: Ford Center for the Performing Arts, New York, January 18, 1998

Songs

"Ragtime"
"Goodbye, My Love"
"Journey On"
"The Crime of the Century"
"What Kind of Woman"
"A Shtetl Iz Amereke"
"Success"
"Gettin' Ready Rag"
"Henry Ford"
"Nothing Like the City"
"Your Daddy's Son"
"New Music"
"Wheels of a Dream"
"The Night That Goldman Spoke at Union Square"
"Lawrence, Massachusetts"
"Gliding"
"Justice"
"President"
"Till We Reach That Day"
"Harry Houdini, Master Escapist"
"Coalhouse's Soliloquy"
"Coalhouse Demands"
"What a Game!"
"Atlantic City"
"New Music" (Reprise)
"Atlantic City," Part II
"The Crime of the Century" (Reprise)
"Harry Houdini, Master Escapist" (Reprise)
"Buffalo Nickel Photoplay, Inc."
"Our Children"
"Sarah Brown Eyes"
"He Wanted to Say"
"Back to Before"
"Look What You've Done"
"Make Them Hear You"
"Ragtime" (Reprise)
"Wheels of a Dream" (Reprise)

Overview

Ragtime is a musical theater adaptation of E. L. Doctorow's acclaimed 1975 novel of the same name. Set mostly in the New York City region during the early twentieth century, the plot weaves a complex blend of interlaced storylines about characters representing three distinct American racial-ethnic groups: native-born whites, native-born African Americans, and recently arrived European immigrants, who all live in uneasy proximity to one another. Doctorow's novel utilized both fictional characters and actual luminaries of the time who interact in surprising ways. Although this device was neither new nor unique to this author, Doctorow employed it in a bold, imaginative fashion. His novel caught the public's fancy, becoming both a critical and commercial success.

A highly anticipated movie version of *Ragtime*, released in 1981, failed at the box office. Subsequently Doctorow expressed dissatisfaction with the screenplay which, he felt, overemphasized one plotline from his novel: the story of Coalhouse Walker, Jr., a fictional African American pianist whose attempt to redress an act of racial injustice results in tragedy. "I think of *Ragtime* as a kind of tapestry," Doctorow explained. "If you pull enough strings out, it falls apart" (Kirchoff 1996).

The tapestry Doctorow had conceived encompassed a broad, expansive portrait of America at the dawn of the twentieth century, a vision more fully realized in the stage adaptation. While *Ragtime* the musical does explore the racial animosities reflected in Walker's storyline, it also examines tensions generated by an enormous influx of non-English speaking immigrants and the impact upon established white communities, who had little prior interaction with foreign émigrés.

Historians usually refer to this period (roughly 1890–1920) as the Progressive Era, owing to the socio-political reform movements for individual rights and improved working conditions that emerged during the period. The Progressive Era is posited variously as following, overlapping with, and/or responding to the earlier Gilded Age, so named for the massive wealth accrued by a very small portion of the population thanks to the ascension of American industrialization following the Civil War. *Ragtime* is akin to a snapshot of the two historical periods meeting up in time.

Music historians also know this period as the age of ragtime: a popular piano-based song-and-composition form of African American origins, generally containing a syncopated lead over a steady rhythmic bass. The diverse storylines of *Ragtime* suggest the three or four contrasting sections of a typical ragtime piece. The musical also coaxes a few visual puns out of the "rag" in ragtime (rag boats, raggedy clothes, etc.) alluding to poverty experienced by African Americans and recently arrived immigrants.

Although a fictional character, Coalhouse Walker's musical career in *Ragtime* bears a strong resemblance to that of ragtime pioneer Scott Joplin, who rose from playing in music halls and saloons to become the most famous ragtime composer and performer in history. Moreover, Walker's interactions with prominent African American educator Booker T. Washington contextualize the breadth of Washington's influence during that period even as those same scenes point to the actual criticisms Washington faced regarding his leadership.

Immigrants arriving from Europe during the Progressive Era were not only escaping horrendous conditions at home but also pursuing an idealized notion of opportunity in the United States. Lured by appealing newspaper reports and letters from friends and family already in America, many immigrants interpreted the nation's popular twin images of a Golden Door and a Melting Pot as a certainty and imagined an America glistening "with connotations of wide acceptance and mutual ascension" (Prchal 2007). Many immigrants ultimately found the better life they sought, but for most it took sacrifice and severe drudgery. Newcomers, such as *Ragtime*'s Latvian Jewish immigrant Tateh, took low-paying, sometimes dangerous, jobs in order to survive. Most immigrant adults had to learn to speak English, adjust to a strange culture, and deal with prejudice and hostility on a daily basis from neighbors and co-workers.

Crowded and unsanitary conditions for immigrants and migrating African Americans in the northeastern United States gave rise to working-class-based political reform movements. The emergence of anarchist Emma Goldman (1869–1940) as a political activist, labor organizer, and charismatic orator predated the 1901 assassination of President William McKinley by Leon Czolgosz, a self-proclaimed anarchist who cited her as an influence. Goldman's appearances in *Ragtime* spotlight her impact on the political climate during a period when anarchism and other expressions of radical anti-establishment political activism could lead to arrest, public rebuke, and, for immigrant activists, deportation.

Dizzying advances in technology affected almost every aspect of American daily life. The automobile in particular had a pervasive impact on society, and *Ragtime* reflects automobile industrialist Henry Ford's central role in that phenomenon. *Ragtime* acknowledges Ford's legacy in several ways. Ford himself is represented in a cameo role, but more importantly his quintessential product, the Model-T Ford, serves a pivotal function in the plot. For Coalhouse Walker, Jr., the automobile represents autonomy and hope for a better future; significantly, it is an attack on his car that provokes *Ragtime*'s tragic denouement.

In the early 1990s, Canadian theater impresario Garth Drabinsky, in search of material, reread Doctorow's *Ragtime* and felt it would make an ideal stage musical. Drabinsky and his production company, Livent, had established themselves on Broadway with the musical *Kiss of the Spider Woman* (1993), winner of seven Tony Awards, including Best Musical and Best Book of a Musical for Terrence McNally. Doctorow, initially wary of permitting another adaptation of his novel, was eventually won over by Drabinsky's sharp assessment of the film version's flaws, his pledge to honor the novel's structure, and a promise of substantial influence over the selection of the creative team. Reassured, Doctorow granted Livent worldwide theatrical rights to *Ragtime*.

Both Drabinsky and Doctorow were eager to work with *Spider Woman*'s librettist Terrence McNally who, despite competing commitments, agreed to write the book for *Ragtime*. Lyricist Lynn Ahrens and composer Stephen Flaherty, then best known for the musical *Once on This Island* (1990), signed on. Frank Galati, a resident director for two prominent Chicago theater companies, Steppenwolf and the Goodman Theatre, was hired to direct.

Starting in summer 1995, Drabinsky and his team invited guests to a series of semi-staged workshop performances held in various Toronto venues. For this process Drabinsky initiated a practice of distributing questionnaires to attendees after each performance. A consulting firm would then analyze the results. When the trade journal *Variety* ran an article drawing disparaging parallels between Drabinsky's audience surveys and similar Hollywood polling techniques, Drabinsky defended the practice. Noting that filmmakers poll viewers after millions of dollars have already been spent on a nearly finished project, Drabinsky argued that staging workshops and polling the audiences amounted to a fraction of what out-of-town tryouts or a mini-tour would cost.

After post-workshop adjustments, *Ragtime* had its world premiere on December 8, 1996, at the Ford Centre for the Performing Arts in Toronto. In another unconventional move, Drabinsky invited New York critics to Canada for the opening night a full year prior to the projected Broadway debut. The premiere was met with considerable excitement; critic John Lahr reported that at the curtain call the crowd stood and cheered for a full five minutes. Reviews ranged from guardedly positive to ecstatic. Once the Toronto run was underway a second company opened *Ragtime* at the Shubert Theater in Los Angeles during summer 1997, yet another unusual move.

Concurrent with all this activity, Livent was deeply involved in the construction of the venue where *Ragtime* would make its New York bow: an entirely new theater on West 42nd Street, where the Lyric and Apollo Theaters formerly stood. This became the new Ford Center for the Performing Arts (not to be confused with the similarly named Toronto theater), a 1,850-seat house that was built using physical elements of both the Lyric and the Apollo. Assembly of the new theater was underway while *Ragtime* was in development. Remarkably, work on each of these complicated projects was completed in time for *Ragtime*'s first Broadway preview on December 26, 1997. *Ragtime* officially opened some three weeks later on January 18, 1998.

While *Ragtime*'s regular production and advertising costs were said to total a higher-than-average $12 million, the decidedly non-regular additional cost of building New York's Ford Center ran the show's real expense to a then-unheard of—and untenable—$35 million or more. Soon after the premiere, an article by *New York Times* journalist Bruce Weber documented Livent's risky tactics and spiraling financial obligations. "Should *Ragtime* not become a mega-hit, selling out the house for months, if not years, to come," he observed, "then the growth of Mr. Drabinsky's highly leveraged, expanding theater empire could be imperiled" (Weber 1998).

It was. Only seven months after the Broadway premiere of *Ragtime*, Livent's board fired founding producer Drabinsky and another founding partner for financial malfeasance; soon thereafter the company filed for bankruptcy.

Plot synopsis

Ragtime's opening number, the title song performed by the entire cast, establishes that the musical is set in the New York City area at the turn of the twentieth century. Members of an affluent New Rochelle family step forward in turn and introduce themselves; they are identified simply as Father, Mother, their son the Little Boy, Mother's Younger Brother, and Grandfather. They are white, Anglo-Saxon Protestants, and their future looks bright. Father declares there are no African Americans in the vicinity. As the music shifts to a syncopated ragtime melody the African Americans of Harlem enter dancing. They introduce pianist Coalhouse Walker, Jr., and Sarah, the woman he loves. Meanwhile the residents of New Rochelle, smugly ensconced in their all-white neighborhood (although standing right next to the African Americans on stage), reiterate that there are no African Americans in their community, nor are there any immigrants. The music takes on a klezmer-like inflection as a group of immigrants appear, waiting to board a ship bound for America. Tateh, a Jewish man from Latvia, steps forward. He and his daughter seek a better life in the New World. As the song builds to a crescendo, members of the three groups sing in unison yet remain in physical isolation from one another—a choreographed tableau that dramatizes reciprocal curiosity, fear, attraction, and distrust. During the opening number, several prominent figures from the period also introduce themselves. This group includes Henry Ford, Booker T. Washington, escape artist Harry Houdini, actress/model Evelyn Nesbit, and anarchist Emma Goldman.

Father prepares to leave New Rochelle and embark on a year-long voyage of exploration to the North Pole with Admiral Robert Peary. Mother bids him farewell ("Goodbye, My Love") and reveals frustration at the constraints of her life. Onboard his ship, Father sees another vessel on the horizon, a rag boat bringing immigrants to America, and expresses admiration for them ("Journey On"). Tateh, a passenger on that boat with his daughter, takes up Father's song, though he is mystified that anyone would want to leave America. Meanwhile, Mother's Younger Brother becomes enamored with glamorous performer Evelyn Nesbit. Nesbit gets involved in a love triangle that results in murder and becomes a notorious scandal ("The Crime of the Century"). The Younger Brother attempts to meet Nesbit, but she rebuffs him.

While digging in her garden Mother finds a newborn baby, an African American boy, and wonders how his parents could have abandoned him ("What Kind of Woman"). When the police apprehend the boy's mother, Sarah, Mother decides to take responsibility for both parent and child. Sarah takes up residence in Mother's attic with her baby. Tateh and his daughter settle in New York City's Lower East Side, where he sets up a sidewalk business peddling silhouettes he cuts from black paper. Anarchist Emma Goldman finds him offering an image of J. P. Morgan, and berates him for glorifying an exploitative capitalist. Tateh declares himself indifferent to politics and anticipates prosperity in America ("Success"). Residents of Harlem sing the praises of pianist Coalhouse Walker, Jr. He is brokenhearted since his beloved Sarah left him but is determined to win her back ("Gettin' Ready Rag"). At the behest of Henry Ford himself, Coalhouse buys a Model-T Ford automobile. Tateh leaves the city with his daughter and heads for Massachusetts. En route they encounter Mother and her son in New Rochelle. Mutual introductions are made ("Nothing Like the City").

Coalhouse arrives in New Rochelle in search of Sarah and is confronted by a racist fireman, Willie Conklin. Evading him, Coalhouse comes to the home of Father and Mother seeking Sarah, but Mother sends him away at Sarah's insistence. In the ensuing weeks he calls on her every Sunday, but she refuses to see him. He ingratiates himself with the family, and plays ragtime tunes for them.

Returning home from the North Pole, Father is confounded by the fact that the new maid does not know him, his wife inexplicably holds a brown baby, and an unfamiliar man is in the parlor playing strange melodies ("New Music"). Soon thereafter Sarah relents and is reunited with Coalhouse. Later, as Coalhouse polishes his new car, he sings to Sarah of the wonderful life ahead for their son ("Wheels of a Dream").

Emma Goldman addresses a political rally about an artist friend who has been reduced to working in a mill over sixty hours a week for a pittance—this is Tateh. Younger Brother is stirred by her words and embraces her cause. Goldman is arrested. Militiamen violently crush a strike at the mill. When strikebreakers attack, Tateh and his daughter escape on a train. He shows her a flip book he has made of silhouette figures skating on a frozen pond ("Gliding"). The conductor, admiring his "movie book," buys it for a dollar. Inadvertently, Tateh has started a new business.

Coalhouse, Sarah, and their son are riding in their Ford when they are stopped by a band of firemen led by Conklin. Coalhouse sends his family ahead on foot. He refuses to pay a bogus "toll" that Conklin demands. The firemen vandalize his car and push it into a pond. Coalhouse's attempts to redress this injustice are thwarted by an indifferent bureaucracy ("Justice"). Sarah takes matters into her own hands when a prominent politician arrives to deliver a speech. But as she rushes toward him to plead her cause, guards mistake her for an assassin and club her to death. At her funeral, Coalhouse expresses his grief ("Till We Reach That Day"). Distraught, he turns to violence to avenge Sarah. Now the leader of a terrorist band, Coalhouse orders his men to shoot firemen and burn down Conklin's firehouse. Coalhouse vows to end his spree only if his demands are met: first, that his Model-T Ford is restored to its original condition, and second, that Conklin is handed over to him for retribution.

Father and Younger Brother argue about the family's role in Coalhouse's rampage. For a respite the family flees to Atlantic City. There they meet Tateh, now known as Baron Ashkenazy, a director for his own filmmaking company "Buffalo Nickel Photoplay, Inc." The Little Boy befriends Tateh's daughter ("Our Children"). Tateh and Mother are drawn to each other.

In Harlem, Younger Brother reveals his expertise in making explosives and is accepted into Coalhouse's gang. The gang seizes the J. P. Morgan Library in Manhattan. Father returns to the city. Mother expresses her belief that their life will never again be the same ("Back to Before"). Aware that Coalhouse respects Booker T. Washington, Father urges authorities to send for the famous African American leader to negotiate an end to Coalhouse's siege. At Washington's behest Coalhouse surrenders in return for safe passage for his men and a fair trial. He insists his actions have made a positive difference ("Make Them Hear You"). After his men depart, Coalhouse emerges from the library and is instantly shot dead.

In 1914, the World War erupts. Younger Brother joins revolutionaries in Mexico. Father dies on the liner *Lusitania*, torpedoed by the Germans. A year later, Mother marries Tateh, who envisions a movie series about children of all races and creeds playing in harmony.

Critical reception

When *Ragtime* finally opened on Broadway at New York's Ford Center, most of the critics in attendance had already seen the show in Toronto or Los Angeles. Several drew parallels between the production and the newly completed venue in which it premiered. "Just as the handsome new building that houses *Ragtime* is a refabrication of two theaters from the era in which the show is set," wrote Ben Brantley of the *New York Times*, "[t]he musical is a carefully constructed pastiche of period charm and contemporary mechanical efficiency. The result itself is less a celebration of theater per se than of theatrical technology and its smooth manipulation" (Brantley 1998). Vincent Canby, in a follow-up piece run by the same paper several days later, echoed Brantley when he observed that the creative team had put the show's elements in place much like the builders of the Ford Center, "with efficiency and a good deal of money, but not with the kind of style that would establish its own urgent identity" (Canby 1998). The *New Yorker*'s John Lahr called the production a "big, brave, passionate gamble" and fashioned a similar parallel between the show and its new home, albeit with a more positive spin. "*Ragtime*," he wrote, "may be the first musical ever to have its central theme built into the architecture of the theater that was created to house it: the Ford Center recreates an ambience of magical comfort in a hard world, and signals, in its sumptuous exaggeration, the era's sense of expectation and alienation" (Lahr 1998).

Linda Winer of *Newsday*, who had sounded a cautiously optimistic note in her review of the Toronto production, allowed that the Broadway *Ragtime* was "vast, handsome, and extremely professional," yet ultimately disappointing. "This is a new-old theater and a new-old musical," Winer observed, in yet another correlation with the building, "both attractively cobbled from things already known and admired." The *Wall Street Journal*'s Donald Lyons dismissed the show's take on American history as "a Marxist cartoon wherein workers, immigrants, and people of color are relentlessly ground down" and questioned whether the capitalists who operate Livent, and surely hoped to turn a profit on this enterprise, truly believed this message" (Lyons 1998). More harshly, Robert Brustein condemned *Ragtime* as "a self-congratulatory waxworks" in the *New Republic* and added that "little is left of Doctorow's broad panoramic view of America except his liberal pieties" (Brustein 1998).

Ragtime did receive positive reviews from other New York journals, including the *New York Post*, the *New York Daily News*, and the *Village Voice*. The *Post*'s Clive Barnes, who attended the Toronto premiere, felt the necessary pre-Broadway fine-tuning had for the most part been successfully accomplished. He observed that the show was thematically and theatrically modern yet "cozily old-fashioned" musically (Barnes 1998). Fintan O'Toole, writing for the *New York Daily News*, deemed it "a tough and truthful parable for our own times" (O'Toole 1998). The *Village Voice*'s Michael Feingold called *Ragtime* "a new show constructed in homage to the old tactics, at once a nostalgic paean to the vanished past and a mordant slap at its own nostalgia," adding that it was the right show for the right time (Feingold 1998).

According to a news story in *Variety*, the show received only four outright pans, five mixed evaluations and eleven positive reviews (Evans 1998). However, the problem for Livent's administrators was that the most prestigious critics were negative or mixed in their appraisals. The largely unfavorable assessments of Brantley and Canby caused particular dismay, as the *New York Times* was widely regarded as the most influential judge of theatrical endeavors. And while *Ragtime* was nominated for an impressive thirteen Tony Awards, it ultimately won only four, while Disney's *The Lion King* took six that year, including Best Musical. But by late summer of 1998, about seven months into the Broadway run, Livent officials were faced with more daunting matters than reviews or awards.

When *Ragtime* opened in New York it was clear that Livent was dangerously overleveraged. A new team was brought in to run the company, while Drabinsky was relegated to a strictly non-managerial role. Rumors flew that his position was precarious, but even so observers were shocked when, in mid-August 1998, it was announced that Drabinsky and Livent co-founder Myron Gottlieb had been suspended pending investigation of serious accounting irregularities dating back years. Both men were subsequently fired. Livent filed for bankruptcy protection in November 1998, and the company folded the following year.

The scandal seemingly had no adverse impact on *Ragtime*'s popularity with theatergoers. During this tumultuous period the show played to packed houses, although it would eventually close in January 2000 at a loss. In 2009, *Ragtime* was revived at Washington, D.C.'s John F. Kennedy Center. The new production was streamlined compared to the lavish Livent version. The text was trimmed, and some of Livent's more extravagant touches, such as fireworks and an on-stage working Model T Ford, were eliminated. Producers and critics alike noted that, in the eleven years since the premiere, significant social changes had occurred in the nation, giving the show's political material a new relevance. Moreover, the election of Barack Obama as U.S. President the previous year put the examination of systemic American racism in a new light. The favorable critical and audience reception in Washington prompted a Broadway transfer.

Broadway's first *Ragtime* revival opened at the Neil Simon Theatre on November 15, 2009, directed by Marcia Milgrom Dodge. Reviews were mixed. In the *New York Times*, Ben Brantley praised the simplified presentation but criticized the adaptation itself more harshly than he had a decade earlier. He complained that McNally's libretto flattened "the kinked currents of history that eddied through Mr. Doctorow's book." Brantley concluded, however, that whatever the show's flaws, the revival "elicits glimmers of delicate beauty that got lost in the fireworks the first time around" (Brantley 2009). In October 2024, a concert presentation of *Ragtime* opened Off-Broadway at New York City Center. The spare production, which employed simple sets, served to emphasize the music. This production ran from October 30 to November 10, 2024, straddling the November 5 presidential election between Democratic Vice President Kamala Harris and former Republican President Donald Trump. More than one critic observed that, depending on one's political leanings, the show's lyrics—whether hopeful or despairing—took on different shades of meaning based on whether one attended before or after the election. A Broadway transfer to the Lincoln Center opened on October 16, 2025 to overwhelmingly positive reviews.

Historical accuracy and context

The immigrant experience 1880s–1914

As the twentieth century dawned, America was faced with the challenge of absorbing an unprecedented influx of immigrants who came to this country seeking a better life. Nearly 22 million people emigrated to America between 1881 and 1914, most of them from Europe. Beginning in 1892, they arrived at the processing center at New York's Ellis Island.

The newcomers included some 1.5 million European Jews, whose experience is exemplified in the story of Tateh (Yiddish for "Dad") and his daughter journeying from Latvia. On their rag boat to America, Tateh drills his daughter on how to answer questions likely to be asked them upon arrival, a brief exchange that speaks to immigrants' first American experiences. At the point of original departure, passengers had to provide answers to over twenty questions, including name, age, family connections in America, professional skills they possessed, whether they had any money, and so on. Their answers were entered into the ship's manifest, which the ship's officers turned over to officials at Ellis Island. In a process that might last a few hours, barring any prohibitive issues, the new arrivals stood before an immigration clerk who had the manifest opened on a desk. The clerk proceeded, often through interpreters, to ask questions based on the manifest information to confirm the answers matched. (After the assassination of President McKinley in 1901 by a self-proclaimed anarchist, albeit a native-born one, immigrants might also be asked whether they were anarchists.) Once through the process, the émigrés were free to leave the harbor port, and settle wherever they wished. Many went no farther than New York City.

Tateh and his daughter first live in a Lower East Side tenement. Later, disillusioned with city life, they migrate to Lawrence, Massachusetts, where Tateh gets a job in a mill. Many immigrants accepted such jobs in textile factories or on construction projects. Language barriers often kept them in these low-paying positions, since many had difficulty with jobs requiring direct interpersonal contact with English-speaking co-workers or customers. Factory owners hired newly arrived workers because they were willing to work longer hours for lower wages, willing to endure unsanitary and/or unsafe working conditions, and less likely to demand wage increases or participate in union activities. (Indeed, Tateh avoids political activism and takes no part in organizing a strike at the mill where he works.) Tateh's later self-reinvention as "Baron Ashkenazy," motion picture producer and director, is reflective of the many Jewish immigrants who made significant contributions to American popular culture in music, theater, and film within a generation after arriving in America.

One such success story in *Ragtime* is embodied in stage performer Harry Houdini, who calls himself "one immigrant who made an art of escape." Houdini (1874–1926), the son of a rabbi, was born Erik Weisz in Budapest, Hungary. When he was four his family emigrated to America. Houdini became renowned for his ability to free himself from any form of restraint, whether cuffs, chains, or manacles. He was revered by immigrants, especially in Jewish communities, not only as an entertainer but also as an inspiration to immigrants seeking to "break those chains" that inhibit their success in America. In *Ragtime*, Houdini is admired by his compatriots as well as the Little Boy from New Rochelle.

Henry Ford and the automotive revolution

In this period of vast technological change, it was the automobile that was most consequential for most Americans. Henry Ford (1863–1947) had the greatest impact on its development. Though he invented neither the automobile nor the mass production assembly line, Ford was an industrialist of genius whose methods helped make cars affordable for middle-class consumers. He revolutionized American society by transforming the automobile from a novelty for the rich into a necessity for the country's growing middle class, and did so in a remarkably brief span of time. In 1900, approximately 8,000 Americans owned an automobile. By 1910, the figure had risen to 500,000, while by 1920, it had risen to 8,000,000 (Miller 2015; Hess 1984/1996). In his time, Ford was among the most famous men on earth, but he was also a polarizing, controversial figure.

The Model T, Ford's archetypal car, plays a significant role in *Ragtime*. Ford himself makes only a token appearance, though he is the subject of the eponymously titled "Henry Ford," an ironically celebratory gospel number. At the climax of this song Ford personally urges Coalhouse Walker, Jr. to purchase a Model T. Introduced in 1908, the Model T was relatively low-priced, and easy to drive and repair. As production costs decreased, the car's purchase price dropped by over 50 percent, from \$825 to \$360. (Adjusted for inflation this latter sum equals about 10,700 in 2025 dollars ["CPI Inflation Calculator" n.d.].) But for Coalhouse and his fiancée Sarah, the car is more than a mere means of conveyance. Like many other Americans aspiring to better themselves, Coalhouse viewed his first car as a harbinger of a better future for himself and his family: "Beyond that road / Beyond this lifetime / That car full of hope will always gleam!"

Tateh works in a mill, not an auto plant, but the employment problems faced by immigrants played a real-life role in Ford's factories. In the early 1900s, almost half of the workers on Ford assembly lines and in his machine shops were foreign-born. An internal study conducted by the company found that their workers represented over fifty nationalities and spoke some 100 languages and dialects. Many did not speak English. In 1914, Ford instituted compulsory classes in English for those employees deemed deficient in English speaking skills. Lessons focused on phrases used in domestic life, commercial transactions, and work situations. Workers who refused to take the classes were dismissed, but most were eager or at least willing to assimilate.

Henry Ford opposed labor unions, a position he made explicit in numerous public statements. He was also openly antisemitic. Those who knew Ford cite many examples of disparaging remarks he made about Jews, but his views became public knowledge when a series of essays under his byline appeared in the *Dearborn Independent*, a newspaper he owned. The pieces ran from 1920 to 1924, and were later collected and published in book form under the title *The International Jew*. Ford declared in a court case that he did not write the pieces, and claimed moreover that he had not even read some of them. However, the *Independent*'s editor William Cameron, Ford's ghost writer, said he composed them after conversations with Ford, and that they represented his views. The essays alleged corrupt and seditious Jewish influence in various aspects of American life, including business, politics, popular culture, and sports.

Doctorow cites Henry Ford's antisemitism in his novel, but there is no mention of it in *Ragtime* the musical. Ford was long dead by the time the stage show was produced. And yet, the company he founded was directly involved in its New York premiere. The Ford Motor Company invested significantly in Livent's construction of the new Broadway theater that provided *Ragtime* with its home, and was therefore granted naming rights for the building. Ironically, the very first show staged at the Ford Center for the Performing Arts featured a number that sardonically saluted the company's founder. After Livent's bankruptcy, ownership of the Ford Center changed hands several times. It was eventually renamed the Lyric, after the theater which once stood on its site.

Emma Goldman and the anarchist movement

Emma Goldman (1869–1940), outspoken anarchist, makes her presence known during *Ragtime*'s opening number. After tycoons Henry Ford and J. P. Morgan (1837–1913) have introduced themselves, she exclaims: "These men are sucking your very souls dry! I hate them!" Prominent financier Morgan indignantly remarks that Goldman should be arrested. (In reality she was arrested many times.) Like Houdini, Goldman was an immigrant, but her attitude towards her adopted homeland differed radically from his.

Goldman was born into a Jewish Orthodox family in Lithuania. From an early age she was interested in political matters, which was decidedly uncommon for a woman of her time and place. At the age of sixteen, having rebelled against the strictures of her tyrannical father, Goldman emigrated to America. In 1889 she settled in New York City, where she met anarchist Alexander Berkman, who became both a political mentor and her lover.

Anarchism was an ideological reaction to industrialization and the expanding power of the economic and political institutions which accompanied it. There were several schools of anarchist thought. Goldman's beliefs evolved over time, but essentially she was committed to communal ownership of property, the distribution of goods and services by collectives, and unfettered freedom of expression. She also advocated open marriage and full equality for women.

In the 1890s Goldman became known as a charismatic, fiery public speaker. She toured the United States and Europe, advocating revolution. When President William McKinley was assassinated in 1901 by self-proclaimed anarchist Leon Czolgosz, who cited Goldman as an inspiration, she was arrested. With the support of new President Theodore Roosevelt the Anarchist Exclusion Act was passed by Congress, permitting immigration authorities to deny entry to immigrants who held anarchist political beliefs.

In *Ragtime*, Goldman embodies fierce political opposition to the prevailing economic system and institutions in America at the turn of the century. Her encounter with Tateh shortly after his arrival in New York provides insight into her sharp debating skills: when he insists he is apolitical, she replies "Work is politics." Goldman's impact upon young people is encapsulated in Younger Brother's unexpected embrace of leftist causes after he hears her speak, a point underscored by her appearances as an inspirational figure expressing the inner feelings Younger Brother cannot articulate. The Younger Brother–Goldman interplay creditably acknowledges Goldman's impact as a thinker and activist, as anti-establishment political movements gained momentum in the Progressive Era.

At the musical's finale, Goldman announces that, with the outbreak of the Great War, her political activism would lead to her arrest and eventual deportation after the Armistice. The reason, not explained in *Ragtime*, was her opposition to American involvement in the war. In 1917 Goldman co-founded the No Conscription League, and urged men not to register for the military, as required by the newly passed Selective Service Act. She was arrested, tried under the Espionage Act, also newly enacted, and jailed. Goldman was deported upon her release in 1919.

Booker T. Washington and race relations

In *Ragtime*'s opening number, Booker Taliaferro Washington (*c.* 1856–1915) introduces himself as the most famous Black person in America, a distinction which redounded to him in 1895 after the death of Frederick Douglass. Washington's fictional involvement with Coalhouse in the show's climactic sequence affirms, albeit in melodramatic terms, Washington's stature as a nationally respected leader, even as it reflects criticism he received from other Black leaders over his strategies for African American advancement.

Born a slave in Virginia, Washington was still a child when the Civil War ended in 1865. Subsequently, Congress passed several bills to help assure full rights of citizenship for Blacks, but these laws were largely opposed by white officials and business leaders in the former Confederate states. Blacks were disenfranchised via state constitutional amendments, local ordinances, intimidation, fraud, and state sanctioned violence. The Ku Klux Klan and other white supremacist terrorist groups intimidated, assaulted, and murdered Blacks who tried to vote, purchase land, or start businesses. White mobs lynched more than 1,750 Black people by 1900 ("Lynchings" n.d.).

Eager to learn as a youth, Washington enrolled in a school for Blacks in Virginia. His progress was rapid, and soon he became an instructor. In 1881, Congress allotted funds to establish a college for Black teachers in Tuskegee, Alabama, and Washington was hired as its principal. Washington and his all-Black staff built the Tuskegee Institute into a thriving university. National recognition came in 1895 when Washington, attending a cotton exhibition, delivered what came to be known as the Atlanta Compromise speech. In this speech, Washington preached economic self-reliance for freed people, but dismissed then-current progressive movements for political and civil rights, contending that fuller recognition would come to Blacks when they had earned it through honest labor. This latter point won him praise from whites, but harmed his reputation with some, though not all, Blacks.

Washington became a celebrity. He published his autobiography *Up from Slavery* in 1901 and dined with President Theodore Roosevelt in the White House, an honor that outraged many whites. But Washington was a figure of controversy in the African American community, especially with the intelligentsia. Civil rights activist W. E. B. Du Bois and other African American intellectuals complained that Washington was an accommodationist, too willing to accept institutionalized racial discrimination.

Washington's role in *Ragtime* plays on his popularly accepted persona. When Coalhouse Walker, Jr. is challenged by racists, Washington appears in ethereal form and urges patience—a familiar theme in Washington's writings on race relations—even as fire fighters demolish Walker's car. But after his beloved Sarah dies, Walker chooses vengeance. Speaking to reporters, Washington laments the irreparable harm Walker's violence has done to the African American cause. (In reality, no such gang of African American guerilla warriors terrorized whites, in New York or any other American city, during this period.) When Walker's gang occupies J. P. Morgan's library and threatens to demolish it, Washington confronts Coalhouse directly: "What has your selfish recklessness cost us, / we who work so hard to still the white man's hate."

The reference to Black people working to "still the white man's hate" conveys a debatable tenet of Washington's accommodationist strategy, namely that Black people bear the ultimate responsibility for making the changes and sacrifices necessary to advance in white-dominated society. Coalhouse's surrender to authorities upon accepting Washington's guarantee of safe passage and his abrupt murder by law enforcement officers invite speculation that *Ragtime*'s creators agreed with Washington's harshest critics: those who considered him a pawn, wittingly or unwittingly, of the white-dominated *status quo*.

In the epilog to *Ragtime*, Washington refers to his Tuskegee Institute as the "capital of Black America." Speaking of himself in the historical past, he announces that upon news of his death, American flags flew at half-staff, and among those in attendance at his funeral were President and Mrs. Woodrow Wilson. Left unresolved are lingering questions posed by the musical's creators concerning Washington's astuteness and the depth of his public commitment to racial equality. And yet most historians agree that Washington was privately committed to the goal of racial equality. He differed from Du Bois and other, more outspoken African American leaders in strategy, but not in terms of the ultimate objectives.

William Charles Morrow

Further reading

Anderson, Ingrid. 2017. "What History Reveals about Surges in Anti-semitism and Antiimmigrant Sentiments." *The Conversation US*, April 2, 2017.

Barnes, Clive. 1998. "*Ragtime* Hits All the Right Notes." *New York Post*, January 19, 1998.

Brantley, Ben. 1998. "*Ragtime:* A Diorama with Nostalgia Rampant." *New York Times*, January 19, 1998.

Brantley, Ben. 2009. "I Hear America Singing, in Syncopation." *New York Times*, November 15, 2009.

Brustein, Robert. 1998. "Musical with a Message." *The New Republic*, March 30, 1998.

Canby, Vincent. 1998. "Big and Beautiful, 'Ragtime' Never Quite Sings." *New York Times*, January 25, 1998.

Cannato, Vincent J. 2009. *American Passage: The History of Ellis Island*. New York: Harper & Brothers.

Carroll, Rebecca, ed. 2006. *Uncle Tom or New Negro? African Americans Reflect on Booker T. Washington and Up from Slavery 100 Years Later*. New York: Broadway Books/Harlem Moon.

"CPI Inflation Calculator." n.d. *Bureau of Labor Statistics*. Washington, DC, https://www.bls.gov/bls/contact.htm.

Evans, Greg. 1998. "Strong BO [Box Office] for *Ragtime*." *Variety*, January 19, 1998, https://variety.com/1998/legit/news/strong-b-o-for-ragtime-1117466850/.

Feingold, Michael. 1998. "Silver Threads." *Village Voice*, February 2, 1998.

Hess, Kenneth. 1984. "The Growth of Automotive Transportation." *KLH.com*. Updated. 1996, https://www.klhess.com/growth-automotive-transportation/car_essy.html.

Kirchoff, H. J. 1996. "Doctorow Sings Praises of *Ragtime* Team." *Toronto Globe and Mail*, June 29, 1996.

Lahr, John. 1998. "Making History." *The New Yorker*, February 2, 1998.

"Lynchings: By Year and Race." n.d. *University of Missouri-Kansas City Law School: Faculty Projects*, http://law2.umkc.edu/faculty/projects/ftrials/shipp/lynchingyear.html.

Lyons, Donald. 1998. "Canada's Musical America." *Wall Street Journal*, January 21, 1998.

Mackintosh, Barry. 1972. *Booker T. Washington: An Appreciation of the Man and His Times*. Office of Publications. Washington, D.C.: U.S. Department of the Interior.

McNally, Terrence and Lynn Ahrens (lyrics). 1996–7. *Ragtime: The Musical*. Unpublished typescript.

Miller, G. Wayne. 2015. *Car Crazy: The Battle for Supremacy between Ford and Olds and the Dawn of the Automobile Age*. Philadelphia: Public Affairs/Perseus.

Mooney, Michael MacDonald. 1976. *Evelyn Nesbit and Stanford White: Love and Death in the Gilded Age*. New York: William Morrow.

Morton, Marian J. 1992. *Emma Goldman and the American Left: "Nowhere at Home*. New York: Twayne Publishers.

O'Toole, Fintan. 1998. "Three Divergent Worlds Collide in a Mosaic of Stunning Power." *New York Daily News*, January 19, 1998.

Prchal, Tim. 2007. "Reimagining the Melting Pot and the Golden Door: National Identity in Gilded Age and Progressive Era Literature." *MELUS* 32, no. 1 (Spring): 29–51.
Watts, Steven. 2005. *The People's Tycoon: Henry Ford and the American Century*. New York: Alfred A. Knopf.
Weber, Bruce. 1998. "Corporate Broadway—A Special Report: Gambling on a Trip from *Ragtime* to Riches." *New York Times*, February 19, 1998.
Winer, Linda. 1998. "A Great Big Show Opens a Great Big Theater." *Newsday*, January 19, 1998.

CHAPTER 16
RAISIN (1973)

Music by Judd Woldin (1925–2011)
Lyrics by Robert Brittan (NA)
Book by Robert Nemiroff (1929–91) and Charlotte Zaltzberg (1924–74)
World Premiere: Arena Theatre Washington, May 30, 1973
Broadway Run: 46th Street Theatre (through December 28, 1974) and Lunt-Fontanne Theatre (January 13, 1975–closing)
Opening Date: October 18, 1973
Closing Date: December 7, 1975
Total Performances: 847

Songs

"Prologue"
"Man Say"
"Who's Little Angry Man"
"Runnin' to Meet the Man"
"A Whole Lotta Sunlight"
"Booze"
"Alaiyo"
"African Dance"
"Sweet Time"
"You Done Right"
"He Come Down This Morning"
"It's a Deal"
"Sweet Time" (Reprise)
"Sidewalk Tree"
"Not Anymore"
"Alaiyo" (Reprise)
"It's a Deal" (Reprise)
"Measure the Valleys"

Overview

Raisin is a musical adaptation of Lorraine Hansberry's iconic play *A Raisin in the Sun* (1959). Premiering eight years after Hansberry's death, *Raisin* adheres closely to Hansberry's original playscript, embracing Hansberry's concept of grounding the fictional "kitchen table" drama of the Younger family in the context of profound historical forces at work in post-World War II America, especially as they impacted African Americans in the North. Co-authored by Hansberry's ex-husband Robert Nemiroff and his theatrical producing and writing partner, Charlotte Zaltzberg, *Raisin*'s plot, like that of the play, is based loosely on Hansberry's childhood recollections of her parents' fight to purchase and occupy a house in a segregated neighborhood of Chicago.

Raisin's storyline, set "sometime" between 1945 and the late 1950s, shows Lena Younger ("Mama"), her two grown children (Walter and Beneatha), daughter-in-law (Ruth), and grandson (Travis) struggling daily and desperately to make ends meet while moderating family squabbles in their deteriorating Chicago apartment.

When Lena receives her late husband's life insurance check, family conflicts boil over as the Youngers realize they now have the financial means to invest in some, but not all, of the family's aspirations for a better life. Hard, painful choices await them. Like the play, *Raisin* mines its dramatic tension from the way the Youngers negotiate the choices and challenges demanded of people seeking to propel themselves out of poverty. For a Northern Black family in the 1950s, there was no greater challenge than buying a new home in an all-white suburb.

In an eerily understated scene in Act One, Lena reveals almost casually that she has taken a large portion of the insurance money and done precisely that. Lena's down payment on a house in a white suburb (the fictional Clybourne Park) transforms the story into an historically creditable test case of the rules governing postwar suburban home expansion: a network of government discriminatory regulations and segregationist private business practices that stymied untold numbers of Black people who, like many white people, sought better lives for themselves after the war. The Youngers are confronted by a neighborhood "improvement" association's efforts to prevent them taking possession of their home, a circumstance that brings to bear upon the story the relatively little-known history of planned segregation in Northern suburbs.

Lena's life insurance check arrives as Chicago and other Northern cities were in the throes of what would become be a twenty-five-year "mass suburbanization" of America's urban areas. A national housing shortage greeted an entire generation of veterans returning home from World War II. In response, the federal government created a series of initiatives in the 1940s, such as the GI Bill, to assist veterans in returning to society as successful middle-class citizens in prospering new neighborhoods. Partnerships between banks and private real estate developers generated myriad new home-buying opportunities as suburban communities sprang up around most major American cities. However, these opportunities were largely closed to people of color, particularly African Americans.

The suburban housing boom grew so quickly that it stampeded over concurrent court rulings which, theoretically, overturned segregationist housing practices nationwide. However, it would be years before those legal protections would take effect in local neighborhoods across the country. New home developers, realtors, and banks openly blocked occupancy by "the colored race," even to the point of separating (or "redlining") neighborhoods earmarked for Black homebuyers from those designated for whites only. Hence in 1959, five years after the Supreme Court declared unconstitutional the principle of "separate but equal" racial segregation (*Brown v. Board of Education*), families like the Youngers would have been very likely to find their soon-to-be white neighbors determined to keep them out of the neighborhood.

Raisin's emphasis on the Clybourne Park Improvement Association fronting the effort to stop the Youngers from taking possession of their new home is historically significant. Banks and realtors pressured the first wave of homebuyers to protect neighborhood property value by keeping neighborhoods "well maintained," effectively code for "all-white." *Raisin*'s association representative, Karl Linder, embodies what Hansberry viewed (and civil rights historians later concurred) to be hypocrisy among Northern white people who professed support for racial equality but were more deeply committed to the "neighborhood stability" presumably afforded by racial segregation. The Youngers' story also invokes the heroism of Black families that took the first step of moving into previously all-white neighborhoods. Although, like the play, *Raisin* ends before the Youngers take physical possession of their house, Hansberry and Nemiroff's audiences would have been familiar with notorious incidents of harassment and violence inflicted upon the first families who crossed segregated housing boundaries in Cicero, Illinois, in 1951 and Levittown, Pennsylvania, in 1957.

When *Raisin* premiered in 1973, *A Raisin in the Sun* was, as it remains, the most influential play ever written by an African American and an established masterpiece of twentieth-century American drama. The play's imposing legacy made a commercial musical adaptation of the Youngers' story possible in the first place. Yet over time, Hansberry's play cast a shadow over *Raisin*'s fortunes, and the musical struggled to establish a legacy of its own. *Raisin* had an auspicious start, garnering strong opening-night reviews, enjoying a fourteen-month Broadway run, winning the Tony Award for Best Musical, and supporting a successful eighteen-month national tour. After that, *Raisin* lapsed quickly into obscurity. It has never been revived on Broadway and there have been no touring productions since the 1970s. Even among predominantly Black communities, schools, and colleges, local productions have been few and far between.

There is likely no single explanation for the short-lived fame of a show that was initially so successful and so closely associated with an American theater masterpiece. Changes that writers Nemiroff and Zaltzberg made to Hansberry's original text generated some debate, but overall, critics and audiences honored the writers' allegiance to Hansberry's original characters. As was conventional for Broadway musicals at the time, *Raisin* expands the play's one-set apartment interior to other locations: that is, a neighborhood bar, a church, and the Southside Chicago street where the Youngers live. The implication that all of Southside Chicago shared the Youngers' story seemed reasonably aligned with Hansberry's original vision.

Key omissions from the play in Nemiroff and Zaltzberg's adaptation drew attention as well. The musical omits Ruth's unexpected pregnancy and the emotionally searing discussions between Lena and Ruth that arise when Ruth considers getting an abortion. *Raisin* also eliminates one of Beneatha's original two suitors: George, son of a wealthy "black bourgeois" businessman and heir to a fortune. George's absence intensifies *Raisin*'s focus on Joseph Asagai, Beneatha's Nigerian classmate and love interest. Their shared fascination with African American cultural connectivity reflected a growing national interest in the African roots of Black culture that had emerged since the premiere of *A Raisin in the Sun*. The additional focus on the Beneatha–Asagai relationship played out as an appropriate updating of the original drama to the extent that no one took notice of George's absence at all.

The score by Broadway newcomers Judd Woldin and Robert Brittan clearly did not help *Raisin* establish a legacy. While the music was not lambasted by critics, praise was tepid. Moreover, the score did not yield a single popular hit song, a fact that has likely deterred touring companies and student theater groups from mounting a production.

Additionally, Hansberry's 1959 success notwithstanding, Black-authored and Black-themed theater—especially full-scale musicals—rarely see production on Broadway, much less develop an enduring legacy. In 1973, important breakthroughs for Black-themed musicals lie ahead, such as *The Wiz* (1975), *Ain't Misbehavin'* (1978), and *Dreamgirls* (1981), but *Raisin* made no such impact.

Ultimately, the primary cause of *Raisin*'s long-term demise probably lies with the constantly evolving historical significance of Hansberry's play. As theater historian Donatella Galella observes, "the visibility of *A Raisin in the Sun* [throws] into relief the obscurity of the musical version" (Galella 2015). Theater artists, critics, scholars, and teachers keep returning to *A Raisin in the Sun*. It houses troves of insight into race, gender, American politics, and family dynamics that reveal themselves anew to successive generations of readers and audiences. Such cannot be said of *Raisin*, or many musicals, or, for that matter, any but the most distinguished works of literature.

Plot synopsis

At night on a street in Southside Chicago, *circa* 1950s, music plays over pantomimed mini-dramas: couples meet, men deal drugs, strangers rescue an assaulted woman, a drunk person staggers homeward, and night melts into day.

Morning in the Younger family's cramped apartment finds Ruth waking up her twelve-year-old son Travis, who sleeps on the living room couch. She makes breakfast as Travis races to beat their neighbor, Mrs. Johnson, to the shared hallway bathroom. Her husband, Walter Lee, enters dressed for his job as a businessman's chauffeur. He flirts with Ruth and mentions that his mother, Lena, is expecting a $10,000 insurance payment in the mail from the recent death of his father. Lena has already committed some of the money to cover medical school tuition for Walter's younger sister, Beneatha. Walter, eager to quit his job and open a liquor store with friends, hopes to persuade Lena to finance his venture with the remaining money.

At breakfast Walter asks Ruth to intercede with Lena, but Ruth evades the subject. Walter accuses her of not supporting his dreams ("Man Say"). Travis, dressed for school, chafes at Ruth's request for a good-bye kiss, but Ruth cajoles him into it ("Whose Little Angry Man Are You?"). As Beneatha enters, Walter questions her about her plans to become a doctor. Knowing that Walter resents her, Beneatha rebukes him for asking. After some gentler family bickering over carfare, Walter and Travis leave for work and school, respectively.

Walter joins other commuters in their rush to work. He vents his frustration about his job: chauffeuring his boss, Mr. Arnold, whose off-stage amplified voice barks commands and criticisms at Walter ("Runnin' to Meet the Man"). Walter sneaks away to phone some friends, insisting they meet to "talk business . . . TONIGHT."

In the apartment, Lena tends a houseplant she treasures for its promise of future growth ("A Whole Lotta Sunlight"). Ruth enters, asking about the insurance money. Lena reaffirms her commitment to Beneatha's tuition but has also considered making a down payment on a new house. Ruth mentions Walter's liquor store plan, pleading that Walter "needs his chance." Unmoved, Lena invokes her sharecropper roots ("we ain't no business people") and religious aversion to liquor. Beneatha enters announcing she is starting conga drum lessons. Her casual use of the Lord's name and expensive jumping from hobby to hobby trouble Lena, who worries about both children: Walter, haunted by money; Beneatha, modern beyond comprehension.

At a bar, Walter and his friend Bobo celebrate their soon-to-be liquor store ("Booze"). Willie Harris, leader of the partnership, enters chastising Walter for not having his investment share in-hand. Willie smooth-talks both men into hastily signing contracts with him, promising to finalize the arrangements once they pay up.

Lena, Ruth, and Beneatha perform Saturday chores. Beneatha invites fellow student, Joseph Asagai, to drop over. Lena is taken aback upon learning he is African. Beneatha lectures Lena on Americans' shallow understanding of Africa's colonial history. Asagai enters, presenting African gifts to Beneatha and charming Lena with his courtly manners. Alone, Beneatha and Asagai "lock eyes," envisioning a merger of African and African American cultures ("Alaiyo"). Asagai invites Beneatha to an African student's reception that night.

An envelope containing the insurance check arrives at the apartment. After sharing her excitement with Ruth, Beneatha, and Travis, Lena celebrates the possibility of a better future ("A Whole Lotta Sunlight" [Reprise]). That evening, Ruth irons clothes as Beneatha enters in African dress. In anticipation of the African student's reception, she puts on a record of celebratory African drumming, and dances energetically. Walter enters intoxicated and joins Beneatha's dance. Walter imagines African villagers (the ensemble) dancing with them. Asagai arrives to escort Beneatha on their date as the dance number recedes. Asagai and Beneatha exit. Ruth advises Walter against pressing Lena for money for the liquor store. Walter rebuffs her heatedly as Ruth laments the loss of tenderness between them ("Sweet Time"). Lena enters; Walter shows her his liquor store contract, but she cuts him off. Lena announces she has made a down payment on a house in Clybourne Park, a segregated white suburb. Ruth cautiously embraces the opportunity to flee the apartment. Walter, assuming that no insurance money remains for him, angrily crumples the contract and exits ("You Done Right").

On Sunday, Lena, Ruth, and Travis attend church. Lena solos in the choir ("He Come Down This Morning"). At church, Mrs. Johnson warns them about likely violence awaiting them in Clybourne Park and mocks them for their matriarchal dominance over Walter. Later, a self-pitying Walter is drunk at the bar as Lena enters. Acknowledging his hurt, Lena entrusts Walter with her remaining insurance money. She directs him to save

$3,000 for Beneatha's tuition but grants him authority over the rest. Overjoyed, Walter sings in celebration ("It's a Deal"). Weeks later, the Youngers are packing up in the apartment to move to Clybourne Park. Karl Lindner from the Clybourne Park Improvement Association enters. Realizing immediately that Lindner intends to block their move, Walter approaches him with ominous silence. On the front stoop, Travis bids farewell to his childhood street ("Sidewalk Tree"). In the apartment (during Travis' song) Walter, Ruth, and Beneatha have rejected Lindner's "offer" to buy their house back, and he has departed. The three of them mock the hypocritical passive-aggressive racism of Northern neighborhood improvement associations ("Not Anymore").

A grief-stricken Bobo enters with news of the liquor store deal; Willie has absconded with all their money. Devastated, Walter cries out in anguish. Sensing correctly that Walter gave Beneatha's tuition money to Willie, Lena in fury prepares to strike him. Horrified, Beneatha shouts her down.

Beneatha mopes on the stoop as Asagai arrives to help with the packing. Beneatha updates him on the crisis including loss of her tuition money. Asagai encourages her to join him in Nigeria. Beneatha agrees to think it over. Walter rushes out of the apartment building as Beneatha verbally scorns him. Lena fears she will never own a house, but Ruth rallies her with pledges to make more sacrifices to keep this one. Walter re-enters, boasting that he has agreed to sell back the house to Lindner's association. He has invited Lindner back to the apartment to force "the Man" to pay for segregation. Walter's betrayal of the family's heritage shocks Lena and cements her resolve to keep the house. Lena proclaims that the Younger family was never so poor as to take money for conceding they were "unfit to walk the earth." Walter holds firm, exiting to the bedroom until Lindner arrives. Beneatha condemns Walter's self-emasculation but Lena reprimands her, noting that harsh judgments are partly responsible for Walter's fractured manhood ("Measure the Valleys"). As Lindner enters, Walter re-emerges, his pride restored. Invoking the Youngers' eight generations in America, he reclaims the house on their behalf.

Lindner retreats almost unnoticed. Movers clear the apartment, singing neighbors gather to help, the Youngers rejoice, Lena's plant gets a spotlighted moment, and *Curtain.*

Critical reception

The legacy of Lorraine Hansberry's 1959 play *A Raisin in the Sun* was so powerful that several critics reviewing the Broadway premiere of *Raisin* in 1973 were drawn into the play's magnetic field. While reviewers of the pre-Broadway runs in Washington, D.C. and Philadelphia showed minimal interest in comparing the two works, some prominent New York theater critics critiqued *Raisin* largely in terms of the degree to which the musical honored or detracted from the legacy of the play, reassessing the fourteen-year-old drama in a way that ultimately ill-served the musical.

Clive Barnes opened his *New York Times* review by asserting that *Raisin* is superior to Hansberry's play. He noted approvingly that *Raisin* retained much of the play's best dramatic moments and Hansberry's "sharp," "honest" dialog. However, in retrospect he considered Hansberry's detailed exploration of African American life to be "oddly . . . dated." Barnes praised *Raisin* for "transcending" the particulars of Black American experiences and achieving a presumptively worthier "universal" appeal: "this is a family that could be anywhere at any time." Harold Clurman in *The Nation* vigorously countered Barnes' argument, ridiculing the idea that *Raisin*'s overlay of songs and dance numbers improved upon Hansberry's "straightforward," "humane" drama in any manner. The entire first half of Clurman's review comprises an energetic defense of the play, which he deemed to be "old fashioned" only in its appropriately realistic effective staging. Peter Bailey in *Ebony Magazine* mildly chastised *Raisin*'s dilution of racially specific content from the original play, singling out a softer political tone for Nigerian student Asagai (reportedly Hansberry's favorite character) in the musical. In 1959, Asagai presented an altogether new image of Africans in American popular culture, not just theater: a young post-colonial intellectual with a forward-thinking consciousness of emerging African liberation movements: "an angry young man . . . quiet in his anger." Bailey laments that *Raisin* does not "see this Asagai." Neither Brendan Gill of the *New Yorker* nor T. E. Kalem of *Time Magazine* particularly admired *A Raisin in the Sun*, and both felt that it absorbed many of the play's weaknesses. Gill, while saluting Hansberry for generating opportunities for future Black theater artists, dismissed the Youngers in both the play and the musical as banal theater stereotypes: "stock Jewish American melodrama translated . . . into black terms." Although Kalem thought *A Raisin in the Sun* conveyed a worthwhile if limited message for the 1950s, the Youngers' story in 1973 seemed to him "hopelessly dated." Setting the story to music made it even more so. If there was a middle voice on the matter of *Raisin* and its roots in Hansberry's play, it came from Catharine Hughes' equivocating review in *America Magazine:* "if [Hansberry's legacy] has not suffered much, neither has it gained much." Hughes characterized *Raisin's* storyline as "strong" and "involving" yet "excessively melodramatic and diffuse." On Hansberry's original story holding up over time, Hughes was artfully enigmatic: "it seems a little dated today [but] very possibly is not."

Other reviewers were less conflicted about the original play and generally enthusiastic about the musical. The *New York Post*, the *Christian Science Monitor*, and Long Island's *Newsday* all ran solidly positive reviews, praising the cast, direction, and the respectful representation of the Younger family. Reviewers from the *Los Angeles Times, Philadelphia Inquirer*, and *Dallas Times-Herald* hailed the Youngers musical return to Broadway as well. Virginia Capers as Lena drew universal and exuberant praise for her acting, singing, and commanding presence throughout the show. Reviewers to near unanimity echoed Barnes' salute to her "strong as Gibraltar matriarchal performance." (Capers won the 1974 Tony Award for Best Actress in a Musical for Lena.) With few exceptions, the rest of the cast received plaudits for their ability to keep up with Capers' performance. Even the otherwise dismissive Gill hailed the cast's "extraordinarily attractive and able performers." The supporting cast member drawing the most attention was eleven-year-old Ralph Carter as Travis. Gill praised him as the production's "scene stealer." Hughes was impressed but cautious: "the hottest child actor in town [Carter] is engaging, if . . . self-consciously precocious." And from Barnes, cheers for the "mighty atom of a child star." Carter received a Tony nomination for Best Featured Actor in a Musical, placing him among the youngest Tony nominees in history. The choreography by director-choreographer Donald McKayle, the only African American among the production's lead creative team, drew some special attention for the show's choreography. Bailey's review in *Ebony Magazine* featured photographs from choreographed ensemble scenes (including "Going to Meet the Man" and Walter and Beneatha's African dance fantasy), which Bailey hailed as "rousing," "outstanding," and "appealing."

For all the critical tributes *Raisin* earned for its cast, writers, and director-choreographer, composer and lyricist Judd Woldin and Robert Brittan attracted little more than polite acknowledgment for serviceable songs and music. Lena's two showcase numbers received some passing complimentary notes—the church-scene gospel song "He Come Down This Morning" and her meditative "A Whole Lotta Sunlight"—but otherwise opening night criticism of the music was generally mixed or indifferent. *Raisin* surrendered a competitive advantage to its challengers in that neither Woldin nor Brittan had a single prior Broadway credit nor had established a track record of success in commercial music of any kind. Moreover, *Raisin* never generated a hit song that the general public could associate with the show. Timing also posed a problem in that, during the mid-1970s, the record and radio industries were retreating from traditional Broadway tunes and gravitating toward songs from recent Rock Musicals, such as *Jesus Christ Superstar* (1971) and *Grease* (1972). *Raisin*'s rookie songwriting team also faced competition from Tony-award-winning composer-lyricist Stephen Sondheim, whose song "Send in the Clowns" from *A Little Night Music* (1973) was on its way to becoming an American songbook standard. However, among industry professionals Woldin and Brittan fared better. They share credit for the show's 1974 Tony Award for Best Musical and won a Grammy in the same year for Best Score from an Original Cast Show.

Notwithstanding its impressive run of 847 performances over fourteen months and strong initial reception, *Raisin* remains a surprisingly obscure work. It appears that, paradoxically, eternal fascination with Hansberry's 1959 play has had the effect of dating its 1973 musical adaptation.

Historical accuracy and context

The GI Bill and "suburbanization"

Although not specifically referenced in *Raisin*, the GI Bill figures prominently in the history behind the Youngers' story. The GI Bill (1944) was a federal benefits program for veterans returning home from World War II. Offering government funding and subsidies for veterans seeking additional education and/or affordable housing, the GI Bill served multiple purposes: rewarding the sacrifices of returning military men and women; stimulating the economy; and rectifying a nationwide housing shortage. Upon returning home, veterans found a generally robust job market, but housing was in short supply. In 1947, approximately one-third of World War II veterans were living "doubled-up with relatives, friends, and strangers" (Jackson 1985). In response, the Truman Administration created the Veterans Emergency Housing Program (VEHP), which incentivized private businesses, banks, and local governments to redirect wartime productivity toward rapid construction of affordable homes for veterans and other eligible homeowners. The GI Bill, the VEHP, and the government's Federal Housing Administration (FHA) fostered a colonial village "American Dream" of pastoral single-family homesteads located outside the town center (Kelly 1987). From this vision, massive postwar suburbanization emerged.

The VEHP plans called for construction of one million new homes in 1947. New home "starts" swelled to an average 1.5 million annually through the 1950s. Many of these homes were built by mass-production housing developers, most notably the Levitt Brothers. Unlike traditional developers, who built and sold twenty-five to fifty new homes in an established community, the Levitts built whole planned towns from scratch, called Levittowns. The first Levittowns (in New York, Pennsylvania, and New Jersey) were each comprised of over 15,000 single-family houses, each set in its own landscaped yard. The developers paved new neighborhood streets, built access routes to city-bound thoroughfares, and secured land for new schools, malls, and community centers. By 1960, over 20 million new homes had been built and purchased on the outskirts of major cities (Nicolaides and Wiese 2017).

This postwar housing expansion, now known as mass suburbanization and similar terms, lasted from about 1945 to 1970. It converted America's cities to "greater metropolitan areas" and transformed almost every aspect of American life. Suburbanization's legacy includes enabling millions of Americans, most from Depression Era lower- and lower-middle-class urban backgrounds, to become the first homeowners in their family's history. However, in almost all cases, the beneficiaries of this phenomenon were white. Moreover, the accompanying abandonment of comparatively integrated urban areas by whites (known as white flight) for white-only suburbs exacerbated segregation in both the cities and suburbs (Miller 2019).

For all its successes, suburbanization thrived in a racially discriminatory social structure that systematically disadvantaged Black people through inequitable distribution of GI Bill benefits and unfavorable mortgage interest rates, and segregated redlined (i.e., older, decaying) neighborhoods zoned for Black homebuyers. In addition to confronting the structural racism of the real estate market, Black families like the Youngers, who broke color barriers as the first Black families moving into their respective neighborhoods, often faced harassment or even violence—sometimes in full view of local authorities.

Suburban segregation: redlining and neighborhood associations

The GI Bill and VEHP housing benefits should have been administered without racial bias. In 1948, the Supreme Court determined that enforcement by state courts of racially restrictive neighborhood covenants and similar agreements violated the equal protection clause of the 14th Amendment (*Shelley v. Kraemer*). In 1954, the Court struck down the separate but equal segregationist doctrine altogether (*Brown v. Board of Education*). Nevertheless, throughout the 1950s African Americans found residential areas in Northern communities—historically touted as more welcoming to African Americans than their Southern counterparts—growing increasingly segregated before their eyes.

Supreme Court decisions notwithstanding, local officials and developers assumed they were building new homes exclusively for white homebuyers (Bennett 2019). Using FHA guidelines, contractors and lenders followed certain criteria for property valuation before issuing mortgages or insurance policies to homebuilders or buyers. These criteria included excellent property condition, limited commercial development, and street-by-street racially exclusive (i.e., whites only) occupancy. To ensure racial exclusivity in new communities, mortgage lenders identified "undesirable colored areas" by drawing red lines around them on their sales maps. Lenders shared these maps with real estate agents who, under an illegal but widespread practice known as redlining, steered Black homebuyers toward red-lined neighborhoods and away from designated white neighborhoods.

The discrimination inherent in the suburban home buying system was actually written into recent FHA guidelines for lenders and insurers. Thus, the federal government's major role in segregating the suburbs was "open, explicit, and well-known" (Rothstein 2017). The practices that led to planned segregation of the suburbs were couched as sound economic outcomes, such as "property valuation" and "neighborhood stability," rather than explicit Southern Jim Crow-type discrimination, that is, "Blacks only" and "whites only." Nevertheless, Black people understood immediately that racism was the engine driving these practices. (*Raisin*'s song "Not Anymore" mocks bureaucratic Northern hypocrisy of "neighborly" racism: "We're a friendly clan . . . / we didn't bring no rope").

Raisin's emphasis on the Youngers' confrontation with the Clybourne Park Improvement Association reflects accurately the prominent role these associations played in fostering segregation in the suburbs. Once the first wave of white owners settled into their homes, bankers, realtors, and homeowners themselves impressed upon new residents their responsibility for maintaining high property values. To meet this challenge, neighborhood associations sprang up throughout the suburbs. (By 1965, over 190 associations had been established in the Detroit area alone.) Originally, neighborhood associations oversaw social activities, such as welcoming new homebuyers and establishing community centers. However, as portrayed in *Raisin*, they also spearheaded efforts to dissuade Black homebuyers from crossing redlined areas into white neighborhoods. As prospective Black homeowners and civil rights organizations protested, sued, and began moving into whites-only neighborhoods, the neighborhood associations became identified almost entirely with segregation efforts (Sugrue 1995).

Many of the first Black families that moved into white neighborhoods faced a frightening pattern of harassment and violence along with indifference or worse from local law enforcement. In 1951, Harvey Clark, an African American war veteran, rented an apartment in the Chicago suburb of Cicero. Over 3,000 people rioted outside his apartment building for several days. They burned and vandalized the building and assaulted Clark. Local law enforcement, overwhelmed or complicit, made little effort to protect him. Eventually the governor called in state militia to restore peace (Kushner 2009; Abrams 1955).

When *A Raisin in the Sun* premiered in 1959, Daisy and Bill Myers' decision to move into the Philadelphia suburb of Levittown, Pennsylvania, was fresh in many people's minds. Bill Myers, a Black World War II veteran, and his wife Daisy moved to Levittown with their three children in 1957. To circumvent Levittown's anti-integration resistance, the Myers bought their house directly from an original owner rather than from Levitt or another realtor. Once the Myers began occupancy, however, the local newspaper ran a story under the headline "First Negro Family Moves into Levittown." By midnight of the day of publication, 200 shouting people crammed onto the Myers' lawn as teenagers threw rocks through their windows. Local law enforcement responded but to little effect. The first of nine consecutive days of volatile harassment, rioting, mob versus police confrontations, and international publicity ended with five arrests, escalating tensions, and local authorities asking state police for help against the "out of control" Levittown citizens (Jonas 2017).

Over the next eight days, outraged residents formed a "Levittown Betterment Committee" to remove the Myers "by legal and peaceful means" or "something else" (Kushner 2009). In defiance of local authorities, citizens harassed the Myers with loud gatherings next to their home. Confrontations between demonstrators and law enforcement produced injuries to both. During the week, two large crosses were burned on the lawns of nearby elementary schools. Local delivery services (heating oil, milk, etc.) were discouraged from providing for the Myers.

News coverage of the crisis in Levittown spread quickly across the nation and beyond. The horrific events combined with embarrassing publicity prompted pro-integration Levittown residents to organize. Led by clergy, Quaker groups, and local Human Relations Council members they sought to end the disturbances and promote integration going forward. However, ultimately, it was an injury to a police officer and an influx of Pennsylvania State police that alleviated the violence. Gradually, court mandates, cooler heads, orders from the governor, the stain on Levittown's reputation, and the Myers' courage and forbearance during the ordeal returned a semblance of normalcy to Levittown. The Myers remained in Levittown for five years.

Although the Myers said they felt on edge during their years in Levittown, they lived without overt harassment and even some measure of acceptance. They were interviewed on *60 Minutes* and regarded as heroes of the Civil Rights Era. Upon publication of her memoir, *Sticks and Stones*, a reviewer called Daisy Myers the "Rosa Parks of the North."

The Hansberrys, the Youngers, and the Supreme Court

In 1937, Carl Hansberry, Lorraine's father, purchased and moved into a family home in the Woodlawn neighborhood of Chicago. An association representing the heretofore all-white community went to court to force the Hansberrys out of their house. The residents association (i.e., Lee et al.) argued that a decades-old neighborhood racially restrictive covenant (written agreements among neighbors) forbade property in restricted areas of Woodlawn to be sold, leased, or occupied by "any person of the colored race." The local court ruled for Lee and against Hansberry. The court determined that racially restrictive neighborhood covenants were constitutional according to Supreme Court decision *Plessy v. Ferguson* (1896) that determined "separate but equal" racial discrimination to be constitutional under the 14th Amendment (Kamp 1987).

Hansberry lost on appeal to the Illinois Supreme Court. However, in 1940 the Supreme Court reversed both lower court rulings and found for Hansberry. The Court did not invalidate Woodlawn's housing covenant for being discriminatory, but rather determined that so few original signers of the covenant were parties to the lawsuit against Hansberry that the covenant had no legal standing as the expressed will of the Woodlawn community. The Hansberrys kept their home.

Two decades later, Lorraine Hansberry memorialized her parents' struggles through the Youngers' fight to move to Clybourne Park. While not a civil rights case *per se*, *Hansberry v. Lee* was a "substantive decision leading directly" to the outlawing of racially restrictive residential covenants (*Shelley v. Kraemer*, 1948) and a precursor to the landmark 1954 *Brown v. Board of Education* decision (Kamp 1987).

The Youngers, Asagai, and African American identity

Even *Raisin*'s detractors conceded that, overall, the musical remains faithful to the Younger family's triumphs and tensions as presented in Hansberry's play. Notwithstanding some plot editing and the infusion of musical numbers, *Raisin*'s creators strove to maintain the insightful connections Hansberry draws between conflicts arising in the Younger household and new thinking about racial consciousness emerging among young African Americans in the late 1950s and 1960s.

Raisin's two plotlines—Mama's new home in a whites-only neighborhood and Walter's pursuit of economic liberation in business—speak to long-standing African American integrationist goals as well as Hansberry's own ambivalence about integration. In the early 1900s, the NAACP's (National Association for the Advancement of Colored People) founding mission prioritized equality before the law and increased opportunities for employment for Blacks. In the 1950s, the Civil Rights movement took up anew the struggle for integrated housing and equal economic opportunity under the banner of Martin Luther King's crusade for a desegregated America.

Purchasing a home where "there's gonna be [Black people] living . . . now," Lena earns a victory for integration and racial equality, having obtained for her family the very freedom her white neighbors sought when they fled city apartments for the suburbs: "Freedom . . . when a man can walk on floors that belong to him." However, Walter's failed attempt to open a liquor store reflects Hansberry's distrust of integrationist visions of Black people achieving equality under American capitalism. Walter's recurring anger over his economic oppression is grounded in integrationist frustration. He rages against white archetypes rooted in segregationist and capitalist power structures: "the Man" and "Mistuh Charlie." Through Walter's failed liquor store scheme and desperate plan to sell the family's house back to the homeowners association, Hansberry manifests her skepticism about African Americans' future in the oppressive American economic system and compromised "civil rights game" (Hansberry 1965).

It is through *Raisin*'s Black college students, Beneatha and Asagai, that Hansberry gives voice to important emerging ideas of Black consciousness to which Beneatha's elders—Mama, Walter, and Ruth—are oblivious. While Walter's anger is narrow and target-specific, Beneatha's anger is fluid and wide-ranging. Her outbursts shift topics, performance styles, and modes of expression. Much like a jazz improvisation, Beneatha's rage embodies an overarching theme of discontent while exploring as-yet-undefined territory (Orem 2017).

Beneatha's seemingly random jumping from moment to moment invigorates *Raisin*, as it did Hansberry's original drama, with the energy of new ideas about Black consciousness emerging in the 1950s. Mama and Ruth ultimately view Walter's business failure as lamentable misfortune that befell a good but sympathetic and underappreciated Black man. However, Beneatha suffers none of that. When Walter loses the insurance money, Beneatha berates him with an insulting monologue, at once a blistering condemnation of capitalism's bogus promises to Black people and a withering mockery of Walter's self-delusional hubris: "*Bitterly, hissingly . . . shouting:* "There he is. Mr. Black Bourgeoisie himself! Entrepreneur! . . . Chairman of the Board!" (92). Beneatha's rage taps the roots of Marxist revolutionary theory that influenced important Black intellectuals of the time, such as Amiri Baraka, Angela Davis, and Franz Fanon. Their writings called for African Americans to embrace an explicitly race-conscious cultural identity that challenged the integrationist goals of Blacks moving all-but-colorlessly into mainstream American society.

Beneatha also performs what came to be known as Afro-centrism: a worldview that challenges African Americans to embrace their connectivity to African heritage as essential elements of self- and collective identity. In a micro-aggressive demonstration of Afro-centrism in Act One, Beneatha interrupts Ruth, who is ironing and singing along to a mainstream popular 1940s record. Beneatha unceremoniously removes Ruth's music, dismisses it as "assimilationist junk," and puts on an African drum record. Beneatha, a drunk Walter, and the ensemble perform an African-inspired dance as Ruth looks on confoundedly.

More significantly, Beneatha perplexes her family when she invites fellow student Joseph Asagai, a Nigerian studying in America, over to their apartment. Asagai was unlike any character ever seen on Broadway. He politely instructs the Youngers on the distinction between African nations and tribes. He sympathetically tolerates Beneatha's initial clumsiness in expressing her interest in her African identity. Nevertheless, Asagai foresees a growing, powerful connectivity between African and African American politics and culture: a vision borne out historically by the subsequent rise of Black Studies school curricula, increased media coverage of African politics and culture, the 1970s Black Arts movement, and other new expressions of African American cultural awareness. Asagai ultimately validates Beneatha's naive embrace of all things Africa by affirming that, her youthful excesses notwithstanding, she is onto something: "there is something terribly wrong in a world—or a house—where all dreams depend upon the death of one man." His pronouncement serves notice that Black liberation will require more than skirmishes won and lost against the "Mistuh Charlies" and Karl Lindners of the world.

Raisin concludes with familiar dramatic resolutions. Walter performs a traditional masculine duty by driving the invader Lindner from their door. The Youngers unite as they embark upon their journey to their new home. But Hansberry's sub-textual argument, that African American liberation lies beyond the limited reach of integration, graces *Raisin* with a measure of *A Raisin in the Sun*'s historical prophetic powers.

Thomas A. Greenfield

Further reading

Abrams, Charles. 1955. *Forbidden Neighbors*. New York: Harper Brothers.

Baily, Peter. 1974. "Raisin: Lorraine Hansberry's Award-Winning Play Becomes Musical Hit on Broadway." *Ebony Magazine* 24, no. 7 (May): 74–80.

Barnes, Clive. 1973. "Theater: *Raisin* A Delight in Musical Form." *New York Times*, Proquest Historical Newspapers, October 19, 1973.

Bennett, Shannon Smith. 2019. "Redlining." In *The American Mosaic: The African American Experience*, ABC-CLIO, 2019, https://africanamerican.abc-clio.com/Topics/Display/1407169?cid=41&sid=1407169.

Clurman, Harold. 1973. "Theatre." *The Nation*, November 12, 1973.

Galella, Donatella. 2015. "Playing in the Dark/Musicalizing *A Raisin in the Sun*." *Continuum: The Journal of African Diaspora Drama* 1, no. 2 (January), continuumjournal.org/index.php/all-issues/current-issue-amiri-baraka/33-volumes/issues/vol-1-no-2-content/ysc-1-2/95-playing-in-the-dark-musicalizing-a-raisin-in-the-sun.

Gill, Brendan. 1973. "A Black Rose." *The New Yorker* 49 (October): 107.

Hansberry, Lorraine. 1959. *A Raisin in the Sun*. New York: Samuel French.

Hansberry, Lorraine. 1965. "The Scars of the Ghetto." Rep. *Monthly Review*, May 1, 2015, https://monthlyreview.org/2015/05/01/the-scars-of-the-ghetto/.

Hughes, Catharine. 1973. "Raisin." *America Magazine*, November 17, 1973.

Jackson, Kenneth T. 1985. *Crabgrass Frontier: The Suburbanization of the United States*. New York: Oxford University Press.

Jonas, Jerry. 2017. "60 Years Later, the Levittown Shame That Still Lingers." *Bucks County Courier Times*, August 12, 2017, https://www.buckscountycouriertimes.com/1cd299e6-7e1a-11e7-92bb-bf5ca2295519.html.

Kalem, T. E. 1973. "The Faith That Faded." *Time Magazine* 102, no. 18 (October): 99.

Kamp, Allen R. 1987. "The History Behind Hansberry v. Lee." *U.C. Davis Law Review* 481, January 1, 1987, https://repository.jmls.edu/cgi/viewcontent.cgi?article=1283&context=facpubs.

Kelly, Barbara. 1987. "The Suburban Revolution." *New York Times*, February 1, 1987.

Kushner, David. 2009. *Levittown: Two Families, One Tycoon and the Fight for Civil Rights in America's Legendary Suburb*. New York: Walker & Co.

"Levittown." 2019. *The American Mosaic: The African American Experience*, https:// africanamerican.abc-clio.com/Search/Display/1514361.

Miller, Karen. 2019. White Flight. *The American Mosaic: The African American Experience*, https://africanamerican.abc-clio.com/Search/Display/1400717.

Nemiroff, Robert and Charlotte Zaltzberg. 1978. *Raisin*. New York: Samuel French.

Nicolaides, Becky, and Andrew Wiese, ed. 2006. *The Suburb Reader*. New York: Routledge.

Nicolaides, Becky and Andrew Wiese. 2017. "Suburbanization in the United States after 1945." *Oxford Research Encyclopedias*, doi:10.1093/acrefore/9780199329175.013.6.

Orem, Sarah. 2017. "Signifyin(g) When Vexed: Black Feminist Revision, Anger, and A Raisin in the Sun." *Modern Drama* 60, no. 2 (Summer): 189–211.

Remington, William. 1947. "The Veterans Emergency Housing Program." *Law and Contemporary Problems* (Winter), https://scholarship.law.duke.edu/lcp/vol12/iss1/11.

Rothstein, Richard. 2017. "A 'Forgotten History' of How the U.S. Government Segregated America." Transcript, *Fresh Air*, National Public Radio, May 3, 2017, https://www.npr.org/2017/05/03/526655831/a-forgotten-history-of-how-the-u-s-government-segregated-america.

Sugrue, Thomas J. 1995. "Crabgrass-Roots Politics: Race, Rights, and the Reaction against Liberalism in the Urban North, 1940–1964." *Journal of American History* 82, no. 2 (September): 551–78.

"What Is the Mission of the NAACP?" n.d. *NAACP* home page, https://www.naacp.org/about-us/.

CHAPTER 17
THE SCOTTSBORO BOYS (2010)

Book by David Thompson (1956–)
Music and Lyrics by John Kander (1927–) and Fred Ebb (1928–2004)
World Premiere: Vineyard Theatre, New York, February 12, 2010–April 18, 2010
Broadway: October 7, 2010–December 12, 2010

Songs*

"Minstrel March"
"Hey, Hey, Hey, Hey!"
"Commencing in Chattanooga"
"Alabama Ladies"
"Nothin'"
"Electric Chair"
"Go Back Home"
"Shout!"
"Make Friends with the Truth"
"That's Not the Way We Do Things"
"Never Too Late"
"Financial Advice"
"Southern Days"
"Chain Gang"
"Alabama Ladies" (Reprise)
"Zat So?"
"You Can't Do Me"
"The Scottsboro Boys"
"Minstrel March" (Reprise)

*Order of songs and listed reprises may vary slightly among published scores, cast recordings, and production programs.

Overview

The Scottsboro Boys is an ironic, purposefully-disjointed retelling of the notorious racial injustices suffered by nine young Black men arrested in 1931 on a train near Scottsboro, Alabama, and falsely accused of raping two white women. At their initial trial—a rushed-through travesty in which all nine defendants' court proceedings, testimony, verdicts, and sentences were dispatched in less than four days—an all-white male jury sentenced eight of the nine to death and one to life in prison. The grotesque mistreatment of the Scottsboro Boys (as they came to be known) attracted national attention almost immediately. As the Scottsboro case metastasized from a quick local trial into years of appeals, retrials, and extended imprisonments, the "attention" evolved into one of the most significant and sobering chapters in the history of American racial injustice. Events surrounding the Scottsboro Boys' protracted ordeal altered the legal, political, and cultural history of race relations in America and set the stage for the transformative Civil Rights Movement of the 1950s and 1960s.

To the extent that the musical *The Scottsboro Boys* presents the major facts and offers a general chronology of the Scottsboro case, it does so responsibly with few specific factual errors. However, the show omits and conflates many details in deference to the intentionally disruptive narrative structure it establishes for recounting this well-documented sequence of historical events. The musical frames the Scottsboro Boys case as a "memory" invoked at the beginning of the show by an elderly Black woman waiting at a corner bus stop. (We learn later that she is Rosa Parks who, in 1955, famously refused a Montgomery, Alabama, bus driver's orders to give up her seat to a white passenger. That incident sparked the Montgomery bus boycott—the first prominent mass Civil Rights action organized and led by Rev. Martin Luther King, Jr.)

The woman's memory unfolds onstage in an incongruously surreal sequence: a nineteenth-century-style minstrel troop bounds on stage with joyous energy, readying itself to perform "the story of the Scottsboro Boys" for the evening's "night of merriment." With the exception of the white master of ceremonies (Mr. Interlocutor), these minstrel performers are Black, nine of whom will portray the Scottsboro Boys in this tale-within-a-minstrel-show-within-a-memory-within-a-Broadway-musical. Black cast members also perform the roles of white southern female accusers, arresting officers, and judges as well as Northern Jewish defense attorneys, further burlesquing the musical's treatment of race, identity, and historical point of view.

The minstrels' high-energy opening number and purposely dated music hall jokes serve as prelude to their telling of the Scottsboro Boys' harrowing story. Notwithstanding the fact that, on this particular evening, the nine key Black minstrel performers insist on telling the "true" story of the Scottsboro Boys, their performance never completely escapes the context of the traditional American minstrel motif: mockery of African Americans for the amusement of white audiences. The disconnect between theatrical form and narrative function is, of course, intentional, as director Susan Stroman found herself explaining repeatedly to dubious journalists and disconcerted audiences: "[We are] taking this racist art form and flipping it on its head" (Clark 2012).

Stroman and the creative team rein in the minstrel format sufficiently to present a coherent, if abridged, retelling of the Scottsboro Boys' story. In the process, the writers give the nine minstrels/Scottsboro Boys some agency in the retelling. The Black players' smoldering resentment of the position they are in escalates and eventually penetrates their white-minstrels-in-blackface personas. Ultimately refusing Mr. Interlocutor's orders to do the show as rehearsed, the nine Black actor-characters ultimately repudiate the blackface minstrel version of the Scottsboro story: a symbolic denunciation of white appropriation and suppression of African American history and culture.

Although many in the Broadway audiences struggled with the shock of seeing a discredited blackface-style "entertainment" in the twenty-first century, *The Scottsboro Boys* sought to illuminate important historical aspects of the Scottsboro trials that transcended the show's minstrelsy context as well as the seven years of legal battles attendant to the case. *The Scottsboro Boys* gives an instructive account of the early uneasy political alliance between the National Association for the Advancement of Colored People (NAACP) and Communist-inspired white Northern activists who took up the defendants' cause for both altruistic and self-serving purposes.

The musical also alludes to two important U.S. Supreme Court rulings on the Scottsboro case, both of which established landmark constitutional precedents for protecting the rights of defendants in criminal cases—especially the rights of African Americans. Most obviously, perhaps, the musical forcefully indicts the American theater—and New York commercial theater in particular—for its long history of promoting blackface entertainment and capitalizing on negative Black stereotypes.

The decision to create a musical adaptation of the Scottsboro case was a purposeful artistic choice by a group of four well-established American theater talents, all of whom were long-time friends, frequent collaborators, legendary successes, and white. The heralded composer-lyricist partnership of John Kander and Fred Ebb, librettist David Thompson, and director-choreographer Susan Stroman (1954–) had, according to Thompson, decided around the year 2000 to develop a musical based on an historical event. They researched American court cases and quickly settled on the Scottsboro case. All four wanted to reexplore a familiar theme in Kander and Ebb's earlier musicals, expressed by Kander as "seductively writing about things that are really awful so people suddenly realize they're having a good time at the expense of others" (Mellini 2010). However, unlike their better-known musicals written in this vein, such as *Cabaret* (1966) and *Kiss of the Spider Woman* (1992), the Scottsboro story was thoroughly documented history. The earlier shows had been fictional stories with historical settings.

In the process of researching the Scottsboro musical, Kander came across a 1930s news account likening the original Scottsboro trial to a "minstrel show" owing to the chaos and absurdity of the courtroom proceedings. The comparison matched his and lyricist Fred Ebb's vision of injecting the shocking historical events with a subversive counter-message: "We [sought] to make it clear that [the Scottsboro Boys] were real people . . . destroyed by the terrible racial injustice in this country. The form of the minstrel show with its Blackface and cliché [*sic*] fit right into that" (Carone 2012).

The death of Fred Ebb in 2004, among other factors, slowed the overall development of the project. However, on March 12, 2010, the show opened for a three-week limited run in New York City's Vineyard Theatre, a well-established Off-Broadway venue specializing in politically, socially, and commercially risky new productions. The Guthrie Theatre in Minneapolis signed on to stage *The Scottsboro Boys* after the Vineyard run as the final production in their 2009–10 season. Stroman directed the Minneapolis show, using that time to further develop the musical that would eventually open on Broadway in October.

The Scottsboro Boys opened on Broadway, October 31, 2010, at the Lyceum Theatre and found itself in trouble almost from the start. Unlike the critical enthusiasm that greeted the Off-Broadway and Minneapolis runs, Broadway reviewers, on the whole, were cooler toward the show. In many cases, even reviewers who found much to admire in *The Scottsboro Boys* either had difficulty with the multilayered irony of the minstrel motif or speculated (correctly) that audiences would have such difficulty. To complicate matters, shortly before the start of the lucrative Broadway holiday season (Thanksgiving through the New Year) a multi-racial coalition of protesters, numbering about thirty, demonstrated outside the Lyceum Theatre to protest the show's use of minstrelsy and invocations of blackface. A widely publicized statement from the demonstrators proclaimed: "This racist play has reduced the tragedy of the Scottsboro Boys case to a 'Step n Fetchit' comedic, minstrel exhibition," further characterizing the show as "an attack on [African American] culture and history" (Jones 2010). *The Scottsboro Boys* closed on December 12 after only forty-nine performances.

The Scottsboro Boys found partial redemption at the Tony Awards, earning no wins but an impressive twelve nominations, including nods for Best Musical, Book, Original Score, Best Director, and Best Actor (Joshua Henry as Haywood Patterson) and two nominations for Best Actor in a Featured Role (Colman Domingo and Forest McClendon, both for multiple roles). Limited-run productions in London in 2013 and 2014 earned rave critical reviews and saw healthy ticket sales. Since then, the show has had several regional productions throughout the United States. The creative team's disappointment at the Broadway run was palpable and something of an anticlimax as the final show of Kander and Ebb's storied forty-plus-year creative partnership. Stroman and Kander were proud of the work, but recognized the ill-fit between *The Scottsboro Boys*' edginess and the less adventurous tastes of Broadway audiences. Lead producer-investor Barry Weissler minced no words regarding the show's inability to find, much less engage, a Broadway audience: "Black audiences made up their mind without seeing the show and the white audience is saying, 'Oh God, we're punishing nine Black boys for something they didn't do and they finally all die. I think I'll see *'Mamma Mia!'*" (Gamerman 2010).

Plot synopsis

An African American woman (Lady) waits for a bus, a cake box resting on her lap. Lifting a box corner she inhales, triggering a flood of memories. The scene around her fades as the remaining cast members enter ("Minstrel March"). Lady reappears onstage throughout the show, moving inconspicuously through the action.

Eleven African American men enter and greet the Lady, forming a traditional minstrel show arc facing the audience. An elderly genteel white man, Mr. Interlocuter, standing center-stage, begins the proceedings with the minstrel show's standard call to action: "Gentlemen, be seated!" Introducing himself as "host . . . and master of these folks," Mr. Interlocutor and company invite the audience to put "sad thoughts out of sight" as they prepare to perform ("Hey! Hey! Hey! Hey!"). As the Interlocutor begins the evening's story of the Scottsboro Boys, one of the African American minstrels (the cast member who will portray Scottsboro defendant Haywood Patterson) asks if tonight the minstrels can tell the true story. Mr. Interlocutor agrees, spinning the request into a joke with the minstrel arc's "end men," Mr. Bones and Mr. Tambo.

The story within the minstrel show opens in 1931 on a railroad boxcar ("Commencing in Chattanooga"). Nine Black males, between the ages of twelve and twenty, are travelling from Tennessee to Alabama in search of jobs. The train stops near Scottsboro, Alabama, where a fight breaks out among the passengers. The men are ushered off the train at gunpoint by two white law enforcement officers (broadly caricatured by Mr. Bones and Mr. Tambo), who accuse them of fighting with white boys on the train.

While the young Black men contend with the police, Victoria Price and Ruby Bates, two white sex workers (played by Black actors in drag), attempt to evade arrest themselves. Victoria and Ruby falsely accuse the nine boys of raping them on the train ("Alabama Ladies"). The boys are arrested solely on the basis of the women's story.

At the trial, presided over by Mr. Interlocutor as judge, the boys are represented by a visibly drunk public defender (played by Mr. Tambo), who presents a clownishly incompetent defense. Haywood defiantly insists that he and the rest of the boys are innocent ("Nothin'"), but they are all found guilty and sentenced to death by electric chair. (In the actual trial, eight were sentenced to death and one of the younger boys, Roy White, was sentenced to life in prison.)

In prison, Eugene Williams, the youngest boy sentenced to death, is plagued by nightmares ("Electric Chair"). As the boys await imminent execution, they commiserate over what they might say in letters they want to write to their families. Their conversation reveals that Haywood is illiterate. Roy offers to teach him to read and write, but Haywood defensively rejects his proposal. Longing for their former lives the boys reflect on the loneliness of imprisonment ("Go Back Home"). Based on appeals filed by Northern lawyers who have taken up their case, and owing to the appeals as well as public outrage over the injustice of their sentences, the boys' executions are stayed. The boys learn that the Supreme Court, having determined that they did not have competent legal representation at their original trial, has ordered a new one. They rejoice, hoping that justice will finally be served ("Shout"). One year passes with the boys still in prison awaiting retrial. Haywood, having been taught to write by Ray, has written a short story about honesty that he shares with the group ("Make Friends with the Truth").

The second trial commences in 1933. Noted New York attorney Samuel Leibowitz arrives in Alabama amid a flurry of publicity, confident in his ability to obtain justice for the boys ("That's Not The Way We Do Things"). During the trial, a surprise witness for the defense takes the stand. Ruby Bates, one of their original accusers, admits that she originally lied about the boys and testifies to their innocence ("Never Too Late"). The boys are elated at Ruby's testimony but their optimism wanes as the Alabama District Attorney claims falsely that Leibowitz bribed Ruby with "Jew money" to lie on the stand ("Financial Advice").

As the boys await the verdict in their courthouse cells, Lady hands the Interlocutor the cake box, a gift he delivers on behalf of an anonymous "admirer." While eating the cake the boys, believing they will not be convicted again of a crime they did not commit, ponder what they will do once freed. As they consider leaving the South to find freedom up North, the Interlocutor enters and scolds them for criticizing their Southern roots. At his request they sing a sentimental tune about the South ("Southern Days"), but, while singing it, the boys subvert the song from a wistful remembrance to an embittered screed about their own experiences.

The jury returns a guilty verdict, and the boys are sentenced to prison. On a chain gang, Haywood learns that his mother is dying. He attempts an escape to visit her but is caught by police ("Commencing in Chattanooga [Reprise]"). The years pass as Leibowitz, bolstered by popular support in the North, particularly among Communists, files additional appeals of the boys' verdict. Nonetheless the boys are found guilty each time. Victoria Price, though wearied by the seemingly endless appeal trials at which she is called to testify, never recants her original false accusation ("Alabama Ladies [Reprise]"). One of the boys, Ozie, is shot in the head during a physical altercation with a prison guard, leaving him permanently brain damaged.

It is 1937. Leibowitz succeeds in getting the four youngest boys freed via plea deals. He tells Haywood, the most resistant to compromise of the nine, that to get out of prison he must give a false confession of the rape charge to the Governor of Alabama and enter a guilty plea to the court. Haywood reluctantly agrees. However, once in court, against advice of counsel, he abruptly proclaims his innocence ("Zat So?"). Haywood is sent back to prison, maintaining his innocence until his death twenty-one years later ("You Can't Do Me").

The Interlocutor introduces the minstrel show finale, in which the eight remaining boys (minus Haywood) appear in top hats, tails, and blackface. While performing a lively closing number, each boy recounts his tragic fate after prison. Haywood alone appears without blackface, still in prison and holding the notebook in which he has written his story. "I told the truth—there's nothing more I can do," he says, handing the book to the Lady, who begins to read it while exiting.

The Interlocutor orders the boys to be seated—but this time they disobey him. They remove their top hats and gloves, resolutely wiping away the blackface makeup with their handkerchiefs. Enraged, the Interlocutor rails at their insubordination. The scene transitions into the show's opening tableau: the Lady with the cake box is now seated on the bus for which she has been waiting. The Interlocutor re-enters, dressed as a bus driver, and orders her to move to the back of the bus. The Lady, whom the audience now realizes is Civil Rights icon Rosa Parks, refuses to move from her seat. Resolutely and firmly, she responds: "No more. I'm going to sit here and rest my feet." Curtain.

Critical reception

The pre-Broadway limited-runs of *The Scottsboro Boys*, one Off-Broadway in New York and one in Minneapolis, likely had little influence upon the producers' and creative team's decision to open *The Scottsboro Boys* on Broadway. Since 2000, Stroman had established herself as the most accomplished woman director-choreographer in Broadway history and had a fanbase as loyal as that of any onstage star performer. As the final collaboration of Kander and the late Fred Ebb, the most prolific Broadway composer–lyricist team of the previous forty years, theater history demanded a Broadway showcase irrespective of content. Moreover, Kander, Stroman, and Thompson all enjoyed their well-earned reputations for adventurousness and risk-taking—qualities that, for better and worse, were on full display in *The Scottsboro Boys*. Not surprisingly, the show's intended—and perhaps some unintended—mixed messaging on race drew the lion's share of attention.

Most reviews were compelled to confront the show's metatheatrical dilemma of bringing forth an indictment of America's pernicious racist history in Broadway's ostentatious "court" of glitz, glamour, and on-the-town high spirits. Notwithstanding that the musical reveals from the beginning a full awareness of its own subversive mixed messaging (the Black cast beckons the audience to "put sadness out of sight" and, essentially, sit back and enjoy the unfolding horror), the show's ironic self-contradictions presented challenges for critics and audiences alike. The *New York Times*' Charles Isherwood asserted that framing the boys' 1930s irredeemably tragic fate inside the revered Rosa Parks' refusal to give up her bus seat to a white passenger "heavy-handedly stresses the inspirational aspects of . . . the civil rights movement" (Isherwood 2010a). Isherwood found the anachronistic pairing particularly off-point in that Rosa Parks' most conspicuous on-stage moments occur within the grotesquely self-mocking minstrel-show motif. Joe Dziemianowicz of the *New York Daily News* argued that the show, while "rousing," suffered from a similar tonal "split personality": "It wants to shock; it yearns to charm. They're not always compatible goals" (Dziemianowicz 2010). Tulis McCall in the *New York Theatre Guide* also found the power of the tale disabled by the telling: "We can only take in such an enormous story one bite at a time. Just about the time that we are getting the hang of the tale, it is over" (McCall 2010). The *Los Angeles Times*' Charles McNulty posited that the show should have remained Off-Broadway, asserting that controversy-averse Broadway audiences were "bound to feel squeamish about tapping their feet to an infectious ragtime beat as police brutality and . . . jokes about lynching pile up" (McNulty 2010). The *Wall Street Journal* also took exception to *Scottsboro Boys*' clashes of tone, calling it "a musical that slathers this terrible tale in a thick coat of musical-comedy frosting that has been spiked with cheap, elephantine irony" (Teachout 2010). Scott Brown of *New York Magazine*, however, viewed the show's discordant juxtapositions of unspeakable degradation and high-powered entertainment essential to its well-aimed disquieting impact: "[*The Scottsboro Boys*] overwhelms our comfortable pieties with pure showmanship, conjuring your applause in waves, then [you ask yourself] . . . Did I just clap for . . . a [racist] shuck-and-jive" dance number? (Brown 2010).

Notwithstanding its destabilizing qualities, *The Scottsboro Boys* received many conventional assessments as well. Isherwood praised the "dazzling verve" Stroman brought to the direction and choreography, and called the production "dynamic . . . thanks in no small part to the dauntless energy of the terrific cast, all fine singers and dancers" (Isherwood 2010a). The *New York Post*'s Elisabeth Vincentelli delivered a rave, calling the production a "grimly thought-provoking . . . thrillingly inventive and entertaining night at the theater" (Vincentelli 2010). The genre-spanning Kander & Ebb score garnered several accolades. David Rooney of the *Hollywood Reporter* called the score "vintage Kander & Ebb, marrying buoyant entertainment with a sinister double edge" (Rooney 2010). Dziemianowicz echoed this sentiment: "[The score] conjures their hits *Cabaret* and *Chicago* in terms of melody and irony" (Dziemianowicz 2010).

Despite having defenders among the critics, the producers felt compelled to contextualize the show's more shocking elements with special inserts placed in *Playbill* programs to pre-empt audience discomfort with the ironic take on racist brutality. Nevertheless, public hostility to *The Scottsboro Boys* grew over the course of the brief Broadway run. Many people flatly objected to representations of minstrelsy and blackface in a show led by an all-white creative team, irrespective of artistic rationales. On November 6, a political action group staged a highly publicized protest outside the Lyceum Theatre as the audience waited for the doors to open. *The Scottsboro Boys* closed early on Broadway after a disappointing two-month run of forty-nine performances.

Notwithstanding its poor financial showing and legacy of public hostility, *The Scottsboro Boys* received a surprising twelve Tony Award nominations, including Best Musical, Best Score, Best Book, and Best Choreography, nearly matching the number of nominations for the season's biggest hit, *The Book of Mormon*. Though *Scottsboro Boys* failed to garner a Tony win, the award notices bolstered its post-Broadway life. Regional productions in the United States and a West End London run were shepherded by the original creative team, and included some original cast members reprising their Broadway roles.

In contrast to its Broadway run, the London production of *The Scottsboro Boys* was a critical and financial success, running for over a year. Sam Marlowe of *The Times* (London) raved, "Susan Stroman's production and choreography are incandescent with energy and invention, and the company deliver performances of gutpunching power" (Marlowe 2014). Lyn Gardner of the *Guardian* echoed this sentiment, proclaiming *The Scottsboro Boys* "a genuinely radical musical, full of stinging indignation and plaintive power" (Gardner 2014).

The production would go on to earn six Olivier Award nominations (the British equivalent of the Tony), including Best Musical, Best Director, and Outstanding Achievement in Music.

Historical accuracy and context

The Scottsboro Boys *and the blackface minstrel tradition*

The nineteenth-century American blackface minstrel tradition, the framework in which *The Scottsboro Boys* recounts the true story of outrageous judicial injustices inflicted upon nine innocent Black young men in the 1930s, bears its own corresponding legacy of racist hypocrisy and cruelty.

Originally, the term "blackface" was a functional descriptor of a specific form of nineteenth-century American music hall entertainment: white performers blackening their faces to caricature white perceptions of African American speech, singing, dancing, and social behavior. American minstrel shows and blackface entertainment originated in the 1830s and 1840s, growing to enormous popularity in the second half of the nineteenth century. From about 1850 to the early 1900s, minstrel shows—the leading purveyor of blackface entertainment for white audiences—were America's most popular form of professional entertainment, drawing large diverse audiences across the country and from all walks of life.

To the dismay of many African Americans, most notably Frederick Douglass, even Northern proponents of racial equality found nothing objectionable in blackface entertainment, or the profusion of commercial handbills, postcards, advertisements, magazine graphics, and decorative figurines that promoted similar outlandish racist images. For Douglass, blackface performers were irredeemably harmful and degrading to African Americans: "the filthy scum of white society . . . have stolen from us a complexion denied them by nature, in which to make money, and pander to [the] corrupt taste of their white fellow citizens" (Douglass 1848). But overwhelmingly white audiences of all social classes embraced blackface minstrelsy: "No [white people] took minstrel shows seriously; they were meant to be light, meaningless entertainment" (Grovesnor and Toll 2019).

The Scottsboro Boys' minstrel-inspired opening, notwithstanding the show's engaging original choreography, invokes traditional nineteenth-century blackface minstrel shows in several ways, with the ironically glaring exception that the show's singers and dancers are Black and, in the first act, perform without blackface. In keeping with traditional minstrel show form, *The Scottsboro Boys* minstrel performers enter carrying simple wooden chairs and place the chairs in a semi-circle facing the audience. Mr. Interlocutor, the straight man and master of ceremonies (not in blackface), brings them to order: "Gentlemen. Be seated." The end men, Mr. Tambo (who plays tambourine) and Mr. Bones (who plays wooden clappers), are stationed at either end of the arc.

As *The Scottsboro Boys*' Mr. Tambo and Mr. Bones make clear, their job is to play "all kinds of characters." The musical coyly avoids specifying the characters they play, but the allusion to minstrelsy's enduring array of stock "Black" characters is unmistakable. By the late nineteenth century, minstrel shows had developed a panoply of Black stereotypes performed by whites in blackface. Over time, these blackface characters became so ingrained in American culture that they and variations of them became fixtures in print media, vaudeville, theater, radio, television, and film long after minstrel shows themselves faded into obscurity. To keep pace with the seemingly boundless popularity of blackface imagery, the term "blackface" itself expanded beyond live stage performances. It now functionally encompasses almost any form of explicit, and sometimes implicit, false representations of African American physical appearance or mannerisms, especially when advanced by white creators for white audiences and consumers (Sammond 2015). Some of these stereotypes originated prior to the minstrel era, while others were the creations of minstrel performers themselves. Sambo, a "simple-minded Black man . . . flourished during the reign of slavery" and embodied the image of a "happy slave" (Green 1998). Jim Crow, the creation of early blackface white performer Thomas D. Rice, was a Black urban fop. A later version of Jim Crow, Zip Coon, was a freed enslaved person, also foppish, who made "clumsy attempts at sophisticated speech" ("Minstrel Structure and Iconography" n.d.). Hannah, a desirable young mulatto woman, evoked suggestions of interracial sex. Mammy, a mother figure and another happy slave or servant, doted extravagantly on children in her care, be they white or Black (Pilgrim 2000).

The popularity of the traditional minstrel show peaked in the late nineteenth century, but blackface minstrelsy left an enduring vexing legacy to American culture and society as a whole. Popular culture research is replete with studies of how nineteenth-century blackface minstrel stereotypes have narrowed white audience expectations for African Americans' capabilities and restricted opportunities for African Americans entering the entertainment, sports, and communications industries. More significantly, as the most popular form of American entertainment in the decades following the Civil War, minstrelsy perpetuated the idea throughout American society that Blacks were inferior to whites (Clark 2019). That legacy's sustained corrosive presence in American culture factored heavily in the original inspiration for and commercial demise of *The Scottsboro Boys* on Broadway.

For the defense: the NAACP versus the Communist Party

The Scottsboro Boys accurately conveys that the American Communist Party (Communist Party USA), headquartered in New York City, became interested in the Scottsboro case shortly after the Scottsboro Boys' original arrests were made public. A representative of the party attended the trial in Scottsboro and quickly persuaded the party's legal arm, International Labor Defense (ILD), to offer legal representation to the defendants in appealing their convictions and sentences. The ILD sent an attorney, Joseph Brodsky (not portrayed in the musical), to Scottsboro in April of 1931 just after the convictions and death sentences were announced. Gaining the confidence of the defendants and their family members, Brodsky became lead counsel for the Scottsboro case. He promptly filed and won a stay of the eight death sentences and filed appeals of the original convictions to the Alabama State Supreme Court.

The National Association for the Advancement of Colored People (NAACP), the nation's pre-eminent African Americans' advocacy organization since its founding in 1909, also sought to involve themselves in the Scottsboro case. More deliberative than the ILD, the NAACP did not commit to offering legal support until after Brodsky and the ILD had secured their position as defense counsel for the defendants. Over the next several months, the NAACP and the Communist Party engaged in a "vicious fight for the allegiance of the defendants" (Mack 2006). As part of the ILD legal strategy, the Communist Party sensationalized the case with demonstrations, protests, letter-writing campaigns, fundraisers, and news releases. The party hoped to arouse public outrage over the Black defendants' plight as well as enhance their organization's recruitment efforts, particularly among African Americans. By early 1932 the NAACP, more accustomed to operating through established channels (courts cases, legislative lobbying, etc.) than inflammatory mass action, temporarily withdrew their outreach to the Scottsboro defendants. However, as the Scottsboro case dragged on, the NAACP soon joined in the defense, finding themselves again both allied and at loggerheads with the ILD.

The tug-of-war between the two organizations over the Scottsboro case served as a microcosm of a larger dispute that had been brewing for a few years among lawyers and other advocates for racial equality. During the 1910s and 1920s, the NAACP had established a strong record of legislative advances on behalf of African Americans (e.g., the anti-lynching bill in Congress) and achieved important Supreme Court victories (e.g., having local ordinances forbidding Blacks from owning real estate declared unconstitutional). However, some racial justice advocates, including attorneys working with the ILD, argued that the NAACP's legal-centered approach to achieving racial equality "should be replaced or supplemented by direct-action and mass-based economic and political activity" (Mack 2006: 38). The NAACP strongly disagreed, advocating staying the course with their strategy of pursuing legal action within established systems and procedures.

The Scottsboro appeals, retrials, and plea arraignments, which lasted from 1931 to 1938, were the principal vehicles for playing out this debate in real time. Although membership in both the NAACP and the Communist Party was open to people of all races, the majority of NAACP's lead lawyers were African American and virtually all of the lead Communist Party lawyers were white. Among the latter, several were Jewish, including the Scottsboro Boys' two most prominent attorneys: Brodsky and Samuel Leibowitz, the latter hired by the ILD in 1933 to handle the first of the retrials ordered by the Supreme Court. (Leibowitz appears in the musical played on Broadway by Black actor Forrest McClendon). For its part, the State of Alabama, which, from Leibowitz's point of view, was fully aware of the egregious injustices being perpetrated upon the Scottsboro Boys, persisted in retrying and resentencing the defendants to death nonetheless ("The Scottsboro Defense Attorney" 2001). The state's persistence was, at least in part, an act of defiance against the campaign of ridicule and disdain being waged against Alabama by the very same Northern Communist Jewish "outsiders" who were mounting the expensive, time-consuming Scottsboro appeals. (The musical reflects accurately that an Alabama prosecutor used Leibowitz's Jewishness to discredit the Scottsboro defendants at trial, stating "Is justice in the case going to be bought and sold in Alabama with Jew money from New York?" [Schloss 2011].)

The ILD's aggressive publicity campaign during the protracted legal proceedings encompassed practically everything surrounding the case and helped reshape the forms and functions of American political activism for years to come: "Scottsboro united radicals, liberals, and moderates, as well as Blacks and whites, in a common—if often contentious—alliance" (Salter 2008). In so doing, the case established a model for issue-centered political coalition-building that has seen numerous reiterations in American politics and protest movements ever since, particularly in the Civil Rights Movement of the 1950s and 1960s and the Vietnam War protests in the 1960s and 1970s.

The Scottsboro Boys and the Supreme Court I

Powell v Alabama Although referenced briefly in the musical, the Supreme Court decisions that overturned the Scottsboro Boys' original and subsequent convictions became landmark cases for bringing matters of race, economic class, and even personal circumstances to bear on legal interpretations of the 6th Amendment to the Constitution. The 6th Amendment guarantees criminal defendants the right to trial including access to a lawyer ("the assistance of counsel") and a jury of one's peers. The first Scottsboro-related Supreme Court case (*Powell v. Alabama*, 1932) marked the first time the Supreme Court ever reversed a lower court conviction for failure to appoint or otherwise ensure "effective counsel" for the defense. The Court's decision "ratified and constitutionalized" *effective* counsel assistance (emphasis added) as a right of all criminal defendants under the 6th Amendment (Mayeux 2014).

Prior to reaching the Supreme Court in 1932, the previous court proceedings for the Scottsboro defendants included the original trial in Scottsboro and an appeal to the Alabama Supreme Court (the latter not referenced in the musical). In the original Scottsboro trial, the prosecution tried the nine defendants in four separate rapid-fire trials before the same judge between April 6 and 9, 1931. All nine defendants were convicted of rape. Eight defendants were sentenced to death and one, Roy Wright, presumed to be the youngest, was sentenced to life in prison. Brodsky's ILD defense team appealed unsuccessfully to the Alabama Supreme Court in July 1932, the court upholding eight of the nine convictions and seven of the eight death sentences.

Brodsky's ILD team then appealed to the Supreme Court on the basis of racial discrimination, arguing that the lower courts violated the defendants' "equal civil and legal rights" granted by the 14th Amendment to "all persons born or naturalized in the United States" (Wallenfeldt 2009). The Supreme Court (Court) ruled favorably on the appeal by 7–2 but, in the majority opinion written by Chief Justice George Sutherland, focused on violations of the defendants' 6th Amendment right to "the assistance of counsel" at the original trial in Scottsboro. The Court noted that the defendants' two court-appointed attorneys for all four trials were assigned on the trial's first day while the first case was already in progress. Both attorneys' lack of preparation and fitness to represent the defendants were baldly transparent through trial transcripts, as was the Scottsboro presiding judge's wholesale disregard of the defense attorneys' incompetence. The Supreme Court held that the Scottsboro court's meager efforts to meet the barest literal requirements to provide defendants with "assistance of counsel" were tantamount to denying them legal representation altogether:

- "Defendants were arraigned, and pleaded not guilty . . . [without ever being] asked whether they had, or were able to, employ counsel."
- "The court inquired whether the parties were ready for trial. The State's attorney replied that he was . . . No one answered for the defendants or appeared to represent or defend them."
- "A defendant should be afforded a fair opportunity to secure counsel of his own choice . . . that [was] not done here . . . such designation of counsel . . . amount[ed] to a denial of effective and substantial aid in that regard" (Sutherland 1932).

The legacy of the Powell decision as it addressed the 6th Amendment right to assistance of counsel was that for criminal defendants, regardless of socio-economic status or individual capability, access to *effective* (emphasis added) legal representation, including competence of counsel and adequate preparation time, is guaranteed under the Constitution.

Although the Sutherland decision was limited to capital cases, over time the Court expanded the application of "Powell" to apply to the rights of effective counsel in all criminal trials. *Powell v. Alabama* established a test, based on the idea of "fundamental fairness," that would guide the Supreme Court over the next fifty years in weighing government's obligation to provide effective counsel to defendants who could not otherwise afford or acquire it ("Understanding Powell v. Alabama" n.d.).

The Scottsboro Boys and the Supreme Court II

Norris v. Alabama and Patterson v. Alabama, 1935 Notwithstanding the Supreme Court's 1932 decision ordering new trials for the eight Scottsboro defendants convicted as adults, delays and legal setbacks continued to plague their case for years. The first Scottsboro defendants retried as a result of *Powell v. Alabama* were Clarence Norris and Haywood Patterson in 1933. Notwithstanding the IDL lawyers' rigorous defense and the transparently flawed prosecution—essentially the same prosecution from the original trial—Patterson and Norris were convicted in a local Alabama court and sentenced to death yet again. The Alabama Supreme Court upheld those convictions on appeal, yet again, in 1934.

In 1935, the Supreme Court agreed to hear Norris and Patterson's appeals of their latest convictions with Leibowitz joining other IDL lawyers on the case. This time Norris and Patterson's attorneys argued that, in their separate 1933 convictions and sentencing, both defendants were denied equal right to an impartial jury by the undisputed fact that local officials had purged all African Americans from the local jury rolls. The State of Alabama did not deny that the jury pool was all-white by design but argued that such action fell rightfully within the purview of state procedure and, therefore, the Supreme Court had no jurisdiction to rule on Norris and Patterson's convictions on that basis. In a unanimous decision, the Court held that systematically excluding African Americans from official jury pools denied the defendants their 14th Amendment right to "equal protection of the laws" by virtue of their race. In so doing the Court invalidated Norris and Patterson's convictions.

The Norris and Patterson cases established the precedent that systematic exclusion of Blacks from jury pools represented a *de facto* violation of a defendant's 6th Amendment right to an impartial jury and 14th Amendment rights of equal protection. The Patterson and Norris cases established that "the South could not return to a system that used all-white juries and expect the federal courts to uphold their decisions" (Roberts 2009).

Thomas A. Greenfield and Mary C. Hanrahan

Further reading

Brown, Scott. 2010. "Theater Review: The Brilliant Blunt Force of *The Scottsboro Boys*." *New Magazine*, October 31, 2010.

Carone, Angela. 2012. "Controversial 'Scottsboro Boys' at Old Globe." *KPBS Transcript*, April 27, 2012, https://www.kpbs.org/news/2012/apr/27/controversial-scottsboro-boys-old-globe/.

Clark, Alexis. 2019. "How the History of Blackface Is Rooted in Racism." *History*, February 15, 2019.

Clark, John. 2012. "Susan Stroman Finds Empowerment in *The Scottsboro Boys*." *Los Angeles Times*, May 4, 2012.

Dixon, Brandon Victor, Colman Domingo, Susan Haskins, John Kander, Michael Riedel, and Susan Stroman. "Theater Talk: 'The Scottsboro Boys'" Composer John Kander, Director Susan Stroman. *YouTube.com*, May 13, 2011. https://www.youtube.com/watch?v=q1PJGnaoSKo.

Douglass, Frederick. 1848. "The North Star." *Uncle Tom's Cabin & American Yorker Culture: A Multi-media Archive*. Charlottesville: University of Virginia. http://utc.iath.virginia.edu/minstrel/miar03bt.html.

Dziemianowicz, Joe. 2010. "'Scottsboro Boys' Review: Split Personality Play Leaves You Zigzagging between Parody and Poignancy." *Daily News*, November 1, 2010.

Gamerman, Ellen. 2010. "Fall Flops: Broadway Season of Early Curtains." *Wall Street Journal*, December 10, 2010.

Gardner, Lyn. 2014. "The Scottsboro Boys Review—A Dazzling Civil Rights Musical." *Guardian*, October 20, 2014.

Green, Laura. 1998. "Summary of Stereotypes: Negative Racial Stereotypes and Their Effect on Attitudes toward African Americans." *The Jim Crow Museum of Racist Memorabilia*. Ferris State University, https://www.ferris.edu/htmls/news/jimcrow/links/essays/vcu.htm.

Grovesnor, Edwin S. and Robert C. Toll. 2019. "Blackface: The Sad History of Minstrel Shows." *American Heritage Magazine* 64, no. 1 (Winter), https://www.americanheritage.com/blackface-sad-history-minstrel-shows.

Healy, Patrick. 2010. "Scottsboro Boys Is Focus of Protest." *New York Times*, November 11, 2010.

Isherwood, Charles. 2010a. "Revisiting an Outrage with Gallows Humor." *New York Times*, October 31, 2010.

Isherwood, Charles. 2010b. "Theatrical Stumbles of Historical Proportions." *New York Times*, December 10, 2010.

Jones, Kenneth. 2010. "Protesters Take Aim at Scottsboro Boys Musical." *Playbill*, November 8, 2010.

Mack, Kenneth W. 2006. "Law and Mass Politics in the Making of the Civil Rights Lawyer, 1931–1941." *Journal of American History* 93, no. 1 (June): 37–62.

Marlowe, Sam. 2014. "The Scottsboro Boys, Garrick Theatre, WC2." *The Times*, October 21, 2014.

Mayeux, Sara 2014. "Ineffective Assistance of Counsel before Powell v. Alabama: Lessons from History for the Future of the Right to Counsel." *Iowa Law Review* 99, no. 5 (July): 2161–84.

McCall, Tulis. 2010. "The Scottsboro Boys." *New York Theatre Guide*, March 11, 2010, www.newyorktheatreguide.com/reviews/the-scottsboro-boys.

McNulty, Charles. 2010. "Theater Review: 'The Scottsboro Boys' at the Lyceum Theatre." *Los Angeles Times*, October 31, 2010, https://latimesblogs.latimes.com/culturemonster/2010/10/theater-review-the-scottsboro-boys-at-the-lyceum-theatre-1.html.

Mellini, Michael. 2010. "What's Up, John Kander?" *BroadwayBuzz*, October 8, 2010, www.broadway.com/ buzz/153832/whats-up-john-kander-the-legendary-composer-talks-scottsboro-boys-cabaret-and-liza/.

"Minstrel Structure and Iconography." n.d. https://exhibits.lib.usf.edu/exhibits/show/minstrelsy.

Pilgrim, David. 2000. "The Mammy Caricature." *Jim Crow Museum of Racist Memorabilia*, https://www.ferris.edu/jimcrow/mammies/.

"Powell v. Alabama." 2008. *West's Encyclopedia of American Law*, Edition 2, https://legal-dictionary.thefreedictionary.com/Powell+v.+Alabama.

Ransdell, Hollace. 1931. "Report on the Scottsboro, Alabama Case." *American Civil Liberties Union*, May 27, 1931. *David Linder, Famous Trials*, https://famous-trials.com.

Roberts, Charles Kenneth. 2009. "Patterson v Alabama." *Encyclopedia of Alabama*, January 7, 2009, www.encyclopediaofalabama.org/article/h-1899.

Rooney, David. 2010. "The Scottsboro Boys: Theater Review." *Hollywood Reporter*, October 31, 2010.

Salter, Daren. 2008. "Scottsboro Trials." *Encyclopedia of Alabama*. Revised 2017, http:// www.encyclopediaofalabama.org/article/h-1456.

Sammond, Nicholas. 2015. "Twenty-first Century Blackface." *Birth of an Industry: Blackface Minstrelsy and the Rise of American Animation*, https://scalar.usc.edu/works/birthofanindustry/index.

Schloss, Eva. 2011. "Scottsboro: A Southern Tragedy, a Jewish Controversy." *Southern Jewish Life*, March 9, 2011.

Scott, Mack. 2014. "From Blackface to Beulah: Subtle Subversion in Early Black Sitcoms." *Journal of Contemporary History* 49, no. 4 (October): 743–69.

"The Scottsboro Defense Attorney." 2001. *American Experience*, PBS, www.pbs.org/wgbh/americanexperience/features/scottsboro-defense-attorney-samuel-leibowitz/.

"Sixth Amendment." n.d. *Legal Information Institute*. Cornell University Law School, www.law.cornell.edu/constitution/sixth_amendment.

Sutherland, George. 1932. "Opinion: Powell v Alabama." *Legal Information Institute*, Cornell University School of Law, www.law.cornell.edu/supremecourt/text/287/45#writing-USSC_CR_0287_0045_ZO.

Teachout, Terry. 2010. "A Perilous Page of History to Turn." *Wall Street Journal*, November 1, 2010.

"Understanding Powell v. Alabama." n.d. *Sixth Amendment Center*, https://sixthamendment.org/the-right-to-counsel/history-of-the-right-to-counsel/understanding-powell-v-alabama/.

Vincentelli, Elisabeth. 2010. "Great 'Scott'! A classic." *New York Post*, November 1, 2010.

Wallenfeldt, Jeff. 2009. "Fourteenth Amendment." *Encyclopedia Britannica*, April 14, 2009.

CHAPTER 18

1776 (1969, REV. 1997)

Book by Peter Stone (1930–2003)
Music and Lyrics by Sherman Edwards (1919–81)
Broadway Premiere: 46th Street Theatre, March 16, 1969–December 27, 1970; St. James Theatre, December 28, 1970–March 24, 1971; Majestic Theatre, March 27, 1971–February 13, 1972
Broadway Revival: Criterion Center Stage Right, August 14, 1997–November 16, 1997; Gershwin Theatre, December 3, 1997–June 14, 1998

Songs

"Overture"
"Sit Down, John"
"Piddle, Twiddle and Resolve"
"Till Then"
"The Lees of Old Virginia"
"But, Mr. Adams"
"Yours, Yours, Yours"
"He Plays the Violin"
"Cool, Cool Considerate Men"
"Momma, Look Sharp"
"The Egg"
"Molasses to Rum"
"Compliments"
"Is Anybody There?"
"Finale"

Overview

1776 explores events surrounding the Second Continental Congress debate in Philadelphia over whether the American colonies should declare their independence from the British monarchy and, if so, upon what specific rationale and terms would such a declaration rest. Covering the period from early May to July 4, 1776, the musical focuses upon the Second Continental Congress itself (hereinafter "Congress"): the delegates' key debates over the pros and cons of declaring independence, the drafting of a declaration document, and the suspense surrounding the independence vote, whose outcome—in both the musical and in Philadelphia at the time—was uncertain until crucial votes were cast.

This two-month period saw the culmination of a decade of escalating friction between the American colonies and their British rulers as well as factionalism among the colonies themselves. In that short period of time, a handful of people confronting an extraordinary moment in American history emerged variously as principled, self-serving, courageous, petty, tedious, and visionary founders of a new country.

In April 1775, long-standing tensions between the American colonies and the British, largely over taxes levied by the British in the 1760s, erupted into full-armed conflict: the Revolutionary War. After the initial battles at Lexington and Concord in Massachusetts, Congress created and dispatched a Continental Army led by General George Washington to fight for the rights of the colonies. At the beginning of the war, Congress favored remaining loyal to the Crown despite Britain's abuses and acts of oppression. The vocal minority that desired independence, most notably John Adams, was considered radical by the majority of the Congressional delegates. However, in 1775, King George III sent British armed forces to America for the purpose of forcibly putting an end to various rebellious actions on the part of the colonials. The British troops escalated their violence against the colonies, deepening American resentments against the king. In January 1776, Thomas Paine's pamphlet *Common Sense*, which entreated the colonists to fight for their "natural right" of independence, sold more than 75,000 copies in a matter of weeks and intensified support for independence throughout the colonies. By early 1776, colonial sentiment for independence had grown significantly among the general population but had not produced a clear consensus within Congress. British loyalists still exercised considerable influence throughout the colonies.

The main action of the musical *1776* recounts a generally accurate, if predictably embellished, calendar-driven order of events leading up to Congress' decision to declare America's independence from Britain. Edwards and Stone place John Adams at the center of the historical moment, as a corrective to perhaps overly bright spotlights typically shone on some other Founding Fathers—Thomas Jefferson and Ben Franklin in particular.

As it did in Philadelphia, suspense surrounding the outcome of the independence debate on stage builds to a climax between June 7 and July 4, 1776—a chronology the musical follows faithfully (with some dating adjustments at the very end). On June 7, Virginia delegate Richard Henry Lee proposed a resolution for independence that already had been approved by the Virginia legislature. The majority of colonies were now supportive of independence and prepared to vote on Lee's resolution. On June 11, Congress theoretically approved the resolution by a vote of 7 to 5 (New York abstained). However, Congress also resolved to postpone a final ratification for three weeks to cool heated tempers before rendering a final decision. In the interim, Congress assigned a committee of five delegates to draw up a written rationale for independence. From the five, Thomas Jefferson was chosen to draft what would become the *Declaration of Independence*. On July 2, Congress reconvened and voted unanimously (with New York abstaining again) to adopt Lee's resolution for independence. Congress deliberated on numerous proposed revisions to the *Declaration*, large and small, until its adoption on July 4, 1776. Five days later, the New York delegation officially approved the resolution. The *Declaration* was actually signed by the majority of delegates on August 2, with several signing thereafter. However, in keeping with audience expectation and national tradition, *1776* enshrines July 4 as *the* day when it happens.

Although no longer a novelty, Broadway musicals featuring real historical characters and well-known historical events were a rarity prior to 1969. The shortlived *Ben Franklin in Paris* (1964) focused on Franklin's diplomatic residency in France during the Revolutionary War, a significant but rather obscure event in most Americans' general understanding of the struggle for independence. *I'd Rather Be Right* by George S. Kaufman and Moss Hart (1937) was a farcical satire on current events. In 1969, the creators of *1776* were exploring relatively new territory for American musical theater productions and they knew it.

Conceptualized by composer-lyricist Sherman Edwards, a New York City-based history teacher and pop hit songwriter ("See You in September," "Wonderful Wonderful"), *1776* is the product of Edwards' scholarly passion for Revolutionary War era and his facility for songwriting. In his early forties, Edwards quit his teaching job to write a musical about the behind-the-scenes story of the *Declaration of Independence*. Once Edwards wrote some songs, he began pitching various playwrights to collaborate with him on a script, only to meet continuous rejection. In the mid-1960s, straightforward patriotic content struck potential collaborators as out-of-step with growing social unrest over civil rights and America's controversial involvement in the Vietnam War. However, two fledgling theater artists in their early thirties, producer-director Stuart Ostrow and writer Peter Stone, saw themes of revolution, insurgency, and social relevance in Edwards' ideas. They teamed up with Edwards and proceeded to develop the full work.

Understanding that virtually every member of the audience would know the main characters and outcome of the plot in advance, the creative team faced the challenge of adhering carefully to historical fact while monitoring closely their exercises of poetic license. Fortunately, the history of Congress' deliberations in 1776 provided several gifts to the writers. First, the "lead up" to the signing embodied its own line of suspense: the relatively unfamiliar fact that the outcome of Congress' vote on the "Declaration" was still in doubt on July 2 and could have gone either way.

History's second gift to the creative team was the eminently "writable" delegate, John Adams. Among the most outspoken and fervent of the early advocates for independence, Adams was relentlessly provocative in pushing Congress toward approval. To his famous self-description, "obnoxious and disliked," his contemporaries added difficult, prone to jealousy, and all but devoid of diplomatic grace. In *1776*, Adams begins as an outsider among his Congressional peers and tirelessly fights his way to victory for American independence. Broadway loves outsiders who prevail. Although Adams' outsider status or "otherness" is not in the order of Liza Doolittle's in *My Fair Lady* or the eponymous musical biographies of Alexander Hamilton or Andrew Jackson, history afforded Edwards and Stone enough evidence to set Adams on a traditional storybook hero's narrative arc from group rejection to triumph, acceptance, and personal redemption.

Most importantly, while political debate can appear lifeless as news coverage, it can also be effective as precisely what it is—a theatrical presentation. Each speaker assumes an elevated space and moment in the room. The "players" are afforded a few improvisational liberties such as minor disruptions of order as well as strategic entrances and exits. An audience of peers judges the performance immediately. Edwards and Stone made the Second Continental Congress' stage their stage as well. In so doing they provided ample opportunity for their Founding Father characters to show off their theatrical chops. History tells us—as do Edwards and Stone—that during the debates over the "Declaration," many of the real Founding Fathers did precisely that.

To underscore the centrality of debate and argument, *1776* contains long stretches of dialogue (sometimes upwards of thirty minutes) without music—a highly unusual occurrence in Broadway musicals, especially considering that in the 1960s original cast record albums were more popular than they are now. Furthermore, the show opens in a blast of verbally contentious rhetoric. A crescendo of triumphant drumming and wind instruments introduces the first song, "Sit Down, John." This number offers a combination back-and-forth debate and verbal gang fight between John Adams and an aggravated exhausted chorus of fellow delegates. "Adams: Vote for Independency / Congress: Will someone shut that man up? / Adams: Never." Here Edwards and Stone serve notice that that verbal oneupmanship, whether by intellectual acuity or emotional intensity, will be the order of the first day and the days that follow. We understand immediately that Adams is going to have to win the delegates and the audience around to independence with something other than "Broadway" charm. Spoiler alert: he succeeds.

1776 was a solid hit show. The first Broadway run lasted for 1,217 performances and nearly three full years, winning three Tony Awards including Best Musical. Strong critical reviews and audience support gave the show enough momentum to inspire Warner Brothers to adapt *1776* for a film (1972), with many original cast members reprising their Broadway roles. A disappointing 1997 Broadway revival closed after only 333 performances. However, interest in *1776* has remained alive and well through tours and local productions. Another Broadway revival, originally announced for the 2020–1 season was postponed due to Covid 19. It opened October 6, 2022 and closed on January 8, 2026. Hoping to benefit from *Hamilton*'s success with radical casting, producers filled the Philadelphia room where it happened with a multiracial cast of women, trans, and non-binary actors. Reviews were mixed but even many detractors saw merit in the casting and the actors' efforts to make a new statement with very familiar material.

Plot synopsis

The play opens to a tableau of the Second Continental Congress in Philadelphia as delegates leisurely sit at tables waiting to discuss the next issue. John Adams, agitated by the lack of serious debate, urges Congress to declare independence from British rule. His pleas are ignored as other delegates, momentarily united, complain about the heat and demand that Adams stop talking ("Sit Down, John"). Adams storms out of the chamber and looks to heaven for guidance ("Piddle, Twiddle and Resolve"). His wife Abigail appears to him in his imagination. He asks if she is making saltpeter for the war effort, but she pleads for straight pins instead. They affectionately bicker and then declare their love for one another ("Till Then").

The next day, Adams meets with Benjamin Franklin and acknowledges his failure to argue persuasively for independence. Franklin suggests finding a more popular member of Congress to propose the issue. Upon Franklin's invitation, Richard Henry Lee enters and, citing his pedigree as a member of America's finest established family, concurs that he is the best man for the job ("The Lees of Old Virginia").

In the Congressional chamber delegates enter and converse with one another before the President of Congress, John Hancock, calls the meeting to order. Lee enters with a resolve for independence. A vote is called and each state is polled. New York abstains, but the rest of the colonies persist in great debate. Congress is closely divided on the question of independence. Adams, leader of the pro-independence delegates, encounters a formidable anti-independence counterpart in John Dickinson of Pennsylvania. Adams argues that Britain's tyrannical rule and oppressive taxes are intolerable, whereas Dickinson extols the virtue of loyalty to the Crown. The delegates eventually determine that they need more time to consider where they all stand. Dickinson moves that a unanimous vote be required for approval of any independence measure in order to ensure that the colonies remain united. A vote on Dickinson's proposal produces a tie, which Hancock breaks in favor of unanimity. Adams, angered by this decision, moves for a postponement to give time for a declaration to be written, defining the reasons and goals for independence. This vote also results in a tie that Hancock breaks in favor of postponement.

Congress appoints five delegates to draft the declaration: Benjamin Franklin, John Adams, Roger Sherman, Robert Livingston, and Thomas Jefferson. The five meet to determine who among them should write the document. Adams passes a pen to each man, but each demurs in turn, explaining why another man is better suited to the task ("But, Mr. Adams"). Ultimately, Adams convinces Jefferson to stay in Pennsylvania and write the declaration instead of returning home to his wife for whom he yearns.

A week later, Adams and Franklin call on Jefferson to assess his progress only to learn that Jefferson, complaining that he is distracted, is unable to write. Adams, having anticipated this difficulty, has summoned Jefferson's wife, Martha, who appears in the room. Jefferson and Martha embrace, unaware of anyone else around them. Adams leaves, imagining another conversation with Abigail. Again, they exchange words and pledge their love for one another ("Yours, Yours, Yours"). The following morning Adams and Franklin return to Jefferson's quarters. As Jefferson continues to sleep, they meet Martha and ask how so lovely a woman as she fell for a man like Jefferson. She responds that his musical talent won her over ("He Plays the Violin").

On June 22, Congress reconvenes. Adams, worried about the impending vote, lobbies some reluctant delegates to vote for independence. A courier delivers a dispatch from General Washington which Congressional Secretary Charles Thompson reads aloud. Washington castigates the unprofessional conduct of the Continental soldiers and requests a Congressional visit to strengthen troop discipline. Adams volunteers and invites Samuel Chase of Maryland to join him, assuring Chase that the war is going much better than Washington says. Chase accepts and promises to support independence if Adams is correct.

All remaining delegates in favor of independence leave the chamber as Dickinson leads fellow royalist delegates in a minuet, proclaiming their desire to keep their land and wealth under British rule ("Cool, Cool

Considerate Men"). Another dispatch from Washington, which Congress ignores, warns about impending British advances. All remaining delegates depart the chamber, leaving custodian Andrew McNair, the courier, and a workman. The courier recounts his gruesome experiences on the warfront including seeing a soldier's mother searching for her son's body ("Momma, Look Sharp").

Outside the chamber Jefferson waits as the secretary reads his declaration to Congress. Adams and Franklin meet him cheerfully, having convinced Samuel Chase to support independence after visiting the Continental Army. They commend Jefferson on the excellence of the document and equate the creation of this new country to the hatching of an egg. The three men debate which bird would best represent America and agree on the eagle ("The Egg").

On June 28, Congress meets to discuss suggested alterations to the "Declaration" document. Jefferson consents to many of the suggestions until Dickinson demands removal of a phrase calling the king a "tyrant," fearing it will offend friends in Parliament. Further complications arise as Edward Rutledge of South Carolina objects to a clause in the "Declaration" condemning the slave trade. Rutledge accuses the Northern colonies of hypocrisy, asserting that the North prospers from the slave trade as much as the South prospers from slave labor ("Molasses to Rum"). When Jefferson refuses to remove the clause, the delegates from the Carolinas and Georgia storm out of the chamber. Other delegates leave as Franklin tells a dejected Adams that the slavery clause must be deleted to secure the vote for independence. Needing encouragement again, Adams consults his image of Abigail to strengthen his morale. Suddenly, kegs of saltpeter from his wife are delivered to him ("Compliments").

Alone in the chamber, Adams rereads a discouraging dispatch from Washington and relates Washington's plight to his own ("Is Anybody There?"). As Adams declares his vision of a new nation, seemingly to himself, Dr. Lyman Hall of Georgia appears. Lyman walks to the vote tally board and changes Georgia's vote in favor of independence.

The action shifts to July 2, as each delegation is called to vote. Except for Pennsylvania, which passes, and New York, which once again abstains, all remaining Northern and middle colonies vote "yea." When the vote reaches South Carolina, Rutledge agrees to vote "yea" only upon removal of the slavery clause. Jefferson reluctantly scratches out the clause as the Carolinas and Georgia all vote "yea." The last colony required for a unanimous approval is Pennsylvania, whose three-man delegation is polled individually. Franklin votes "yea" and Dickinson votes "nay." James Wilson, a lawyer from central Pennsylvania, hesitates . . . and votes "yea." With the motion passing, Hancock submits that all Congressional delegates must sign the "Declaration." Dickinson refuses to do so and resigns from Congress.

On July 4, 1776, Hancock leads the delegates in a signing ceremony. McNair rings the Liberty Bell as each delegate is called up to sign their name to the *Declaration of Independence*. As the last man signs, the delegates freeze in a tableau. The bottom half of the *Declaration of Independence* featuring the signatures is revealed to the audience.

Critical reception

1776 premiered on Broadway at the 46th Street Theatre on March 16, 1969. At first, the novel premise of the musical concerned some critics. Many shared the initial apprehensions of *Des Moines Register* critic William Glover: "Whoever heard of a musical enacted in powdered wigs, with no chorus girls [and] little dancing . . . And about history—American history at that?" (Glover 1969). However, to the surprise of many the show was an instant hit. Despite the seemingly incongruous juxtaposition of the musical's flag-waving patriotic content against the tumultuous political climate of the day, critics such as the *New York Times*' Clive Barnes saluted the show's improbable achievement: "few historical incidents seem more unlikely to spawn a Broadway musical . . . Yet, *1776* . . . is consistently exciting and entertaining" (Barnes 1969). Theophilus Lewis in *America Magazine* was so taken with *1776* that he considered "describing the production as great and then work up from there" (Lewis 1969). Peter Stone's book was praised frequently. Writing in *Newsweek*, Jack Kroll saluted the script's "intelligence and style," sentiments echoed by Barnes in the *Times* (Kroll 1969). The *Wall Street Journal* was also fulsome in its praise: "first-rate as musical entertainment and as a semi-documentary. It is absorbing and exciting" (Cooke 1969). In a hyperbolic retrospective on the original production, critic Peter Filichia channeled John Adams' appraisal of the *Declaration of Independence* to praise Stone's libretto: "It's a masterpiece, I say; they will cheer ev'ry word, ev'ry letter" (Filichia 1997). But for a few dissenters, critics were impressed by the realistic characterizations and the actors' portrayals of the historic figures. The *New York Post*'s Richard Watts appreciated that *1776* "makes no attempt to romanticize the Founding Fathers. It shows the delegates to the Continental Congress . . . as a group of highly fallible, quarrelsome and sometimes pig-headed men" (Watts 1969). Barnes felt the "characterizations are most unusually full for a musical" and that director Peter Hunt "encouraged his actors to behave precisely as if they were in a play rather than a musical" (Barnes 1969). Barnes also hailed William Daniels' portrayal of John Adams as embodying a "beautiful mixture of pride, ambition, an almost priggish sense of justice" (Barnes 1969). Kroll, however, while praising the cast as a whole, offered a rare rebuke of Daniels' "small-scale emotional range" (Kroll 1969). Nevertheless, Daniels and Howard Da Silva (as Ben Franklin) were so popular that they were invited to reprise their lead roles in the Warner Brothers 1972 film adaptation of *1776*. Several other members of the original Broadway cast also reprised their roles in the film.

The Broadway production of *1776* ran for an impressive 1,217 performances over the course of three years. The show received five Tony nominations, winning three: the highly coveted Best Musical as well as Best Direction of a Musical for Peter Hunt and Best Featured Actor in a Musical for Ronald Holgate as Richard Henry Lee.

Following the initial production, *1776* toured for two years. The show was revived on Broadway nearly thirty years later at the Criterion Center Stage Right Theatre on August 14, 1997. Although not as successful as the original production (only running for 333 performances), the revival garnered positive reviews, many echoing those of the original production. While declaring it to be "gratingly corny" and the "squarest thing on Times Square," Ben Brantley reviewing for the *Times* acknowledged that the *1776* revival "finds dramatic suspense in a most familiar plot" (Brantley 1997). The *Daily News*' Howard Kissel found himself caught up in the unlikely suspense of the musical, admitting to having spent three hours "on the edge of his seat" wondering how the musical would come out (Kissel 1997). As with the original production, critics hailed Peter Stone's superb book and characterizations. Brantley admired the "specific, discrete identities of each of the score of delegates at the Congress" and noted that the writing had imbued the story with "enough troubled shading . . . to remind us that great events are often shaped by mixed motives and less-than-noble emotions" (Brantley 1997). Linda Bloom, writing in *Curtain Up*, agreed: "the well-tuned ensemble delivers an entertaining and, at times, compelling production in which even the smallest of parts is sharply drawn" (Bloom 1997). Greg Evans of *Variety* lauded Stone's ability to "give each of the 20 representatives and seven other characters a personality as easily identifiable as it is [*sic*] captivating." Evans also praised the revival cast: Pat Hingle's Benjamin Franklin "strikes the perfect blend of wisdom, compassion and humor" and Brent Spiner's John Adams "brings the prickly character to life" (Evans 1997). The Broadway revival of *1776* was nominated for three Tony awards in 1997, including Best Revival of a Musical, but garnered no wins.

Notwithstanding Sherman Edwards' background as a successful composer of hit pop songs, critics of both the original production and the 1997 revival tended to be less enthusiastic about his score and songs than they were about the show's book and cast performances. Astoundingly, the original *1776* production won the Tony for Best Musical without producing one hit song for radio airplay or record sales. By contrast, the score for *Hair*, which *1776* bested for Best Musical, generated no fewer than five hit singles. Critical response to the 1997 revival reflected mixed and ambivalent feelings about the music. Brantley found the strongest songs, such as "Sit Down, John," to be "full of cantankerous life" and "invigorating musical metaphors for the political process." However, "The Egg" and "He Plays the Violin" were not at all inspiring. The *Daily News* described the score as "cute" as well as "musically richer and more powerful" than expected. However, the songs "Momma, Look Sharp" and "He Plays the Violin" lacked the impact of the stronger pieces (Kissel 1997).

Since the opening of *Hamilton* (2015), the spectacularly successful historically-based musical about the Revolutionary War period, several professional theater companies have mounted productions of *1776*, hoping to capitalize on *Hamilton*'s success. To some extent, the attempt to wed *1776*'s fortunes to *Hamilton*'s has been successful. A Broadway revival of *1776* had been announced for the 2020–1 season with a subsequent run in Los Angeles. Writings on American history in film and theater (such as this book) touch on comparisons between the two musicals. Notably among these pairings is one that *Hamilton* composer and lyricist Lin-Manuel Miranda offered on behalf of the earlier show: "*1776* certainly paved the way for *Hamilton*—not just in that it's about our founders, but also in that it engages fully with their humanity" (Weinstock 2019).

Historical accuracy and context

John Adams: obnoxious, disliked . . . and underappreciated?

Aside from relatively minor fictionalizations, the representation of John Adams in *1776* is fundamentally accurate and based largely upon well-documented historical research and his own writings, as well as those of his wife Abigail and others who knew him. A Massachusetts-born, Harvard-educated lawyer, Adams became an early, unsparing critic of British policies toward the American colonies from the start of King George III's reign in 1760. Adams' speeches and writings against Writs of Assistance (1760), the Stamp Act (1765), and the Townshend Act (1767), which imposed restrictions on Americans' rights and new taxes on goods purchased in the colonies, established his reputation as a champion for independence prior to his election to the First Continental Congress in 1774.

"Obnoxious and disliked" (a phrase Stone and Edwards apply throughout the musical), Adams was aware of the negative perception others had of him and mindful that "my early and constant zeal in promoting [independence]" had complicated Congress' deliberations on the matter ("John Adams Autobiography" n.d.). To the writers' credit, the book for *1776* not only extracts dramatic tension and comedy from Adams' famous temperament but also sentimentality and touches of redemption in Adams' self-awareness—especially as he reveals himself in the imagined dialogs with wife Abigail. Although presented in the musical as Adams' interior monologues, the John-and-Abigail exchanges are grounded in the more than one thousand known letters John Adams and Abigail wrote to one another during the course of their marriage. Among the issues from their correspondences adapted for the musical are the need for saltpeter for the warfront and pins for the women, their children's illnesses, and a letter addressing Abigail's "Faults, Imperfections, Defects, or whatever you please to call them" ("Letter from John Adams . . . " n.d.). If *1776* has a petition to make, it is that America and history afford John Adams exalted status among the Founding Fathers to a degree comparable to that of more famous fellow delegates Thomas Jefferson and Benjamin Franklin. In Stone and Edwards' telling, Adams plays a singularly critical behind-the-scenes role in driving Congress and the nation to independence: pressing the issue even when support falters; winning over persuadable doubters; outmaneuvering entrenched opposition; playing to his own strengths; and strategically cultivating allies to shore up his shortcomings. Over time, Jefferson received more laurels for the sweeping, enduring power of his words, and Franklin earned iconic status as America's first internationally famous scientist, inventor, diplomat, and celebrity. Stone and Edwards' petition to secure Adams' greater glory is a question of historical interpretation not historical accuracy, but they have impressive support among American historians. David McCullough, Pulitzer Prize-winning biographer of Adams, deems Adams "the force behind the 'Declaration of Independence'" (McCullough 2006). Another biographer, John Ferling, credits Adams for "masterminding the arduous struggle" for independence in Congress (Ferling 1996). To be sure, as second President of the United States and father of the sixth, John Adams is hardly a victim of historical neglect. But for a musical to step credibly into a substantive debate in presidential history, as indeed *1776* does on this point, attests to the creators' serious-minded approach to the history behind the show.

1776 and the Congressional state delegations

With the main stage action focusing on two months of deliberating and politicking on the floor of the Second Continental Congress—activity for which no consensus authoritative transcripts or eyewitness accounts exist—Stone and Edwards annotated the published libretto of *1776* with a semi-confessional accounting of how they handled historical matters. In addition to proclaiming the historical accuracy of most of their work, Stone and Edwards detail things they knowingly altered, added, deleted, or rearranged. To make matters better, a Harvard University study group published a fact check of Edwards and Stone's treatment of the show's historical content (Sneff 2017). Overall, the Harvard study and other documents affirm that *1776*, within the confines of a two-hour scripted entertainment theater piece, is commendably researched and historically valuable.

The writers' most obvious and clearly necessary alteration comes in the number of Congressional delegates onstage versus the number of delegates at the Second Congressional Congress. The thirteen Congressional delegations sent a total of fifty-six delegates, including Congressional President and presiding officer John Hancock. The 46th Street Theatre struggled to contain the twenty delegates with named speaking roles (standing, strutting, cross-walking, etc. throughout) and the no more than twenty-six delegates and staff members (custodian, courier, etc.) in the chamber at any one time. In the musical, each colony has a three-member delegation, but in reality, delegation sizes varied. Among them, only Delaware actually had three delegates. All other delegations had four or more members.

Apart from their aforementioned positioning of John Adams as the key figure in the ratification process, Stone and Edwards fleshed out the personal dynamics among the delegates with a great deal of informed speculation about how they might have interacted. Perhaps the portrayal that plays most strikingly against audience expectation is that of the *Declaration's* heralded lead author Thomas Jefferson, pointedly *not* the central focus of the story. The musical introduces Jefferson as one of five potential but reluctant drafters of the *Declaration* in a gentle satire of how committees function ("But, Mr. Adams"). However, Adams' autobiography offers the more likely explanation that, by virtue of his renowned writing skills, Jefferson was Adams' first choice all along: "Jefferson had the Reputation of a masterly Pen . . . consequence of a very handsome public Paper which he had written for the [Virginia] House of Burgesses" (Butterfield 1961). Doubtless, it would have also surprised audiences to see Jefferson assume a largely passive role in the intense verbal exchanges leading up to and during the Congressional vote on the *Declaration*. But here again history supports Jefferson's reserved, low-profile stage persona in *1776* (again, Adams on Jefferson): "Jefferson attended his Duty [in Congress] . . . a very small part of the time and when there had never spoken in public . . . in Congress, I never heard him utter three Sentences together" (Butterfield 1961).

The portrayal of Pennsylvania's John Dickinson, leader of the anti-independence forces, is accurate with regards to representation of the basic facts, if, perhaps predictably, casually dismissive of the case against pursuing independence from Britain. As the musical accurately demonstrates, Dickinson opposed independence to the bitter end. He resigned from Congress on principle rather than sign the ratified *Declaration*. However, the musical caricaturizes Dickinson and the anti-independence delegates as entirely self-serving wealthy imperialists, smugly complacent about the wealth, property, and privilege they enjoy as colonial allies of the Crown. True, Dickinson and other anti-independence delegates were wealthy, propertied men—as were Adams, Jefferson, Lee, and many proponents of independence. But they were hardly complacent. Dickinson led a faction profoundly troubled by what America would lose after a failed (or even a successful) war for independence when weighed against the benefits of remaining subjects of the British Empire. Hoping that Parliament would eventually temper the king's repressive behavior and facilitate a reconciliation between the colonies and the Crown, Dickinson sincerely believed that Adams was leading the colonies toward ruin. Perhaps nodding to popular expectation and patriotic sentiment, the musical decidedly underplays the persuasive power of the anti-independence argument.

Washington's dispatches from the front

The onstage reading aloud of Washington's war dispatches juxtaposes the bureaucratic, verbose, sometimes petty deliberations of Congress with the dire and deteriorating circumstances of the war-weary Continental Army. If anything, the five dispatches read aloud during the musical understate the historical reality of Washington's epistolary presence in Congress during the summer of 1776. From May through July, Washington peppered Congressional President John Hancock with communications from the war—several per week and sometimes one or more per day. Some communications amounted to routine updates, but frequently Washington's unflinching words bore sad news from the front and laid the blame at Congress' door.

Following the clash at Lexington and Concord, colonial forces suffered defeats at Bunker Hill and the Battle of Quebec in addition to smaller skirmishes elsewhere. Combat losses and soldier fatigue were exacerbated by chronic shortages of supplies, disorganization in civilian leadership (including that of Congress itself), and lack of the promised funds for recruiting and paying soldiers. Although Washington never appears before the audience, through his writings the general and his exigent military mission loom over the proceedings on stage.

Appointed Commander-in-Chief of the Continental Army on June 14, 1775, George Washington, an experienced if not entirely successful military officer in the French and Indian War, aspired to organize the colonial army into a disciplined, effective fighting force. Yet, this mission would prove to be excruciatingly difficult, as even the modest support promised by Congress and the colonial legislatures often failed to materialize. Washington regularly reported progress (and lack thereof) to Congress in care of Congressional President John Hancock, often delivering stern protests, doomsday predictions, and itemized grievances in the process:

> May 5: "[I have received] complaints from [recruiting] Officers in the Eastern Regiments . . . [who] have never yet been allowed anything [for pay or out-of-pocket expenses]."
>
> June 8: "Troops at Boston are extremely uneasy and almost mutinous for want of pay . . . several months of which being now due."
>
> July 14: [*with understated patrician sarcasm—Ed.*] "I have the *pleasure* to Inform Congress, That If their design is to keep the Armies from provision, that the Commissary has told me upon Inquiry, he has forwarded supplies to Albany."
>
> *"Washington Papers" 2010*

As presented in the musical, Hancock had some of Washington's communications read aloud to the Congressional delegation. However, since many of Washington's complaints had to be referred to Congressional committees anyway, the body of fifty-six delegates stayed up to date on Washington's reports as a matter of course. Hancock typically responded to Washington quickly and in good faith, frequently conceding that Congress had been too overrun with other matters to tend properly to its obligations to the army. Hancock pledged to make Congress more responsive and occasionally succeeded: for example, writing on May 13, 1776, "I have delivered . . . four Hundred Thousand Dollars, contained in six Boxes, for the Use of the Troops in New York, and Massachusetts Bay" ("Washington Papers" 2010). But in many respects, Hancock's hands were tied. The Continental Congress, disorganized and ill-prepared to act on such matters, often declined or otherwise failed to address Washington's pleas directly. Many delegates had little faith in the Continental Army's ability to defeat the British forces, especially in light of the waning number of soldiers able and willing to fight for the colonies. Moreover, delegates who remained sympathetic and loyal to the Crown often resisted giving full-on support and treasure to their own colonial uprising.

Slavery and the Declaration of Independence

Whether on stage or in history, the issue of slavery did not dominate the deliberations of the Second Continental Congress. However, slavery briefly made its presence felt when in late June Thomas Jefferson submitted his draft of the Declaration, in which a condemnation of the African slave trade appears in the list of grievances the document presses against the king: "He has . . . violated most sacred Rights of Life and Liberty in the Persons of a distant People who never offended him, captivating and carrying them into Slavery in another Hemisphere."

That this and any other testament against slavery would be excised from the final *Declaration of Independence* was practically a forgone conclusion. Since early June, Congress had determined that approval of any formal declaration of independence would require the unanimous approval of the congressional delegates. Anti-slavery language was opposed by representatives of both the agricultural colonies in the South, whose economic structure relied heavily on slave labor, and representatives of Northern shipping and mercantile interests who profited from the slave trade. (The musical sensibly addresses America's nationwide profiteering from slavery when Edward Rutledge of South Carolina sings "Molasses to Rum" to his fellow delegates: "who sailed the ships outta Boston / the slavers have come / [from] New England with Bibles, and rum.")

In 1776, no white, wealthy, property-owning male had an abundance of moral leverage over any other propertied male on matters of abolition. Slavery and the slave trade were legal in all thirteen colonies. Delegates to the Second Continental Congress, white males either from or connected to the propertied classes, owned slaves unapologetically, owned slaves with some regrets, or did not own slaves but benefitted, directly or indirectly, from those who did. In the course of debating and drafting the *Declaration*, Jefferson never puts forth an argument to abolish slavery. In an early draft of the *Declaration*, he blames the "Christian King of Great Britain" for keeping open a market where "men could be bought and sold." Yet he avoids altogether the complicity of slaveholders, including his own, in sustaining the king's "cruel war against human nature itself." Jefferson's positing of slavery in the colonies as a grievance against the king was highly dubious, since numerous factors and actors were involved in supporting slavery in the states. The final ratified version of the *Declaration* has no specific mention of slavery at all. However, in the list of grievances against King George the delegates added the statement: "He has excited domestic insurrections amongst us," which most historians understand as a reference to slave rebellions ("Jefferson's 'Rough Draft'" 1776).

Indeed, Jefferson's ambivalent positions and behavior with respect to race and slavery persist as open questions in contemporary studies on Jefferson and the Revolutionary War era. Adams' position was not appreciably better, although Adams opposed slavery in principle and never owned slaves. However, in 1776 he was in no hurry to rid the country of slavery, notwithstanding the musical's implication to the contrary. Adams feared what he took to be the religious radicalism of abolitionists (who were largely identified with Quakerism). In 1801, twenty-five years after the signing of the *Declaration of Independence*, he was still hesitant about abolition, writing that he could only support it if it was done in a "gradual way [with] . . . much caution and circumspection" ("John Adams . . . Slavery" n.d.).

Minor fact checks

The staging of the action in *1776* brought forth a few historical oddities and inaccuracies worth noting.

- Throughout the play, a tally board on the chamber wall kept a running record of all votes made by the delegations. Although helpful to the audience, the Congressional Chamber did not have a tally board. Votes were most likely tallied by the Secretary, Charles Thompson, and recorded on parchment.
- The votes for independence and the revised *Declaration of Independence* were actually held on different days, with the resolution for independence being approved on July 2 and the Declaration on July 4. The musical ends with a signing scene that freezes to a tableau, invoking the famous Trumbull and Pine paintings of the signing and implying that all delegates signed on the same day. However, most delegates did not sign until August 2, and some signed even later. As Sneff writes, "it makes sense that July 2nd, July 4th, and August 2nd were conflated, so that the play can quickly transition from debating independence itself to debating the document, to signing the document."
- References to extreme heat and hovering flies recur throughout the musical. Historians take the delegates at their word and deduce that a typical Philadelphia summer day would have been about 80 degrees, humid, with a high chance of discomfort brought on by thick frockcoats and heavy wigs in a room with poor ventilation.
- In the musical, Adams hopes to persuade on-the-fence Maryland delegate Samuel Chase to support independence by inviting Chase to join him and Benjamin Franklin on a troop inspection to New Brunswick, New Jersey. This trip never occurred and appears to be a plot device to get Adams offstage at that moment. Adams and Ben Franklin did stay in New Brunswick for a night in September 1776 as a stopover on a trip from Philadelphia to New York on other Congressional business.
- In another fictional sojourn, Martha Jefferson never visited husband Thomas in Philadelphia during the summer of 1776. Having recently suffered a miscarriage, she was unable to travel and not likely requested by Adams, secretly or otherwise, to rush to Thomas's bedside and dispel his writers' block.

Thomas A. Greenfield and Christina M. Baurle

Further reading

1776. 1972. Directed by Peter Hunt. Sony Pictures Home Entertainment, 2007. DVD.

Barnes, Clive. 1969. "Theater: Spirited '1776.'" *New York Times*, March 17, 1969.

Bloom, Linda. 1997. "A *Curtain Up* Review: *1776*." *Curtain Up*, Summer, http:// www.curtainup.com/1776.html.

Brantley, Ben. 1997. "Singing the Course of Human Events." *New York Times*, August 15, 1997.

Brindell Fradin, Dennis. 2002. *The Signers: The 56 Stories Behind the Declaration of Independence*. New York: Walker & Company.

Butterfield, L. H., ed. 1961. *Diary and Autobiography of John Adams*. Cambridge, MA: Harvard University Press. Re-posted in *Adams Family Papers: An Electronic Archive*. Massachusetts Historical Society, http://www.masshist.org/digitaladams/.

Chapman, John. 1969. "1776 Opens at the 46th Street; It's Funny, Moving and Artistic." *Daily News*, March 17, 1969.

Cooke, Richard P. 1969. "1776." *Musical Theatre International Catalog*, https://www.mtishows.com/print/node/925.

Edwards, Sherman and Peter Stone. 1969. *1776*. New York: Penguin Books.

Evans, Greg. 1997. "1776." *Variety*, August 24, 1997.

Ferling, John. 1996. *John Adams: A Life*. New York: Henry Holt & Company.

Filichia, Peter. 1997. "Stagestruck by Peter Filichia: The Spirit of *1776*." *Playbill*, November 12, 1997, www.playbill.com/article/stagestruck-by-peter-filichia-the-spirit-of-1776-com-72109.

Ford, Worthington Chauncey, ed. 1889–93. *The Writings of George Washington*. New York: G.P. Putnam's Sons.

Glover, William. 1969. "Timing Is Right for the Message." *Des Moines Register*, May 18, 1969.

Green, Jesse. 2016. "Theater Review: The Encores! Revival of 1776 Adds Modern Touches to a Powerful and Deserving Show." *Vulture*, March 31, 2016.

Janes, Joe. 2015. "Declaration of Independence Deleted Passage, 1776." *Documents That Changed the World*. Podcast audio, October 20, 2015.

"Jefferson's 'Original Rough Draught' of the Declaration of Independence." 1776. *The Papers of Thomas Jefferson*. Princeton, NJ: Princeton University, jeffersonpapers.princeton.edu/selecteddocuments/jefferson%E2%80%99s-%E2%80%9Coriginal-rough-draught%E2%80%9D-declaration-independence.

"John Adams on the Abolition of Slavery, 1801." n.d. *The Gilder Lehrman Institute of American History*, www.gilderlehrman.org/content/john-adams-abolition-slavery-1801.

"John Adams Autobiography, Part 1." n.d. *Adams Family Papers: An Electronic Archive*. Massachusetts Historical Society, http://www.masshist.org/digitaladams/.

Kissel, Howard. 1997. "Revival Captures the Spirit of '1776'." *Daily News*, August 15, 1997.

Kroll, Jack. 1969. "Birth of a Nation." *Newsweek*, March 31, 1969.

"Letter from John Adams to Abigail Smith, 7 May 1764" [electronic edition]. *Adams Family Papers: An Electronic Archive*. Massachusetts Historical Society, http:// www.masshist.org/digitaladams/.

Lewis, Theophilus. 1969. "1776." *America Magazine*, March 31, 1969.

McCullough, David. 2006. *1776*. New York: Simon & Schuster.

Rakove, Jack. 2010. "The Patriot Who Refused to Sign the Declaration of Independence." *American History Magazine*, June 3, 2010.

Scheck, Frank. 2016. "'1776': Theater Review." *Hollywood Reporter*, March 31, 2016.

Sneff, Emily. 2017. "Presenting the Facts: 1776." *Declaration Resources Project*, Harvard University, March 28, 2017, https://declaration.fas.harvard.edu/blog/facts-1776/.

Syse, Glenna. 1969. "Finale of Musical '1776' a Moment for Goosebumps, Little Gulps in the Throat." *Des Moines Register*, May 18, 1969.

Thomas Jefferson Foundation. 2019. "Thomas Jefferson Monticello," https://www.monticello.org/.

"Washington Papers Online: Washington Hancock Correspondence." 2010. *Founders Online*, National Archives, www.archives.gov (searchable homepage).

Watts, Richard. 1969. *Musical Theatre International Catalogue*, https://www.mtishows.com/print/node/925.

Weinstock, Matt. 2019. "Lin-Manuel Miranda and William Daniels Talk *Hamilton*, *1776*, Mr. Feeny, and More." *Playbill*, July 1, 2019.

CHAPTER 19
SHENANDOAH (1974)

Book by Peter Udell (1929–), Philip Rose (1921–2011), and James Lee Barrett (1929–89)
Music by Gary Geld (1935–)
Lyrics by Peter Udell
Based on James Lee Barrett's original screenplay for the 1965 film *Shenandoah*
World Professional Premiere: Goodspeed Opera House, East Haddam, Connecticut, August 12, 1974
Broadway: Alvin Theater, January 7, 1975–August 7, 1977

Songs

"Raise the Flag of Dixie" (Prologue)
"I've Heard It All Before"
"Pass the Cross to Me"
"Why Am I Me?"
"Next to Lovin' (I Like Fightin')"
"Over the Hill"
"The Pickers Are Coming"
"Next to Lovin' (I Like Fightin')" (Reprise)
"Meditation"
"We Make a Beautiful Pair"
"Violets and Silverbells"
"It's a Boy!"
"Freedom"
"Violets and Silverbells" (Reprise)
"Papa's Gonna Make It Alright"
"The Only Home I Know"
"Papa's Gonna Make It Alright" (Reprise)
"Meditation II"
"Pass the Cross to Me" (Finale)

Overview

Shenandoah is a fictitious Civil War tale set in the Shenandoah Valley of Virginia west of the Blue Ridge Mountains. One of a long line of theatrical and cinematic fictional representations of the American Civil War (including the 1965 film from which it was adapted), *Shenandoah* differs from traditional Civil War depictions in its focus on a white patriarchal Virginia landowner who openly dissents against his state's secession from the Union, the Confederacy, and wars fought in the name of noble causes and slavery.

Widower Charlie Anderson and his seven children (six sons and one daughter, ages twelve to twenty-eight) comprise the entire workforce of their struggling but moderately successful family farm. In 1861, less than one year into the war, Charlie and his family have thus far been spared the burdens of warfare. Neither he nor his sons have joined the Confederate forces nor have hostile Northern Union soldiers shown a notable presence in their Shenandoah Valley town. Living over a hundred miles inland from Virginia's populated seaports and the Confederate capital at Richmond, Charlie expects to spend the war tending to his own household and sheltering his family from the violence of war. Charlie views his farm and family as an island apart from the Confederacy—essentially, a sovereign neutral territory where he exercises familial and political authority via his dissident moral code: ambivalence about the Confederacy; dismissiveness toward his presumptive "duty to the state" of Virginia over America; and opposition to slavery on his property. (Charlie is not an abolitionist nor is he involved with any antislavery reform movements.) Most distressing to Charlie is his sense that the South has succumbed to an all-consuming self-destructive fever for war in the name of states' rights and Southern independence—although he is not opposed to violence in defense of one's self or property.

Although presented as a traditional Broadway entertainment piece, *Shenandoah* possesses qualities of an historical fable: an instructive and cautionary lesson for principled, informed citizens confronted with choices that test their convictions. From the outset of the war and the musical, Charlie is aware that many Virginia families have already suffered wartime losses of family members and rendered other sacrifices toward the war effort. His dissident opinions are drawing criticism very close to home. His children, respectfully but pointedly, question his outright rejection of a "duty to Virginia." His anti-Confederacy beliefs are alienating close friends and neighbors. His local preacher delivers sermons on the Lord's desire to see Northern invaders driven from the South.

Anti-war sentiment among whites was prevalent in both the North and the South during the Civil War. Dissention in the South took numerous forms and sprang from many rationales, some of which *Shenandoah*'s plainspoken, thoughtful Charlie Anderson reflects in his beliefs. Much of Charlie's disaffection from the Confederacy is rooted in the economic status of the Southern yeoman farmer during the Civil War years. Yeomen were the owners of small, family-run farms throughout the Confederacy. They comprised upward of 50 percent of the white population of the South during the war. They owned few if any slaves. Yeomen farmers like Charlie Anderson who lived in hill country regions and the Upper Southern states sought little contact with the Confederate government and did not become economically dependent upon slave labor. As with Charlie in *Shenandoah*, the yeomen's first extensive contact with the Confederate government often took the form of an uninvited communication from an official stationed in the nearest Confederate military outpost (Ambrose 1962). In all likelihood the official would dispatch orders compelling the yeomen's sons to join the Confederate Army and/or "impressing" the yeomen's crops and animals in support of the war (i.e., seizing them outright or coercively buying them at below-market prices). Such intrusions grew more numerous as the war progressed, engendering further resentment on the part of the yeomen towards the Confederate government.

Religious and faith-based dissent also bred opposition to the Civil War in both the North and the South. In *Shenandoah*, Charlie declares himself to be "nonreligious." However, in meditations at his wife's grave, he speaks mournfully of how the war is tearing families apart. He professes his own religious-based objection to the war which, even as an internalized expression of feeling, invokes anti-war doctrines associated with nineteenth-century Quaker, Mennonite, and other faith-based conscientious objector movements: "I've got just enough belief in me to know that God didn't create war," he says.

There are some admirable and thought-provoking moments in *Shenandoah*'s admittedly limited but serious-minded presentation of Charlie's alienation from the Confederacy. However, in their attempt to address slavery and race relations in the context of Charlie's antislavery beliefs, *Shenandoah*'s creators took an inexplicably simplistic, hands-off approach to the subject. There is not one adult African American character in the show. What little exposition *Shenandoah* musters on slavery and race relations is delivered by three minor characters in an innocuous song about freedom being a "state of mind" and pointedly not a consequence of race, economics, culture, or law. The empty pieties of their freedom song are garnished by ostensibly heartwarming dialog between two twelve-year-old friends, one Black and one white. Gabriel, a slave youth belonging to Charlie's neighbor (and the only African American character in the show), Charlie's twelve -year-old son Boy, and Charlie's daughter-in-law Anne imbue the play with a cliched "brothers-and-sisters-under-the-skin" prescription for the Civil War era's troubled legacy of race relations. Beyond that, the musical conspicuously dispenses with subjects related to race altogether.

Such sentimentality and naïveté about race may have found a fairer hearing when the original film of *Shenandoah* was released in 1965. Congress had just passed the Civil Rights Act, and the nation's outlook for progress on race relations, while hardly childish or simplistic, embraced a measure of justifiable optimism and reasoned expectation that less-troubled pathways lay ahead. *Shenandoah* the musical, however, premiered in 1974, six years after the assassination of Martin Luther King and in the midst of racial conflict over federal court rulings to desegregate public school systems in the North, Midwest, and West. Moreover, America's controversial, decades-long divisive military involvement in the Vietnam War was coming to an unsettling and inconclusive end. However well intentioned at the time, *Shenandoah*'s dismissive approach to slavery and race relations undercut its implicit promise to treat serious social issues responsibly even within the format of a sentimental, traditional, feel-good Broadway musical.

Shenandoah achieved considerable success at the Broadway box office. Its upbeat, perky music and unapologetic sentimentality kept the show running for 1,050 performances. It won two major Tony Awards (Best Book of a Musical and Best Actor in a Musical for John Cullum in the role of Charlie Anderson). Gary Geld and Peter Udell's score blended conventional Broadway melodies along with strains of old-time country and mountain music. The production contains enough Virginia reels and song arrangements in mountain music traditions to convey the location and time period of the action. The 1975 Broadway opening coincided with commercial country music's steady growth from an American niche or regional musical genre to a major market within the recording and AM radio industries. By the time *Shenandoah* opened, pop and rock musicians such as John Denver, Linda Ronstadt, and the Eagles were gaining audiences and fanbases that crossed over from country music. Reciprocally, several country music artists, such as Willie Nelson, Mac Davis, Tammy Wynette, and Lynn Anderson had charted radio hits on AM pop radio. *Shenandoah*'s composer-lyricist team Geld and Udell were very familiar with the genre crossover phenomenon in commercial American music. As professional songwriters before writing *Shenandoah*, they had written many popular hit songs, including Bryan Highland's pop hit "Sealed with a Kiss" and the Skeeter Davis song "He Says the Same Thing to Me," the latter reaching top 20 status on both *Billboard*'s Country Music and Adult Contemporary charts. However, *Shenandoah* did not yield a signature hit song that found a commercial audience on its own.

Plot synopsis

In the prologue, the stage is full of Confederate and Union Civil War soldiers singing a rousing war song ("Raise the Flag of Dixie"). Trading insults, each army promises to win this war quickly. The stomping and hollering subside as the two armies exit right and left respectively, revealing Charlie Anderson standing at his late wife Martha's gravesite. Addressing Martha, Charlie laments that the fires of war are consuming Virginia, but he vows to keep their family safe.

At dinner the Anderson family engages in a spirited but civil discussion about the war. Charlie, his six sons (Jacob, James, Nathan, John, Henry, and twelve-year-old Robert ["Boy"]), daughter Jenny, and pregnant daughter-in-law Anne (James' wife) all participate. James expresses concern that they cannot ignore the war any longer because they owe a duty to Virginia. Charlie answers that since they do not own slaves, they are not getting involved. Henry agrees with Charlie, asserting that they should not have to fight a war they don't believe in. As dinner ends, Charlie, distressed by rising pressure on his family to join the war, sings an antiwar manifesto ("I've Heard It All Before").

As the Andersons head for Sunday church services Robert (called "Boy" throughout) detours to talk to his friend Gabriel, a neighbor's slave his own age. Boy complains that he does not want to go to church while Gabriel reveals that his "massa" prevents him from going. In church, the Andersons hear a sermon admonishing everyone to do their duty as Virginians and support the war against the "northern barbarians." After church, Sam, a shy young lieutenant about to join the Confederate militia, expresses a wish to call upon Charlie's daughter Jenny. Charlie grants permission. The family exits as Jenny's brothers tease her about her awkward new beau. Boy stays behind fishing with Gabriel, who restates his interest in attending church. Boy responds that he wouldn't mind being a slave like Gabriel if it meant not having to go to church. The two sing an upbeat song about fate and identity ("Why Am I Me?").

Confederate soldiers appear at the Anderson farm to conscript Charlie's sons, who immediately pick up their rifles. Charlie, approving of his sons' armed defensive stance, explains that they have no slaves, never will, and will not join the Confederate Army. The soldiers leave reluctantly, warning Charlie that the Yankee army will eventually make it impossible for him to avoid the war. Charlie departs for his fields as his sons, excited from handling their guns and talking of war, perform a raucous mountain song and dance number ("Next to Lovin', I Like Fightin'"). Sam arrives to court Jenny. His reticence leads her to lament that by the time he gets over his shyness and kisses her, she will be too old to enjoy it ("Over the Hill"). Overhearing the couple, Charlie ponders his daughter's maturity, referring to Jenny as his "ripe plum" who will be "picked any day now" ("The Pickers Are Coming"). The Confederate soldiers return, this time hoping to confiscate the family's horses. A fight ensues, ending with the bruised soldiers limping away from the farm empty-handed.

Charlie revisits Martha's grave. He declares that the Andersons do not owe any duty to Virginia and sings a bittersweet ballad recalling his and Martha's life together ("Meditation"). Sam asks Charlie for Jenny's hand in marriage. After Charlie gives his blessing, preparations for the wedding ensue. A pregnant Anne helps Jenny into her wedding dress, and they sing about marriage ("We Make a Beautiful Pair"). At their wedding, Jenny and Sam declare their love for each other ("Violets and Silverbells"), after which Sam receives his orders to join his battalion. Gabriel and Boy go into the woods to check rabbit traps. Anne goes into labor. Charlie and his other sons presume to welcome in song Anne's new baby boy, which they soon discover is a girl ("It's a Boy!").

Gabriel reappears and reports that Yankee soldiers have taken Boy, who was wearing a Confederate Army cap he found in the woods. Most of the family prepare to leave in search of Boy as Charlie acknowledges that the war now concerns them. Charlie, Jenny, Jacob, Nathan, John, and Henry take off on their search. James, Anne, and the baby, named Martha, remain alone on the farm.

Weeks later, Gabriel approaches Anne at the Andersons' farm with news that Yankees have burned down his master's farm, and his master has run away. The Union soldiers told Gabriel and the other slaves that they are free. As Gabriel wraps his head around this concept, Anne and Gabriel sing a duet, proclaiming that true freedom is a "state of the mind" ("Freedom"). Gabriel says he is heading further south to find his parents. After he leaves, Anne and James reprise the love song from his sister's wedding. Anne enters the house to care for their baby, while a ragtag trio of scavenger soldiers (in Union, Confederate, and civilian clothes, respectively) approach James in the yard. They ask for water but stab James when his back is turned. James dies and the scavengers head toward the house in pursuit of Anne. Charlie, his four sons, and daughter Jenny are camping out after traveling many miles looking through Yankee camps for Boy. Charlie comforts Jenny, who is fearful that her brother and husband Sam are dead ("Papa's Gonna Make It Alright"). They seize a train full of Confederate prisoners, looking for Boy among the wounded and sick men. They do not find Boy, but unexpectedly discover a battered, exhausted Sam; Jenny and Sam embrace joyfully.

The only officer among them, Sam tells the other Confederate soldiers on the train that the war is lost and they should go home. The freed soldier-prisoners sing about families torn apart by war ("The Only Home I Know"). Charlie and his sons burn the empty train.

That evening, Jacob stands watch over the Andersons' campsite. A Confederate sniper kills Jacob, mistaking him for a Yankee. In retaliation, Charlie takes up his rifle as the sniper, tearfully acknowledging his tragic error, pleads for Charlie's forgiveness. Unmoved, Charlie shoots the now unarmed sniper repeatedly, slaughtering him. Stunned at Charlie's violent turn, his children stare at him in disbelief. Grieving, they all give up on finding Boy and take Jacob's body home for burial.

Back home the Andersons learn that their preacher, Reverend Byrd, found the murdered bodies of James and Anne. The baby Martha has survived. Charlie sings to his granddaughter, reprieving the lullaby he sang to Jenny. Later, Charlie visits his wife's grave again, singing about the loss of Jacob, James, Anne, and Boy. He also voices regret for killing the sniper who shot Jacob ("Meditation II"). Hearing church bells, Charlie realizes it is Sunday and insists the family go to church.

The Andersons arrive at church as the congregation is singing a hymn. The congregation pauses as Reverend Byrd and all gathered greet the Andersons. As the congregation resumes its song, Boy hobbles into the church in tattered clothes. He limps slowly towards his father, who rises tearfully to greet him and escort him to the family's seats ("Pass the Cross to Me").

Critical reception

Shenandoah premiered at the Goodspeed Opera House, East Haddam, Connecticut, August 12, 1974, and transferred to Broadway's Alvin Theater on January 7, 1975. In a season that included such urbane musicals as *Chicago*, *A Chorus Line*, and *The Wiz*, the creators of *Shenandoah* may have unknowingly taken a risk with the show's homespun sentimentality. Every critic who wrote about the musical mentioned its saccharine simplicity. Even those who acknowledged that the play capably presented its appealing humble, virtuous characters felt that the production's folksy cuteness was hard to swallow. Clearly disappointed, composer Geld expressed surprise at the critics' lack of appreciation of the traditional nature of the show, telling the *New York Times* "I was shocked at what seemed to be a backlash against the old-fashioned virtues and values … When did Rodgers and Hammerstein become dirty words in American Theater?" (Wilson 1975b).

Clive Barnes' *New York Times* opening night review seemed to damn *Shenandoah* with faint praise, calling it a likeable, old-fashioned American musical, the kind that seemed to be fading away. Although he found *Shenandoah* to be full of "high principles and strong ballads, simple truth and simpler sentiments," Barnes thought the musical was weighed down by unambitious music and lyrics, as well as mediocre staging and choreography. Citing lead actor John Cullum (Charlie Anderson), for elevating the sometimes-maudlin material, Barnes accurately predicted that *Shenandoah*'s cloying sweetness would make it a commercial success (Barnes 1975). Harris Green, writing in the *New York Times* about recent Broadway trends, offered a brutal condemnation of *Shenandoah*. Green asserted that the show demonstrated how unsuitable the musical genre was for handling serious themes or, for that matter, history itself: *Shenandoah*, a show set in Virginia during the anything but toe tappin' time of the Civil War … looks and sounds as if its creators' ingenuity had been exhausted in trying to avoid, or play down, such inescapable topics as slavery, rebellion and death" (Green 1975). Brendan Gill was also patronizingly harsh, writing in the *New Yorker* that the play was drowning in "conventional claptrap." While lauding Cullum, who "lends a surprising degree of conviction to an implausible role," Gill blasted the show for its meaningless treatment of slavery: if "freedom is not in the state of Maine, etc., but rather in the 'state of mind' [as Gabriel, the newly freed slave youth, declares] … why bother with emancipation?" (Gill 1975). Offering a defense for *Shenandoah*'s traditional feel, Catharine Hughes, writing for *America*, argued that the show's box office numbers confirmed that theatergoers had not yet become too sophisticated for Rodgers and Hammerstein-type musicals. Despite the implausibility of the plot, Hughes felt that Americans were "yearning to believe again" in virtuous, simple country folk. A fan of the score, Hughes took the book to task for failing to make believable Charlie Anderson's quick change from "pacifist to violent revenge-seeker" (Hughes 1975). Writing about the cast recording in the *New York Times*, John S. Wilson agreed with Hughes that *Shenandoah* was highly reminiscent of Rodgers and Hammerstein. Moreover, Wilson felt that the show's "musical déjà vu" sensibility was warranted since the nineteenth-century setting called for Southern mountain music to set the tone and mood of the play (Wilson 1975a).

Jack Kroll rendered a self-described "split decision" on *Shenandoah* for *Newsweek*. Acknowledging a temptation to dismiss *Shenandoah* as "pure corn," he admired the show for audaciously trying to "heal psychic wounds" in an age of unrest. Noting that Geld and Udell had created songs that fit the show's idealism, Kroll found the emotion that poured out on the stage to be "a little cringe-worthy at times" (Kroll 1975). Moira Hodgson, reviewing for *Dance Magazine*, expressed surprise that *Shenandoah* was such a "compelling show." Despite being an oversentimental cliché, "the honest, humble, and hardworking characters draw you in," Hodgson wrote. She also noted that the homespun songs, though far from original, lent a "surprising freshness" to the predictable plot. She admired the two major dance numbers, both farmyard jigs set to thigh-slapping Virginia reels. Noting they were performed by men only (Charlie and/or his sons), Hodgson deemed the staging appropriate as in mid-nineteenth-century America "ladies' dancing was often frowned upon" (Hodgson 1975).

Shenandoah closed on Broadway on August 7, 1977, after 1,050 performances. The show won two Tony Awards and earned three additional nominations, including Best Musical. Revivals over the years have done little to strengthen its artistic or commercial legacy. A limited-run Broadway revival in 1989 earned lackluster reviews. A Washington, D.C. revival in 2006 caused critic J. Wynn Rousuck to write in the *Baltimore Sun* that three decades after the show debuted in a post-Vietnam maelstrom, "the nation is at loggerheads over our involvement in another foreign conflict," this time in the Middle East. Rousuck also recoiled at the sexism in the musical associated with Jenny's "gun-toting, trousers-wearing" persona (Rousuck 2006).

Tony Frankel's review of a 2012 Los Angeles production offers one of the clearer summative explanations as to why *Shenandoah* has struggled over the years to secure its footing with audiences, critics, and the musical genre itself. Calling it "oddly schizophrenic," Frankel explained:

> On the one hand [it] is traditional Broadway comedy fare. Full of romanticism [a wedding, a Poppa's lullaby] and corniness [knee-slapping dances] . . . On the other hand, it contains socially conscious propaganda and high principles that are meant to be taken very seriously . . . It is completely family friendly in one scene and then horrifyingly inappropriate for kids the next . . . Its split-personality book has three authors and it shows.
>
> *Frankel 2012*

Critics and audiences found *Shenandoah* as uncomfortably out of its element as was its hero Charlie Anderson, neither fully the grounded traditionalist it thought it was, nor convincingly the arbiter of historical complexities it aspired to be.

Historical accuracy and context

Economics, slavery ownership, and the white yeoman farmer

Like Charlie Anderson and his family, a large number of white farmers and business people in the Southern states prior to the start of the Civil War were not slave owners. They relied largely on family members and hired hands for their livelihood, even if expedience led many to hire slaves temporarily or borrow slaves from friendly neighbors to assist with a harvest or other specific task. In 1860, the demographic profile of the Confederate states' population was 41.8 percent non-slaveholding whites, 37.4 percent slaves, and 18.7 percent slaveholding whites (Watson 1985). However, in the Shenandoah Valley of northwestern Virginia—the setting for *Shenandoah*—slaves made up approximately 16 percent of the population ("Population of Virginia" 1970). Many non-slaveholding yeoman farmers not only supported the institution of slavery, believing it to be beneficial to the South if not to themselves directly, but also aspired to own slaves themselves. Even in their disdain for the pretentions of the "despised" aristocratic slaveholding planters, non-slaveholding yeoman farmers remained "loyal to the slave regime" through their opposition to centralized political power rooted in the North. Furthermore, as long as the slaveholders of the large plantations "made few demands on these regions, [non-slaveholding yeoman farmers'] claims to being champions of freedom and autonomy appeared perfectly legitimate" (Genovese 1975). The circumstances which led to a large number of non-slaveholding white households in the Confederacy were varied and subject to change over the course of the war. Some Southerners saw Christianity and slavery as mildly incompatible, viewing slave-ownership in much the same light that Charlie Anderson does in *Shenandoah*: a personal decision not to be flaunted in front of neighbors, much less one's home state or the Confederacy, who felt differently about the subject. A white farmer or planter with strong abolitionist beliefs had few practical options but to maintain secrecy on the subject. To express these views openly, as some few did, risked being run out of their homes, assaulted, and/or murdered.

However, some white farmers and business owners questioned slavery's economic effectiveness, particularly in regions like the Shenandoah Valley, whose climate, topography, and staple crops differed from those of the large politically influential Virginia plantations. While *Shenandoah* does not specify what crops Charlie harvests, the Shenandoah Valley's staple crop in the nineteenth century was wheat (Koons 2015), a crop with a relatively distant relationship with slavery, even in the antebellum South. By contrast, the more prosperous slave-owning planters tended to grow tobacco, cotton, and/or sugarcane.

Shenandoah leaves unanswered the question of whether Charlie Anderson, a white farmer opposed to slavery and dismissive of the current war and its "higher cause," is an anomaly or a representative of a significant number of likeminded white property owners who remained in the Confederacy throughout the war. Certainly, as the economic and military fortunes of the Confederacy declined after 1863, many earlier supporters became disillusioned with the South's conduct in the war. Charlie's alienation as expressed in *Shenandoah* is consonant with the cumulative resentment registered by many poor and middle-class whites who came to view the conflict as a "rich man's war, poor man's fight" that disincentivized non-slaveholding whites to continue fighting for the wealthy planters' slave system (Tatum 2000). For example, when the Confederate Congress passed the Conscription Act in 1862, the law included several amendments giving wealthy plantation and farm owners the chance to avoid military conscription via a "twenty-slave rule." This rule exempted a white male adult, either an owner or overseer, from military service on plantations of twenty or more slaves.

However, white property owners' disillusionment with the Confederacy's management of the war, especially in the wake of several military defeats in 1864 and 1865, did not translate into a weakening of support for slavery. In the Shenandoah Valley alone, slaves were bought, sold, and traded into the final months of the war. Most Southern states—including the four states that did not secede (Missouri, Kentucky, Maryland, and Delaware)—maintained their status as "slave states" for as long as feasibly possible. The cultural resilience of slavery—the principal means by which the South maintained social and political power over the region's large Black population—was reborn in the racism of post-Civil War Reconstruction and Jim Crow segregation. The Charlie Andersons of the Civil War-era South likely stood very much alone among their peers, as did Charlie himself in *Shenandoah*.

Pacifists and conscientious objectors in the Confederacy

Shenandoah does not assign a specific Christian denomination to Charlie, his family, or the church he attends regularly, if unenthusiastically, to honor his late wife's wishes. Nonetheless the musical highlights Charlie's moral objections to the Confederacy in general and the Civil War in particular. Charlie's condemnation of all wars as undifferentiated affronts to God broadly aligns with pacifist doctrines associated with nineteenth-century religious-based anti-war activists' groups: " . . . always a holy cause to march you off to war / I've heard it all before . . . God didn't create war." Doctrinaire Quakers and Mennonites would have related to Charlie's anti-war stance even though Charlie is neither affiliated with any formal anti-war group nor a student of pacifist teachings.

Some critics took *Shenandoah* to task for its seemingly implausible juxtaposition of Charlie's God-fearing pacifism and the mini-arsenal of rifles he and his children wield casually in the name of self-defense. However, both semantics and the pragmatics of history support *Shenandoah*'s more nuanced if inconsistent representation of Charlie's anti-war beliefs. Modern philosophical debates on pacifism have drawn a clarifying distinction between pacifism as an all-encompassing commitment to non-violence and a narrower anti-war position that applies specifically to wars among nation states. (A still narrower controversial definition of pacifism allows for principled objections to specific "unjust wars," i.e., a form of pacifism that, by extension, embraces the concept of a "just war.")

In wartime, principled opponents of war often confront complex dilemmas and make difficult compromises in their struggle "to balance the conflicting duties of citizenship in both an earthly state and a heavenly kingdom" (Scott 2009). *Sheandoah*'s creditable if cryptic presentation of Charlie's anti-war sentiments has instructive value as a presentation of Confederate "conscientious objections" even though the terms "conscientious objector" and "pacifist" do not appear in the show.

The Confederacy included over 2,000 Quakers (members of the Society of Friends). The largest concentration of Friends in the South lived in North Carolina. The Shenandoah Valley was home to approximately 400 families of Mennonites and a few German Baptist Brethren (sometimes referred to as "Dunkers" owing to their full immersion Baptism rites), both Christian denominations whose foundational religious principles include opposition to war. Many members of these communities were also opposed to slavery, resulting in many pacifists escaping the Confederacy altogether by fleeing to the North. Many conscientious objectors who remained in the South, at least at the beginning of the war, were able to avoid military service legally based on their religious beliefs. Several states made provisions for these men to file as conscientious objectors, usually requiring an affidavit on their behalf signed by an official of a recognized "peace church." State conscientious objector laws generally offered such options of paying a commutation fee for as much as $500 in lieu of serving in the Confederate Army or serving in alternative ways that did not require active combat.

Like Charlie, many conscientious objectors faced rebuke and worse from soldiers and civilians who subjected them to taunts, reproaches, and sometimes violence, although extreme cases of abuse were the exception. Even military officials tried to coerce pacifists to join the fight, especially late in the war, but most eventually simply allowed members of the peace churches to stay home and grow food for the army. Mennonites in the Shenandoah Valley, many of whom had emigrated to America in the early 1800s to avoid military service in Europe, hoped to live in Virginia as an isolated, self-sustaining community. However, the Civil War compelled them to interact with mainstream Virginia society and adapt to "the contingencies of war in order to protect their distinctive and countercultural religious beliefs." Such contingencies included serving in the military as "non-shooting" soldiers and losing farms and personal property in the Northern Army's sweeps through the South (Scott 2009). In North Carolina, Quakers providing alternative service in Confederate coastal salt mines drew the ire of Confederate military authorities who suspected the Quakers of making illegal subversive contact with nearby occupying Union Army officials. In addition, many Quaker men were coerced into joining the Confederate Army by local army officers desperate for manpower despite state laws and regulations established specifically to assist Quakers in living their faith during the war.

All Southern dissenters were taking dangerous risks that contributed in large part to the Confederacy's downfall. Through his principled neutrality, Charlie Anderson suffered the tragic loss of three family members and accomplished little if anything for the cause of peace. However, the creators of *Shenandoah*, apparently no more eager than Charlie to immerse themselves in the complex historical issues in front of them, allow Charlie to garner what modern tragic characters often take from their most costly errors: a life more wisely lived after a painful lesson learned.

The Shenandoah Valley in the Civil War

If there is an altogether implausible historical assumption operating in *Shenandoah*, it is that Charlie believes the remoteness of his farm nestled inconspicuously in the northwestern hills of Virginia would keep his family insulated from the raging war. He is buoyed in this belief by the fact that several months into the war the Shenandoah Valley has seen no major military conflict (an accurate representation). The musical deludes Charlie into thinking his family can remain safe indefinitely since, but for the prologue and a brief appearance by a "scavenger" dressed in Union garb, no Union soldier appears or speaks throughout the entire play. All information about Union Army activity is conveyed by Southern characters. In reality, the Shenandoah Valley failed to do its part in upholding Charlie's apolitical de-militarized wartime vision. The Valley was the battleground for two major military campaigns and several smaller bloody confrontations between Union and Confederate forces. Sustained Confederate military control of the Shenandoah Valley actually prolonged the South's war effort. From the start of the war, the fertile grain-producing Shenandoah Valley helped feed Confederate soldiers throughout the South once the state of Virginia connected existing rail lines in the eastern centers of Richmond, Petersburgh, and Portsmouth-Norfolk to new tracks running westward to the Shenandoah Valley and Blue Ridge Mountains.

Quiet and largely free of military action early on, the Shenandoah Valley did not stay that way for long. In the spring of 1862, several Union Army units comprising 50,000 soldiers occupied parts of the Valley, establishing a front for the Union. However, those units were called to Richmond to join up with other Union forces in attacking the Confederate capital city. Thomas "Stonewall" Jackson, then a relatively unknown Confederate general, marched a force of 17,000 Confederate troops to the Valley to prevent the Union Army from joining the planned attack on Richmond. In a series of divide-and-conquer maneuvers, Jackson's vastly outnumbered forces defeated half a dozen Union Army generals in as many different locations throughout the Valley. Jackson's forces inflicted significant losses on the Union, broke the North's stronghold in the Valley, and established both Jackson himself and the Shenandoah Valley as mythic figures in Confederate lore and legend.

On the other hand, the North won a decisive victory in an 1864 Shenandoah military campaign that influenced the 1864 presidential election and hastened the end of the war. By 1864, the Shenandoah Valley had become a vital source of food and supply movement for the Confederacy as its army had maintained control of the area for most of the period following Jackson's 1862 victory. Confederate troops moved with relative ease throughout the Valley while often thwarting Union troops that sought to use it to advance on Richmond and other points east. In a see-saw series of battles, Union General Philip Sheridan's army sought to seize Valley land and destroy crop-producing farms. Sheridan eventually won a final decisive victory over Confederate General Jubal A. Early and brutally laid waste to vast amounts of farm land (an attack sometimes referred to as "the Burning"). The overwhelming victory that occurred in late October was one of the last major battles before the 1864 presidential election. Coming on the heels of Union General William Sherman's capture of Atlanta in September, news of Sheridan's victory in the Shenandoah Valley helped propel Lincoln to a November victory over Democratic candidate and former Union Army general George McClellan.

Lincoln defeated McClellan in the Electoral College by 212 vote to 21, an election Lincoln himself had believed he would lose only three months earlier.

Thomas A. Greenfield and Sue Ann Brainard

Further reading

Ambrose, Stephen E. 1962. "Yeoman Discontent in the Confederacy." *Civil War History* 8, no. 3 (September): 258–69.

Anderson, Paul Christopher. n.d. "The Shenandoah Valley during the Civil War." *Encyclopedia Virginia*. Charlottesville: Virginia Humanities, www.encyclopediavirginia.org/Shenandoah_Valley_During_the_Civil_War.

Barnes, Clive. 1975. "*Shenandoah* Is [*sic*] Musical of Civil War." *New York Times*, January 8, 1975.

Barrett, James Lee, Peter Udell, and Philip Rose. 1975. *Shenandoah*. New York: Samuel French.

Brock, Peter. 2002. *Liberty and Conscience: A Documentary History of the Experiences of Conscientious Objectors in America through the Civil War*. New York: Oxford University Press.

Downing, David. 2007. *A South Divided: Portraits of Dissent in the Confederacy*. Nashville, TN: Cumberland House.

Frankel, Tony. 2012. "Los Angeles Theater Review: *Shenandoah*." *Stage and Cinema*, June 15, 2012, https://www.stageandcinema.com/2012/06/15/shenandoah-mtg/.

Genovese, Eugene D. 1975. "Yeoman Farmers in a Slaveholders' Democracy." *Agricultural History* 49, no. 2 (April): 331–42.

Gill, Brendan. 1975. "The Theatre." *New Yorker* 50 (January): 61.

Green, Harris. 1975. "Is the Broadway Musical Changing Its Tune?" *New York Times*, July 20, 1975.

Gutman, Jon. 2006. "Review: The Shenandoah Valley Campaign of 1862." *Civil War Times*, November/December 2006.

Hodgson, Moira. 1975. "Warming Up on Broadway." *Dance Magazine* 49 (March): 34.

Hughes, Catherine. 1975. "Buying American." *America* 132 (February): 93.

Koons, Kenneth. 2015. "Our Once Beautiful but Now Desolated Valley." *Shenandoah at War, Shenandoah Valley Battlefields Foundation*, New Market, VA, June 2015, http://www.shenandoahatwar.org/our-once-beautiful-but-now-desolated-valley/.

Kroll, Jack. 1975. "Split Decision." *Newsweek* 85 (January): 82–3.

"Population of Virginia—1860." 1970. *Inter-university Consortium for Political and Social Research*. Ann Arbor, MI, http://virginiaplaces.org/population/pop1860numbers.html.

Rousuck, J. Wynn. 2006. "'Shenandoah': A Musical at War with Itself." *Baltimore Sun*, March 28, 2006, 1C.

Scott, Sean A. 2009. "Review: *Mennonites, Amish, and the American Civil War*." *Ohio History* 116: 133–5.

Tatum, George Lee. 2000. *Disloyalty in the Confederacy*. Lincoln: University of Nebraska Press.

Watson, Henry L. 1985. "Conflict and Collaboration: Yeoman, Slaveholders, and Politics in the Antebellum South." *Social History* 10, no. 3: 273–98.

Wilson, John S. 1975a. "Recordings View: 'The Wiz' Is Not a Subtle Soul." *The New York Times*, June 1, 1975.

Wilson, John S. 1975b. "The Shenandoah Saga." *New York Times*, February 16, 1975.

Wright, Edward Needles. 1931. *Conscientious Objectors in the Civil War*. Philadelphia: University of Pennsylvania Press.

CHAPTER 20
WAR PAINT (2016)

Composer: Scott Frankel (1963–)
Lyricist: Michael Korie (1955–)
Book: Doug Wright (1962–)
World Premiere: The Goodman Theatre, Chicago, June 28, 2016
Broadway Premiere: Nederlander Theatre, April 6, 2017

Songs

"Best Face Forward"
"Behind the Red Door"
"Back on Top"
"My Secret Weapon"
"My American Moment"
"Step on Out"
"If I'd Been a Man"
"Better Yourself"
"Oh, That's Rich"
"Face to Face"
"Inside of the Jar"
"Necessity Is the Mother of Invention"
"Best Face Forward" (Reprise)
"Now You Know"
"No Thank You"
"Fire and Ice"
"Dinosaurs"
"Pink"
"Forever Beautiful"
"Beauty in the World"

Overview

War Paint chronicles the thirty-year professional and personal rivalry between cosmetic industry pioneers Helena Rubinstein (1870–1965) and Elizabeth Arden (*c.* 1878–1966). The musical takes its inspiration from Lindy Woodhead's 2003 "dual biography" of the same name. The storyline, adapted for the stage by Pulitzer Prize-winning playwright Doug Wright, faithfully advances Woodhead's basic premise—namely, that Arden and Rubinstein's intense rivalry fueled their outsized ambitions, abetting their shared dominance of the burgeoning commercial cosmetics industry in the first half of the twentieth century. The long silent feud (apparently, by choice, they never met) turned the two adversaries into unwitting collaborators on the road to becoming America's first women self-made founders and CEOs of multi-million-dollar companies.

Arden, a native Canadian, and Rubinstein, born in Poland, both fled personally and financially troubled childhood homes. They emigrated to New York City as part of the "last great wave" of emigration to America (Foner 2013). Arden arrived in 1908. Rubinstein, having left Poland in 1902 to live with relatives in Australia, emigrated to New York City around 1915. Arden, aged twenty-four, arrived with virtually no money. Rubinstein arrived in America in her forties, having already become an extraordinarily successful cosmetics entrepreneur in Australia. Both women began their ascent to prominence in America just as powerful forces were changing the country's socio-economic landscape—forces that would shape their early careers and that they, in turn, would help define with their success and legacies.

New York City met Elizabeth Arden and Helena Rubinstein when all three were moving toward the peak of their powers. In the early part of the twentieth century, Arden and Rubinstein's ambitions fed and were fed by the city's burgeoning wealth and emerging national dominance in many fields: finance, women's cosmetics and fashion, advertising, celebrity journalism, culture, entertainment, the arts, and customer-based merchandising ("New York City in the Gilded Age" 2017). Arden and Rubinstein's business and personal lives ventured into all of those areas.

In the 1910s, New York City figured prominently in the women's suffrage movement when Arden and Rubinstein were achieving their earliest successes. New York state ratified a woman's right to vote in 1917, three years before Congress passed the 20th Amendment to the Constitution. However, the state had held an earlier women's suffrage referendum in 1915 that failed, losing narrowly among voters both in New York City and the rest of the state. The successful 1917 referendum passed narrowly, but it lost among voters outside of New York City: "It was the City with its large Catholic, Jewish, immigrant, and working-class population which carried the state for women's suffrage" (Lerner 1981).

New York City newspapers and magazines increasingly featured profiles of famous entrepreneurs and their families, turning them into celebrities and cultural icons for their charitable work and extravagant lifestyles along with their financial conquests. Arden and Rubinstein would soon join their ranks. Arden famously designed a line of cosmetics especially for crusading suffragists. A prominent figure in the thoroughbred horseracing industry, Arden was the sole owner of the 1947 Kentucky Derby winner, Jet Pilot. Rubinstein became a renowned art collector, exhibitor, and patron of Europe's and America's leading artists of the day.

While Arden and Rubinstein made history throughout their professional lives, those "Gilded Age" years in New York City prior to 1930 arguably comprised the most compelling period in their rivalry. This was the period in which Arden and Rubinstein destroyed long-standing taboos against "respectable" women wearing makeup and forged what became America's multi-billion-dollar beauty culture market: "They created an industry. When [Arden and Rubinstein] started their businesses cosmetics were w[o]rn mostly by prostitutes and performers . . . they changed all that" ("The Powder and the Glory" 2007). And they had done so well before 1930. Woodhead's biography devotes a great deal of attention to that period. However, Wright's script for *War Paint* opens the story in 1935 and proceeds chronologically through the early 1960s. The musical has no flashback scenes and few references to the early years in New York.

The decision to skip over the first twenty years of the Arden–Rubinstein biography was itself the result of two business decisions: one made by the *War Paint* creative team in pre-production, and one made by Helena Rubinstein in 1928. For the creatives' part, the Arden–Rubinstein narrative offered a rare vehicle for two "star power" Broadway actresses (and no male leads). The team cast revered Broadway headliners Patti LuPone as Rubinstein and Christine Ebersole as Arden, a marquee pairing that drove the show's overall design and promotional campaign. Time limitations and the fact that both Ebersole and LuPone were in their sixties militated against having the actresses play their characters as twenty-somethings during the show.

In one of Rubinstein's shrewdest business decisions, she sold her American business holdings in 1928 to Lehman Brothers holding company. Lehman paid her $7.3 million, the equivalent of $110 million in 2020 (Cavendish 2015). Rubinstein moved to Paris with her husband to enjoy her wealth, manage her European interests, and collect art. However, when the Great Depression hit America a year later, the value of her former company's stock plummeted. Lehman could not turn the company's fortunes around and, in 1935, sold Rubinstein's American interests back to her for about one-fifth of what they paid her originally. In an effort to restore her American company to primacy—especially since Arden had surpassed Rubinstein Inc. in sales while Lehman Brothers owned it—Rubinstein returned to New York City to resume command of her company.

The musical *War Paint* takes up the Arden–Rubinstein rivalry with Rubinstein's return to New York in 1935.

War Paint is no coming-of-age musical—in 1935, Rubinstein is sixty-five, Arden is fifty-eight. Both are fabulously wealthy and at the top of a game for which they wrote most of the original rules. The show understandably gives Ebersole and LuPone lots of time to unfurl their character studies: Arden's flamboyance; Rubinstein's brooding intensity; and their shared qualities—unbridled ambition, obsessive competitiveness, authoritarianism, and business genius. The storyline sprints through the decades stopping briefly at signature historical events along the way. In the 1930s, Congress compels cosmetics giants (Arden and Rubinstein among them) to label their products honestly. The 1940s saw the rivals honor women serving in World War II by creating special cosmetic lines for women in the armed forces (Arden) and women performing essential jobs replacing men who joined the military (Rubinstein). Both women are caught off-guard in the 1950s by a new generation of cosmetic entrepreneurs (embodied by Revlon founder Charles Revson), who are more adroit at marketing in the new age of television. A purely fictionalized accidental meeting between Arden and Rubinstein in the 1960s closes the show with a reconciliation between the two that never occurred.

War Paint lightly brushstrokes feminist criticism of the cosmetic industry and beauty culture that began drawing national attention toward the very end of Arden and Rubinstein's careers. Nevertheless, the musical briefly acknowledges the criticism as part of the women's legacy. In the fictional reconciliation scene, Arden and Rubinstein own up to their own storied manipulations of their customers. In so doing, the show's creators honor the audience's twenty-first-century feminist perspective on the Arden–Rubinstein legacy without undercutting the two women's unique place in American history: "Did we make women freer / Or did we help enslave them . . . [But] Who else will stand for Beauty in the World?"

War Paint premiered at the Goodman Theatre in Chicago on June 28, 2016, for a pre-Broadway trial. The show was well received although the creatives made some song substitutions and scene edits before the Broadway opening on April 6, 2017. Ultimately, many found the Broadway run disappointing for a number of reasons, not the least of which was that Patti LuPone, performing for months in pain with a weakened hip, withdrew from the show in early November to have hip surgery. Rather than replace her, the producers closed the show seven weeks earlier than anticipated. Expectations may also have been elevated over the fact that Ebersole, author Doug Wright, composer and lyricist team Frankel and Korie, and director Michael Greif had all worked together on the critically acclaimed musical *Grey Gardens* (2006), for which Ebersole had won the Tony for Best Actress and the rest of that team had all received Tony nominations. Several reviewers noted, however, that *Grey Gardens* was a better show, and the paucity of Tony nominations for the company suggested that their peers felt similarly.

Plot synopsis

In Manhattan, 1935, Society Ladies check their appearance in their compact mirrors. Radio announcers recite ad copy that resonates in their minds: "Has your husband lost interest? . . . The right face cream can work miracles." The ads invoke the ladies' anxieties over having to remain beautiful throughout their lives ("Best Face Forward"). At the Red Door Salon, Elizabeth Arden's exclusive house of beauty, the Society Ladies enter. They are greeted by lovely Arden Girls enumerating the splendors awaiting them in Arden's salon ("Behind the Red Door"). Elizabeth Arden regally descends a staircase. Awestruck by Arden's beauty and celebrity, the women hang on Arden's every critique as she greets them. Tommy Lewis, Arden's assistant and husband, enters with urgent business. Arden halts him, forbidding any disruption of her clients' outpouring of adulation.

Later, Arden reminds Tommy that at work she is his boss not his wife. Chastened, Tommy informs Arden that Helena Rubinstein is returning to Manhattan from Paris to resume control of her company. New York newspapers have dubbed Rubinstein's return a declaration of war against Arden. Eager for the challenge, Helena Rubinstein arrives at the port of New York with her executive assistant Harry Fleming ("Back on Top").

Rubinstein's beauty lab is a study in contrast with Arden's salon. Staffed by "fierce, burly beauty technicians," Rubinstein's company champions the science of beauty for all women, not Arden-style glamour and surface luxury. Rubinstein and Harry unveil a new product: estrogen-based skin cream, hoping to make it the "secret weapon" for every woman ("My Secret Weapon").

In her office, Arden prepares for Rubinstein's return. Having acquired a jar of Rubinstein's soon-to-be-released cream, she is impressed by the product but finds Rubinstein's bland labeling design laughable. Declaring "Arden Pink" the color of "every woman's childhood," she orders Tommy to announce a new Arden line: twelve shades of pink lipstick. Within weeks, Arden's creams, repackaged in pink jars, are outselling Rubinstein's estrogen cream. Harry suggests that Rubinstein mount a counteroffensive, "Twin Youthifiers": re-packaged estrogen cream in two different jars—one for day, one for night. Rubinstein agrees.

Rubinstein's Twin Youthifiers soon outsell Arden's best creams. Tommy presses Arden to grant him the near-partnership status Rubinstein affords Harry so that Tommy can work as effectively. To Tommy's dismay, Arden rebuffs him: "the moment I credit you is the moment they discredit me . . . I'm the one wearing a skirt." Fuming, Tommy exits.

Arden and Rubinstein dine at the same restaurant unaware of each other's presence. Rubinstein, with Harry, delights in her recent triumph over Arden ("My American Moment"). Harry requests a raise on the strength of their new success. Rubinstein suspects disloyalty and informs Harry, a closeted gay man, that she knows about his sexuality, adding it is "bad for the company." Sickened by her statement, Harry leaves. Arden, dining alone, intercepts Harry at the restaurant doorway and encourages him to contact her.

Arden interviews Harry and offers him a senior-level position plus assurances that his private life is his own business. Tommy enters unexpectedly. Understanding immediately that Arden has hired Harry, Tommy storms out of the office. As he leaves the building, the Arden Girls mock Tommy by saying "good night, Mr. Arden." Further incensed, Tommy taunts the girls into joining him for a joyously spiteful night of revelry ("Step on Out").

Harry informs Rubinstein that he now works for Arden. Devastated, Rubinstein tries to make amends but to no avail. Tommy and Harry cross paths on the street; briefly if coldly, they acknowledge their parallel circumstances. Arden and Rubinstein each despair over the challenges confronting a woman who wants a normal family but has more career success than every man she knows ("If I'd Been a Man").

Charles Revson, an aggressive, fast-talking young cosmetics developer, hangs around the Red Door lobby hoping to pitch a product to Arden: colored enamel nail polish. Persuading an Arden model he meets in the lobby to help him make his pitch, Revson barges into Arden's office. Contemptuous of men who think they understand women's beauty, Arden dismisses Revson and cautions the model not to tie herself to a man if she wants to be successful ("Better Yourself").

At her home, Rubinstein poses for a portrait by the famous French painter Raoul Dufy (1877–1953). Tommy appears and asks for Harry's former job. Enticed by his desire to topple Arden, Rubinstein hires Tommy, who suggests they report Arden to the Food and Drug Administration for using toxins in her products ("Oh That's Rich").

In Washington, D.C., senators interrogate Arden about her products' ingredients. Between committee sessions, Harry advises Arden to report Rubinstein to the government for using bizarre animal byproducts in her cosmetics. Rubinstein appears before the same Senate committee, which rebukes both women as charlatans preying upon women's vanity. Henceforth, both women must list all ingredients on the labels of their products. Harry and Tommy protest, but privately Arden and Rubinstein understand that, through their ruthless ambition, they brought this rebuke upon themselves ("Face to Face").

In 1942, women in stores examine Arden and Rubinstein's newest products, reading the labels with wonder and curiosity ("Inside of a Jar"). The government has limited manufacture of luxury items in wartime and has called upon all citizens to aid the war effort. Rubinstein designs a perfume, Heaven Sent, especially for women machinists, nurses, and others performing critical civilian jobs. Arden releases a new lipstick, Montezuma Red, and stenciled leggings in honor of the WACS and women's other armed services ("Necessity Is the Mother of Invention").

In 1951, Rubinstein learns that the board of a Park Avenue property where she has made a cash offer on a luxury flat has rejected her bid. The board's too-polite letter exposes their unmistakable antisemitism. Rubinstein recoils in disgust: "the USA with its grand promises." Arden basks in the success of her new groundbreaking luxury spa-retreat and accolades as co-owner of a Kentucky Derby-winning horse. Expecting acceptance into an exclusive association of society women, she is rejected because her wealth is self-acquired and not inherited from a distinguished family. In parallel, Arden and Rubinstein condemn the prejudicial disregard of their accomplishments ("Now You Know").

Confronting growing industry competition, Harry proposes a new Arden campaign: "Ten minutes that last ten hours." Arden objects to promoting beauty "shortcuts," but Harry counters that new competitors Revlon (Revson's company), Estee Lauder, and Helene Curtis are successfully marketing time-saving cosmetics. Tommy wants to add sex appeal to Rubinstein's line with a "bare shoulder" campaign, but Rubinstein is similarly repulsed ("No, Thank You").

Tommy brings William Paley, President of CBS, to meet Arden, hoping she will sponsor CBS's forthcoming television show, *The $64,000 Question*. Dismissing television as "down-marketing" for dog food and cigarettes, Arden declines. Paley subsequently approaches Rubinstein, who sees no point in presenting cosmetics in black and white. The *$64,000 Question* premiers sponsored by Revlon's nail products ("Fire and Ice"). Rubinstein and Arden watch the show in disgust. Revlon's television advertising strategy succeeds and the company soon overtakes Arden and Rubinstein in sales. Tommy and Harry, fired by their respective bosses after Revlon's surge, bump into each other yet again. They bury their hatchets and bond over battles they both lost ("Dinosaurs").

In 1963, Arden's is notified that her board of directors wants to find her successor—someone "more in touch with the times." Arden roars her outrage that her legacy is so unappreciated ("Pink"). At home, Rubinstein and her attorney draw up her will. She wants to keep her magnificent residence and establish a charitable foundation but struggles upon learning she must sell off the collection of portraits she has commissioned from leading artists. She resists at first, asserting that portraits do what cosmetics cannot: freeze a woman's beauty in time ("Forever Beautiful"). Ultimately, she relents and sells them.

A prestigious women's association inadvertently invites both Arden and Rubinstein to receive a lifetime achievement award intended for only one of them. Backstage, they are startled to discover each other. Acknowledging coldly this first-ever meeting, the two lifelong rivals reconcile over their shared singular place in history: "For fifty years we led the way / [But] . . . who else will stand for beauty in the world?" ("Beauty in the World").

Critical reception

Nearly all critics agreed that *War Paint*'s appeal lies in the star power and talent of the lead actresses, with costumes by Catherine Zuber coming in a close second. Many reviewers went so far as to compare LuPone and Ebersole's respective positions atop the musical theater profession with Arden and Rubinstein's towering legacy in the cosmetics industry. Critics also tended to agree that Doug Wright's book, although skillful and faithful to its subjects' representation, provided little in the way of compelling dramatic action. However, opinions on the degree to which the script's limitations detracted from *War Paint*'s overall effectiveness varied considerably.

No critic was more forgiving of weaknesses than David Rooney of the *Hollywood Reporter*: "LuPone and Ebersole and their contrasting turns here are simply mesmerizing. If this review ends up unfinished, just assume I died and went to show-queen heaven." Anticipating that other critics would take *War Paint*'s book to task for lacking dramatic intensity (some did), Rooney rebuts them before they can say a word: "[*War Paint* is] compelling and masterfully entertaining throughout. It's an intelligent, character-driven musical about two innovators . . . and it's been given a suitably deluxe production co-piloted by two star turns for the ages" (Rooney 2017). As Rooney predicted, *Variety*'s Marilyn Stasio described the show as "book-lite," but saw nothing that took away from the glamor of *War Paint*'s epic lead characters or the artists that brought them to life:

> *War Paint* is a musical about Catherine Zuber's fabulous costumes and magnificent hats, as modeled by the great Patti LuPone as Helena Rubinstein and her Highness, Christine Ebersole, as Elizabeth Arden . . . Luckily, there's not much plot to distract from these carefully nuanced characters, their amazing careers and dazzling wardrobes.
>
> *Stasio 2017*

amNY's Matt Windman also minimized the book's impact upon the show:

> The musical is built around an unwieldy and repetitive Ping-Pong structure of shifting back and forth between the two characters. However, *War Paint* still has a lot going for it, including self-empowered protagonists, high-powered performances, well-crafted period-style songs, the classy aura of old-school New York, and the smooth direction of Michael Greif.
>
> *Windman 2017*

Benjamin Brantley, writing in the *New York Times*, was less impressed than Rooney or Stasio but, perhaps in deference to Lupone and Ebersole's extraordinary track records, his protests were remarkably diplomatic and restrained. He lavished praise upon Lupone and Ebersole but let it to be known that they had done better work in the past. Brantley also faulted Doug Wright's slavish allegiance to Lindy Woodhead's biography for weighing down the production: "the compression of extensive research can make *War Paint* sound like a singing Wikipedia entry . . . Ms. Ebersole and Ms. LuPone go a great distance in disguising the show's essential sameness" (Brantley 2017). Linda Winer of *Newsday* also found the stars to be stronger than the show they were in but, owing to considerable appreciation of the show's historical content, considered *War Paint* a success overall:

> *War Paint* may not be one of the great musicals, but it is an enormously satisfying one. Yes, it is a showcase for established artists hungry for new material. But the show . . . looks at American women from 1934 to 1964 through a new lens—from the lives of two business titans who took lipstick from harlots to high society.
>
> *Winer 2017*

Decidedly less forgiving of the book's limitations, Joe Dziemianowicz wrote in the *New York Daily News* that *War Paint* "isn't very good even though Patti Lupone and her co-star Christine Ebersole are great . . . through it all [Arden and Rubinstein] lived parallel lives. As in they never met . . . That's a problem and it's one the creators haven't solved." Dziemianowicz considered that Wright's effort to repurpose for the stage biographer Woodhead's concept of pairing the women's similarities while emphasizing the presumptive fact that they never actually met disrupted rather than authenticated the story: "The structure of the show doesn't help. Arden starts a song, only to have Rubinstein chime in to give her side of the same story—or vice versa. All the back and forth makes it like musical ping pong" (Dziemianowicz 2017). Even less impressed was Adam Feldman, writing in *Time Out New York*. Offering passing praise for LuPone and Ebersole, Feldman has little good to say about the "tame battle" the two play out on stage:

> With two narratives to track, and a lot of time soaked up by musical numbers about customers and sales pitches, the show is heavy on primer and contours but light on blending and shading . . . much of *War Paint* is a blur . . . [and] doesn't make a persuasive case that its stories must be told.
>
> *Feldman 2017*

While some critics singled out for praise the show's two character-defining anthems, Ebersole's "Pink" and LuPone's "Forever Beautiful," few critics went out of their way to either lavish praise upon or excoriate Scott Frankel and Michael Korie's score. The consensus of kudos went to the stars and the costumer; the slings and arrows generally found their way to the librettist.

War Paint closed on Broadway after seven months and 236 performances, closing early when LuPone had to have hip replacement surgery. The show did not do well at the Tony Awards, earning no wins and nominations for Lupone, Ebersole, costumer Zuber, and scenic designer David Korins alone. The director, writer, composer, lyricist, and all the featured actors were passed over for nominations.

Historical accuracy and context

Arden, Rubinstein, and the "Heroic Age of Invention"

Elizabeth Arden and Helena Rubinstein's respective ascents to power, each in its own way, reflected both typical and atypical aspects of the countless success stories that arose during the later part of the American Industrial Revolution. From approximately 1890 to 1920, a period often referred to as the Gilded Age, the modern American city came into being. An industrialized urban economy centered in the Northeast and upper Midwest emerged, driven by rapid expansion of "heavy industry": large-scale metal, chemical, fuel, and machinery production. This expansion was powered by "waves" of immigrants, approximately 20 million of European descent, who, along with their immediate descendants, made up most of the industrial labor force for much of the twentieth century (Hirschman and Mogford 2009).

As large industrial companies gained increasing influence over the American economy, their founders became familiar figures in daily news reports, politics, "society" columns, and even popular culture. Industrialists like Henry Ford (Ford Motor Company), Andrew Carnegie (U.S. Steel), and John D. Rockefeller (Standard Oil) became celebrities owing to their wealth, political influence, charitable work, and, at times, extravagant lifestyles. In the process, their names became closely associated with their products' commercial brand. (For the likes of Henry Ford and airplane manufacturer William Boeing, the name became the brand itself.) They were invariably male, white, and, for the most part, born in the United States. However, Arden, Rubinstein and many other business successes rose to prominence in the context of another phenomenon of the Gilded Age: the "Heroic Age of Invention."

The years following the Civil War saw a dramatic rise in inventions and design creations that generated whole new ways of managing life and production. Engineers, designers, machinists, and tinkerers devised innovations that radically changed the American home and workplace ("Invention" 2020). This Heroic Age of Invention produced its own celebrated names: Thomas Edison, Alexander Graham Bell, and George Westinghouse. Prior to 1920, however, most of America's inventors functioned independently of affiliation with established firms: "Research laboratories, such as the Thomas Edison's in Menlo Park, New Jersey, were rare." Most of these innovators conducted their experiments and made their design models using space and materials acquired on their own (Akcigit et al. 2017). From family kitchens, basements, and converted workspaces emerged a legion of independent inventor-entrepreneurs. Many were women, newly arrived immigrants, and people of color—people generally excluded from centers of economic power earlier in the Industrial Age. Elizabeth Arden and Helena Rubinstein became towering figures among these American inventor-entrepreneurs.

The ingenuity and vast output of inventor-entrepreneurs gave rise to a newly emerging "modern corporation" (Heinze 2009). Unlike many heavy industries, the modern corporation sold directly to everyday customers through their own outlets or other stores: "[They] sought to attract and retain consumers through new forms of packaging, marketing, and advertising" (Heinze 2009). The modern corporation manifested itself in the rise of department store chains (such as Macys, Sears, and J.C. Penney), as well as mail order companies and variety stores. These companies put an array of home and self-improvement products into the hands of middle- and working-class consumers, including products from the new fields of cosmetics. The modern corporation was particularly welcoming of products from inventor-entrepreneurs. Many, including Arden and Rubinstein, were immigrant self-starters who began with little capital and no prior influence in American business. Moreover, immigrant entrepreneurs often used knowledge and experiences from their "pre-American" lives to establish their American business success—something Arden and Rubinstein did with a vengeance.

Arden (born Florence Nightingale Graham), who emigrated from Canada, was of Anglo-Scottish descent and grew up on a struggling family farm. She abandoned early studies in nursing but developed a life-changing fascination with the medical and restorative powers of salves, lotions, and creams used in treating burns and skin disorders. Fleeing the family farm, she moved to New York City in 1908. She landed a job as a clerk for a large pharmaceutical company and later worked as an assistant at a beauty salon. In 1910, confident in the knowledge she picked up from these jobs, she opened the Red Door Salon in Manhattan. She changed her professional name to Elizabeth Arden, making it the brand for her company (Elizabeth Arden, Inc.). Possessed of extraordinary instincts for product innovation, marketing, package design, and consumer psychology—to say nothing of a flare for the dramatic—Arden became known throughout the world for her salons, her cosmetics, and as a corporate celebrity in her own right. Fifty years after her death, the company is still a major cosmetics brand. Elizabeth Arden is currently owned by former rival the Revlon Company, which purchased it in 2016 for $870 million (Wahba 2016).

Rubinstein's American immigrant success story is more complicated than Arden's and took some decidedly different turns along the way. Helena (born Chaja) Rubinstein, was born in Krakow, Poland, and was the eldest daughter of struggling Jewish shopkeepers. In her mid-twenties, she had a falling-out with her father and left Poland to live with an uncle's family in Australia. Over the next twelve years she built a highly successful business in Australia, creating and marketing cosmetics. She eventually opened two beauty salons in Melbourne, whose extraordinary success enabled her to establish a salon in Paris and another in London before ever traveling to America.

Accounts vary on how Rubinstein achieved success in Australia. She claimed that her mother created extraordinary beauty creams in the family home in Poland and informed women in Australia that she had brought her mother's secret exotic formulas with her. Rubinstein sold creams and beauty treatments, passing on the fruits of her mother's old-world beauty secrets to enthralled Australian women. However, other accounts have Rubinstein waiting tables in Melbourne, putting together ad hoc creams with a local chemist from ingredients at hand, befriending a Melbourne tea company executive, and securing a generous investment to start her Melbourne salons (Maher 2018). Unlike Arden, Rubinstein became a prosperous self-made businesswoman before ever setting foot in New York City. What is not in dispute is that, like Arden, Rubinstein was a tireless innovator, inexhaustible self-promoter, shameless exaggerator, commandant of every aspect of her business ventures, exuberant profiteer, and an early master of consumer psychology.

Rubinstein moved to New York City in 1914, finding Arden established as the rising name in commercial beauty products. Rubinstein opened her first New York salon in 1915 and by 1920 had opened salons in New Orleans, Chicago, Atlantic City, and Boston. Like Arden, she was selling her products in modern department stores and other outlets as well as her own salons and shops. Like Elizabeth Arden's company, the Helena Rubinstein company remained a prominent brand long past its founder's death. In 1973, Colgate Palmolive acquired the company for $142 million (approximately $850 million in 2020), although the company has seen variations in its value since then (Levin 1988).

Arden's brand marketed beauty as a luxury to which every woman is entitled and for which she should pay handsomely. She expressed this sentiment succinctly in two of her most famous quotes: "Every woman has a right to be beautiful" and "Nothing that costs only a dollar is worth having." Arden promoted high society style, celebrity self-pampering, and gorgeous presentation. Rubinstein's company promoted women's beauty as an essential element of modern life:

> [Rubinstein] sold cosmetics as one component of a larger lifestyle. She pushed for women's self-improvement in all areas of life, believing that a beautiful woman was a confident, liberated woman. Her stores were the first beauty salons modeled after the intellectual salons of Europe which fostered the discussion and dissemination of grand ideas
>
> *Schneider 2015*

A case of label: Arden, Rubinstein, and the Federal government

Toward the end of Act One, Arden and Rubinstein are summoned separately to testify at a Senate committee hearing on product safety. It is 1938. Outraged senators interrogate the women over reports of dangerous toxic materials in their products, whose ingredients they do not disclose in labeling, advertisements, or any public information. We learn that government officials have been tipped off about hazardous ingredients in the women's "secret formulas" by their own former chief aids, Tommy and Harry, who switched allegiances and took their respective ex-bosses' secret formulas with them when they departed. Under questioning, Arden and Rubinstein are shamelessly evasive, affronted, and otherwise magnificently uncooperative. The appalled senators order the women to henceforth list every ingredient "from rose petals to formaldehyde" on every product they sell.

Setting aside the show's loose command of Congressional committee procedures, the exchanges between the women and the senators amount to a wildly distorted representation of a significant occurrence in the history of consumer protection law: Congress' decision to bring commercial cosmetics under the same labeling regulations as required for many foods and drugs, as well as to expand pre-market safety testing and inspections for cosmetics and a wide range of other products.

The scene itself is ludicrously fictionalized. Neither Arden nor Rubinstein were hauled before any government body to testify, much less forced to sit through a face-to-face hammering by outraged officials.

Moreover, their *aide-de-camps* did not alert authorities to the companies' secret wrongdoing. By 1938, there was nothing secret about it. Consumer groups and journalists had been conducting investigations and publishing muckraking exposés about high-profile companies since the turn of the century and had started catching up to the cosmetics industry long before 1938. In 1934, M. C. Phillips' bestselling book *Skin Deep* detailed widespread use of dangerous ingredients in cosmetics—including ingredients found in Arden and Rubinstein's lines. The American Medical Association (AMA) had been publishing research on the presence of hazardous chemicals in commercial products for years, even offering to oversee pre-market safety studies and grant AMA safety "seals of approval" to products that passed muster. (Neither Arden nor Rubinstein cared about AMA approvals, believing that lack of AMA approval did not impact sales or product reputation [Woodhead 2003].)

Regulating the burgeoning cosmetics industry was part of a larger goal President Franklin D. Roosevelt established for his first term (1933–7): update the 1906 Pure Food and Drug Act. The 1906 Act had many good consumer-safety provisions, including requiring widespread labeling of a number of food and drugs as well as prohibiting interstate transport of unlawful food and drugs. But it offered very little in the way of oversight of pre-market product safety and did not regulate cosmetics, a thriving industry even during the Depression. Administrators in the Food and Drug Administration had been frustrated over their limited enforcement powers under Roosevelt's predecessors, Herbert Hoover and Calvin Coolidge. However, with Roosevelt's inauguration in 1933, the agency and consumer groups found an advocate for expanding government regulation of food, drugs, and cosmetics sold throughout the country.

Business owners, industry associations, and their congressional allies opposed Roosevelt's expansion efforts and were often dismissive of the motives behind the initiative (attitudes nicely represented in the fictional, yet hilarious, scenes of Rubinstein and Arden misbehaving at the Senate committee hearing). The struggle to get the legislation through Congress took Roosevelt into his second term. However, in 1938 the updated Food, Drug, and Cosmetic Act was passed by Congress, requiring detailed product labeling on cosmetics and strengthening the government's power to inspect and approve consumer products prior to sale.

Movie rights: Elizabeth Arden, Max Factor, and Hollywood's "Powder Puff War"

Broadly speaking, the narrative premise of *War Paint*—both the musical and Woodhead's book—is that the modern women's cosmetics industry came into being between 1910 and 1930 on a four-block stretch of Manhattan between Arden's Red Door Salon and Helena Rubinstein, Inc. However, aficionados of West Coast culture might beg to differ.

During that same time period, Los Angeles-based cosmetics pioneers Max Factor (1877–1938) and the House of Westmore were leading a cosmetics boom that attached itself to the burgeoning film industry and the glamorous celebrity culture that grew up along with it. While the Arden–Rubinstein rivalry saw both corporate chieftains alternately gain and lose advantage to each other over time, Max Factor (Factor) convincingly surpassed the Westmores and other competitors, eventually achieving primacy in cosmetics for major studio film work.

Factor opened his first Los Angeles establishment in 1908—a wig, toupee, and hair-costuming shop. By the early 1910s, he had developed a loyal A-list Hollywood clientele. In 1910, there was no such thing as movie "make-up" (a term Factor is credited with coining); film actors used heavy grease paint and other traditional stage facial concoctions. An apothecary's assistant in his native Poland (born Maksymilian Faktorowicz), Factor's adroitness at chemical experimentation led him to create original cosmetic formulas that worked much better on film than did theatrical makeup. One of his hair shop clients, film director Cecil B. DeMille, began using Factor's makeup in his films as early as 1914. Almost immediately, Factor and his makeup became Hollywood fixtures. By the 1920s, Max Factor makeup was available nationwide, battling Arden and Rubinstein for market share by "enabling women to emulate the looks of their favorite movie stars" ("Our Heritage" n.d.).

Rubinstein and Arden expanded their respective product lines, global reach, and sales volume throughout the 1920s. While both had celebrity clients and ad models, they ceded the Hollywood studio filmmaking territory to Factor. That is, until the "Hollywood Powder Puff War" broke out. In 1935 *Becky Sharp*, the first studio-released feature film in color, was met with excoriating reviews for the distracting, unaesthetic skin tone colors emanating from the screen. Outrage from critics, audiences, and industry insiders left the studios no choice but to find a new approach to makeup that could accommodate new color-film technologies. Most studio stakeholders assumed that if anyone was going to make that discovery it would be Max Factor. However, well-connected friends of Arden in the Hollywood film industry (people she likely befriended through her thoroughbred horse business ventures) enticed her to develop a new product line to compete against Factor for the studios' business. Thus, the battle for the new Technicolor cosmetics market was "principally fought between two (new) brands and their respective products: Max Factor's Pan-Cake Make-Up and Elizabeth Arden's Screen and Stage MakeUp" (Dootson 2016).

Clearly the underdog in this contest, Arden went full-in nonetheless. She acquired an established makeup laboratory in Los Angeles from which she launched a "Screen and Stage" division and promoted the new line with grandeur worthy of a Hollywood premiere: "Screen and Stage Make-up, acclaimed by the greatest artists of stage and screen—is a complete departure from ordinary heavy greasepaint. It is perspiration proof, light-and-heat proof, and clings for hours without renewal . . . made of the purest ingredients obtainable, it feels extremely cool, comfortable and satin smooth on the skin" (Bennett 2019).

Arden managed to place "Screen and Stage" makeup in a few studio films, most notably Selznick International Studio's *A Star Is Born* (1937). However, Max Factor debuted his new Pan-Cake cream that same year and won the studios over: *Variety* declared Pan-Cake "the clincher for the success of colored film" (Dootson 2016), ending Arden's hopes of becoming Hollywood's go-to makeup brand for color filmmaking. Nonetheless, "the lure of show business [that] ran deep in Elizabeth's veins" and her brand's identification with up-scale glamour may account for the fact that her name and legacy are sometimes associated with Hollywood's golden era, notwithstanding her limited time and influence in the industry: "The whole modern cosmetics industry is nothing but the offspring of Max Factor and Elizabeth Arden, make-up artists to the Hollywood stars" (Woodhead 2003; Morin 2005).

Thomas A. Greenfield

Further reading

Akcigit, Ufuk, John Grigsby, and Tom Nicholas. 2017. "Immigration and the Rise of American Ingenuity." *American Economic Review: Papers and Proceedings* 107, no. 5 (May): 327–31.

Bennett, James. 2019. "Arden Screen and Stage Make-up." *Cosmetics and Skin*, February 10, 2019, https://cosmeticsandskin.com/bcb/arden-screen-stage.php.

Brantley, Ben. 2017. "War Paint Review: LuPone and Ebersole Shine in Smart, Rousing Musical." *New York Times*, April 6, 2017.

Cavendish, Richard. 2015. "Helena Rubinstein Dies in New York." *History Today* 65, no. 4 (April), https://www.historytoday.com/archive/helena-rubinstein-dies-new-york.

"Color Comes into Its Own in 37." 1937. In Kristy Sinclair Dootson, "'The Hollywood Powder Puff War': Technicolor Cosmetics in the 1930s." *Film History* 28, no. 1 (2016), doi:10.2979/filmhistory.28.1.04.

Dootson, Kristy Sinclair. 2016. "'The Hollywood Powder Puff War': Technicolor Cosmetics in the 1930s." *Film History* 28, no. 1, doi: 10.2979/filmhistory.28.1.04.

"Drug and Cosmetic Industry." 1935. In James Bennett, "Arden Screen and Stage Makeup." *Cosmetics and Skin*, Updated February 2019, https://cosmeticsandskin.com/bcb/arden-screen-stage.php.

Dziemianowicz, Joe. 2017. "Patti LuPone and Christine Ebersole Wage a Tame Battle in War Paint—Theater Review." *New York Daily News*, April 6. 2017.

Feldman, Adam. 2017. "War Paint." *Time Out New York*, April 6, 2017.

Foner, Nancy 2013. "Immigration Past and Present." *Daedelus* 142, no. 3 (Summer): 16–25.

Heinze, Andrew. 2009. "Advertising and Consumer Culture in the United States." *Jewish Women: A Comprehensive Historical Encyclopedia*, February 27, 2009, https:// jwa.org/encyclopedia/article/advertising-and-consumer-culture-in-united-states.

Hirschman, C. and E. Mogford. 2009. "Immigration and the American Industrial Revolution from 1880 to 1920." *Social Science Research* 38, no. 4 (December), doi: 10.1016/j.ssresearch.2009.04.001.

"Invention: Topic Essentials." 2020. In *American History*, ABC-CLIO. americanhistory.abc-clio.com/Topics/Display/1187723?cid=141&sid=1879197.

Lerner, Elinor. 1981. "Jewish Involvement in the New York City Woman Suffrage Movement." *American Jewish History* 70, no. 4 (June): 442–61.

Levin, Doran P. 1988. "L'Oreal Buys Rubinstein in Shrouded Deal." *New York Times*, October 15, 1988.

Maher, Louise. 2018. "Cosmetics Queen Helena Rubinstein Launched International Empire from Australia in 1902." *ABC Radio Canberra*, August 7, 2018, www.abc.net.au/news/2018-08-08/helena-rubinstein-launched-empire-from-australia/1006069.

Morin, Edgar. 2005. *The Stars*. Translated by Richard Howard. Minneapolis: University of Minnesota Press.

"New York City in the Gilded Age." 2017. *Smithsonian Associates*, February 2017, https:// smithsonianassociates.org/ticketing/tickets/236621.

"Our Heritage." n.d. *Max Factor*, https://www.maxfactor.com/en-gb/our-brand/our-heritage.

"The Powder and the Glory." 2007. Movie Download. Directed by Ann Carol Grossman and Arnie Reisman. Producer: Powderglory Productions. Distributor: Amazon Prime.

Rooney, David. 2017. "War Paint: Theater Review." *Hollywood Reporter*, April 6, 2017.

Schneider, Ivy Sanders. 2015. "For Helena Rubinstein, Beauty Was Power." *Yale University Press Blog*, February 24, 2015.

Stasio, Marilyn. 2017. "Broadway Review: War Paint Starring Patti LuPone, Christine Ebersole." *Variety*, April 6, 2017.

Wahba, Phil. 2016. "Revlon Comes to the Rescue of Elizabeth Arden in $870M Deal." *Fortune*, June 16, 2016.

Windman, Matt. 2017. "'War Paint' Review: LuPone and Ebersole Shine in Smart, Rousing Musical." *amNY*, April 6, 2017.

Winer, Linda. 2017. "War Paint Review: Patti LuPone, Christine Ebersole as Cosmetics Queens Rubinstein, Arden." *Newsday*, April 6, 2017.

Woodhead, Lindy. 2003. *War Paint: Madame Helena Rubinstein and Miss Elizabeth Arden—Their Lives, Their Times, Their Rivalry*. Hoboken, NJ: Wiley.

Wright, Doug, Scott Frankel, and Michael Korie. 2018. *War Paint*. New York: Samuel French.

CHAPTER 21
SUFFS (2024)

Book, Music, and Lyrics by Shaina Taub (1988–)
World Premiere: The Public Theater, New York City. April 6, 2022
Broadway Run: April 18, 2024–January 5, 2025

Songs (from Shaina Taub, *Suffs*. New York City: Theater Communications Group, 2024)

Act One	**Act Two**
"Let Mother Vote"	"The Young Are at the Gates"
"Finish the Fight"	"Respectfully Yours, Dudley Malone"
"Find a Way"	"Hold It Together"
"Wait My Turn"	"Wait My Turn" (Reprise)
"Terrell's Theme"	"The Report"
"The March (We Demand Equality)"	"Show Them Who You Are" (Reprise)
"Great American Bitch"	"Insane"
"Ladies"	"Fire & Tea"
"A Meeting with President Wilson"	"Let Mother Vote" (Reprise)
"Worth It"	"She and I"
"If We Were Married"	"A Letter From Harry's Mother"
"The Convention Part I"	"I Was Here"
"This Girl"	"If We Were Married" (Reprise)
"The Convention Part II"	"August 26th 1920"
"Alva Belmont"	"Lucy's Song"
"Show Them Who You Are"	"Finish the Fight" (Reprise)
"The Campaign"	"Keep Marching"
"How Long?"	

All quotes from the musical are from Shaina Taub's *Suffs*, Theater Communications Group, 2024.

Overview

Shaina Taub's *Suffs* recounts Alice Paul's (1885–1997) crusade to radicalize the American suffrage movement and push the country toward the adoption of the 19th Amendment. A young scholarly Quaker from New Jersey, Paul joined the American suffrage movement in 1911 following a three-year period in England working with the militant British Women's Social and Political Union (WSPU). Targeting America's largest suffrage organization, the National American Woman Suffrage Association (NAWSA), Paul believed the suffrage movement's long-standing strategy of cajoling one state legislature at a time to grant women the vote was too slow and bound to end in failure.

From 1913 until 1920 Paul and a cohort of like-minded suffragists launched national campaigns for a constitutional amendment guaranteeing universal women's suffrage. Through Paul's organizational skills and flair for public spectacle, they devised loud, visually arresting, and confrontational displays of outrage that by turns embarrassed, shocked, and intimidated their political opponents while also educating the public on the necessity of women's political equality. These included a mass protest march in Washington, D.C., the first-ever picket protests at the gate of the White House, and hunger strikes by jailed suffragists that spurred nationwide outrage. With the ratification of the 19th Amendment in 1920, Alice Paul's place in American suffrage history was secure. However, her story is still little known to this day beyond the cloistered realms of historical scholarship and niche museum collections. Shaina Taub wrote *Suffs* to help change all that.

A self-proclaimed student enthusiast of history and social movements, Taub was unpleasantly surprised that she had never heard of Alice Paul until a few years after graduating from college. A friend had given her Doris Stevens' 1920 book, *Jailed for Freedom: A First-Person Account of the Militant Fight for Women's Rights*. Stevens, a member of Alice Paul's inner circle, was also the designated chronicler of the organizations Paul led along the way. Taub read the book, loved it, and rued that this dramatic "treasure" of a story is not a prominent part of our American history education. Paul's obscurity perhaps as much as her astonishing accomplishments moved Taub to bring Stevens' story front and center before the American public.

Suffs is remarkably attentive to the historical record. The main characters are all historical figures who participated in documented events. The characters often repeat speeches, letters, and other documents word for word. Nevertheless, the musical strays from historical accuracy at certain moments in relation to President Woodrow Wilson and factionalism within the suffrage movement.

As much as *Suffs* stays true to Stevens' historical point of view and honors her writing, Taub dissents from Stevens, semantically at least, on one intriguing point. Taub conspicuously demurs on the *Jailed for Freedom* author's prolific use of the term "militant" to characterize Paul, her followers, and their politics, though the word "Militant" is in the book's subtitle. Stevens identifies Paul's brigade of activists as the "militant suffragettes of America" (7). She further dubs Alice Paul the "Militant General," touting Paul as channeling the "militant spirit" of Susan B. Anthony (5). Seeming to take pains to avoid the term, Taub may have taken to heart historian Elaine Weiss' fervent objection to describing Paul as militant. In *The Woman's Hour*, a book Taub admires, Weiss writes: "Unlike the [militant British suffragettes], whose forces attacked shops and office windows with hammers, planted small bombs in post boxes, and set fire to government property, Alice Paul and the Woman's Party was never violent and anything but 'militant'" (62).

Although *Suffs* represents Taub's Broadway debut as actor, writer, and composer, few Broadway neophytes ever brought a better résumé to their first gig. She had been a popular singer/songwriter, freelance musician, and theater artist in New York City for over ten years prior to opening *Suffs* at the Music Box Theater. Her numerous credits with the Public Theater in lower Manhattan, a launching pad for dozens of Broadway shows including *Hair*, *A Chorus Line*, *Fun Home*, *Hamilton*, and, of course, *Suffs*, all but preordained a Broadway career for her. After *Suffs* closed on Broadway, Taub played radical activist Emma Goldman in a Broadway revival of *Ragtime*, a show Taub cites as an inspiration for *Suffs*.

Several aspects of *Suffs*' early development broke new ground on Broadway and garnered some favorable pre-show "buzz." Once a Broadway opening date was confirmed, Taub became only the second woman ever to write the book, music, songs, and lyrics as well as star in a full-length Broadway musical. (Micki Grant accomplished the same feat in 1972 with *Don't Bother Me, I Can't Cope*.) Taub's early commitment to the story's educational mission attracted high-profile backers, including former Senator, Secretary of State, and First Lady Hillary Rodham Clinton and Nobel Peace Prize winner Malala Yousafzai, who may now add "Broadway Producer" to their distinguished résumés.

Taub's decision to cast only women and non-binary performers for all roles, including the male characters, offered a novel take on the sometimes contentious issue of identity-conscious casting (i.e., selecting actors for roles with similar life experiences as the characters they play, including identities of race, nationality, gender, and/or sexuality). The casting of *Suffs* conveyed an unmistakable message: for these two and a half hours on this stage, American politics and history are women's sacred spheres. However, some saw the portrayal of male characters, especially President Woodrow Wilson's comedic drag representation, as diminishing the higher purpose of the fighting, marching, and "finding a way" that the Suffs sing about so earnestly.

Despite closing its run earlier than expected, *Suffs* shows signs of having an impact on culture and media beyond the measure of its box office receipts. PBS has scheduled a filmed live performance for broadcast in its "Great Performances" series. Taub, in collaboration with the Educational Theatre Foundation, established a well-received grant program to fund ten high school productions of *Suffs* during the 2025–6 school year, even as the first post-Broadway national tour of *Suffs* is in progress. The Tony Award-winning score generated an Original Cast CD which garnered a Grammy nomination and a number one spot on the *Billboard* charts in its genre. Individual songs, such as the anthem "Keep Marching" and the ironic salute to female deference "Let Mother Vote," are finding online enthusiasts even if the score did not generate a breakout pop hit song while the show played on Broadway.

Plot synopsis

In 1913 Carrie Chapman Catt, introducing herself as President of the National American Woman Suffrage Association (NAWSA), addresses an audience of male lawmakers in the hope of garnering their support for women's suffrage. She appeals to the men's idealization of their mothers and wives, assuring them that women will vote in accordance with their husbands' wishes. After the speech, Alice Paul, a young intern with the NAWSA, introduces herself to Carrie and Mollie Hay, Carrie's domestic partner and a leader in the New York State suffrage movement. Alice criticizes Carrie's "strategic sweetness" approach to winning support for suffrage as being catastrophically slow. She proposes that NAWSA organize a first-ever march on Washington, D.C. to compel the President to support a constitutional amendment. Carrie declines and exits. Alice reflects on the risks of creating her own team to organize the march and "finish the fight" begun by earlier suffragists.

In a dilapidated Washinton storefront, Alice establishes her headquarters for planning the march to be held on March 3, 1913, the day before Woodrow Wilson's first-term inauguration. Her leadership team enters: Lucy Burns, a fellow suffragist whom Alice knew "in college"; Inez Milholland, a lawyer and glamourous New York socialite; Ruza Wenclawska, a working-class Polish immigrant and strike organizer; and Doris Stevens, a young writer whom Paul appoints as group secretary. (In this synopsis, "Suffs" refers collectively to these five women.)

The Suffs secure a parade permit from a resistant Washington chief of police after Inez threatens to use her influence with a senator to get him fired. They secure participation commitments from a range of delegations of suffragists representing all forty-eight states, including marching bands, dozens of university contingents, and numerous professional associations.

The Suffs receive letters from Southern donors threatening to pull their support of the march if "colored women" are allowed to participate. Alice recommends appeasing the donors by giving Black marchers a special delegation at the back of the procession. Ida B. Wells, a Black suffragist and anti-lynching activist, enters and rejects this diminished status for Black women marchers. Ida berates the committee for capitulating to age-old racist denigrations of Black people. Ida exits as the Suffs acknowledge their fault in this matter. On the morning of the march, Ida greets Mary Church Terrell, a southern Black activist who has worked on anti-lynching laws with Ida. Mary's social activism leans toward mainstream lobbying ("dignified agitation") compared to Ida's confrontational style. Mary announces that her delegation of university women will march in the college section alongside white university women.

The march proceeds down Pennsylvania Avenue, led by Inez on a white horse. The Suffs and fellow marchers shout and sing their demands. Ostensibly addressing President Wilson, the Suffs are aware of their historical reach ("I want my mother . . . sister . . . students . . . great granddaughters to know I was here"). Suddenly mobs of men rush and assault the women in an effort to halt the march. The police do not respond to their calls for help, but the Suffs resist and finish the march.

Later that night in their headquarters, the Suffs tend to their wounds and joyfully toast the positive newspaper and public response to the march. Alice proposes they reach out to Carrie Catt and NAWSA and jointly build upon the march's success to get a meeting with President Wilson. Doris is shaken by having been called "a bitch" by a heckler. The Suffs assure her that the word is an unintended compliment from men in that it validates their agency and power.

Carrie enters the headquarters and surprises the Suffs with her approbation of the march. Carrie suggests the two groups work together going forward and offers them status and support as an official NAWSA committee. As Carrie and Alice toast their new alliance, their sharp differences in strategy and temperament are evident.

After the march, the Suffs, now representing NAWSA, meet with President Wilson in the White House several times. Briefed by Chief of Staff Dudley Malone, Wilson asserts that although he adores "the ladies," men must shield them from burdensome civic responsibilities. As Wilson welcomes the Suffs, Alice tells the President that they want his support for a constitutional amendment guaranteeing women's suffrage. He brushes the issue aside, citing tariff reform as his all-consuming priority and dismisses them with a perfunctory "promise" to consider the issue.

The scene repeats itself in rapid succession to caricature the futility of the Suffs' meetings with Wilson between 1913 and 1916. The President dismissively rattles off a "carousel of excuses" for not endorsing a constitutional amendment. At the final meeting, Wilson hints at putting "in a good word for suffrage" during his re-election campaign. Alice offers to help write his endorsement as Dudley escorts the Suffs out.

In the Suffs' D.C. office, Alice takes a call from Carrie, who scolds the Suffs for disrupting Wilson's campaign speeches. Alice counters that Wilson broke his promise to campaign on votes for women and the disruptions drew favorable publicity to their cause. Alice is about to call a man she has been seeing and Lucy and Inez question Alice about her feelings for him. Alone, Alice questions whether her dedication to the movement is worth the sacrifices.

At a D.C. bar, Ruza and Doris warn Dudley that suffragists will oppose Wilson's election if he does not endorse women's suffrage. Ruza exits. Dudley tells Doris that Wilson plans to support women's suffrage eventually. Intimating mutual attraction, Doris and Dudley discuss the state of women in marriage. Dudley acknowledges his ignorance of the legal burdens that marriage imposes on women. Doris then invites Dudley to attend the upcoming 1916 NAWSA convention in Atlanta.

At the start of the NAWSA convention, Mary sees Ida and chides her radical friend for having joined the mainstream, white-dominated suffragist organization. Ida responds by saying that she is attending the NAACP convention and criticizes Mary for agreeing to be a NAWSA convention speaker – a wealthy "prop" for a group that does not also prioritize equal rights for Blacks. Mary counters that tolerating the white suffragists is necessary to gain their attention. Mary urges Ida to support President Wilson in the upcoming election.

Just prior to delivering her committee report, Alice tries to ask Carrie to support her proposal that NAWSA formally oppose Wilson's re-election unless he endorses votes for women. Carrie cuts her off, countering that NAWSA should support Wilson's opposition to American military involvement in the European war. Carrie insists that Alice, as a committee chair, support Wilson's re-election as well. At the podium, Alice and the Suffs unfurl a "VOTE WILSON OUT!" banner and raucously chant that slogan. Alice calls on NAWSA to ignore "old fogies" and take a united stand against Wilson.

Carrie, the next speaker, watches silently. Enraged by Alice's gall and divisiveness, Carrie berates herself for having given Alice the platform to undermine her leadership. Carrie takes the convention podium and rebukes Alice's speech and the Suffs' outburst. She assures the membership that NAWSA will not indulge the "reckless ventures" of a rival organization within its ranks. Reaffirming NAWSA's support for President Wilson's commitment to keep American troops out of Europe, Carrie offers hope that Wilson will soon "let mother vote." Alice confronts Carrie backstage for implying that she is a disloyal suffragist. Carrie countercharges that Alice dishonestly used NAWSA's name and funds to undermine the Association. Carrie expels Alice and her committee from NAWSA, withdrawing the Association's funding and support.

Alice proposes that the Suffs form a new party. She introduces the Suffs to Alva Belmont, a wealthy philanthropist and long-time suffragist who is aware of the conflict between Carrie and Alice. Alva supports Alice's radical stance and agrees to finance the Suffs' new National Woman's Party (aka "NWP" and "the Woman's Party") and fund a party headquarters near the White House. Alice has dispatched Inez, the NWP's most famous member, on a rigorous national tour that pushes Inez to exhaustion. Inez tells Alice she needs a respite, so Alice persuades her to take some time off and rejoin the campaign later. After a brief rest, Inez returns to campaigning. On election night, November 7, 1916, an optimistic NWP convenes in Washington to await the election results. When Wilson's re-election is confirmed, the women are stunned. Lucy enters with news that Inez had died while campaigning. The Suffs gather at Inez's memorial service where Alice eulogizes Inez as the movement's charismatic star. The service expands out "holistically, across the country." Alice hints that her next move involves the White House.

In January 1917, Alice, Ruza, Lucy, Doris, and other NWP protesters block the White House entry gate, vowing to remain until Wilson supports a constitutional amendment for women's suffrage. Carrie and Mollie Hay arrive for a scheduled meeting with Wilson, but Dudley informs them that Wilson has postponed it because of the NWP demonstrations. Enraged, they exit. Alice and the NWP Suffs celebrate the rapid growth of their party.

On April 6, 1917 Congress, at Woodrow Wilson's request, declares war on Germany. The White House decrees that "unpatriotic" opposition to the war effort "shall be punished." Alice, aware of the risks, exhorts her NWP protesters to discredit Wilson openly for refusing to support women's suffrage. They continue their protests against Wilson and are attacked by police, arrested on President Wilson's orders, put on trial, and sentenced to six months in jail.

In the Oval Office, Dudley fails to extract from Wilson any sympathy for the suffragists' maltreatment by authorities. Dudley resigns his position, publicly declaring full support for women's suffrage. In prison, Alice, Doris, Lucy and, Ruza declare themselves to be political prisoners, refuse prison officials' orders to eat, flip over trays, and begin a hunger strike. Elsewhere, Carrie addresses a male audience on how mainstream suffragists, unlike Alice Paul's NWP, support Wilson's patriotic war effort. Mollie shames Carrie for supporting Wilson's war policy, implying her rivalry with Alice has clouded her thinking.

In prison, Ruza attempts to eat, but Alice stops her, triggering anger among the other Suffs. They blame Alice for their years of life-threatening sacrifice under her leadership without success. Alice promises that Wilson will be publicly shamed into pardoning them. Posing as Doris' husband, Dudley visits Doris and secures her release from jail.

In Chicago, Mary visits Ida, who is writing an anti-war editorial. Invoking Alice's imprisonment, Mary warns Ida that public opposition to the war jeopardizes both the suffrage and anti-lynching movements. Ida counters that compromise prolongs the struggle for success. Mary and Ida share their mutual fear that the pressures of advocacy may overwhelm them both. Meanwhile, the imprisoned suffragists write letters detailing their daily beatings and force-feedings. Alice smuggles out the letters to Alva, who delivers them to Lucy, Doris, and Dudley. As press rumors circulate about the women's mistreatment, President Wilson releases an "official report" claiming that the imprisoned women are well treated and taking proper nourishment. Simultaneously the imprisoned Suffs debunk the report point by point. Dr. White, author of Wilson's bogus report, threatens to have Alice committed if she does not eat voluntarily. Alice dreams of a visit from Inez, who warns Alice her hunger strike will kill her and destroy their cause.

Doris leaks the jailed Suffs' letters to the press. The suffragists are soon released from jail. The freed Suffs rally supporters near the White House and burn Wilson in effigy. Carrie meets with Wilson, who commends her politeness but declines to discuss suffrage. Carrie angrily confronts Wilson for his years of evading the issue and weaponizing NAWSA's support for him against the women of the NWP. She tells Wilson to support suffrage for women publicly or else his "proper ladies" will join his violent opposition. Wilson addresses Congress, urging them to legalize women's suffrage, denying that "foolish agitators" have influenced his stance.

In Nashville, Tennessee, Doris writes "it's been two years of clawing our way through state ratifications." She doubts if Tennessee or any state will be the 36th state to ratify the women's suffrage amendment. Carrie and Alice, both in Nashville for the Tennessee vote, bump into each other. After initial pleasantries, their mutual bitterness surfaces. Carrie admits to herself that she sees in Alice her own youthful rebelliousness and recalls her mentor, Susan B. Anthony, reigning her in during confrontational outbursts.

In the Tennessee State House, the Suffs, Carrie, and Mollie wait in the gallery for the final vote. Senator Harry Burn, a conservative presumed to be an anti-suffragist, casts the aye vote that breaks a tie and the amendment passes. He reveals that he changed his mind upon receiving a letter from his mother just before the vote. She had written that, although she hates Wilson for taking the country into a war that killed her husband, she told Burn that he owes his own baby daughter an "Aye" vote. "Surprising himself, and the world," Burn votes aye. The amendment is ratified.

The women celebrate finishing the fight. Mary calls Ida. They celebrate on the phone, aware that Black women and men will face a new struggle to exercise their right to vote. Dudley and Doris pledge to marry. Carrie and Mollie dream of a day in which they can marry. The Suffs return to the Washington, D.C. office and toast the victory. Alice proposes a new struggle: win an equal rights amendment to the Constitution. The other Suffs decline the challenge and exit. Doris wants to write a book about their crusade, while Ruza heads off to become a professional actor. Lucy confesses she is not an activist at heart but joined Alice's crusade as an admirer and friend. Alice is left alone in the office.

Seamlessly it becomes 1972. Robin, a young videographer with the National Organization for Women (NOW), approaches Alice, who coordinates phonebanks in support of the Equal Rights Amendment. She assumes Robin is volunteering to make calls, but she informs Alice that NOW wants to film Alice for a campaign video presenting thirty demands to President Nixon, who is running for re-election. Alice objects, noting that "*one* persistent demand" won the 19th Amendment. Robin counters that only white women benefitted from the 19th Amendment and that one-demand strategies are outdated. Feeling like an old fogey herself, Alice unconsciously echoes Carrie by urging Robin to channel her energies toward an achievable goal. Unknowingly echoing Alice, Robin kicks off "her own musical" and vows to finish the fight. Alice joins Robin and the entire cast in the affirmation that everyone must march for justice in their lifetime.

Critical reception

Reviews of the Broadway production of *Suffs* were generally favorable. Nearly all critics praised Taub's supporting ensemble cast; Ida B. Wells' defiant showstopper "Wait My Turn"; the production's successful transformation from its decidedly weaker 2022 Off-Broadway premiere; and Taub's singular achievement in writing, composing, and starring in an exceptionally ambitious show. Plaudits for Taub even came from critics who otherwise took issue with her acting, writing, lack of humor, excessive humor, misplaced seriousness, and so on. Much of the critical ambivalence about *Suffs* spoke to Taub's handling of the Aristotelian mandate she imposed upon herself: "to please *and* instruct."

The *New York Times*' review was typical in that respect. Jesse Green felt "jubilant but dissatisfied" with the show he called "smart and noble and a bit like a rally." He lauded Taub's ability to craft lyrics and song structure to expand the narrative, an achievement particularly evident in the reprise of "If We Were Married." Introduced early as a flirtation between Dudley and Doris, Taub reprises the song in the second act as a post-ratification "I Want" number on marriage equality. However, Green felt that Taub "prioritized intelligence over expressiveness, making Paul seem not just driven but robotic" (Green 2024).

Variety's Frank Rizzo, on the other hand, lauded everything about the show. "[*Suffs*] captures the sweep of history in all its complexities without sacrifice of character or credibility." He had unqualified praise for composer Taub's "rich musical palette," actor Taub's "offbeat underdog charisma," and writer Taub's rejection of "facile men-against-women tropes" for explorations of "internal challenges within the movement and within the women as individuals" (Rizzo 2024). The *Chicago Tribune*'s Chris Jones, only slightly put off by the moralistically stiff "cleared by committee" feel of the show, ultimately saw what Rizzo saw: "*Suffs* does what all of the best Broadway musicals do: it humanizes and empowers, and it entertains and moves an audience" (Jones 2024). Elizabeth Vincentelli of the *Washington Post*, a fierce critic of Taub's "didactic overstuffed mess" that premiered off Broadway in 2022, was ultimately impressed by *Suffs*' "tight, confident, rousing, entertaining" Broadway comeback (Vincentelli 2024).

Many critics honed in on the characterization of President Woodrow Wilson, played for laughs as the suffragists' foil, to gauge Taub's use of humor in a show that takes its message very seriously. *Exeunt*'s Cameron Kelsall, who faulted the show for trying too hard to be "likable," praised Taub as well as actor Grace McLean for the "slippery fun" representation of the "detestable" President (Kelsall 2024). *Variety*'s Rizzo also cheered McClean's "dazzling vaudevillian turn" as the "snide condescending" Wilson. Green, in the *Times*, while finding nothing problematic in casting women and non-binary actors in male roles, found "Wilson, presented here as a cartoon fop, too silly to take seriously." Catherine Sawoski, writing in Columbia University's *Columbia Spectator*, agreed that Wilson's one-dimensional villainy undermined the show's presumptive serious intent but believed that casting was, in fact, part of the problem: "male characters are played by women wearing suits and fake facial hair, often leaving them feeling more like cardboard cutouts of the patriarchy than free-thinking agents" (Sawoski 2024). Sara Holden, writing for *Vulture*, admired the show but cited Wilson's characterization and featured song "Ladies" as examples of Taub stretching her "music-hall streak too far" at the expense of the character (Holden 2024).

Among the more negative-leaning reviews, Sawoski's *Columbia Spectator* piece took issue with Taub's perspective on feminism. Writing for the university's student paper under the headline "Broadway's *Suffs* Suffers from Activism Your Aunt Will Love," Sawoski remarked that "[*Suffs*] leaves a younger generation wondering if there is such a thing as too much self-congratulation." That said, Sawoski ultimately congratulated the show on its originality and for presenting a "revolutionary story . . . that even ardent feminists may not know in detail" (Sawoski 2024). Johnny Oleksinski in the *New York Post* admired Taub's score, especially "Wait My Turn" and the recurring "Find a Way." However, he struggled with the slow pace of the first half and its chain of "historical meetings and conferences . . . informative and sometimes touching . . . but hardly ever compelling" (Oleksinski 2024). Kelsall (*Exeunt*) found that *Suffs* was "a pleasant historical diversion" that failed to convey "the painful struggle to cement equality for all sexes" (Kelsall 2024).

At 300 performances on Broadway, the show was not a hit (numerous critical comparisons with *Hamilton* notwithstanding), but *Suffs* made a respectable showing in the major theatrical awards. Taub personally won

Tonys for Best Original Score Written for the Theater and Best Book of a Musical. The show itself was a Best Musical nominee as was Leigh Silverman for Best Direction of a Musical, Nikki M. James (Ida B. Wells) for Best Performance by an Actress in a Featured Role, and Paul Tazewell for Best Costume Design of a Musical. Taub also won a Drama Desk Award for Outstanding Music and Tazewell won a Drama Desk Award for Outstanding Costume Design of a Musical.

Historical accuracy and context

Pankhurst suffragette and American suffragist: the British roots of Alice Paul's radical American politics

Taub keeps *Suffs* laser-focused on how American suffragists navigated the political twists and turns between Woodrow Wilson's first inauguration in 1913 and the Tennessee legislature's vote in 1920 that ensured ratification of the 19th Amendment. Taub's characters resolve to "finish the fight" but otherwise allude only occasionally to the better-known early history of the American suffrage movement, such as the work of Susan B. Anthony or the 1848 Seneca Falls convention. Alice Paul, *Suffs*' protagonist and driving force, reveals almost nothing about her past. However, the biographical record on Paul quite literally speaks volumes about her involvement with the militant faction of the British womens' suffrage movement between 1907 and 1910. That period radicalized her politics, steeled her self-confidence, and prepared her for leadership in the fight for the 19th Amendment.

In 1907, Paul accepted a one-year fellowship at an English Quaker school, whose proximity to the University of Birmingham allowed her to attend classes and lectures. In November, Paul attended a lecture by Christabel Pankhurst, twenty-seven-year-old attorney, suffrage advocate, and eldest daughter of Britain's foremost militant suffragette Emmeline Pankhurst. (In England the term "suffragette" was coined by critics of the Pankhursts to mock their disruptive anti-establishment politics. The Pankhursts seized upon the derisive term as a badge of honor, flaunting the distinction it drew between themselves and their moderate counter parts—who were commonly referred to as "suffragists." The American movement, as Taub and *Suffs* make clear, preferred the term "suffragists," which is gender-neutral and sheds the diminutive "ette" suffix.)

Accustomed to the civil, genteel political debates she knew from her New Jersey Quaker upbringing, Paul was shocked when male Birmingham students began harassing Pankhurst before she even started speaking. The students "sang, yelled, whistled, blew horns, played rattles, so that no one heard a word" beyond the front seats, Paul would recall later. "Watching men silence the formidable Christabel Pankhurst became a crystalizing moment in Alice Paul's existence," wrote her biographers (Zahnister and Fry 2014: 46–7).

The summer of 1908 saw a rush of suffragist activity in London. Two major organizations planned extravagant rallies for successive weekends in June. The National Union of Women's Suffrage Societies, the larger, older, more conservative of the two (somewhat analogous to America's NAWSA), set their march for Saturday, June 13. The smaller, radical Pankhurst-led Women's Social and Political Union (WSPU) planned "Women's Sunday" for Sunday, June 21.

Although she had not yet joined any of London's numerous suffragist societies, Paul marched in both events and was profoundly influenced by the experience. She noted the "mixed gender message" of the women's "almost-military precision coupled with a stereotypically feminine talent for display." Additionally, she witnessed the women's power to organize on a large scale, fundraise, speak movingly to thousands, create their own publicity, drive press coverage, and mobilize vast numbers of women to action.

Paul's first significant participatory role in the WSPU was that of a street newsie for the organization's newspaper, *Votes for Women*. She was recruited by Rachel Barrett, an older student at the London School of Economics and WSPU operative, who scouted and trained women to hawk the paper's latest editions. With distribution of up to 30,000 copies per week, Barrett's streetwise force of young women generated essential public support and attendance for WSPU events (Brook 2017).

Barrett knew talent when she saw it. She guided the heretofore "timid" American Quaker through the rigors of standing alone in the streets; speaking directly to passing strangers; facing catcalls and assaults; and eventually winning over people drawn to her message, delivery, and emerging command presence. Through this improbable education, Paul soon excelled at speaking persuasively and forcefully to anyone—a competence in women that defied "the boundaries of social convention" for its time (Zahniser and Fry 2014: 60). WSPU's leadership took notice and increasingly called upon Paul for ever-more ambitious speaking duties. In a span of two years, Barrett's teachings empowered Paul to become a respected leader and influential voice within the British militant suffragette movement.

There appears to be no record of police aggressively arresting suffragists in connection with the June 1908 demonstrations. That chapter in Paul's suffrage journey commenced shortly thereafter. During the winter of 1908–9, the WSPU invited Paul to participate in a July march to Parliament to confront Prime Minister H. H. Asquith over his opposition to a bill that, if passed, would allow some women to vote. The invitation warned of possible arrest or imprisonment and demanded acceptance of those risks as a condition of participation. With some trepidation, Paul accepted.

The march was actually a series of smaller contingents arriving at Parliament throughout the day to thin out the police ranks. On orders from march leaders, Paul's contingent charged a police line in an effort to enter Parliament. Police shoved them back. Many suffragettes were injured in the confrontations and approximately 100 were arrested—including Americans Alice Paul and Lucy Burns (who met for the first time while in police custody). Although uninjured themselves, Paul and other detainees witnessed battered suffragettes "being brought into the police station half-fainting and their clothes torn to pieces." The police detained the suffragettes until Parliament adjourned at 1 am. The experience sealed Paul's "identification with the Pankhursts' righteous indignation . . . Alice was [now] engaged at a visceral and intellectual level" (Zahniser and Fry 2014: 72).

Doris Stevens v Carrie Chapman Catt: a battle of the books

Taub aligned *Suffs*' book with Doris Stevens' *Jailed for Freedom* to the point of writing Stevens into the action as chronicler of the story she inhabits. On the whole, *Suffs* remains faithful to Stevens' record of events but also advances many of Stevens' debatable interpretations of the movement's place in history, especially her commentary on conflicts between Alice Paul's start-up radical Congressional Union of the NAWSA (which became the National Woman's Party, in 1916) and the older, conservative, mainstream, "ladylike" NAWSA establishment embodied in the musical by Carrie Chapman Catt.

Suffs breathes new life into several of Stevens' historical arguments. Stevens holds that Paul and her disruptive suffragist allies "had a clear understanding of the forces that prevail in politics." As such, Paul and Stevens viewed Catt and NAWSA's strategy of travelling state-by-state soliciting men's support of votes for women as "ineffective" and "no longer necessary" (Stevens 2020: vii). *Suffs* reinforces this argument at almost every turn.

No one, least of all Carrie Chapman Catt, would deny that NAWSA pursued a long-game strategy of working to gain universal suffrage by winning over state legislators one state at a time. However, Stevens also argues that NAWSA, and particularly Catt, believed almost to the end that a constitutional amendment ensuring universal suffrage for women was a wildly unrealistic goal. Furthermore, both Stevens and *Suffs* strongly imply that the conservative leadership of NAWSA ultimately acknowledged, if begrudgingly or even cynically, that the political pressure exerted by Alice Paul's disruptive confrontational tactics was *the* deciding factor in swaying President Wilson to publicly back the proposed amendment in 1918.

Stevens acknowledges that her "interpretations" in the book are "arguable" (Stevens 2020: viii), and no one found them more so than Carrie Chapman Catt. Catt published her own account of the suffrage movement in 1923. *Woman Suffrage & Politics*, co-written with fellow NAWSA leader and ally Nettie Rogers Shuler, recounts the suffragists' "startling experiences . . . when woman suffrage once crossed the devious trail of American politics" (Catt and Shuler 2024: vii). Within its 500 pages, Alice Paul receives a scant two mentions and Doris Stevens' name does not appear at all. However, the weight of Alice Paul and her cohort's words and actions make their presence clearly evident in Catt's recollection of events.

In an obvious rebuttal to Stevens' assertion that Catt and NAWSA opposed fighting for a constitutional amendment until the tail end of the struggle, Catt details a series of long-standing mainstream suffrage actions to convert state-level success to federal action, including systematically mobilizing the growing number of pro-suffrage delegates to press for pro-suffrage planks at both parties' national conventions in 1916 (Catt and Shuler 2024: 216, 226). Moreover, in advance of Woodrow Wilson's 1916 presidential re-election campaign, NAWSA's state-based efforts gained momentum by winning women's suffrage in five states over a period of two years (1912–14), doubling the number of states that had approved women's suffrage in the previous twenty-four years.

As for Paul's British-rooted tactic of baiting police into arresting protesters, Catt concedes to Paul credit for garnering public support for women's suffrage through news stories of the suffragists' horrendous treatment in prison. Yet Catt rebuked Paul's political theatrics for alienating politicians and handing them an excuse to discredit the entire women's suffragist campaign (Catt and Shuler 2024: 232).

Catt further condemns as counter-productive Paul's British parliamentary-style 1916 campaign against Woodrow Wilson and the "party in power" for its indiscriminate opposition to all Democratic candidates, including state and local Democratic supporters of women's suffrage. Catt cites fallout among alienated Democratic convention delegates and state referendum workers who saw Paul's tactics "swell opposition to a considerable degree" (Catt and Shuler 2024: 244). Not surprisingly, Catt denies ever conceding that Paul and the radical National Woman's Party ultimately chose a net-positive course of action.

The early histories of the suffragist movement tended toward "intensely partisan account(s) . . . usually [examining] one group or the other, separately" (Mayo 1995: 32–3). Both Stevens' and Catt's memoirs fit comfortably under this umbrella. The facts support Stevens' assessment of Paul's unconventional leadership, mastery of public relations, and uncanny ability to keep Wilson "off balance" as key elements in winning the fight for the amendment. However, Stevens dismisses too easily the important role that dozens of NAWSA state chapters and other state-based suffrage organizations played in recruiting participants and swelling the ranks for the March 3, 1913 march in Washington. Additionally, Stevens makes no mention of Catt's leadership in the hard-won fight for suffrage in New York State in 1917 that readied the state's large congressional delegation to support the amendment two years later. More than anyone else, Catt corralled and delivered New York's critical body of votes in support of the 19th Amendment.

African Americans and the suffragist movement

Although Black women operated on the margins of the NWP, Shaina Taub gives two leaders—Ida B. Wells and Mary Church Terrell—prominent roles in *Suffs*. Because the musical takes place in the era of Jim Crow repression, the issue of racial inequality could hardly be avoided, although many tried to. In *Jailed for Freedom*, Stevens never mentions either Black leader or refers to any Black person by name. Only in the last thirty years have historians sought to integrate women of color into the history of the suffrage movement.

Ida B. Wells-Barnett (she took the name of her husband, Ferdinand Barnett, in 1895) had been an activist and journalist for several decades when she joined the suffrage movement. She was well known for her anti-lynching writings in the 1890s. Later, she founded the Alpha Suffrage club—the first Black female suffrage organization in Chicago—to coincide with the campaign to secure presidential and municipal suffrage in Illinois. In March 1913, she traveled to Washington, D.C. for Alice Paul's march, one of sixty-five suffragists from the Illinois delegation. But as *Suffs* explains, the organizers insisted that state delegations should only include white people, ostensibly to appease white Southern women who opposed suffrage for Black women. The poignant song "Wait My Turn" expresses despair, frustration, and determination that Wells-Barnett and other Black women felt as they worked alongside racist white suffragists. But Wells-Barnett did not accept this slight, as the song "The March (We Demand Equality)" describes; she stepped out from the crowds and joined her Illinois sisters in the march.

Taub builds dramatic tension by contrasting the radicalism of Wells-Barnett with the more conservative approach of Mary Church Terrell, much like the differences between Paul and Catt. In truth, Wells-Barnett and Terrell did not differ much. Terrell marched at the back of the 1913 parade with her sorority, but she later picketed the White House in 1917, a radical protest that surely Wells-Barnett (who was focused at the time on mobilizing the Black vote in Chicago) would have approved. Both women were co-founders of the National Association of Colored Women's Clubs, known for its motto "Lifting as We Climb." Their club involvement and activism addressed several social justice causes, not just women's suffrage.

Wells-Barnett and Terrell were far more closely aligned in terms of tactics and strategy than Paul and Catt ever were. Their shared approach has much to do with living in an era of widespread disdain for Black equality. Some suffragist leaders publicly advocated for Black women's right to vote, but neither Catt nor Paul did so. Even more daunting was the vocal intransigence of white supremacists towards the suffrage amendment. Ratification required the support of a handful of Southern states. In the pivotal Tennessee showdown, one broadside warned lawmakers "that Woman Suffrage means a reopening of the entire Negro Suffrage question, loss of State rights, and another period of reconstruction horrors." Many racists warned that the 19th Amendment was a harbinger for racial equality under the law, which, of course, it was.

Wilson and the suffragists

President Woodrow Wilson is the main antagonist in *Suffs*. While it is true that Alice Paul's suffrage strategy hinged on prodding the President to endorse the amendment, the musical credits Wilson with more power than he had and neglects several other factors that contributed to the passage of the 19th Amendment. Paul and the NWP kept the suffrage movement in the newspapers through innovative protests: a countermarch at Wilson's inaugural; picketing the White House; choosing jail terms over accepting fines; hunger strikes; and burning the President in effigy. But Catt's "Winning Plan" was equally if not more effective in changing votes and winning elections in state legislative elections to secure suffrage.

Following the success of the 1913 march, Paul and the Congressional Union (the forerunner of the NWP) stepped up pressure on Wilson and the Democrats, leading to the suffragists' campaign in 1916 to oust them from office. There is no doubt that they campaigned strenuously. Inez Milholland did collapse (in Los Angeles) and later died from overexertion, but not on election day, as *Suffs* portrays. Despite their efforts, the NWP failed to thwart Wilson's re-election, and Democrats maintained their control of Congress.

Paul shifted tactics in January 1917 by picketing the White House. No one had ever attempted a protest like this before. After several weeks of mildly irritating demonstrations, the Silent Sentinels, as they were called, increased the pressure on the Wilson administration. On Bastille Day, July 14, several upper-class Sentinels were arrested, but instead of paying a fine, which they had the means to do, they opted for a sixty-day incarceration at a notorious workhouse. The prospect of society ladies in such a degrading place prompted the President to pardon them and dress down the D.C. police commissioner.

The Sentinels also mocked Wilson's dedication to democracy during World War I. One banner insisted that Wilson was "deceiving" officials from Russia's new revolutionary government and implored them to help "make this nation really free." Subsequent banners ridiculed Wilson's hypocrisy, calling him "Kaiser Wilson," for championing democracy yet denying women the vote. Angry men mobbed these pickets and prompted the police to arrest more of the NWP women. In the context of government censorship of leftist groups and anti-war activities, the subsequent trials resulted in sentences that ranged from two to seven months.

Wilson received many protest letters that decried the plight of the suffragists, especially the forced feedings. This pressure led him to inquire about the conditions in the prison, as *Suffs* depicts. Indeed, Dr. William White, Superintendent of the Government Hospital for the Insane in Washinton, D.C., did try to portray Alice Paul as hysterical in order to incarcerate her for an undefined period of time at his asylum. Ultimately, Wilson caved and released Paul and the other picketers, partly because, as Paul stated, they could not "suppress us," but also because Wilson feared investigations once Congress reconvened.

Suffs conflates the release of the Sentinels from prison with the burning of papers and other objects in urns, but these events took place a year apart. Following New York state's vote for extending the suffrage to women in November 1917, Wilson publicly endorsed the suffrage amendment in January 1918. This endorsement seemed decisive in convincing six previously uncommitted Democrats and thus securing a two-thirds majority in the House of Representatives. Wilson's support was decisive because of the unusual partisan politics of suffrage. Most Republicans in Congress supported women's suffrage, but because they did not have a majority, Democrats had to provide the other votes, despite the fact that suffrage deeply divided the party.

The musical builds up to Wilson's speech before the US Senate in support of women's suffrage on September 30, 1918. This indeed was a major event. It was the first time a President had made a direct appeal in the chamber for a Senate action. *Suffs* mostly quotes accurately from this speech, although it concludes with the line "if you give them this . . . thing" when in reality Wilson had said, "if you do this just thing." But Wilson's speech did not produce a victory for the suffragists. The vote fell two votes short of the two-thirds majority needed for passage. In hindsight the defeat of the measure calls into question Paul's strategy. Wilson had neither the constitutional power nor sufficient influence to bring about women's suffrage to begin with.

Tennessee and ratification victory

After Wilson's endorsement of the suffrage amendment, *Suffs* jumps ahead two years to the ratification vote in Tennessee, but those skipped-over months help explain the ultimate success of the 19th Amendment. It was clear that Wilson could not deliver enough Democratic votes, so NAWSA targeted anti-suffrage senators in the upcoming 1918 midterm elections. Republicans, who were more favorably disposed toward women's suffrage than Democrats, were swept into power. Before the new Republican majority was seated in March 1919, Paul tried once more to force the Senate's hand. In *Suffs*, the setting of fires in urns at the White House protests takes place before Wilson's Senate speech, but in truth, the burnings began in January 1919 and were intended to force another Senate vote before the next Congress was seated. The burning of Wilson's effigy, in particular, was a tactical error on Paul's part. These incendiary protests failed to gain any votes, and they proved to be divisive within the ranks of the NWP. Some equated it to a lynching.

The new Republican majority in Congress promptly passed the amendment, but suffragists did not celebrate excessively. They knew that a hard fight lay ahead to convince thirty-six states to approve ratification. Some states, such as Wisconsin and Illinois, raced to become the first to ratify the amendment, others approved the measure but not quickly, and then there were some states, particularly in the South, that strenuously opposed ratification. Both the NWP and NAWSA deployed supporters and strategists in several grueling campaigns.

By the summer of 1920, thirty-five states had ratified the amendment, and all eyes turned to Tennessee. Suffragists referred to the occasion as Armageddon. Catt spent a month in Nashville coordinating the lobbying of lawmakers, but Paul, contrary to what *Suffs* portrays, stayed away for fear that her radical reputation would discourage support for ratification. The vote in the Tennessee House came down to Harry T. Burn, but the *Suffs* account includes several inaccuracies. Burn was a member of the general assembly, not a senator. His mother, Febb (not Phoebe) Burn, sent a letter, not a telegram. Harry brought his mother's letter in his coat pocket to the vote. *Suffs* does not quote exactly from the letter, but the song "A Letter from Harry's Mother" does convey the context of her life.

On August 26, 1920, the 19th Amendment was added to the Constitution. It was not just a victory for Paul and Catt but also for the tens of thousands of women across the country who protested at state capitols, sent letters and telegrams to lawmakers, signed petitions, and used their power and influence behind the scenes to prohibit gender discrimination in voting.

Behind the scenes: an historical miscellany

Rev. Anna Howard Shaw, proud President of NAWSA. In *Suffs*' opening scene, Carrie Chapman Catt addresses a crowd of male politicians gathered in 1913. Identifying herself as the "proud president of NAWSA for twenty years now," she deferentially cajoles them to let women vote. Following her speech, Alice Paul approaches Catt and proposes that NAWSA organize a march in Washington, D.C. to force President Wilson to support a constitutional amendment guaranteeing suffrage for women. Catt dismissively declines.

In this scene the character of Carrie is an amalgam of Carrie Chapman Catt and Reverend Anna Howard Shaw, an ally of Catt's who served as NAWSA President from 1904 to 1915. According to Catt, Alice Paul approached NAWSA's board in 1912 during Shaw's presidency, not Catt's, to request permission to organize a "parade" in Washington and raise money to fund it. The board accepted Paul's proposal with Shaw's approval, yet Anna Howard Shaw is not represented as a named character in *Suffs*.

Catt served as a NAWSA board member during Shaw's presidency. As a delegate to the 1913 NAWSA annual convention, Catt confronted Paul from the audience over the latter's leadership of NAWSA's Congressional Union. Following Paul's Committee chair's report, Catt inaccurately accused Paul of acting without authorization from the Association. Additionally, Catt accused the Committee of promoting itself at the expense of the Association, pointing specifically to their decision to publish their own independent newsletter. In contrast to Catt, Anna Howard Shaw did not openly oppose Paul's radical approach to securing votes for women and was reluctant to criticize Paul publicly.

The White House, the Chief of Staff, and the "heckling variety." Taub presents Dudley Malone as Woodrow Wilson's White House Chief of Staff. Dudley Field Malone was, as *Suffs* correctly portrays him, a trusted confidant of President Wilson who broke with the President publicly over Wilson's unwillingness to declare support for a women's suffrage constitutional amendment. Taub also integrates Malone and Doris Stevens' real life love affair and marriage into *Suffs*' story. In Act 2, Scene 2, Dudley composes his open letter of resignation to Wilson, which made national headlines and embarrassed the Wilson Administration.

All of this is historically accurate except that Malone never worked in the White House, much less served as Chief of Staff. Malone was an influential New York Democratic party leader who aided Wilson in his 1912 presidential campaign. Wilson rewarded Malone with a prestigious appointment—Collector of Customs for the Port of New York, the job from which Malone resigned in his famous letter.

Wilson's Chief of Staff for both terms was John Patrick Tumulty, a New Jersey lawyer and Democratic campaigner who backed Wilson in his 1910 run for Governor of New Jersey. Correspondences involving Tumulty in Woodrow Wilson's Papers suggests that, in presenting Paul's and Catt's respective maneuverings to garner Wilson's endorsement of a suffrage amendment, Taub got the tone of the Wilson Oval Office just right.

On one occasion in 1917, Tumulty forwarded to Wilson a request from Carrie Chapman Catt for a ten-minute meeting with a small group from NAWSA. Not certain as to who was whom in the suffragist movement, Wilson sent a memorandum to Tumulty asking, "Are these ladies of the 'Congressional Union' variety?" Tumulty replied in his memorandum that NAWSA was "the conservative body . . . the Congressional Union people are of the 'heckling' variety and their methods are not approved by the National Association" (Dodd 2013: 390).

The Suffs confront President Wilson. In Act 1, Scene 5, Alice Paul's NAWSA Congressional Union, deputized by the Association to press President Wilson to endorse a constitutional amendment, initiates a series of White House meetings with Wilson that occur between 1913 and 1916. At their first meeting, Wilson deflects the Suffs' efforts to discuss votes for women, citing economic priorities in a clumsy attempt to mask his opposition to women participating in the public sphere. The characters remain on stage for a few minutes as three years of Wilson's condescension and evasiveness spin by on "a carousel of excuses" (tariffs, Congress, the *Lusitania*) for not discussing votes for women. For all its satiric folly, the scene conveys infuriating paternalistic authority to considerable effect.

The onstage presentation of these meetings, however, only hints at how Doris Stevens chronicled them in *Jailed for Freedom* and belies Paul's elaborate strategy in staging these confrontations with Wilson. According to Stevens, no two were alike. Paul orchestrated the various meetings so that Wilson would not know in advance what women or how many were coming to see him until he met each group. One group included Paul and a dozen prominent women journalists and other professionals. Another was comprised of a large group of suffragists from his home state of New Jersey. Still another even larger deputation comprised the delegates to the 1915 NAWSA convention in Washington. In that meeting, NAWSA President Alice Howard Shaw fronted the delegation, cross-examining Wilson for failing to endorse an amendment during his ongoing re-election campaign. The overall impact of Paul's strategy was to keep Wilson "off balance" and create "a forceful impression of a highly organized well-educated responsible battalion of women who wanted to vote" (Mayo 1995: 33).

Thomas A. Greenfield and Justin Behrend

Further reading

Adams, Katherine H. and Michael L. Keene. 2008. *Alice Paul and the American Suffrage Campaign*. Urbana: University of Illinois Press.

Berg, A. Scott. 2013. *Wilson*. New York: Berkley.

Brook, Penny. 2017. "Remembering the Suffragette movement on International Women's Day." *Blog: British Library Untold Lives*, March 2017, blogs.bl.uk/untoldlives/2017/03/remembering-the-suffragette-movement-on-international-womens-day.html.

Cahill, Cathleen D. 2020. *Recasting the Vote: How Women of Color Transformed the Suffrage Movement*. 2020. Chapel Hill: University of North Carolina Press.

Catt, Catherine Chapman and Nettie Rogers Shuler. 2024. *Woman Suffrage and Politics: The Inner Story of the Suffrage Movement*. Garden City, NJ: Dover (New York City: Charles Scribner's Sons, 1923).

Dodd, Lynda G. 2013. "Parades, Pickets, and Prison: Alice Paul and the Virtues of Unruly Constitutional Citizenship." *Journal of Law and Politics* XXIV: 340, 433, https://ssrn.com/abstract=2226351.

DuBois, Ellen Carol. 2020. *Suffrage: Women's Long Battle for the Vote*. New York: Simon and Schuster.

Green, Jesse. 2024. "In *Suffs*, the Thrill of the Vote and How She Got it," *New York Times*, April 18, 2024, https://www.nytimes.com/2024/04/18/theater/suffs-review-broadway-shaina-taub.html.

Holden, Sara. 2024. "Living is Harder: *Suffs* and *Grenfell*," *Vulture*, April 18, 2024, https://www.vulture.com/article/theater-review-suffs-and-grenfell.html.

Jones, Chris. 2024. "Suffs' on Broadway Explores the History of Women's Suffrage in the United States." *Chicago Tribune*, April 18, 2024, https://www.chicagotribune.com/2024/04/18/review-suffs-on-broadway-explores-the-history-of-womens-suffrage-in-the-united-states/.

Kelsal, Cameron. 2024. "Shaina Taub's Likable Suffragist Musical Could Use Some of its Own Advice," *Exeunt*, April 25, 2024, https://exeuntnyc.com/reviews/review-suffs-at-the-music-box-theatre/.

Mayo, Edith. 1995. "Forward." In *Jailed for Freedom: American Women Win the Vote*, edited by Doris Stevens and Carol O'Hare, Troutdale, OR: New Sage Press.

Mickenberg, Julia L. 2014. "Suffragettes and Soviets: American Feminists and the Specter of Revolutionary Russia." *Journal of American History* 100, no. 4: 1021–51.

Oleksinski, Johnny. 2024. "A Moving Musical March that's Not Quite There Yet," *New York Post*, April 18, 2024, https://nypost.com/2024/04/18/entertainment/suffs-review-a-moving-musical-march-thats-not-quite-there-yet/.

Rizzo, Frank. 2024. "Broadway Musical About Women's Fight for the Vote Gets Thrilling and Entertaining Musicalization." *Variety*, April 18, 2024, https://variety.com/2024/legit/reviews/suffs-review-musical-broadway-1235974881/.

Sawoski, Catherine. 2024. "Broadway's *Suffs* Suffers From Activism Your Aunt Will Love." *Columbia Spectator*, April 20, 2024, https://www.columbiaspectator.com/arts-and-culture/2024/04/29/review-broadways-suffs-suffers-from-activism-your-aunt-will-love/.

Spruill, Marjorie J., ed. 2021. *One Woman, One Vote: Rediscovering the Woman Suffrage Movement*. 2nd edition. Tillamook, OR: New Sage Press.

Stevens, Doris. 2020. *Jailed for Freedom: A First-Person Account of the Militant Fight for Women's Rights*. New York City: Workman Publishing Company (New York City: Boni and Liveright, 1920).

Taub, Shaina. 2024. *Suffs: Book, Music, and Lyrics*. New York City: Theater Communications Group.

Terborg-Penn, Rosalyn. 1988. *African American Women in the Struggle for the Vote, 1850–1920*. Bloomington: Indiana University Press.

Vincentelli, Elisabeth. 2024. "Spirited Musical About Suffragists is not a Triumph, But Much Improved." *Washington Post*, April 24, 2024, https://www.washingtonpost.com/entertainment/theater/2024/04/18/suffs-broadway-review.

Weiss, Elaine. 2018. *The Woman's Hour: The Great Fight to Win the Vote*. New York: Penguin Books.

Zahniser, J. D. and Amelia R. Fry. 2014. *Alice Paul: Claiming Power*. New York: Oxford University Press.

ABOUT THE AUTHOR AND CONTRIBUTORS

Thomas A. Greenfield is Professor of English Emeritus and former dean of the College at the State University of New York at Geneseo. His previous books include *American Musicals in Context, Broadway: An Encyclopedia of Theater and American Culture* (2010), *Radio: A Reference Guide* (1989), and *Work and the Work Ethic in American Drama, 1920–1970* (1982). His articles and essays have appeared in *The Arthur Miller Journal, Comparative Drama, The Crisis, Critical Insights: The Crucible, Liberal Education, South Atlantic Bulletin*, and *Twentieth-Century Literary Criticism*, among other publications.

Christina M. Baurle is a theater teacher and Director at Port Chester High School in Westchester, New York. She is a member of the Connected Arts Network, a professional learning community for arts educators. She is also the Vice President of the Eastern Student Artist Guild, an organization that recognizes emerging high school theatre artists in non-musicals and helps them to grow through mentorship and creative opportunities. Christina holds a master's degree from St. Joseph's College and a bachelor's degree from the State University of New York at Geneseo.

Justin Behrend is a Professor of history at the State University of New York at Geneseo. He teaches courses on the Civil War era and African American history. He has published on Reconstruction, emancipation, and slave rebellions. He is the author of *Reconstructing Democracy: Grassroots Black Politics in the Deep South after the Civil War* (2015).

Melanie Blood is Professor of English and Music at the State University of New York at Geneseo, where she also serves as Associate Provost for Curriculum and Dean for Workforce Development. She has published articles and reviews in the *Journal of American Drama and Theatre, Modern Drama*, and *Theatre History Studies*, and as well as numerous anthologies: *Angels in American Theatre, Broadway: An Encyclopedia of Theater and American Culture*, and *The Gay and Lesbian Theatrical Legacy.* Melanie is also past secretary of the Association for Theatre in Higher Education and American Theatre and Drama Society. She regularly teaches about, directs, and choreographs for the musical stage.

Sue Ann Brainard is Research Librarian Emeritus at the State University of New York at Geneseo, where she specialized in teaching research technology for English, History, and Theater. She was a contributing author and Senior Research Associate for *Broadway: An Encyclopedia of Theater and American Culture.* Her work as a research librarian earned her two major American Library Association collaborative awards: Innovation in Instruction (2016) and Excellence in Academic Libraries (2018) .

Kenneth J. Cerniglia is a veteran dramaturg, writer, creative consultant, and organizational leader. His dramaturgy includes the Broadway hits *Hadestown* and *Peter and the Starcatcher.* During a sixteen-year tenure at Disney Theatrical, he developed over seventy titles for Broadway, touring, international, and licensed productions, including *Aladdin, Freaky Friday, High School Musical, The Hunchback of Notre Dame, The Little Mermaid, Newsies, Tarzan*, and the Marvel Spotlight plays. Kenneth is Board Co-chair of the Literary Managers and Dramaturgs of the Americas and holds a PhD in theatre history and criticism from the University of Washington.

Carissa Cordes is an IATSE Local One Union stagehand. Carissa was a contributing author to *Broadway: An Encyclopedia of Theater and American Culture* and has written theater reviews for the *New York Theatre Review* and nytheatre.com. Carissa was associate director for Theatre 1010's production of *The Cradle Will Rock* in New York City (2010) and has performed, designed, and worked behind the scenes in numerous other productions. Carissa has a BFA in Theatre Arts from New York University and has earned a MSTOM in Traditional Chinese Medicine from Pacific College.

Charlie Freeman is a Distinguished Teaching Professor at SUNY Geneseo in the Department of Physics and Astronomy and is a recipient of the SUNY Chancellor's award for Excellence in Teaching. Charlie's research interests are in accelerator physics and ion beam analysis. He serves as director of the 1.7 MV Pelletron accelerator and has supervised scores of undergraduate students on numerous research projects in collaboration with scientists at the University of Rochester's Laboratory for Laser Energetics. Charlie is also an avid baseball fan who has lectured on the physics of our national pastime to many groups.

Mary C. Hanrahan is the Senior Business Affairs Manager for Sephora's Creative Production and Marketing Operations department. Based in New York City, she was a contributing author and research associate for *Broadway: An Encyclopedia of American Theater and Culture*. Mary has also published theater reviews and theater-related columns for BroadwayWorld.

Jessica Hillman-McCord is a Professor in the Department of Theatre and Dance at the State University of New York at Fredonia. She has published in numerous journals including *Studies in Musical Theatre*, *TDR: The Drama Review*, and *Theatre Survey*. Jessica's first book, *Echoes of the Holocaust on the American Musical Stage*, was published in 2012. She is the editor of and contributor to *iBroadway: Musical Theatre in the Digital Age* (2017). An Actors' Equity Association member, Jessica is a professional actress, director, and choreographer.

William Charles Morrow is a librarian at the New York Public Library for the Performing Arts at Lincoln Center, where he catalogs moving image material for the Theatre on Film and Tape Archive. He was a contributing author and senior research associate for *Broadway: An Encyclopedia of Theater and American Culture*. In addition, William has written articles on the performing arts for various publications. In the 1980s, he wrote and directed radio plays for WBAI-FM in New York City, including *The Ministry of Progress* that was adapted as a musical and produced Off-Broadway in 2004.

INDEX